TOTAL GEEK-ART

A CELEBRATION OF POP CULTURE

THOMAS OLIVRI

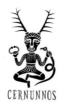

CERNUNNOS

Director of publication: Rodolphe Lachat
Cernunnos logo design: Mark Ryden
Interior design: Benjamin Brard
Cover design: Devin Grosz

ISBN: 978-1-4197-4777-9

Front cover credits (clockwise from top left): Steve Seeley,
She Said (Humm-mmm); Boneface, Guy (detail); Nychos,
Transluscent Mickey; Alex Gross, Mona Lisa (detail)

Back cover credits (clockwise from top left): Isabel Samaras,
Spero Melior (detail); Mike Wrobel, Cersei (detail); Joshua Budich,
Mia Wallace (detail); Brad Albright, BoJack Secretariat (detail)

Published in 2020 by Cernunnos, an imprint of ABRAMS.

Printed and bound in China
10 9 8 7 6 5 4 3 2 1

Abrams books are available at special discounts when purchased
in quantity for premiums and promotions as well as fundraising
or educational use. Special editions can also be created to specifi-
cation. For details, contact specialsales@abramsbooks.com or the
address below.

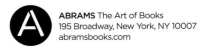

ABRAMS The Art of Books
195 Broadway, New York, NY 10007
abramsbooks.com

TABLE OF CONTENTS

INTRODUCTION
by Isabel Samaras

When *Star Wars* came out in 1977 there were no toys associated with the movie. NO TOYS! George Lucas was worried people were gonna rip off his cool ideas, and Kenner Products, an American toy company that had purchased the *Star Wars* toy-merchandising license, thought perhaps this weird outer space movie was going to be a huge flop, so they decided to just wait and see. (Forty-three-year-old spoiler: It was not a huge flop.) This was pretty lousy for those of us itching to play in a galaxy far, far away, and I dunno what other kids did (because I did not have a surplus of friends), but I made paper dolls. This magical act of creating something out of nothing was a trick I'd learned from my mom, a single working mother who made "toys" for me out of swiped office supplies. It was completely miraculous how she could convert my wishes into reality. An entire family of mermaids? Done. Incredible paper wardrobes for everyone? Voila! It is 100 percent why I became an artist, mesmerized by that ability to transmute gossamer fantasy into solid matter. My desire to pull off that kind of wizardry is why I've spent the bulk of my life hauling my weirdo thoughts out into the open and turning them "real" for everyone to see.

Clearly this obsession with making the unseen seen started early. As an oddball kid, I had many hours (days, weeks, years) to hone my craft. A true nerdling on so many levels, I used to fantasize about having an Egyptian-style burial, and being sealed up in a room packed to the ceiling with science fiction books and horror movies and comics and toys. A hearty diet of sci-fi novels and *Twilight Zone* episodes had raised me to ponder "What if?" an awful lot, but by the time I was an adult the question was shifting into "Why not?" This manifested in repainting old tin lunch boxes with very grown-up—bordering on pornographic—images. I worked on vintage metal TV trays to further the connection between my childhood infatuations and all manner of "mature" activities. These things weren't created for galleries, they weren't made for other people, I didn't expect anyone to like them or even ever *see* them. Like Geppetto carving a son out of wood, I just really needed them to exist. I wanted them to be real, so I made them.

The first time I showed my work to a gallery, the director got up and walked into the next room. Maybe this was my cue to leave? I felt like Joseph Merrick, the Elephant Man: "People are frightened by what they don't understand," and I was prepared to limp away. Imagine my shock when she came back a second later with a contract. Honestly, you could've knocked me over with a feather.

And that's how many of us found each other—in small, brave galleries or in the pages of magazines like *Juxtapoz* or *Hi-Fructose*. Maybe my questions weren't the same ones others were asking, but we were all armpit deep in our kooky revels and starting to declare our outcast selves to the world. Turns out while we were nonconformists, we weren't alone after all, that there was a pack of us that had grown up nourished by eating the scraps of our "modern" civilization and spitting out art inspired by it. The wayward geeks, freaks, and oddballs shunned by the rest of the art scene found a home in the lowbrow art scene, a populist/underground art movement that bubbled up on the West Coast. It was a big clubhouse, with wide doors and no bouncers—all were welcome. Suddenly the misfits had a tribe, and an audience that resonated to the same frequency that we did. It truly didn't matter if your art was tiny or massive, soul searching or lighthearted, beautifully decorative or willfully ugly. Somehow it all hung together, connected by the thread of our mutual artistic compulsions, all our childhood hang-ups and loves, percolating and distilled in the hot little cauldrons of our skulls. We let our geek flags fly high.

The people who opened galleries and showed this work took a chance on all these new artists, and luckily there were collectors just as obsessive and nerdy as we were, as if we all shared that feeling, could see a thing and hear something inside whispering: "Yes, *that*." Our world felt inclusive—what are you into? No shame in that, we'll own it, we'll celebrate it. We were wide open to the siren song of games, manga, sci-fi, cartoons, music, toys, movies, TV, fantasy, monsters, filtered through our various life experiences. We lashed ourselves to the mast and let it drive us all deliciously mad.

This seemed to coincide with the rise in popularity of comics and other nerdy pastimes. Comic-Con, which started out with three hundred devotees in a hotel basement, exploded into a star-studded event that swallows up half of downtown San Diego and now draws one hundred thirty-five thousand people in an annual pilgrimage. The eccentric was now normal, cosplay and dragons entered the mainstream consciousness. In the eighties geeks were friendless dorks, the ones sporting pocket calculators and carrying ragged copies of *Dune*. Now everyone's got techie gadgets and knows what an Infinity Gauntlet is. Suddenly we were "belonging" to something. We'd become legion. While "geeks" were originally the carnival performers who bit the heads off live chickens, today people proudly proclaim their nerd fandoms on "geek chic" T-shirts. A rising tide raises all boats, and some of us ascended right out of the lowbrow scene, through pop surrealism, and straight into blue chip art land. Some of us were happy to keep building the clubhouse, adding more rooms, expanding and ever welcoming.

But this is my favorite thing: That geek art is a flag that anyone can plant, the criteria seem to be only the depth of your love and passion. Why judge when you can enjoy? Why sneer at us when you could laugh or cry with us? So say "Yes, absolutely, oh *Hell* yes." All you misfits and obsessives, I see you. Welcome to the clubhouse.

Secrets of the Batcave
2002

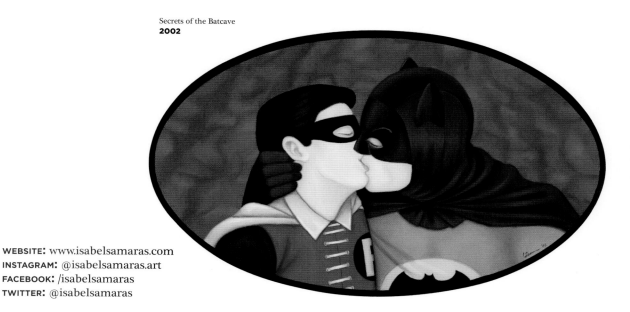

WEBSITE: www.isabelsamaras.com
INSTAGRAM: @isabelsamaras.art
FACEBOOK: /isabelsamaras
TWITTER: @isabelsamaras

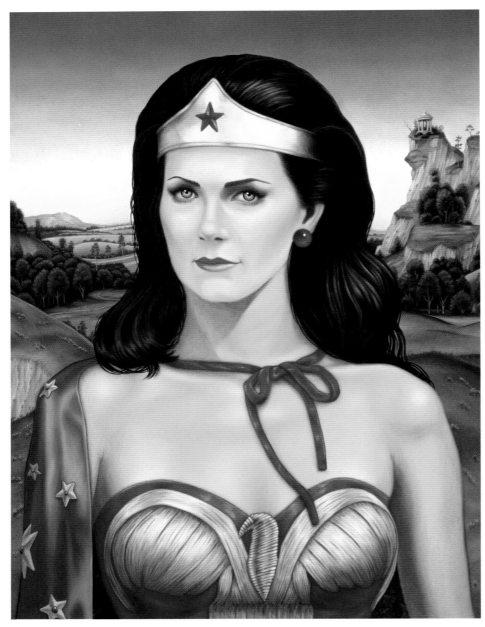

Spiro Spero (While I Breathe, I Hope:
Marita's Linsday)
2004

Spero Melior (I Wish for Better Things)
2017

There was a kind of purity and optimism in the bold women of my childhood—Wonder Woman and the Bionic Woman had this bright charm that made you believe things were absolutely gonna be OK. (Simpler times.) I find myself painting them when I'm in doubt about the state of things, and they become talismans that I hope can put some kind of positive energy back into the world. Powerful and direct, they're looking right at us, challenging us, inviting us to do better and to keep hope alive.

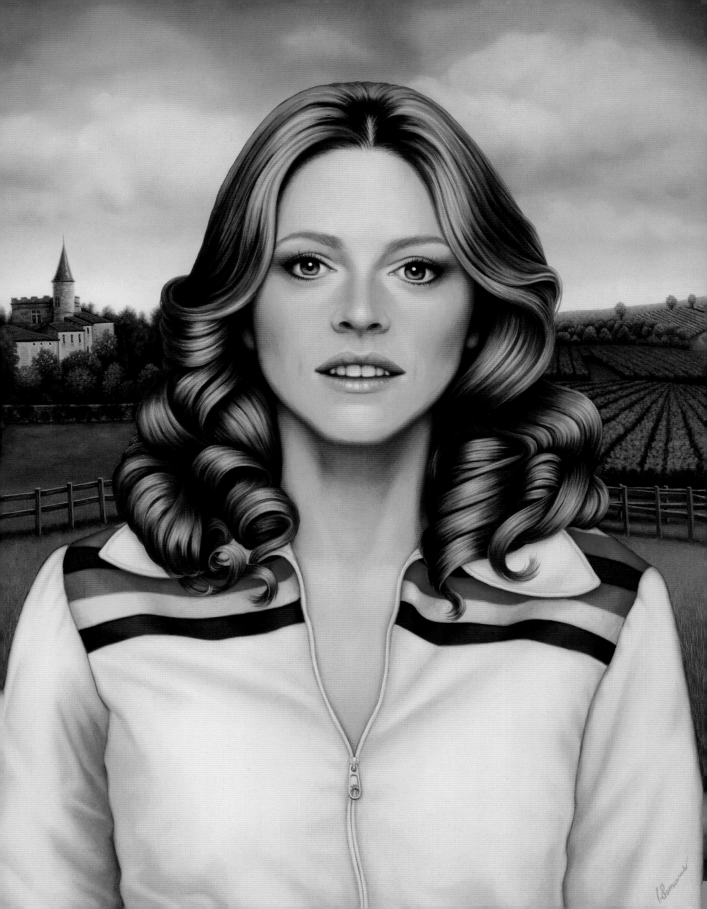

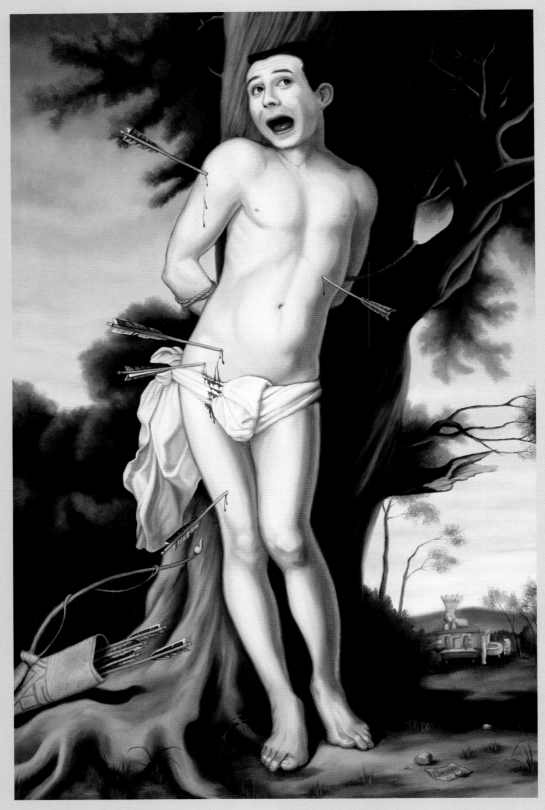

The Martyrdom
of Pee Wee
2004

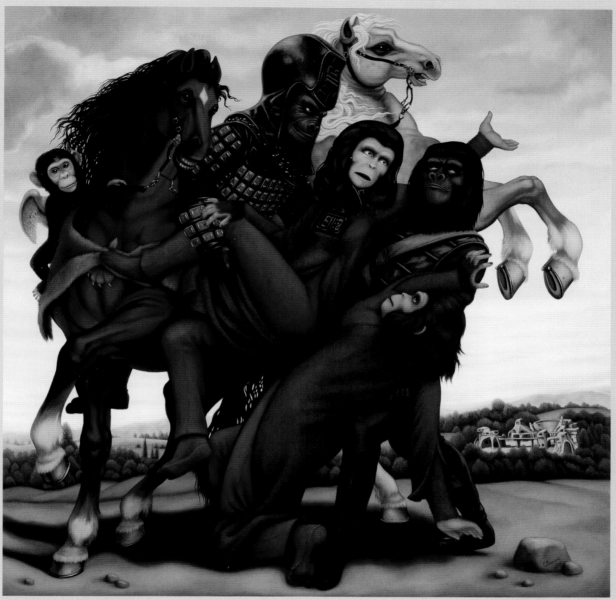

Abduction of the Simian Women
2012

To follow your muse is something like grabbing on to a tiger with a thousand tails: You playfully want to pull them all, but then you need to hang on so you can find out where that curiosity will take you. I've followed my tiger-muse into the forest to chronicle the lost girls of fairy tales all grown up; into the bedrooms of beloved childhood TV characters to spy on their naughty shenanigans; to sit quietly at the feet of monsters and listen to their stories of isolation. Making art like this often felt like sending up a signal flare in the dark: I have some pretty strange thoughts sometimes . . . do you? Am I weird? Am I alone? Will anyone understand? If I reveal to you what's inside me, will you turn away?

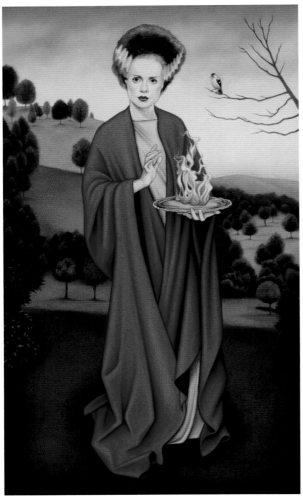

Song of the Goldfinch
2007

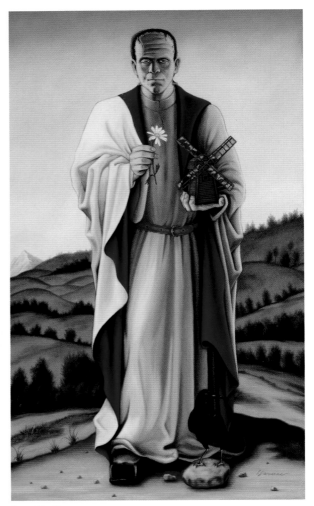

Song of the Raven
2007

While watching classic horror movies as a kid, it seemed clear to me who the real monsters were (humans), and my child-heart would break for all the misunderstood creatures. I keep coming back to them as symbols of social rejection, because anyone who's ever felt like an outcast can relate to feeling alone, stumbling around in the woods just wishing there was someone like you out there somewhere. In "Song of the Goldfinch" and "Song of the Raven" they go a step further, by becoming martyrs. (Did either of them ask to be dug up and reanimated? No they did not.)

"N.W.A (Nuthatches with Attitude)" is my homage to the work of John James Audubon and the hip-hop group N.W.A. (and I spent an absurd amount of time deciding who would go where). Some of the members are more obvious—MC Ren is a wren, while Eazy-E was "not tall in stature" and as luck would have it there's a pygmy nuthatch! (I love the universe.) The rest are proper nuthatches with Dr. Dre, one of the founders of N.W.A., up top, DJ Yella in the middle, and Ice Cube in the lower left about to take flight (he split from the group over royalty disputes).

N.W.A. (Nuthatches With Attitude)
2011

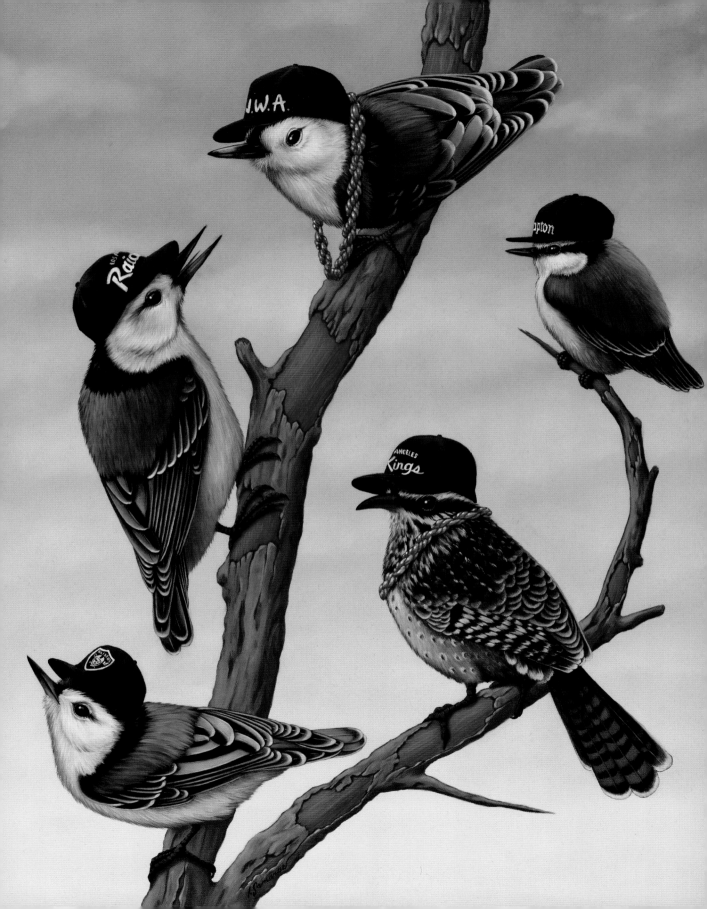

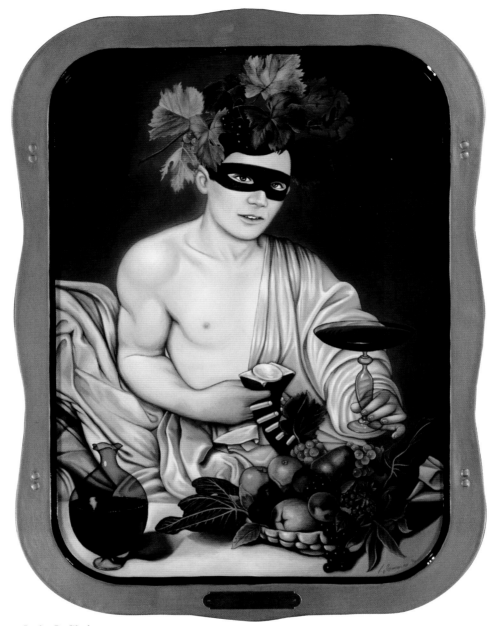

Bacchus Boy Wonder
1999

So many of the old master paintings were filled with characters that would have been known to viewers of the time—they would recognize a Greek goddess by her props and costume, or a Biblical story by the location and poses. I wanted to work with some of those same narratives but use characters from my childhood, who might be recognizable to people now in the same way. (What we lack in knowledge of classical mythology we more than make up for with years planted in front of the TV.) Baroque master Caravaggio had painted a moist young Bacchus, and I couldn't resist dragging Robin into that world.

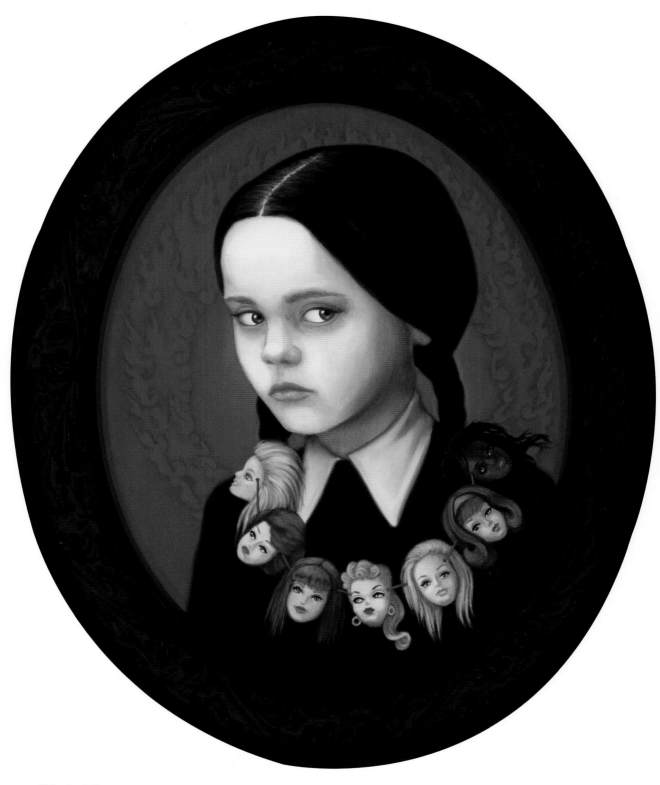

Wednesday the Destroyer
2003

JOEL ABAD

Born and raised in Manresa, Spain, Joel was the kid who was drawing all the time. He attended drawing classes where he was influenced by the American underground comic artists of the 1970s. He got a degree in graphic design in Barcelona and worked at various companies leading graphic departments. In 2005 he started his own graphic design studio, Grafficants, and as time went by he mainly focused on illustration projects. Nowadays, what he does the most is draw merch and posters for bands and the music industry, create brand identities for companies, and paint personal murals. He has worked for Vans, Harley-Davidson, Warner Music Group, Arnette, RockZone magazine, HFMN Crew, Ripper Seeds, Crème International, and RockAction Productions among others. He has also drawn for bands such as NOFX, Lagwagon, Against Me!, the Queers, Marky Ramone, the Ataris, MxPx, Biohazard, Blowfuse, Crisix, Pennywise, Bad Religion, the Toy Dolls, Sick of It All, and Satanic Surfers.

WEBSITE: www.joelabad.com
INSTAGRAM: @joelabad

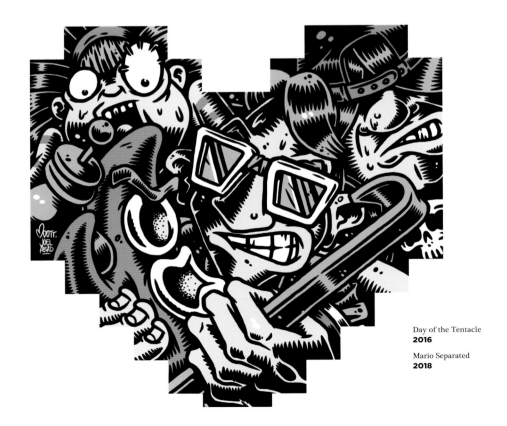

Day of the Tentacle
2016

Mario Separated
2018

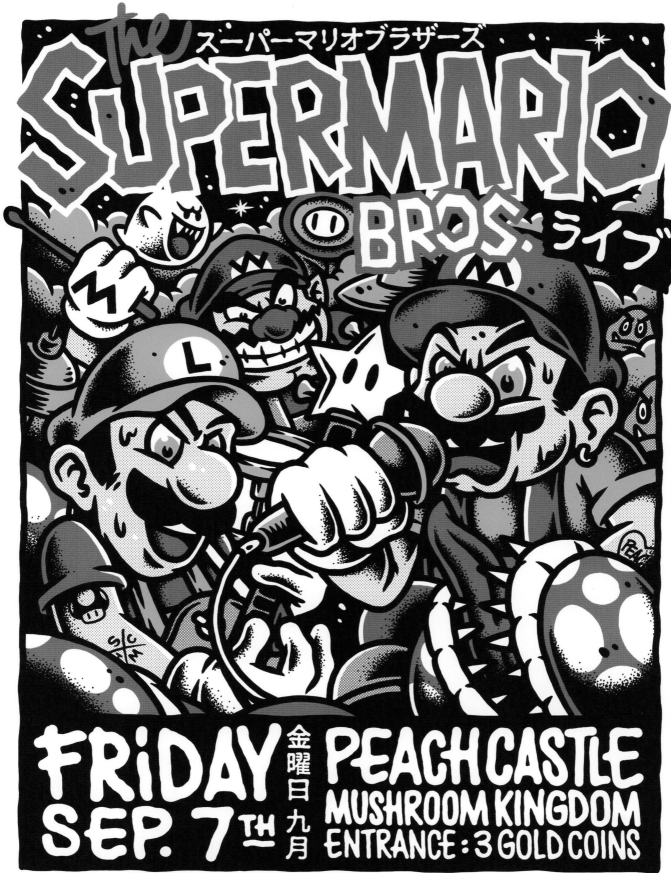

/30

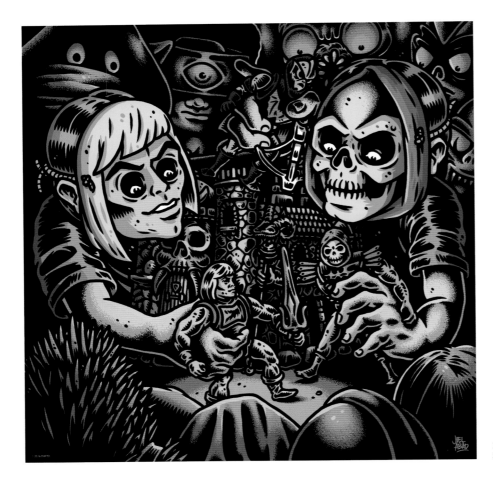

He-Man
2016

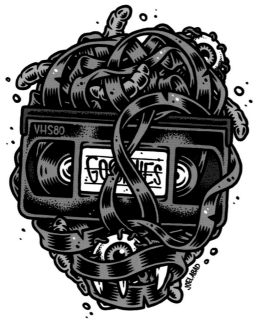

Goonies
2017

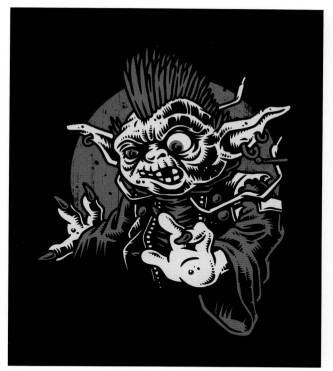

Back 3
2019

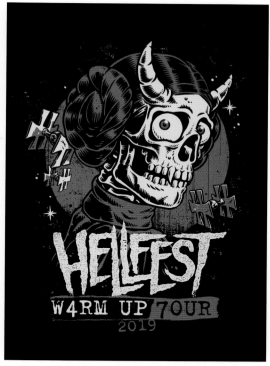

Front Separated
2019

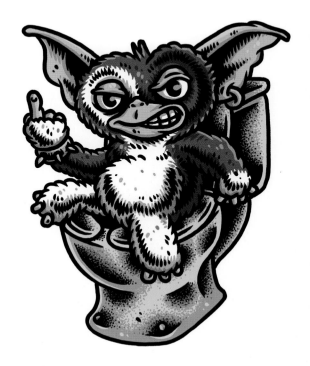

Gizmo sin fondo
2017

" It amuses me how art is influenced by pop culture and pop culture is influenced by art. For years, art has represented the artists' environment, and it still does. It is reproduced in illustrations, paintings, music, movies, whatever. But art also changes the way we see the world, the culture. Our ideas are altered by books and music, how we see people in movies or all the fashion industry. Pop culture is transformed by art and art is transformed by pop culture!"

JONATHAN ADRIAN

nspired by traditional children's book illustrators and animators of the 1950s, Jonathan Adrian's use of vivid colors and whimsical character design are meant to evoke the wonder and joys of youth. Layers of shape are used to direct the eye while complimentary color palettes play with the imitation of light and shadow, pulling the viewers' focus. Jonathan studied illustration and design at Lesley University and has worked on a number of freelance projects, both traditional and digital. Though his styles and mediums vary, his favored technique is traditional gouache-painted illustrations, as seen in this book.

WEBSITE: www.jadrian728.wixsite.com/jonathan-adrian

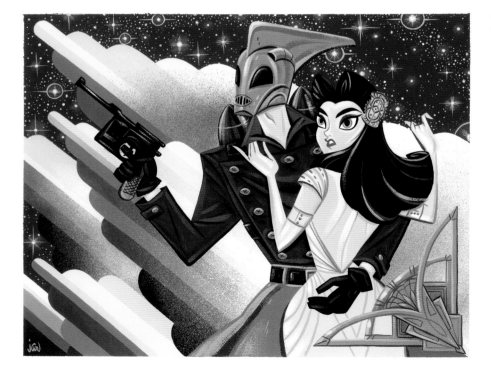

Rocketee Onliner
2015

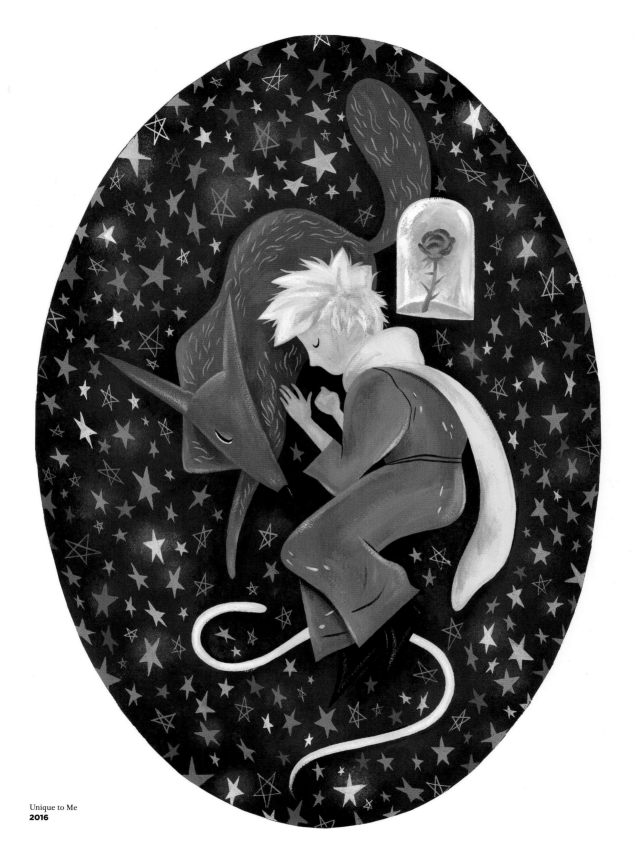

Unique to Me
2016

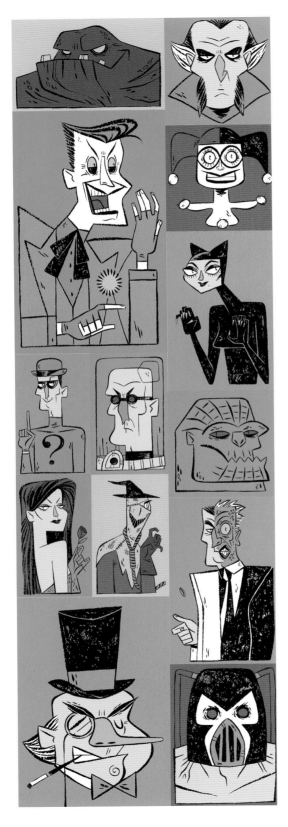

“ For me, geek culture and pop culture are centered around nostalgia and connection. I grew up in the '80s and was pretty much a loner. Cartoons, movies, and comics were my first friends, and they planted a love of anything and everything fantasy in me that has only grown with age. I think my vision of pop culture always comes back to that feeling of joy and wonder I felt as a kid. My work as an artist has become about remembering those feelings and being able to evoke them in others.”

Rogues Gallery
2014

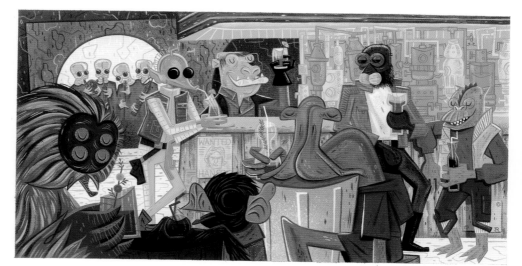

Cantina
2015

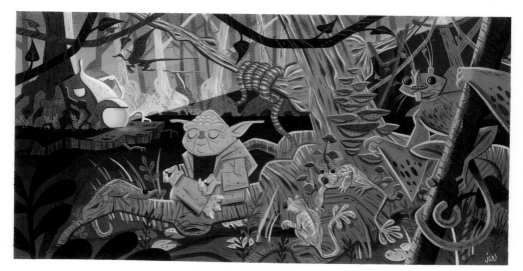

Dagoba
2015

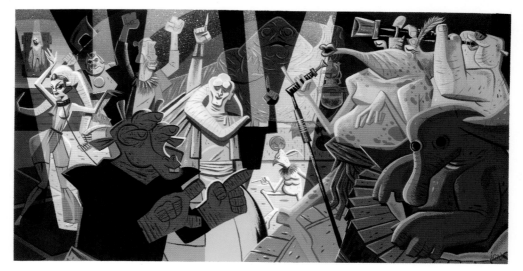

Jabba's Palace
2015

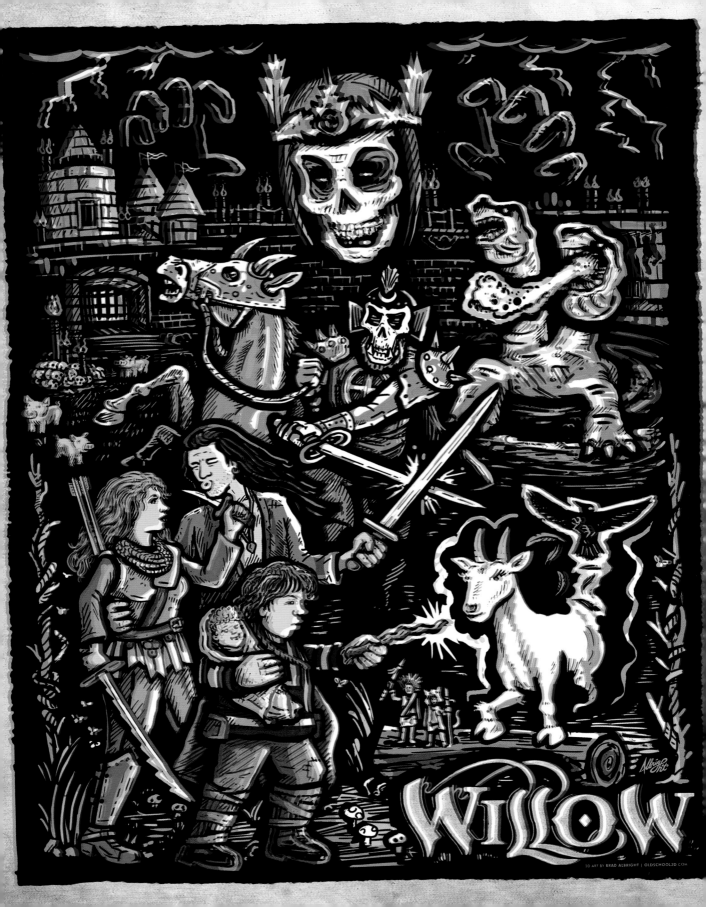

BRAD ALBRIGHT

Brad Albright is an illustrator and gallery artist based in Dallas, Texas. Growing up in American suburbs, his earliest and most enduring influences were pop-culture narrative entertainment. Drawing in a line-art style reminiscent of underground comics and classical woodcut engravings, he is equally inspired by comics, album covers, band tees, literature, film, and television. His work reflects the thematic influence of pop-culture entertainment, with techniques marrying traditional fine art training with modern digital tools.

Whether translating the influence of pop culture, exploring the alluring danger of the Wild West ("Texan Gothic"), or celebrating the multi-sensory live music crowd experience ("Concerto Collection"), his work is regularly presented in old-school 3D, surprising and engaging viewers with red/blue glasses for a fun, nostalgic interactive experience.

WEBSITE: www.albrightillustration.com

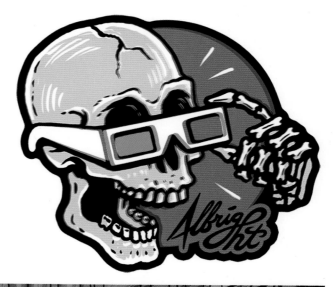

Willow
2018

General Admission
2016

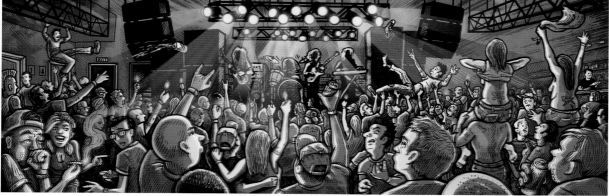

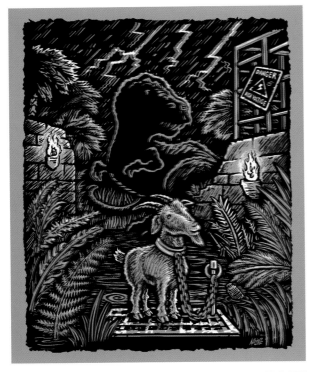

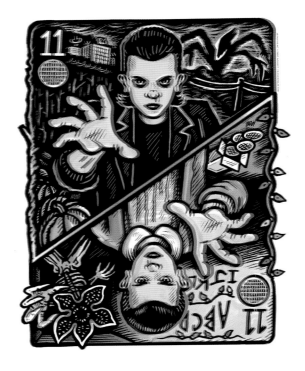

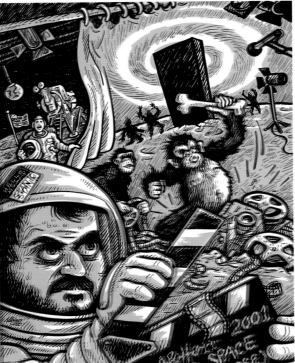

Kubrick's 2001 and the Alleged Apollo Hoax
2012

> " Grounded by narrative storytelling, pop-culture entertainment is as much art as what we find in museums and galleries . . . its ability to communicate, entertain, and inspire is vast and versatile. The masters of today may just be the animators, writers, illustrators, directors, and myriad names you see in the rolling credits of a film or television program. It's a broad and inexhaustible world of sights, sounds, and stories."

Evil Dead
2017

Predator / There's something in those trees...
2018

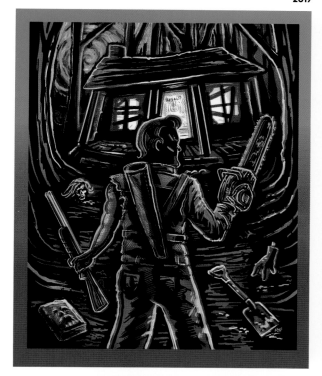

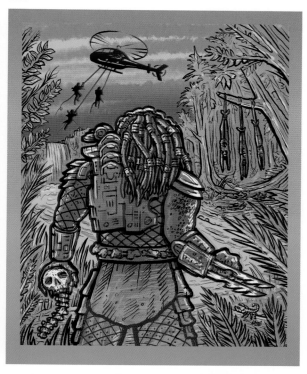

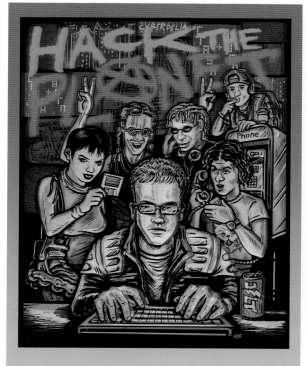

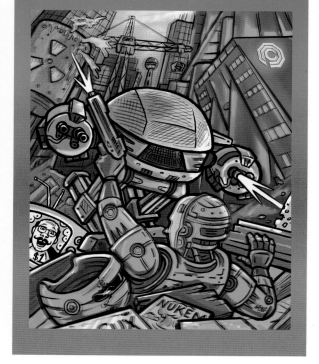

Hack the Planet
2017

Robocop VS ED209
2017

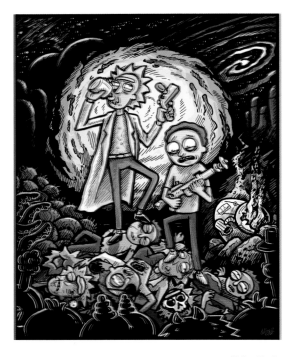

Rickor Mortis
2016

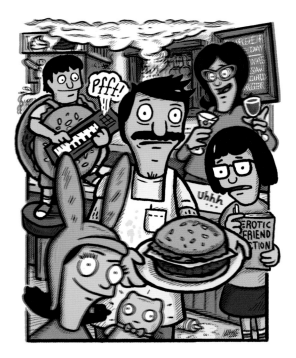

Bob's Burger of the Day
2017

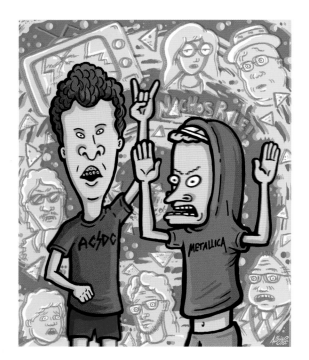

Nachos Rule!
2018

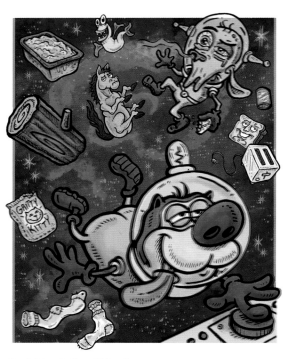

Ren & Stimpy in "Space Madness"
2017

BoJack Secretariat
2017

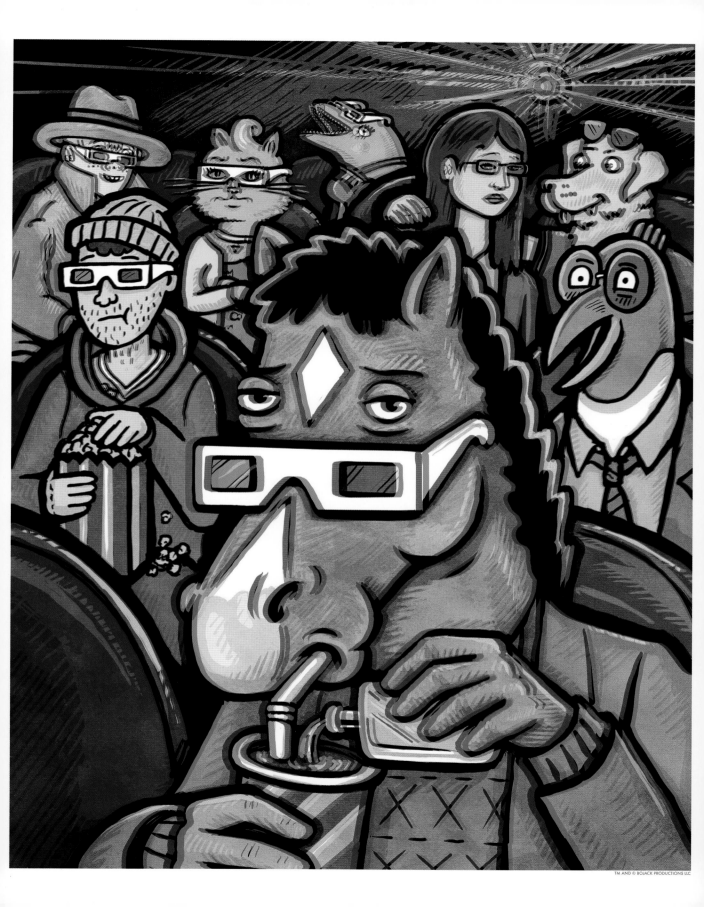

VADU AMKA

Vadu Amka is the creator of the eponymous blog Vaduamka.com which she began at the end of 2011. The initial concept of "machine customization" came from her projects as a freelance artist. Passionate about the art of recovery, design, and retrogaming, she is inspired by urban art as well as other more contemporary movements with a strong fondness for everything related to the eighties and nineties. Since 2015, her projects focused on video games have been carried out in collaboration with publishers and major players in the industry in order to develop unique, ultra-limited promotional pieces for collectors. In 2017, she started a long collaboration with two artists who became partners, mastering new technologies and prototyping. This is how the Random Print Creation Studio was born.

WEBSITE: www.vaduamka.com
INSTAGRAM: @vaduamka
FACEBOOK: /VaduAmka
TWITTER: @VaduAmka

" I am passionate about the art of recycling, design, and retrogaming."

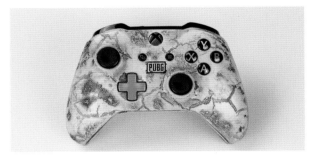

PUBG
2018

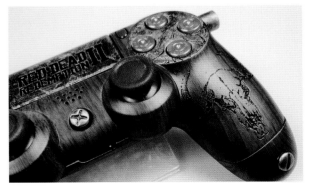

Red Dead Redemption
2018

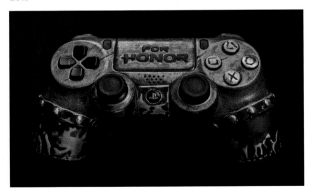

For Honor
2017

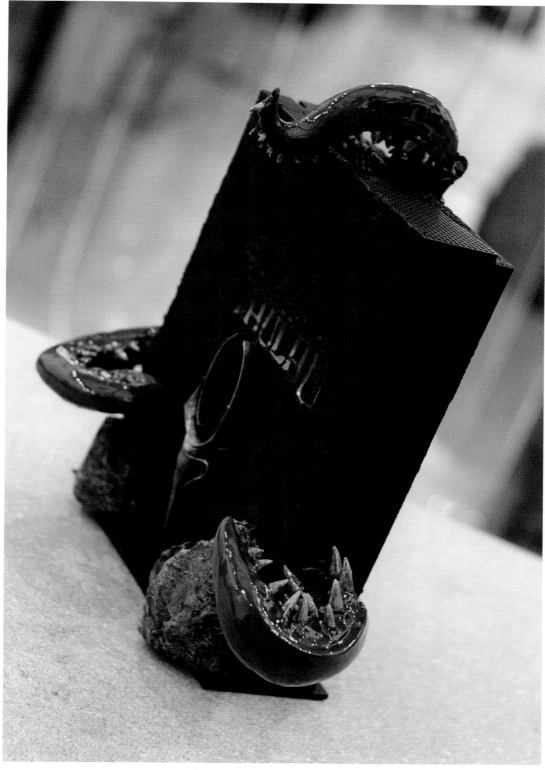

Call of Cthulhu Xbox One S
2017

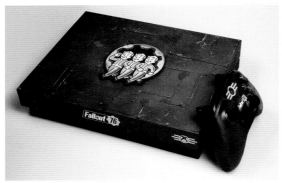

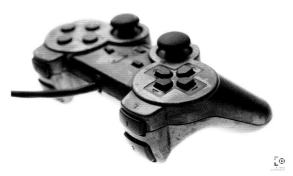

Shelter // Fallout 76 Xbox One X
2018

Castlevania manette PS1
2017

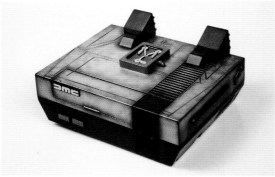

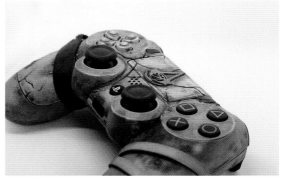

De LoreNES
2018

Assassin's Creed Origins PS4
2017

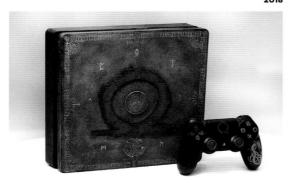

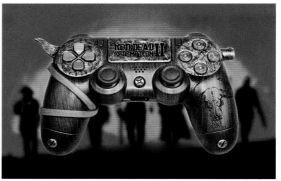

God of War PS4
2018

Red Dead Redemption II
2018

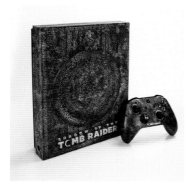

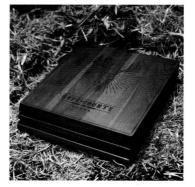

Shadow of the
Tomb Raider
Xbox One X
2018

FarCry 5 PS4
2018

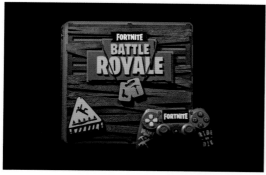

Fortnite Battle Royale PS4
2018

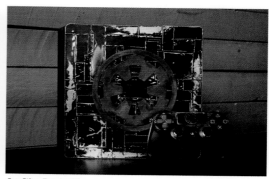

Star Wars Empire PS4
2017

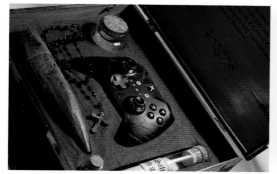

Vampyr Hunting Kit Xbox One S
2017

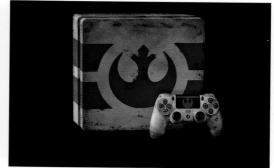

Star Wars Alliance rebelle PS4
2017

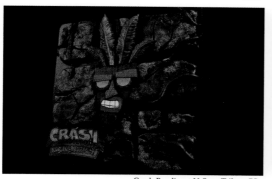

Crash Bandicoot N. Sane Trilogy PS4
2017

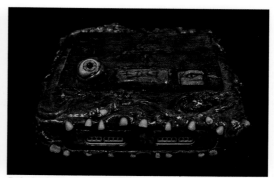

Rudy the abomination Super Nintendo
2017

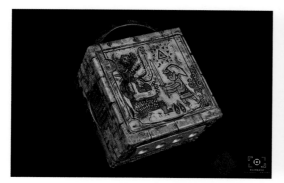

The Legend of Zelda: The fall of Ganondorf GameCube
2018

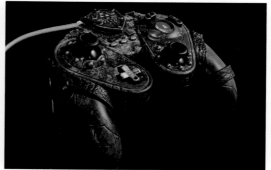

Zelda Fightpad Wii U
2017

ORLANDO AROCENA

Orlando Arocena (Mexifunk) is an artist and graphic designer who works in traditional and digital mediums. After graduating from Pratt Institute in Brooklyn, New York, in 1994, he drew his way through Europe, co-founded Uptown Arts, and discovered he had a knack for digital commercial communications. In addition to a twenty-two-year track record of delivering creative solutions for some of the world's most recognizable brands, he has established himself as a nonconventional vector illustrator who explores cultural iconography, pop culture, and speculative narratives within the majority of his movie studio commissions. His vector art has also been commissioned by Adobe to be the face of their Illustrator CC 2014.

He is a dedicated member of the Poster Posse, a creative and prolific international pop-culture group of artists who service the Hollywood Film Industry. In addition to commercial endeavors, he has exhibited his artwork at Art Basel Miami, the Odessa Museum of Western and Eastern Art in Ukraine, the Metropolitan Museum of Art in New York, and recently exhibited with the official *Star Wars* exhibition in Marseille, France.

In 2017, Arocena was awarded a prestigious Clio Entertainment Gold Award for his nineteen-piece Día De Los Muertos Horror DVD series for 20th Century Fox/MGM Studios. He is currently a global brand ambassador for Z by HP computers.

BEHANCE: /orlandoarocena
INSTAGRAM: @mexifunk
FACEBOOK: /OrlandoArocenaIllustrator
TWITTER: @OrlandoArocena

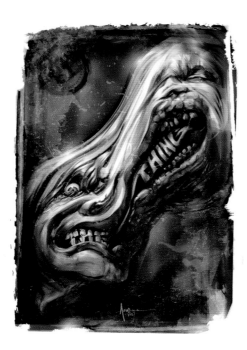

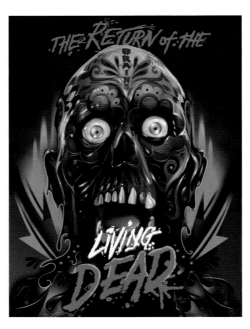

Child's Play
2017

The Thing
2018

The RETURN of the LIVING DEAD
2017

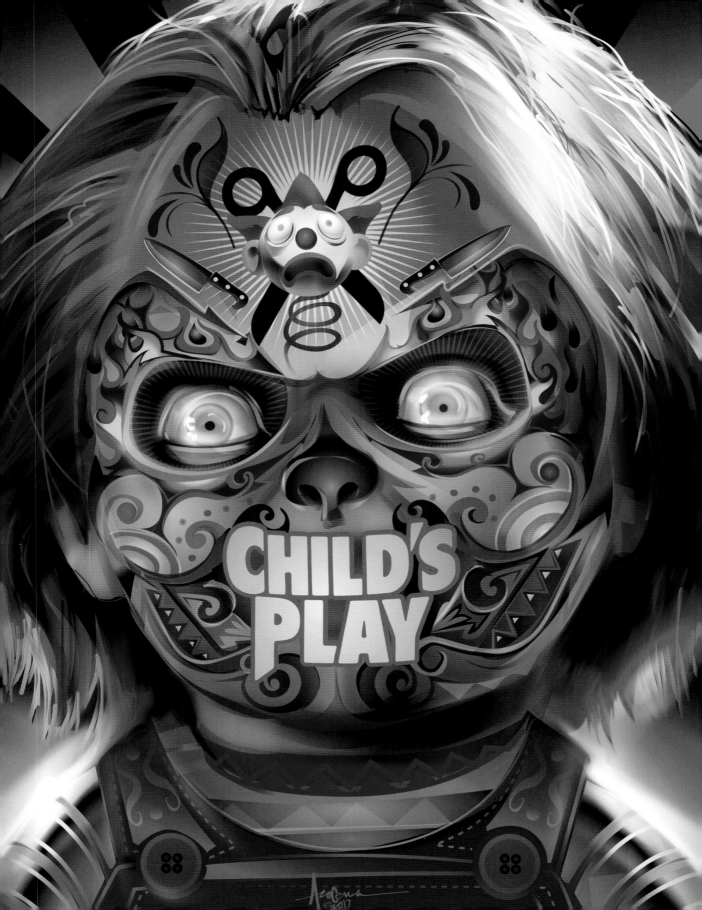

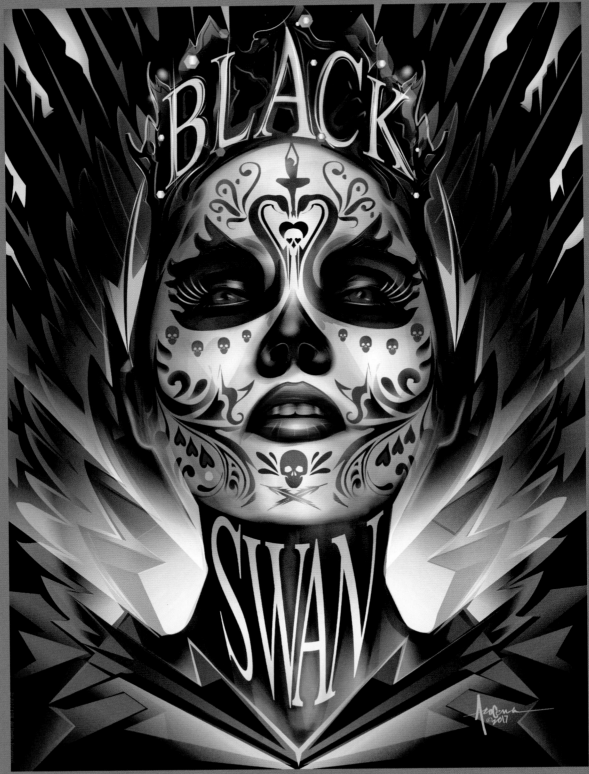

Black Swan
2017

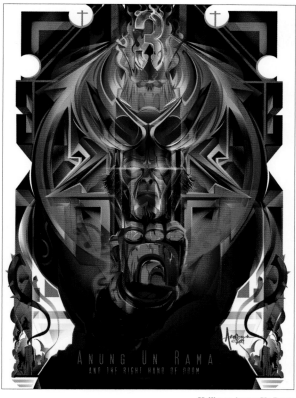

Hellboy 3 Anung Un Rama
2014

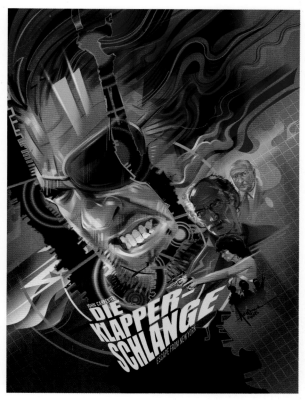

Die Klapperschlange / Escape from New York
2018

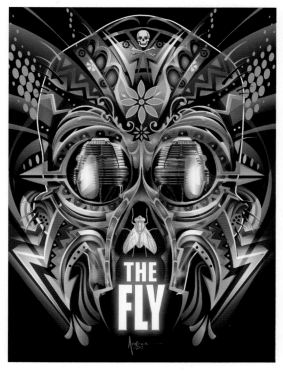

The Fly
2017

" Be like a shark. Why? Because a shark, in order to exist, must always move forward. Never backward."

JOHN BAJET

John Bajet is a Los Angeles–based designer working in animation and publishing. He is currently working on *The Tom and Jerry Show* as a color stylist and he also creates picture books for kids on the side. Past clients include Hasbro, PI Kids, and Cottage Door Press. His most notable books are the "Baby Shark" series for Scholastic.

WEBSITE: www.johnbajet.com
TWITTER: @JohnJohn_Bajet

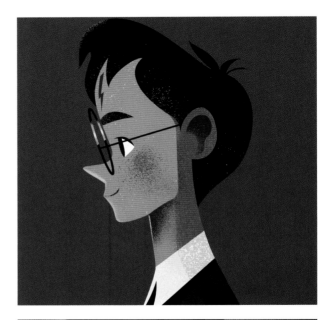

" Color is a
beautiful thing."

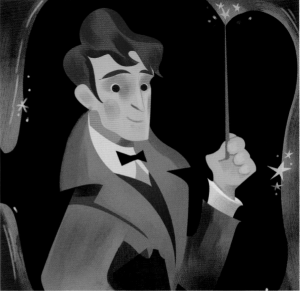

Harry Potter / The Boy Who Lived
2016

Newt
2016

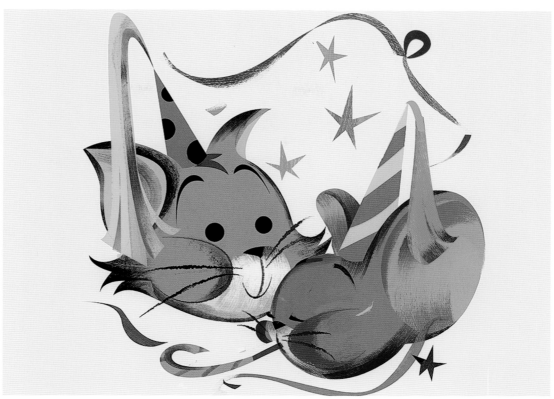

Tom & Jerry
2016

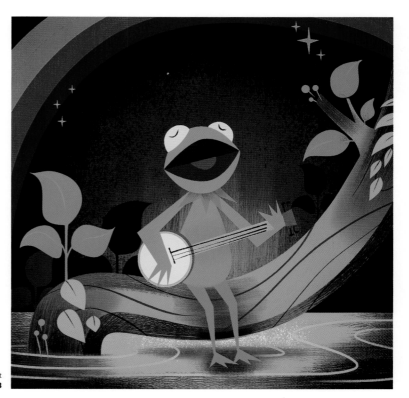

Kermit / Someday we'll find it
2018

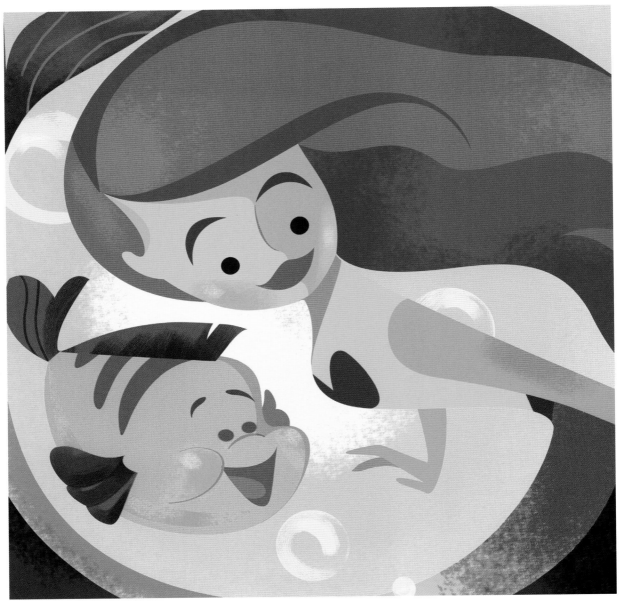

Ariel
2017

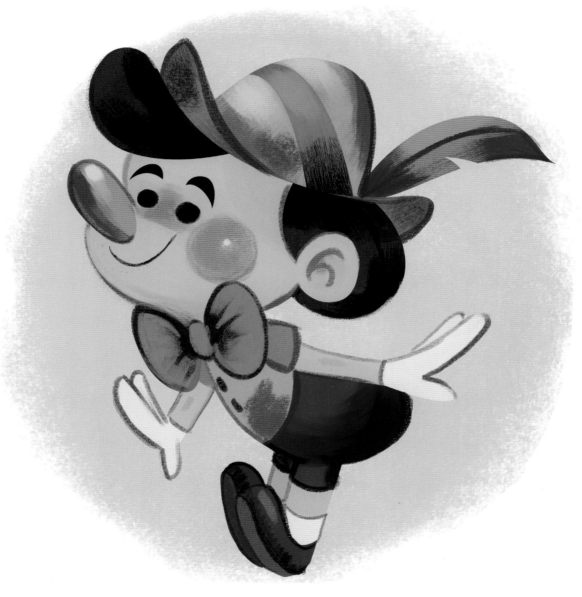

Pinocchio / I've got no strings to hold me down, to make me fret, or make me frown
2017

SCOTT BALMER

Scott is an illustrator who is currently based in Scotland. He sees himself as a person who solves problems of the visual nature and has been doing so since graduating from Duncan of Jordanstone College of Art & Design. Whether it be towering monoliths or conceptual spot illustrations, no illustrative design problem is too small.

He has produced artwork for numerous clients and galleries from around the world, from magazines to newspapers, conceptual works to books.

WEBSITE: www.scottbalmer.co.uk
INSTAGRAM: @scott_balmer
TWITTER: @scott_balmer
CONTACT: illustration@scottbalmer.co.uk

" Popular culture is a strange beast. On one hand, it is seen as disposable since it relies on current interests of the here and now, and for many it is seen as being unimportant, but future generations can learn a lot of valuable lessons about the time period and culture through things like pop culture which makes it truly priceless in my eyes."

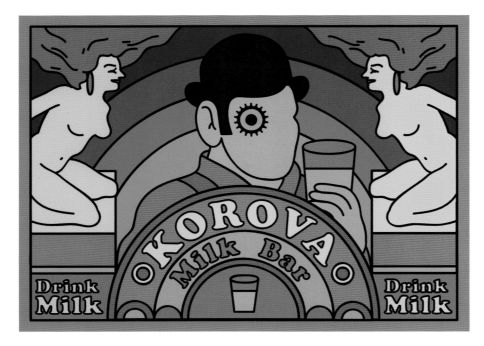

Korova Milk Bar
2016

Ultra Violence
2016

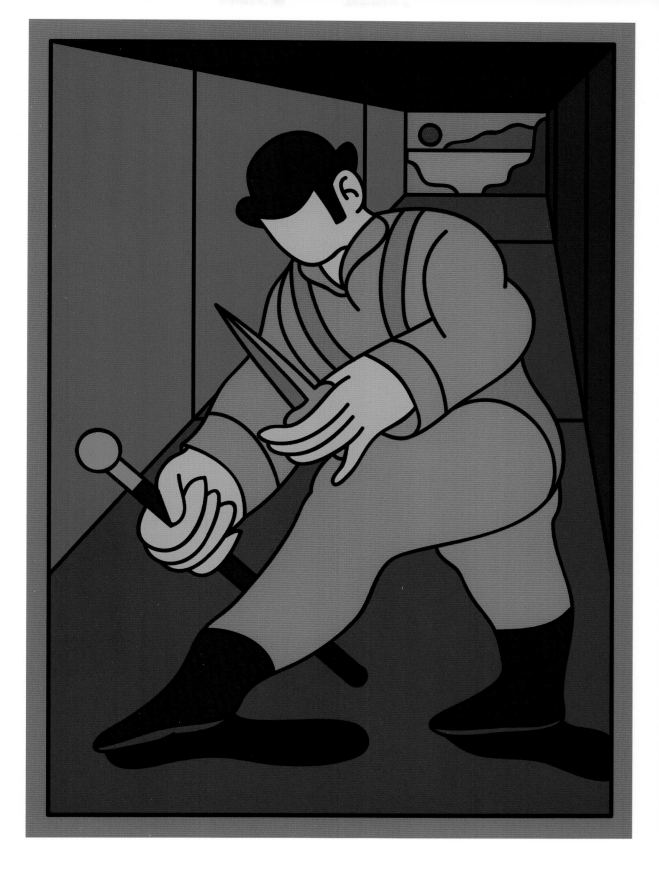

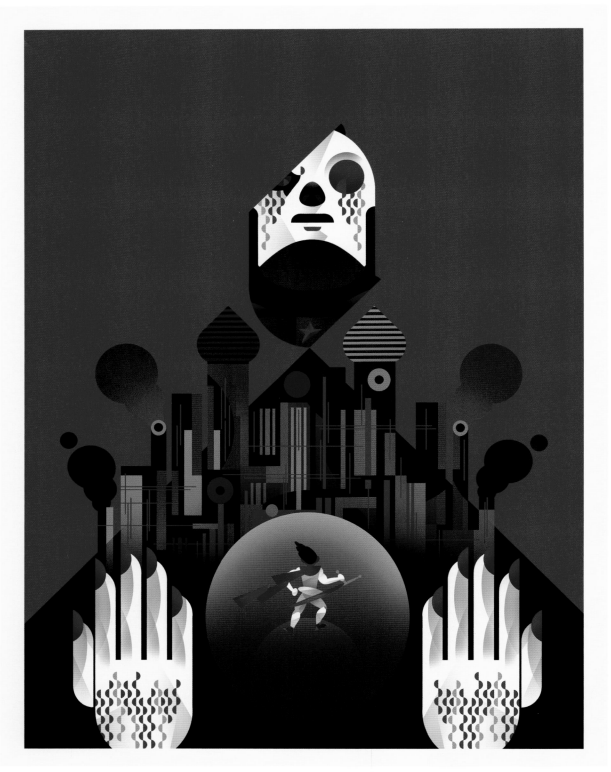

Strider Hiryu, you will never leave Eurasia alive
2015

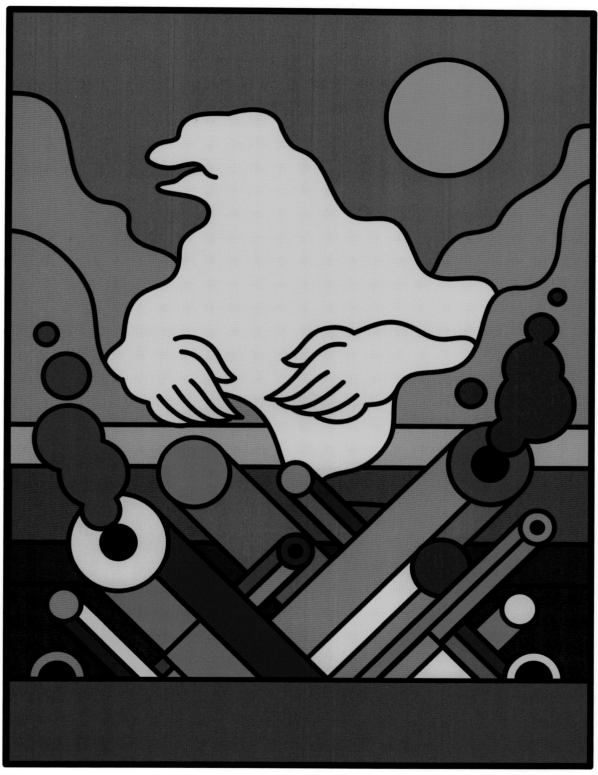

Monster on a Rampage
2016

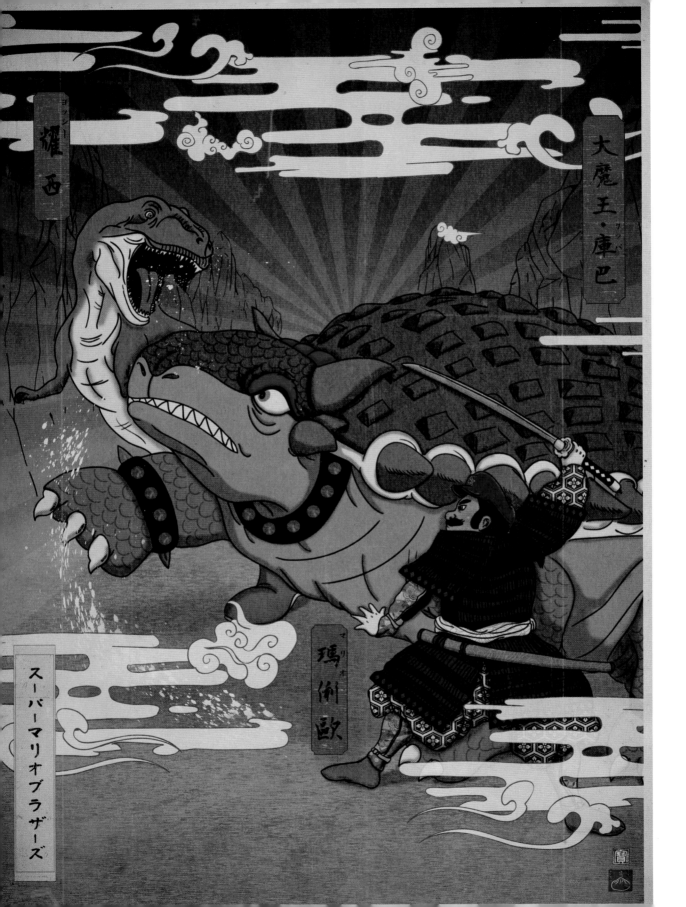

XIAO BAO

Xiao is freelance illustrator based in Singapore who believes in creating something out of nothing as an artist and is heavily influenced by Japanese and Chinese culture.

WEBSITE: www.xiaobaosg.com
INSTAGRAM: @xiaobaosg
CONTACT: xiaobaosg@gmail.com

Hunting Season
2009

Hero's Lullaby
2011

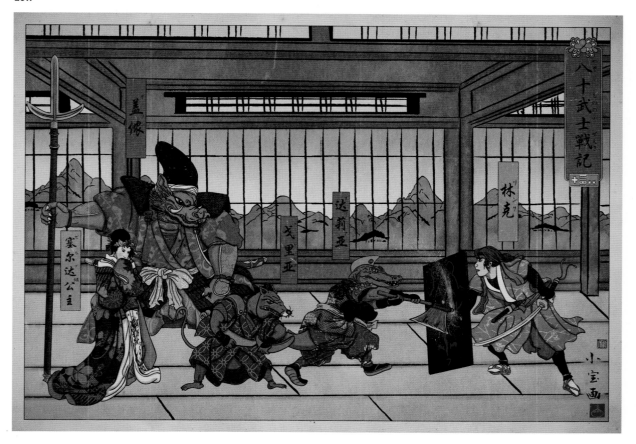

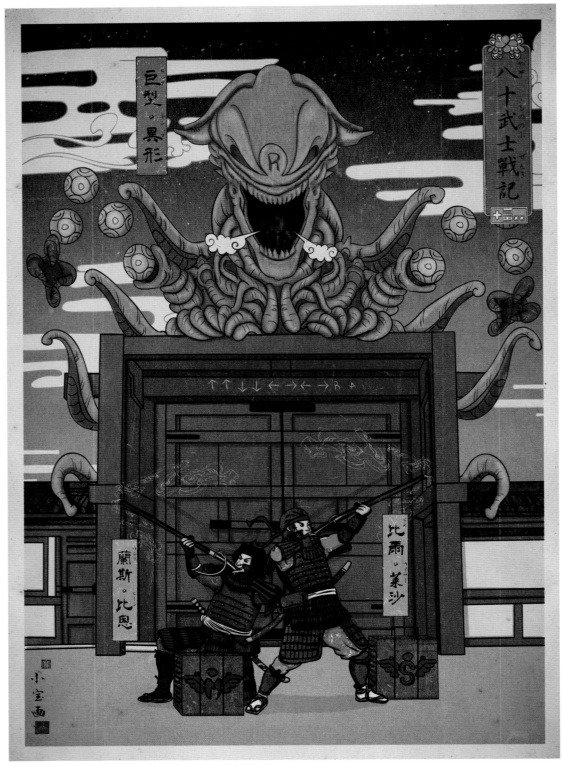

Rescue Dawn
2011

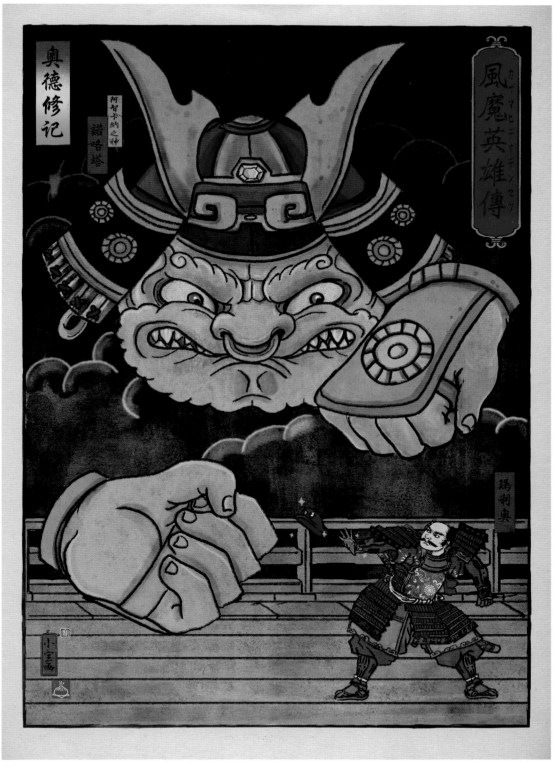

Odyssey
2017

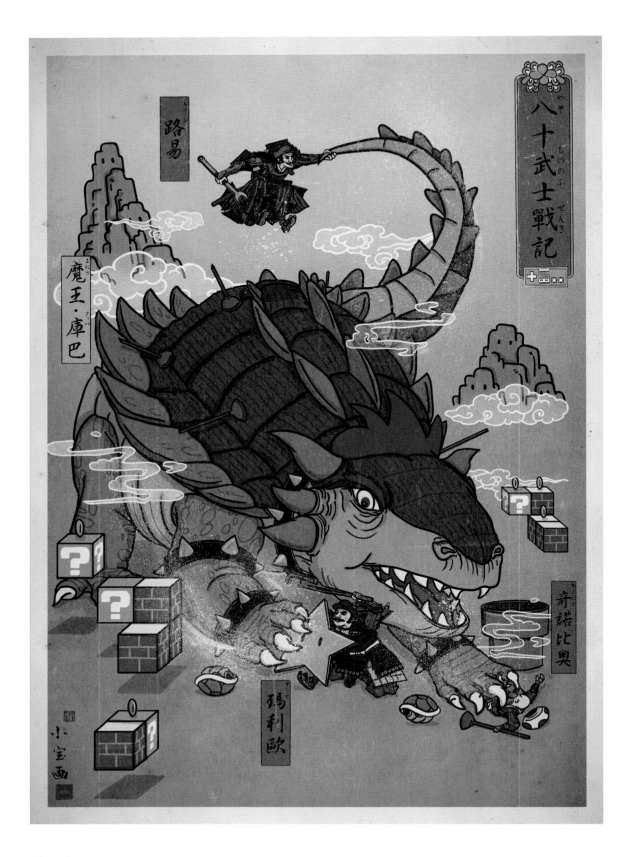

"
To me, pop culture is an essence of movie, TV series, or game summarized into an artwork."

Monster Dogma
2013

Battle Royale
2015

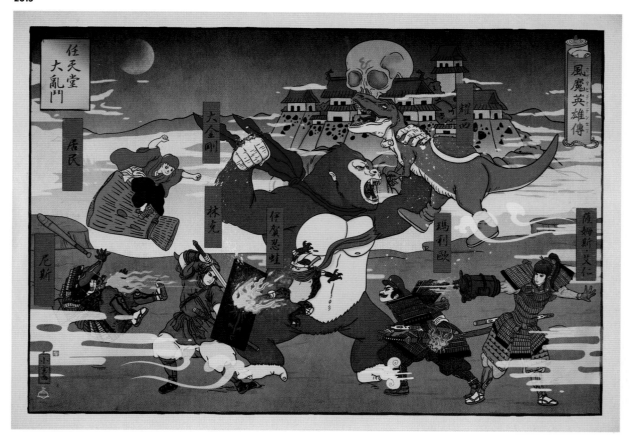

BEASTWRECK

Jared Moraitis was raised on a steady diet of Saturday morning cartoons, comic books, fantasy and sci-fi pulps, monster movies, and eighties toys, and it has infected his brain. He now sells the things he makes with his partner Belle Dee at BeastWreckStuff.com.

WEBSITE: www.beastwreckstuff.com
INSTAGRAM: @beastwreck
FACEBOOK: /beastwreck
TWITTER: @BeastWreck

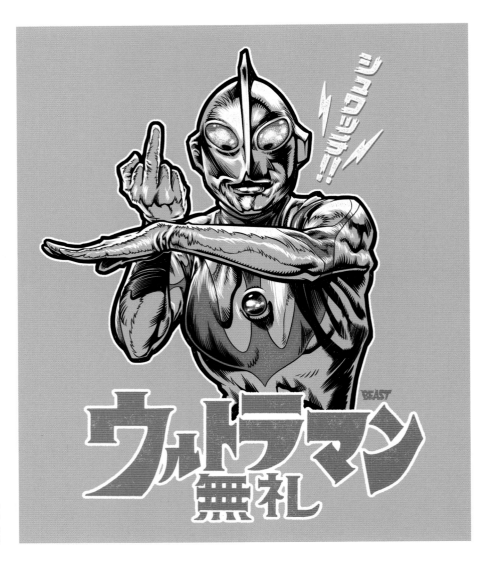

F.U.Ltraman
2018
Sewer Pipe Teens
2014

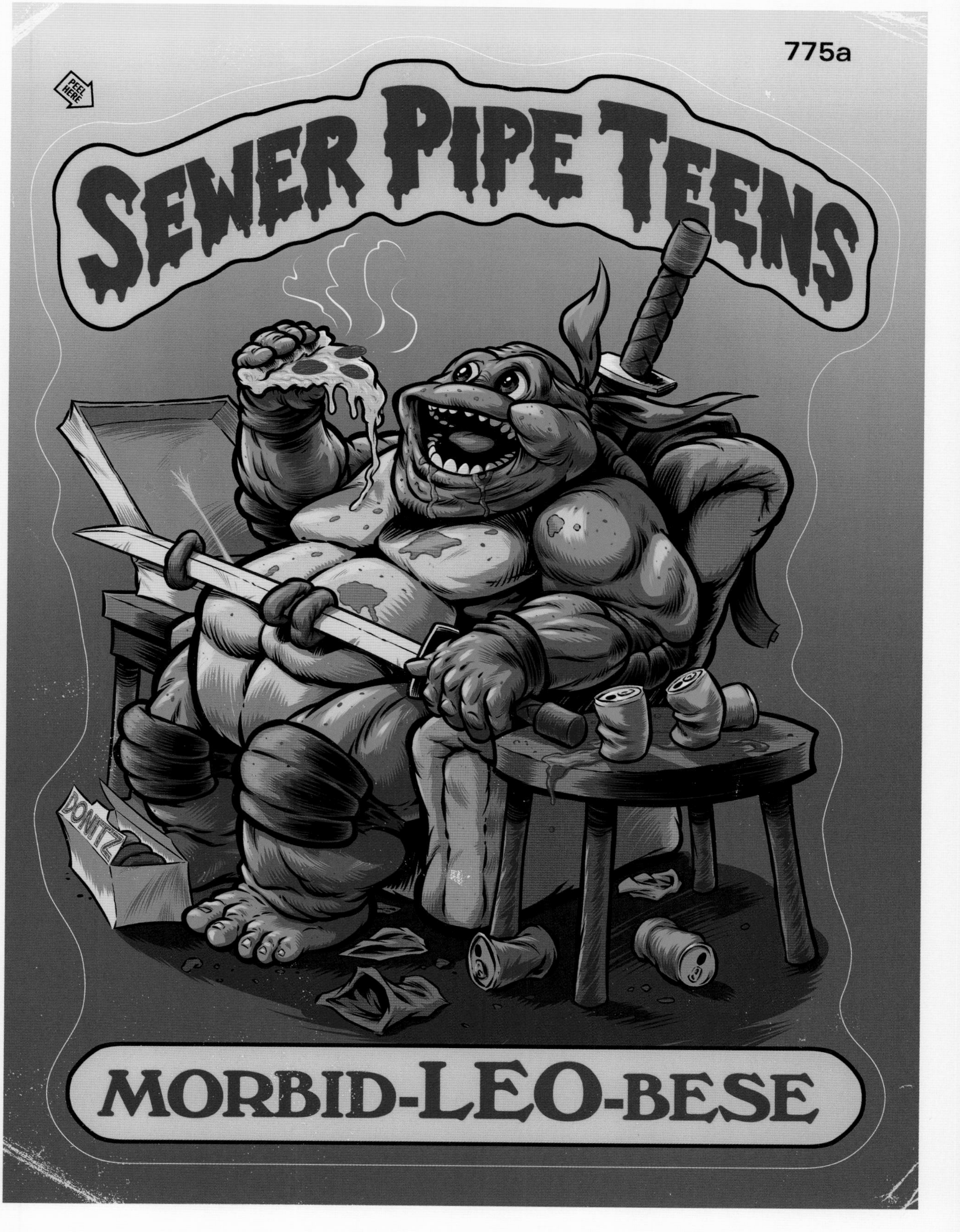
775a
PEEL HERE
SEWER PIPE TEENS
DONITZ
MORBID-LEO-BESE

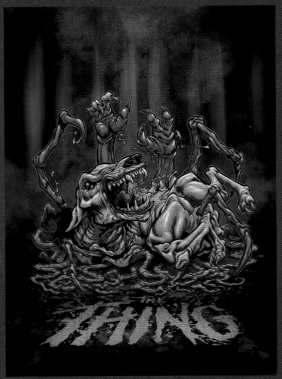

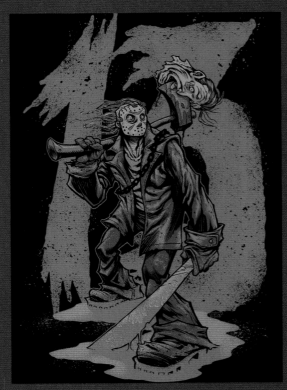

Dog Thing
2017

TGIF 13
2015

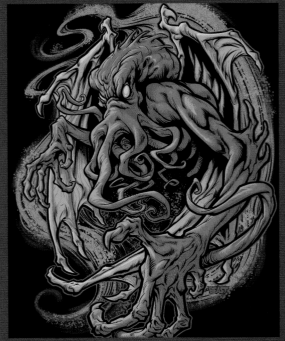

Terror of Cthulhu
2016

"Pop culture is in his blood (but he tries not to take things too seriously)!"

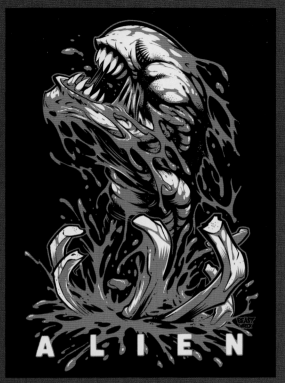

Chestburster
2016

Long Live The Queen
2016

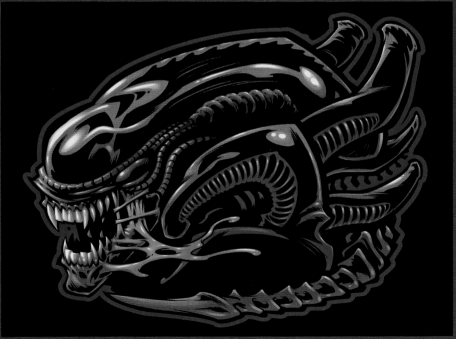

Alien Warrior
2016

BONEFACE

He came from another dimension, where others looked just like him. Boneface's secret lair is now located somewhere in the wastelands of Liverpool, England. His works of evil have been shown around the world, including in galleries in San Francisco and Sydney. His mad campaign to conquer the entire world is slowly coming together . . . Described as "slimed pop-art," Boneface's work is jammed with the color schemes of early nineties Marvel comics and fifties monster comics. Featuring superheroes and villains, leather-clad ghouls and skulls galore, Boneface's art combines dark imagery with badass characters.

WEBSITE: www.boneface.co.uk
INSTAGRAM: @boneface
TWITTER: @boneface

" " Just don't ask what's underneath their masks."

Mad Max Fury Road Sleeve 1
2015

Mad Max Fury Road Sleeve 2
2015

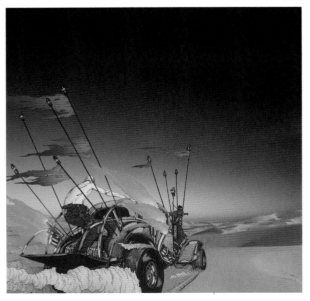
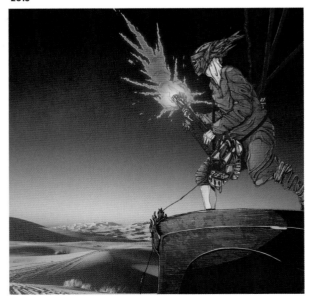

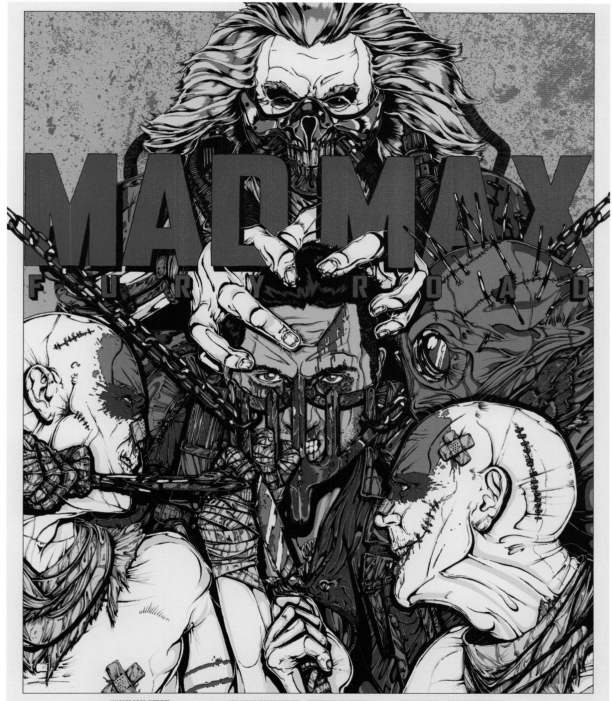

WARNER BROS. PICTURES PRESENTS IN ASSOCIATION WITH VILLAGE ROADSHOW PICTURES A KENNEDY MILLER MITCHELL PRODUCTION A GEORGE MILLER FILM "MAD MAX: FURY ROAD"
TOM HARDY CHARLIZE THERON NICHOLAS HOULT HUGH KEAYS-BYRNE ROSIE HUNTINGTON-WHITELEY RILEY KEOUGH ZOË KRAVITZ ABBEY LEE COURTNEY EATON EDITED BY MARGARET SIXEL
MUSIC BY JUNKIE XL COSTUME DESIGNER JENNY BEAVAN PRODUCTION DESIGNER COLIN GIBSON DIRECTOR OF PHOTOGRAPHY JOHN SEALE, ASC, ACS
EXECUTIVE PRODUCERS IAIN SMITH GRAHAM BURKE BRUCE BERMAN WRITTEN BY GEORGE MILLER BRENDAN McCARTHY NICO LATHOURIS PRODUCED BY DOUG MITCHELL GEORGE MILLER PJ VOETEN DIRECTED BY GEORGE MILLER

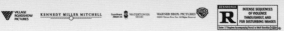

Mad Max Fury Road
2015

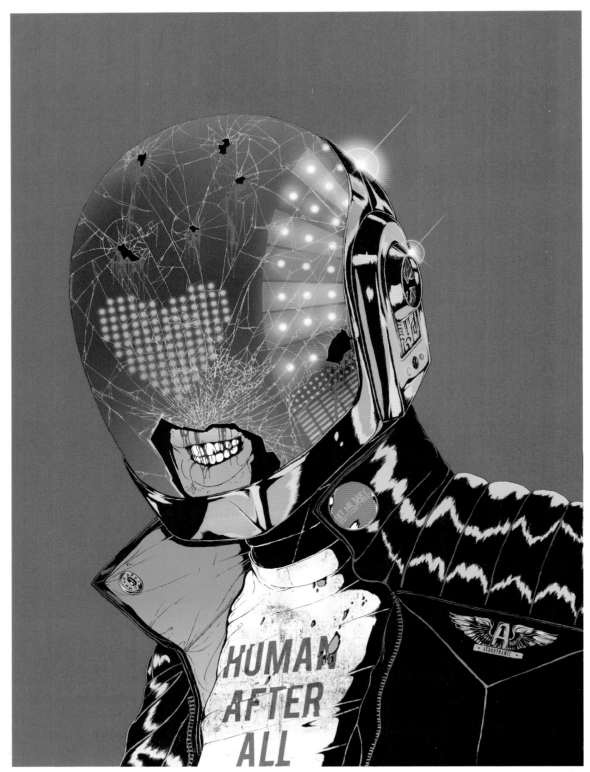

Guy
2014

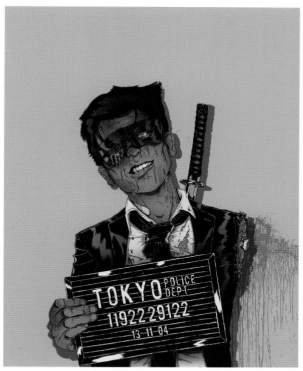

Crazy88
2014

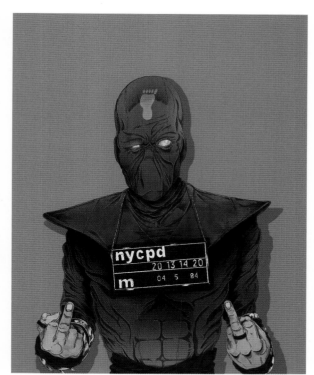

Foot Clan
2014

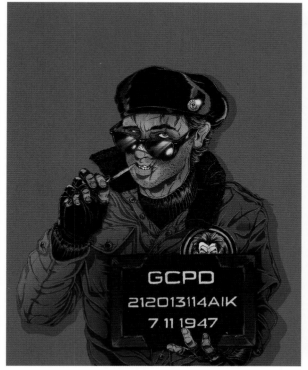

Joker Goon
2014

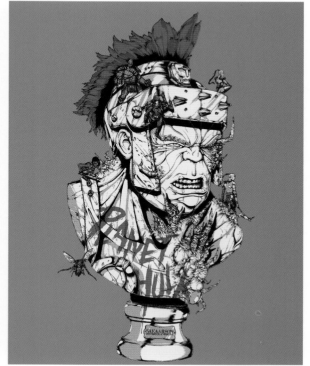

Planet Hulk
2015

RYAN BRINKERHOFF

Ryan Brinkerhoff is a graphic designer/illustrator with ten-plus years of experience in the design industry. Having worked in an agency environment and as an in-house designer, he is constantly pursuing passion projects outside of his nine-to-five job to keep the creativity flowing. He has a love for pop culture and enjoys making posters that showcase his interests, allowing him to be creative, and above all, make people smile!

WEBSITE: www.banditodesignco.com

Stay Puft Marshmallows
2018

Dinosaurs of Dinosaur Land
2018

Beetlejuice
2018

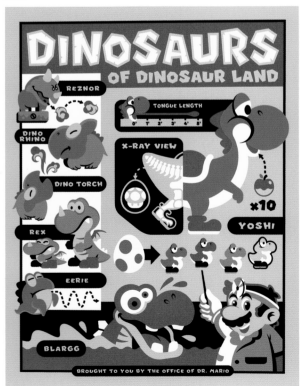

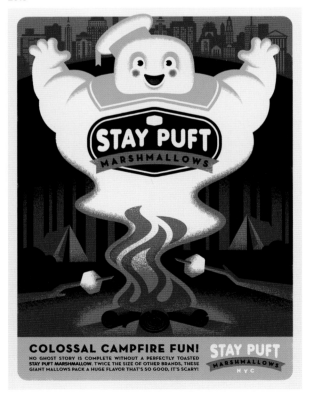

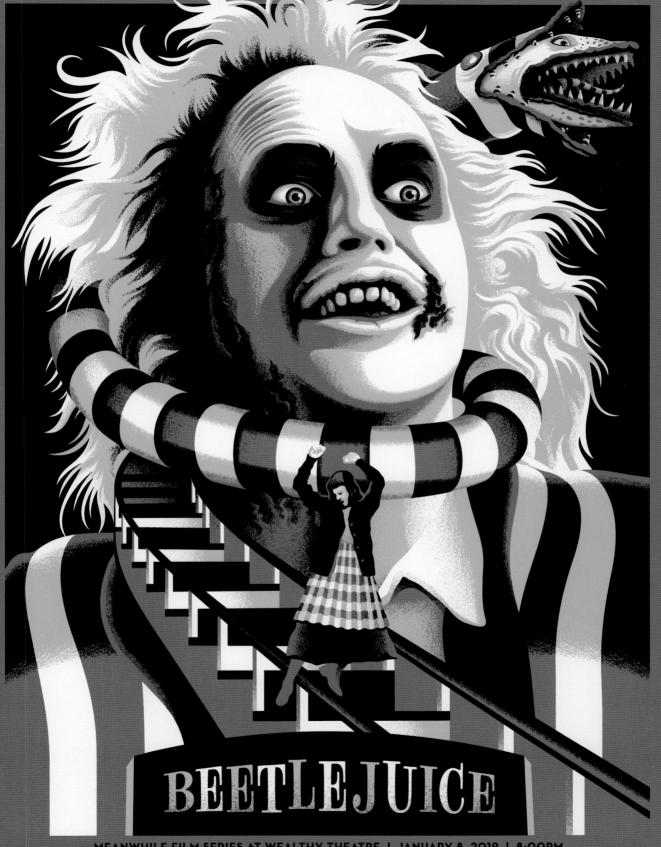

BEETLEJUICE

MEANWHILE FILM SERIES AT WEALTHY THEATRE | JANUARY 8, 2019 | 8:00PM

Meanwhile
BAR

WT

BANDITO
Design Co

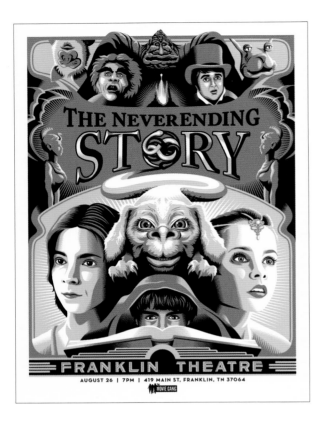

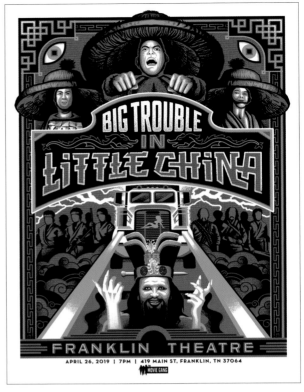

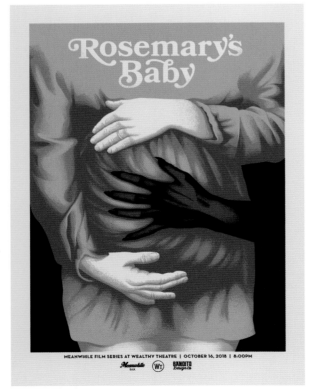

> **"** It doesn't have to be high art; it just has to be fun art!"

Get to Know Your Enemy: Jungle Hunter
2018

Big Trouble in Little China
2019

Rosemary's Baby
2018

The Neverending Story
2017

JUNGLE HUNTER

THE ULTIMATE PREDATOR

PHYSIOLOGY

UNATTRACTIVE, ARTHROPOD-LIKE MANDIBLES.

BRUTAL, INTELLIGENT, AND ADHERES STRICTLY TO RITUAL AND TRADITION.

ENHANCED STRENGTH AND CONSIDERABLE BODY MASS.

COLLECTS TROPHIES, CONSISTING OF THE SKULLS AND/OR SPINAL COLUMNS OF ITS VICTIMS.

SMALL TROPHIES DECORATE THE HUNTER'S ATTIRE. THIS IS AN ATTEMPT TO INTIMIDATE.

LUMINESCENT BLOOD. IF IT BLEEDS, WE CAN KILL IT.

SKILLED CLIMBER, KNOWN TO MOVE FROM TREETOP TO TREETOP IN PURSUIT.

ARSENAL OF WEAPONS

WRIST BLADES
TWO RETRACTABLE RAZOR SHARP BLADES

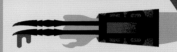

BIO-MASK
ENHANCED SPECTRUM OF VISION AND TARGETING AID

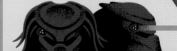

PLASMACASTER
SHOULDER-MOUNTED ENERGY CANNON

CLOAKING
ACTIVE CAMOUFLAGE INVISIBILITY SYSTEM

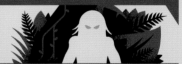

SELF-DESTRUCT DEVICE
POWERFUL TIMED EXPLOSIVE

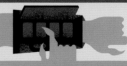

COUNTDOWN

AFTER BEING MORTALLY WOUNDED, THE HUNTER WILL ACTIVATE A SELF-DESTRUCT DEVICE TO ENSURE IT DIES WITH HONOR AND GETS THE **LAST LAUGH**

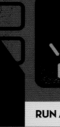

RUN AWAY!   CRITICAL SIGNIFICANT MODERATE   ◀ THREAT LEVEL

GET TO DA CHOPPA!

U.S. ARMY SPECIAL FORCES

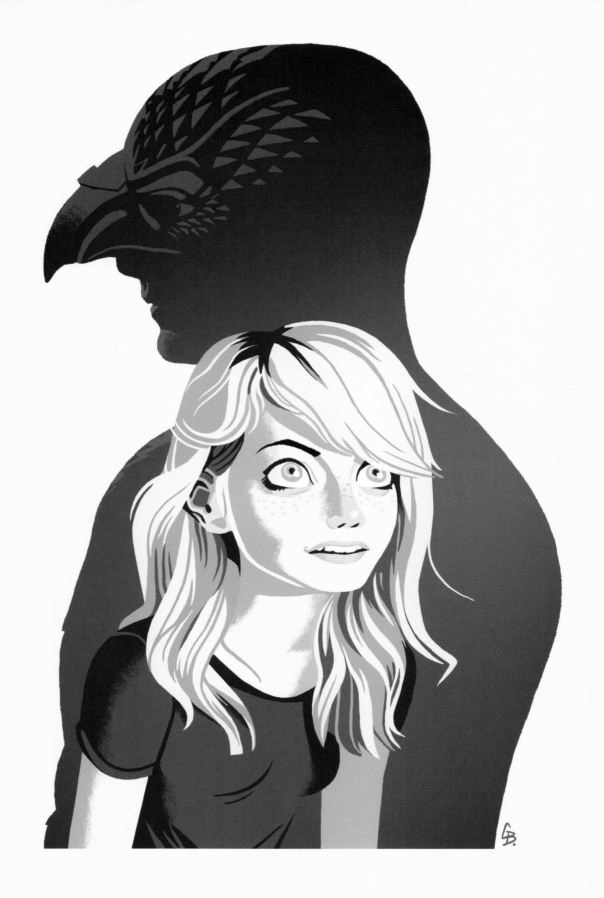

GLEN BROGAN

Glen Brogan is an illustrator operating out of Charleston, West Virginia. He used to get in trouble at school for drawing cartoons all day but now he makes a living at it. His body of work consists of pop-culture drawings and designs that have been featured worldwide in gallery shows, websites, magazines, and art books. He has collaborated with organizations and brands such as *Sesame Street*, Marvel, DC Comics, Disney, *Stranger Things*, *Breaking Bad*, *Ghostbusters*, *Star Trek*, *Overwatch*, the Coen brothers, Laika, and Cartoon Network.

WEBSITE: www.glenbrogan.tumblr.com

" Pop culture is the only thing that sets us apart from the animals . . . Oh, and forks."

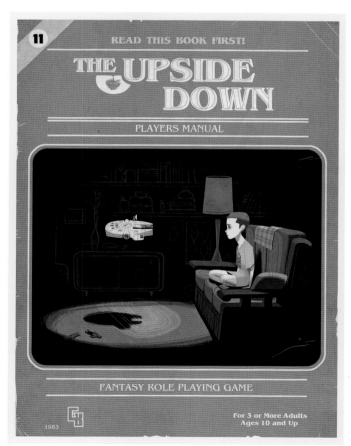

Birdman
2014

Stranger Things / Players Manual
2016

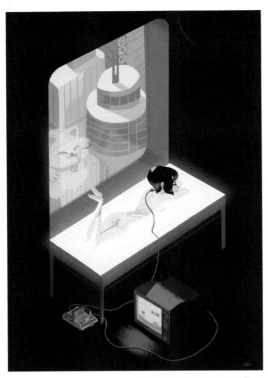

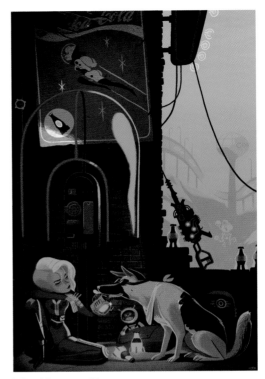

Ghost in the Shell / Famicom Ghost
2017

Fallout / Commonwealth
2017

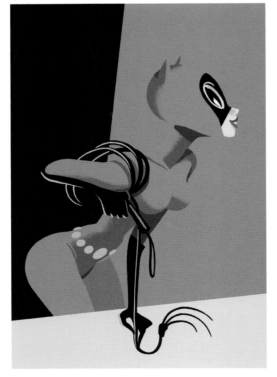

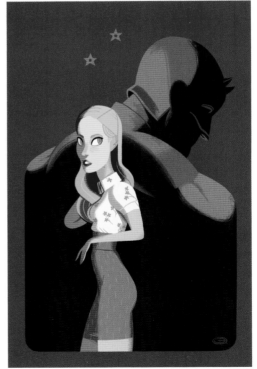

Catwoman
2016

Daredevil / The Devil
2018

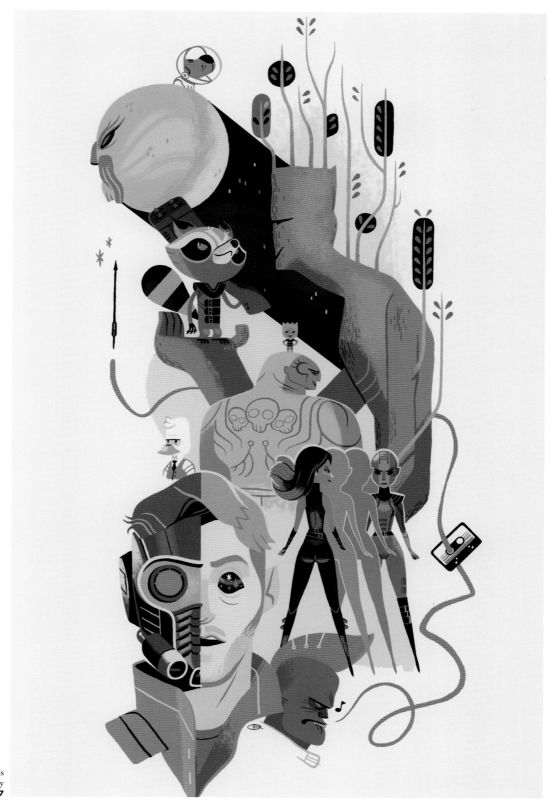

JOSHUA BUDICH

Joshua Budich is an independent illustrator working for numerous galleries, including Gallery1988, Spoke Art, and Hero Complex Gallery; movie studios; and media outlets around the globe. Inspired by a love for the pop culture of his youth, his primary focus is on screenprints that celebrate popular movies (*Star Wars, Star Trek, The Big Lebowski*), television series (*Lost, Marvel's Agents of S.H.I.E.L.D.*), animated shows (*The Simpsons, My Neighbor Totoro, Akira*), and more. Budich graduated from the University of Maryland, Baltimore County with a bachelor of fine arts (imaging and digital arts) in 2000. He enjoys cooking with his wife, drawing with his son, and reading to his daughter. He lives in the Baltimore/District of Columbia area.

WEBSITE: www.joshuabudich.com
INSTAGRAM: @jbudich
FACEBOOK: /joshuabudich
TWITTER: @jbudich

" I don't paint religious icons. I don't worship athletes. I don't follow politicians. I draw what I love. Pop culture."

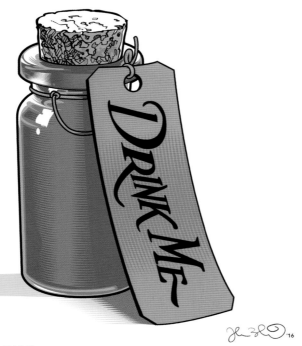

Fictional Food – Alice Drink Me
2015

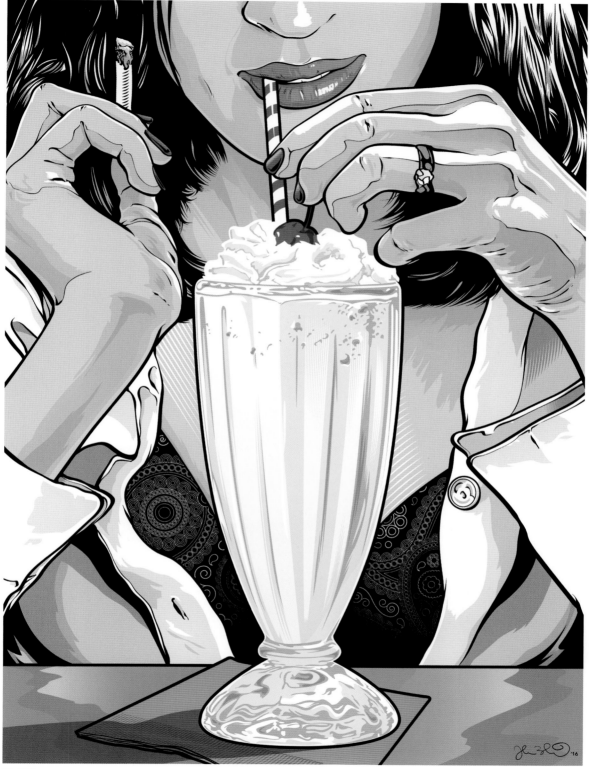

Mia Wallace
2015

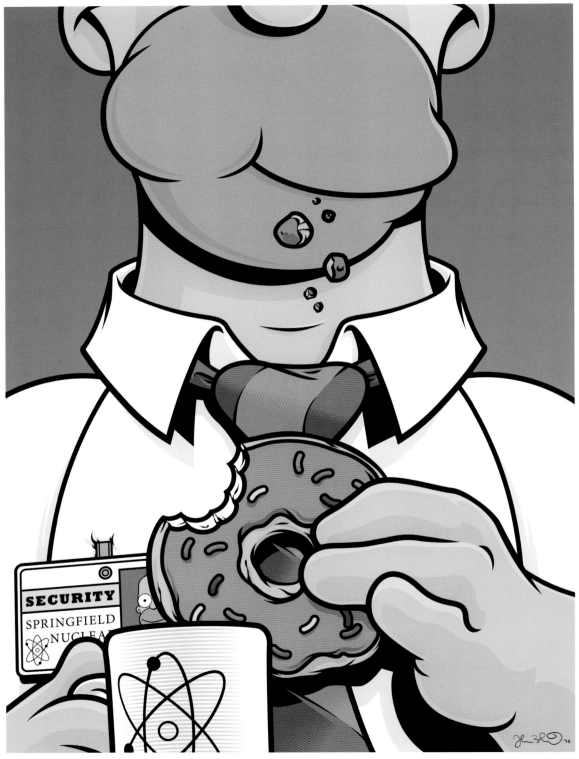

Homer Simpson
2015

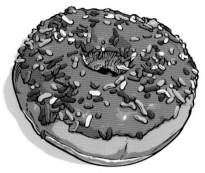

Simpsons – Donut
2015

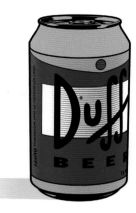

Simpsons – Duff
2000

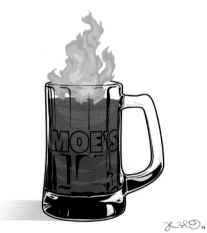

Simpsons – Flaming Moe
2015

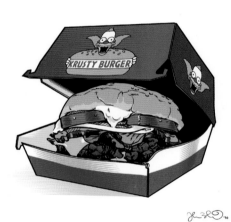

Simpsons – KrustyBurger
2015

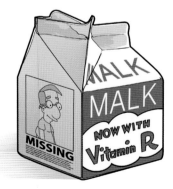

Simpsons – Malk
2015

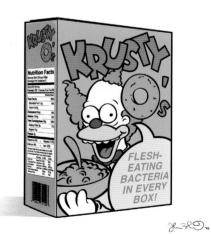

Simpsons – Krusty Os
2015

Fictional Food – Dharma Beer
2014

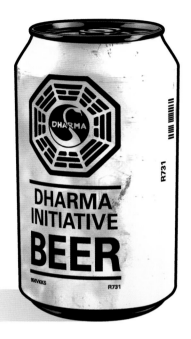

Fictional Food – Dharma Wine
2014

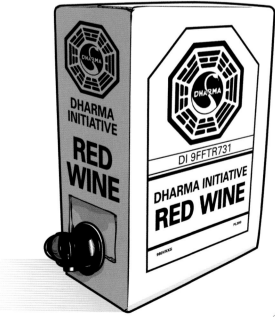

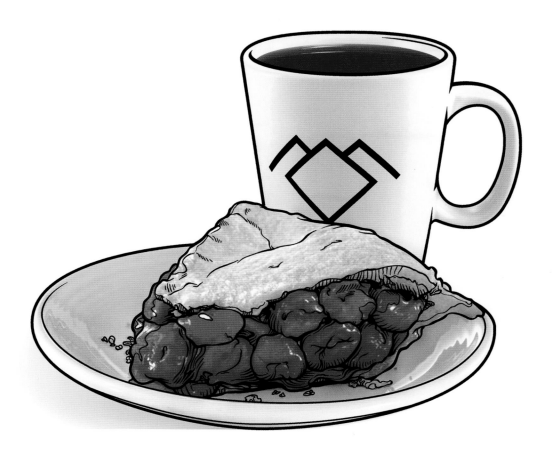

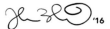

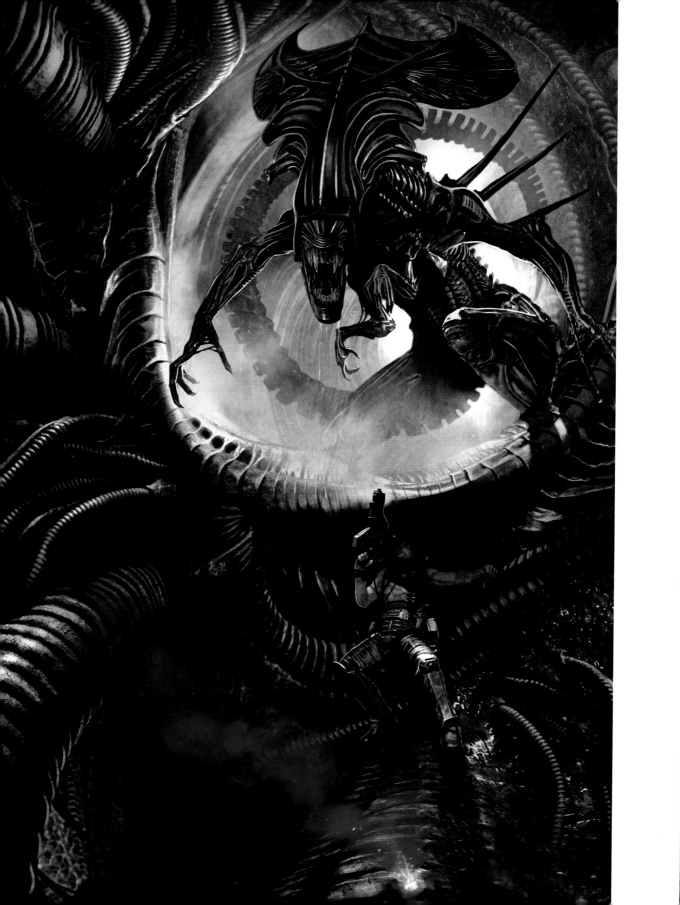

BENJAMIN CARRÉ

S ince 1997, Benjamin Carré has worked for the largest publishing houses, illustrating more than a hundred covers of science fiction, fantasy, and young adult novels. He also illustrates comics books for *Star Wars*, *Blade Runner*, and *Halo*, among others. He created and co-illustrated the comics *Smoke City*. The illustrator of role-playing games and board games (*Nephilim*, *Zombies*, *T.I.M.E Stories*, and *Marvel Noir*), he is also very present in the world of video games as a concept artist on *Alone in the Dark: The New Nightmare*, *Cold Fear*, *I Am Alive*, *Star Wars Journey*, *Heroes of Might and Magic*, and *League of Legends*. He has created concept art for the films *Walled In*, *La Traque*, and *Transformers: Age of Extinction* as well.

WEBSITE: www.artstation.com/ornicar

Desperate Housewife
2016

Metal Death
2019

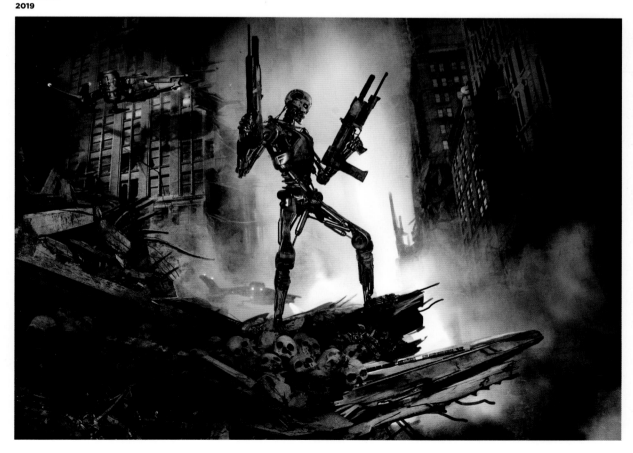

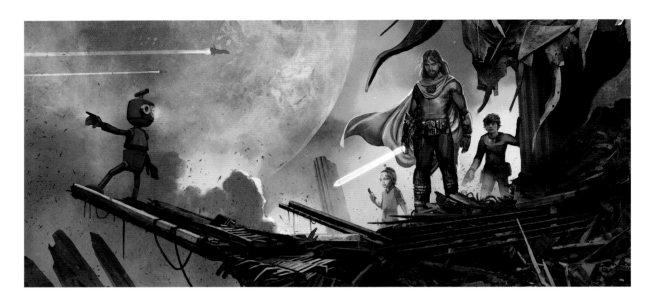

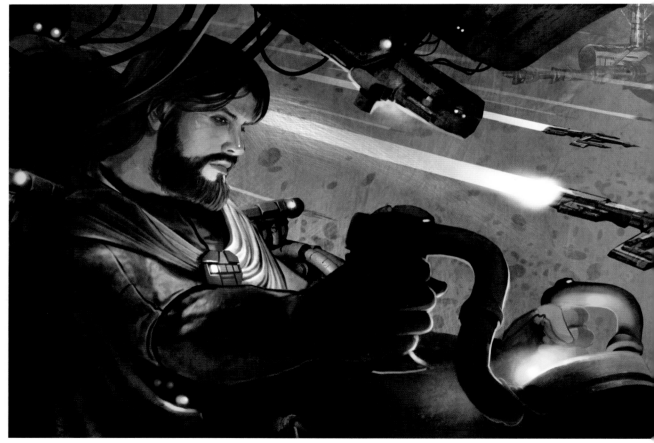

Ulysse 31
2018

Odysseus
2018

" " Today's pop culture is nothing more
than the classics of tomorrow."

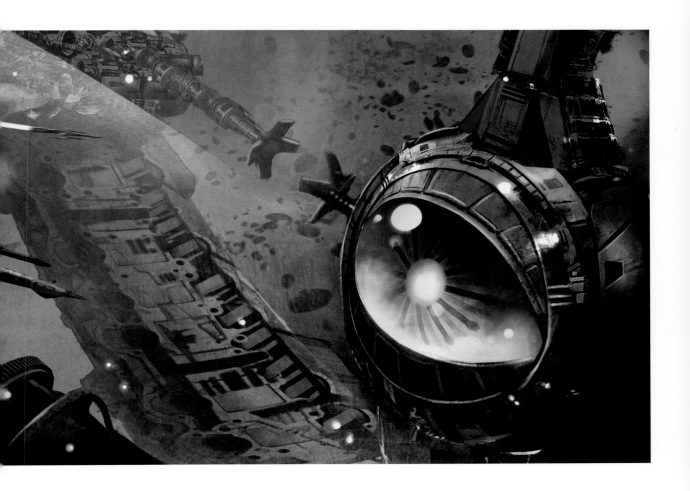

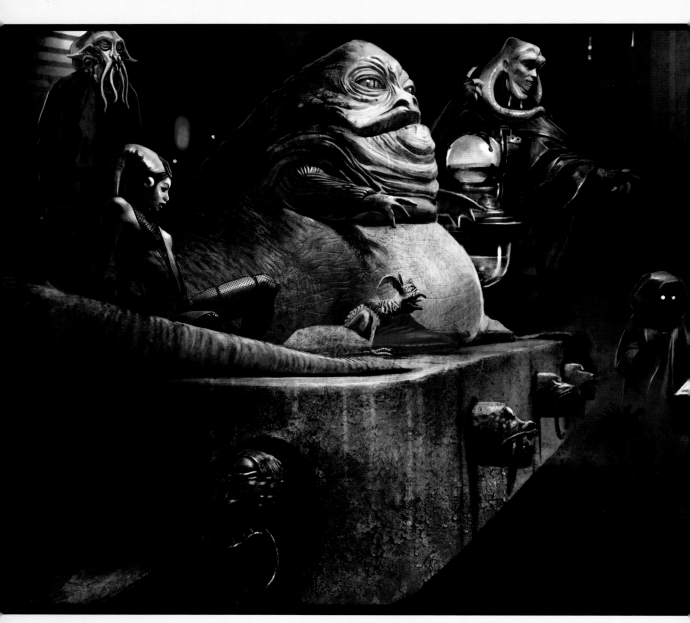

The Trophy
2016

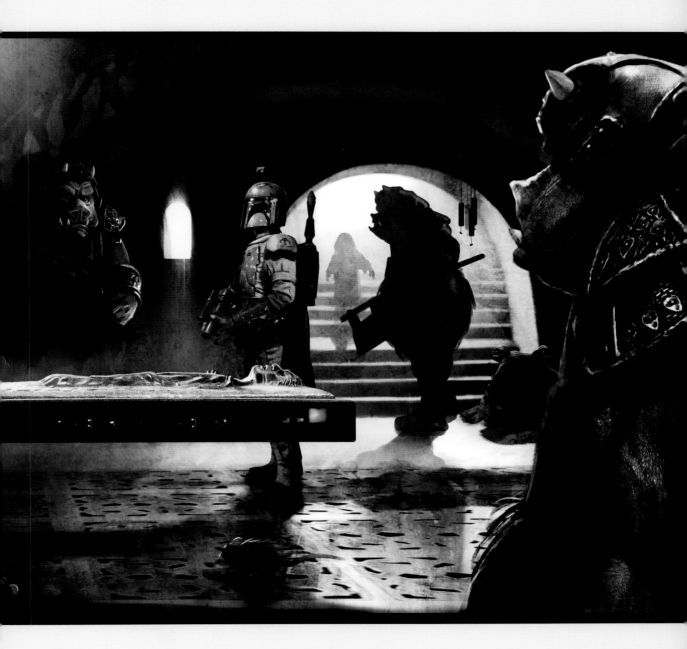

CLOGTWO

Clogtwo is a graffiti practitioner and visual engineer, as well as co-founder of the visual duo collective the Ink&Clog, and Singapura's urban art store, Utama.co, with his partner, Inkten.

Clogtwo's body of work explores numerous mediums, from spray paints to digital media. His body of work focuses on intricate mechanical designs and components, merging them into a style he calls the "MechaSoul." The MechaSoul revolves around the ideology between the psychological bond between mankind and technology.

In two decades, his obsession toward creating has taken him to Japan, South Korea, the United Kingdom, Europe, the United States, Mauritius, Australia, and the South East Asian Region .

Clogtwo has also been commissioned by renowned brands such as Mercedes-Benz, G-Shock, Google, Adidas, Microsoft, Apple, Converse, Mighty Jaxx, Oracle Digital Prime, and the Singapore Tourism Board.

WEBSITE: www.inkandclog.bigcartel.com
INSTAGRAM: @clogtwo
BEHANCE: /clogtwo

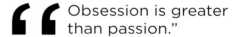

" Obsession is greater than passion."

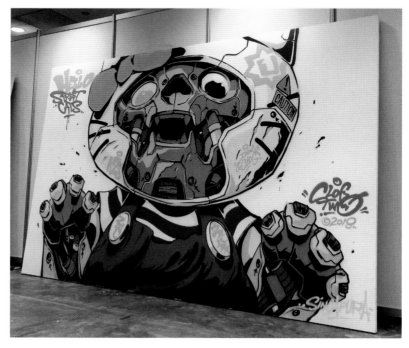

Mechasoul Hello Kitty
2018

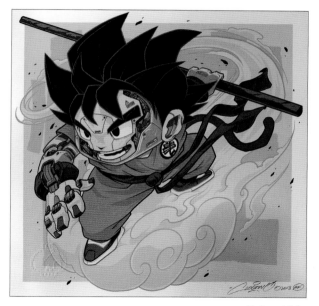

Mechasoul Goku
2018

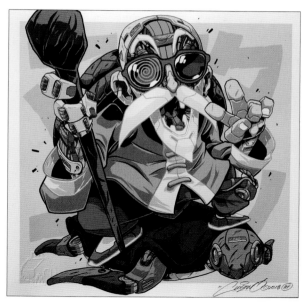

Mechasoul Master Roshi
2018

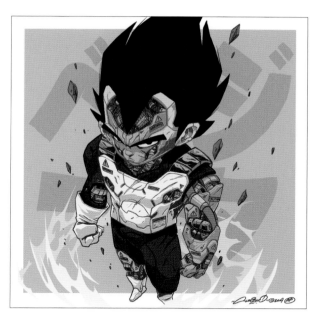

Mechasoul Vegeta
2019

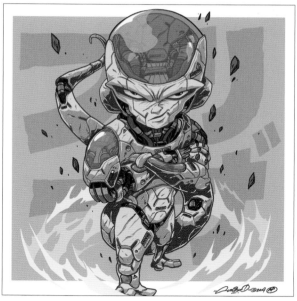

Mechasoul Frieza
2019

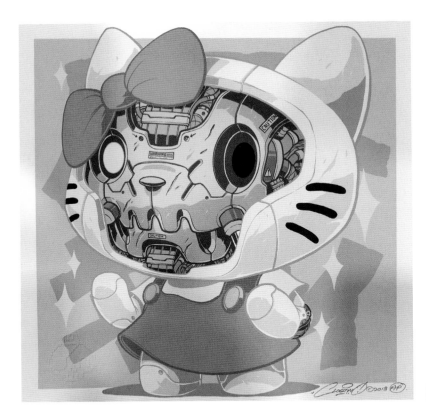

Mechasoul Hello Kitty
2018

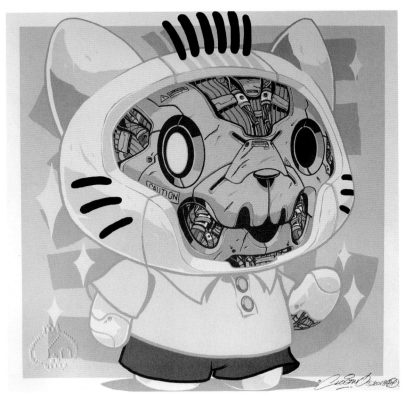

Mechasoul Hello Daniel
2018

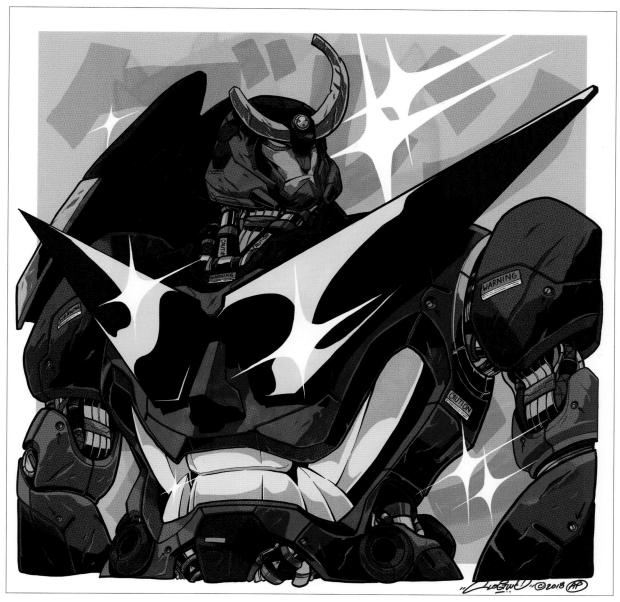

Mechasoul Gurren Lagann
2018

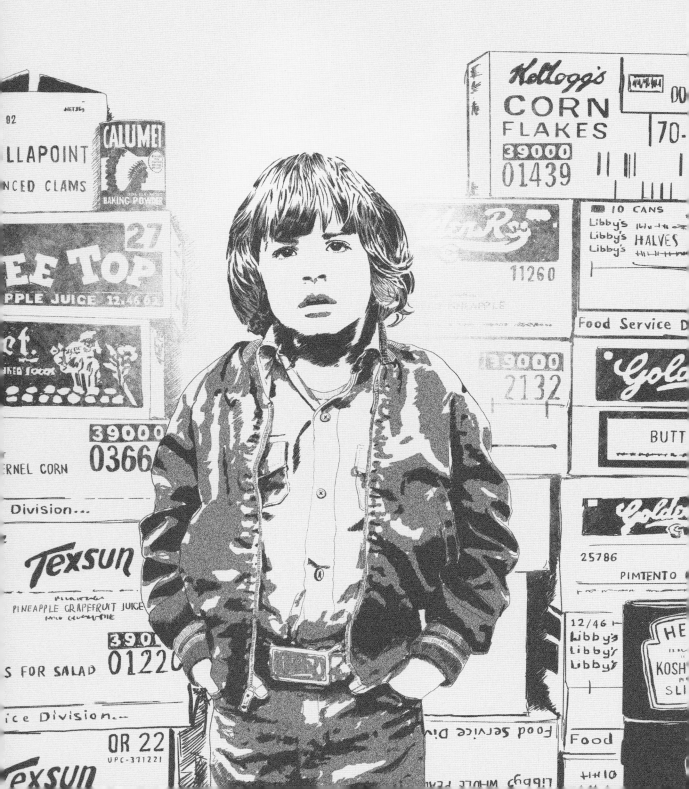

ADAM COCKERTON

Adam Cockerton is a freelance creative art director living in London, England. He's been a graphic designer for more than a decade and has been lucky enough to work with film studios and entertainment clients on some leading projects as well as being in-house art director at Legendary Entertainment for five years. Illustration and "geek art" are recent additions to Adam's portfolio.

"I've been noodling and doodling since I was a boy, but the illustration thing is quite new though; it's my side hustle. I'm mostly self-taught and always learning new things on every illustration project and it's fun rediscovering drawing after designing for such a long time."

BEHANCE: /adamcockerton
INSTAGRAM: @adamcockertonart

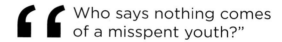

"Who says nothing comes of a misspent youth?"

The Shining
2016

Godzilla
2014

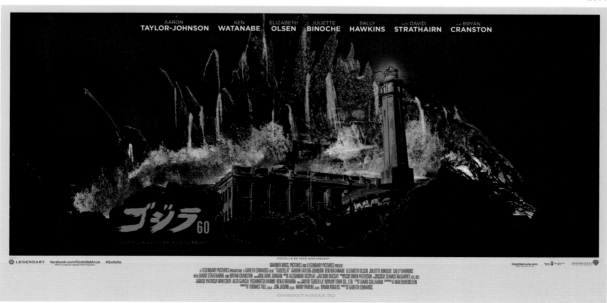

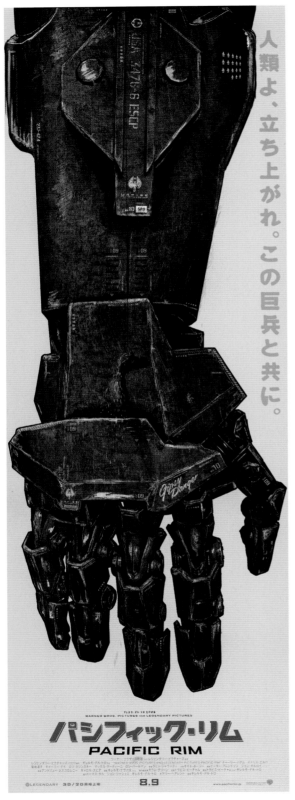

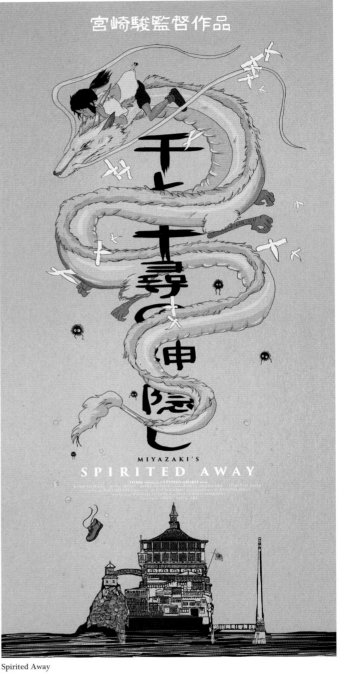

Spirited Away
2016

Pacific Rim
2017

Hood Thing
2017

JOHN CARPENTER'S
THE THING
The ultimate in alien terror

TURMAN-FOSTER COMPANY presents JOHN CARPENTER'S THE THING starring KURT RUSSELL screenplay by BILL LANCASTER special visual effects by ALBERT WHITLOCK
special make-up effects ROB BOTTIN music by ENNIO MORRICONE director of photography DEAN CUNDY edited by LARRY FRANCO associate producer WILBORE STARK produced by STUART COHEN
executive producers DAVID FOSTER & LAWRENCE TURMAN produced by JOHN CARPENTER based on the story "WHO GOES THERE" written by JOHN W. CAMPBELL JR.

Mr. Robot
2016

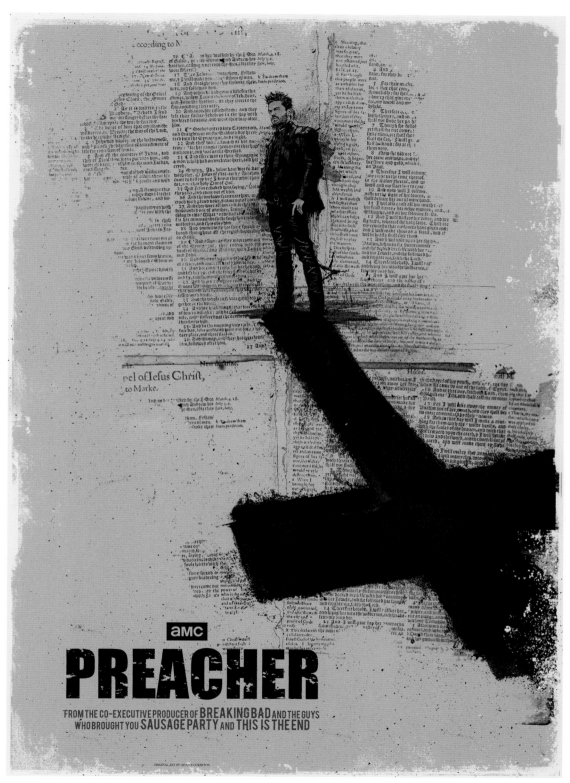

Preacher / In the Shadow of the Cross
2017

GRAHAM CORCORAN

Graham Corcoran is an illustrator from Dublin, Ireland. He developed his unique illustration style from a love of the classic mid-century designers and illustrators of the fifties and sixties. Specializing in pop-culture illustration, he has exhibited his work at Gallery Nucleus, Bottleneck Gallery, and Gallery1988. Graham's commercial work can be found on book covers, magazines, and advertising campaigns around the world. He also works as an art director in the animation industry and has designed several cartoon series, such as the hit show *Kiva Can Do!* for Nick Jr.

WEBSITE: www.grahamcorcoran.com
INSTAGRAM: @GrahamArtwork
CONTACT: graham.corcoran@gmail.com

> " I like to bring a retro whimsical style to modern pop culture subjects."

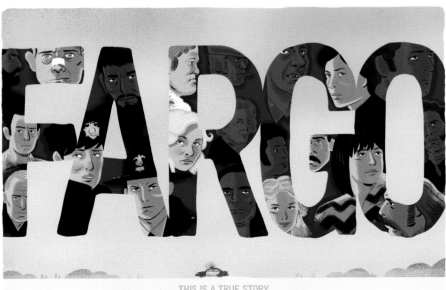

Fargo
2018

THIS IS A TRUE STORY.

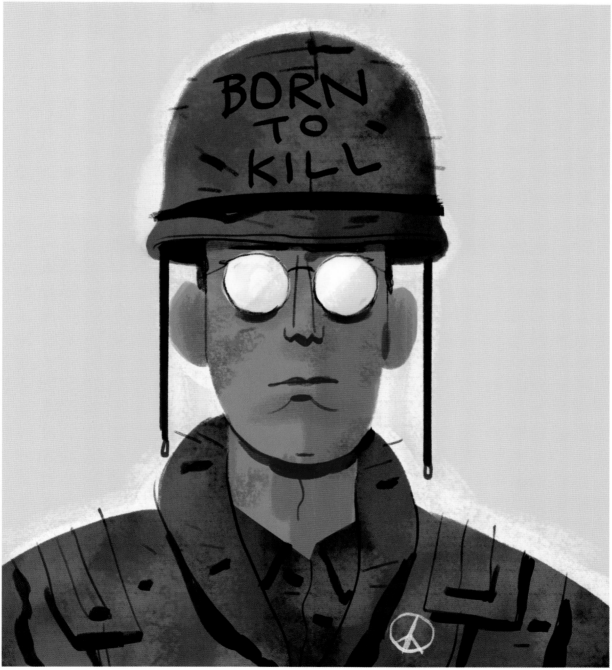

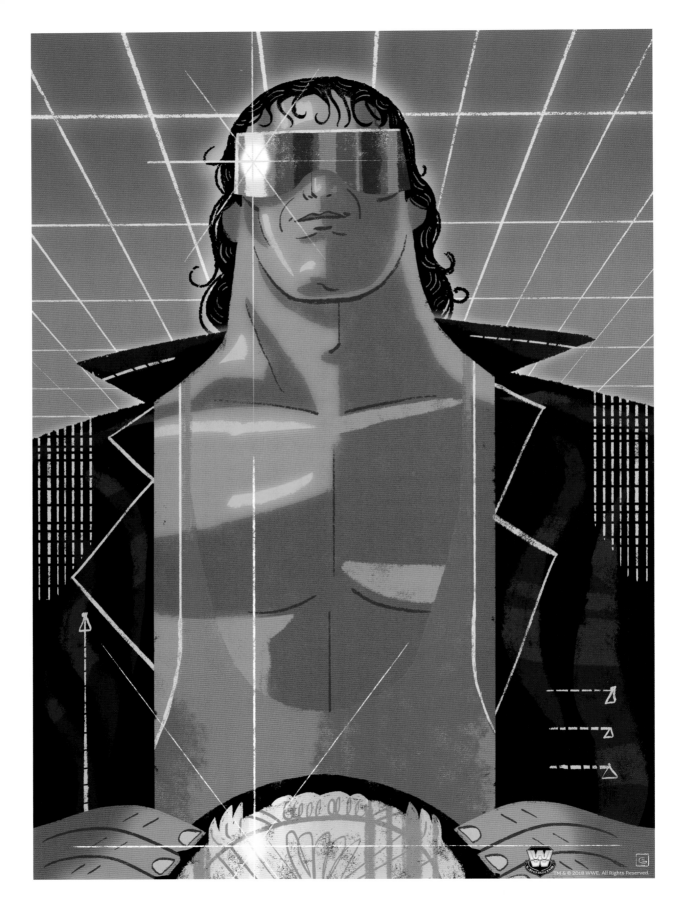

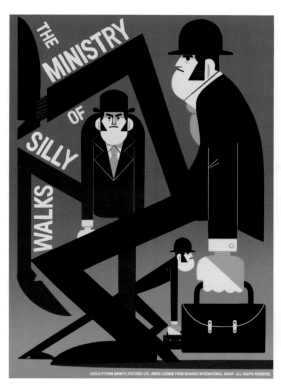

Ministry Of Silly Walks
2018

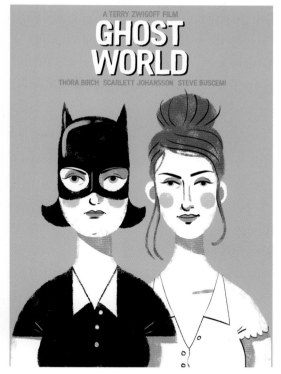

Ghost World
2018

Bret 'The Hitman' Hart
2018

The Good The Bad
and The Ugly
2018

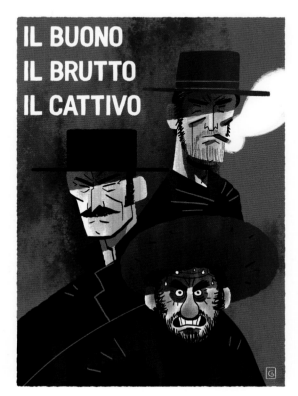

NICOLAS DELORT

Nicolas Delort is a French Canadian illustrator specializing in black and white illustration. He is strongly influenced by symbolist and romantic painting, as well as by nineteenth century printmaking, and when he's not drawing, he spends most of his time watching TV series (ranging from *X-Files* to *Game of Thrones*, to *Twin Peaks*, *Oz*, and *True Detective*) or reading fantasy novels (Joe Abercrombie, Brandon Sanderson, Robin Hobb). Also passionate about classical music, this extraordinary artist routinely practices the clarinet, the piano, and the flute.

WEBSITE: www.nicolasdelort.com
TWITTER: @nicodelort
TUMBLR: nicolasdelort

Nosferatu, Phantom der Nacht
2014

Harry Potter
2012

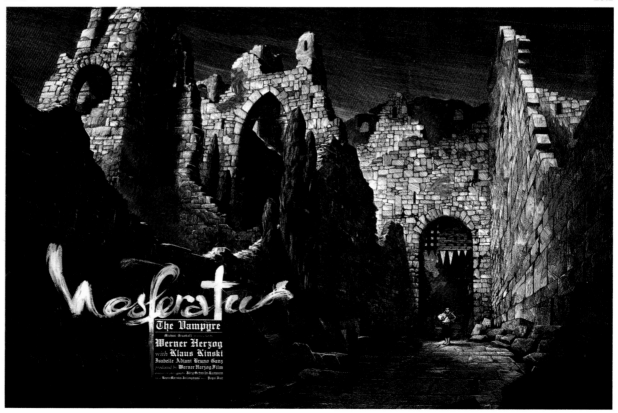

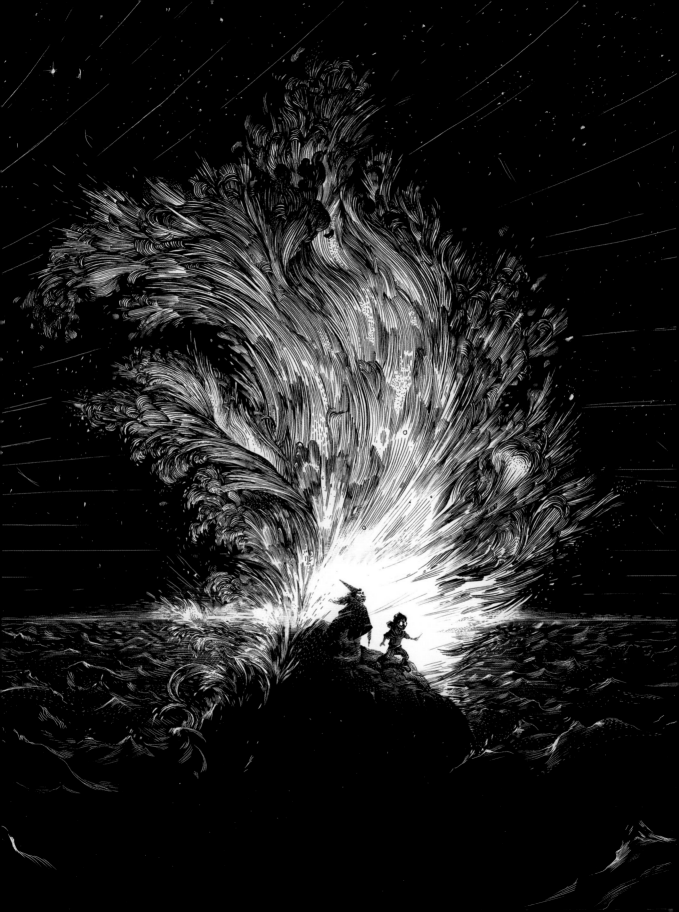

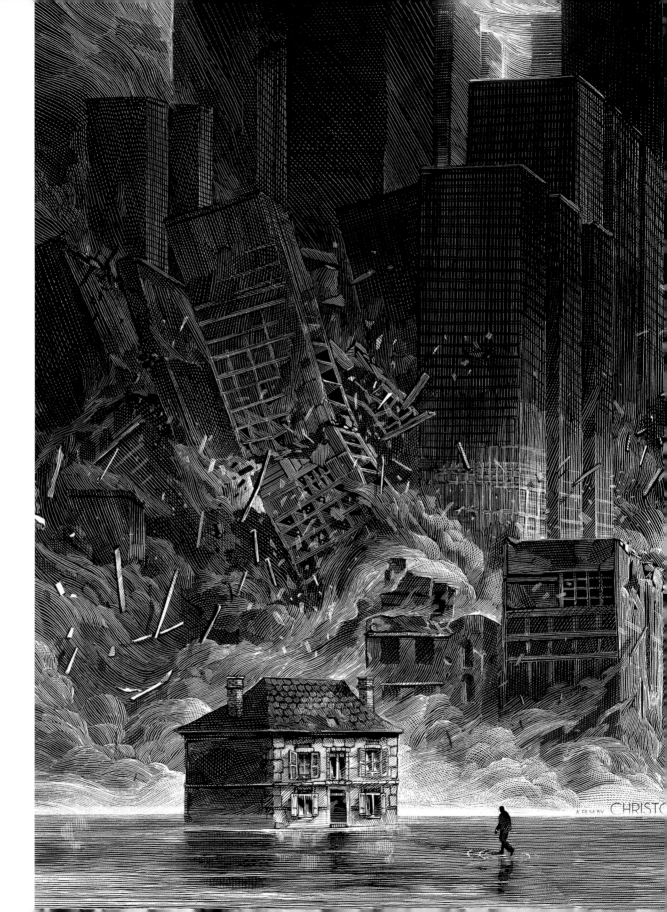

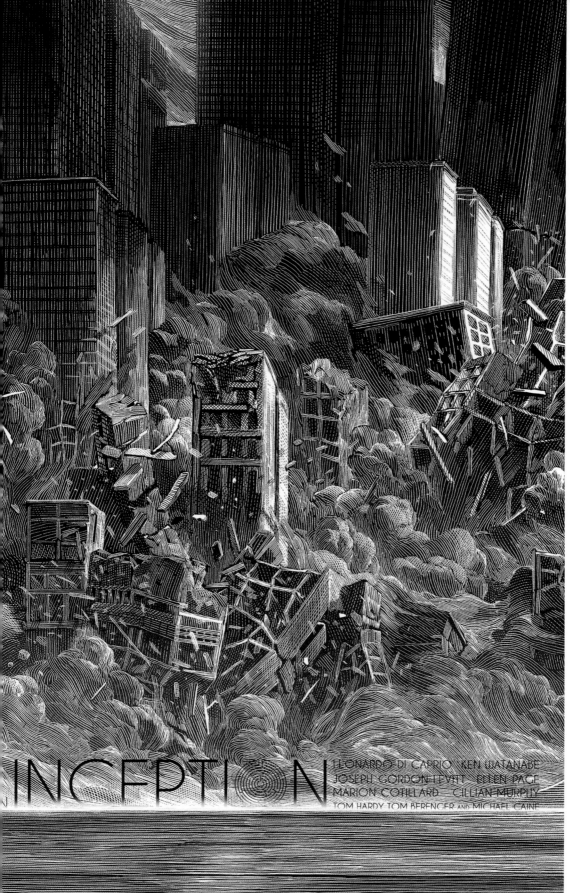

INCEPTION

THE LEONARDO DI CAPRIO   KEN WATANABE
JOSEPH GORDON-LEVITT   ELLEN PAGE
MARION COTILLARD   CILLIAN MURPHY
TOM HARDY TOM BERENGER AND MICHAEL CAINE

Inception
2015

PETER DIAMOND

Peter Diamond is a Canadian illustrator based in Vienna, Austria, working with clients and collaborators around the world in publishing, editorial, and advertising. His work has won awards from the Society of Illustrators, Graphis, 3x3 Design, and the Society of Illustrators Los Angeles, among others. He has been published by Taschen and Die Gestalten, and has exhibited in Asia, Europe, Australia, and North America.

WEBSITE: www.peterdiamond.ca

> **"** To me the border between pop culture and high culture is largely artificial, and I prefer to think of them in concert rather than in contrast. I see a river of stories, sound, and pictures thousands of years long, and it's a daily honor to contribute even the tiniest drop to its flow."

Breakfast At Banksy's
2015

Ayahuasca
2019

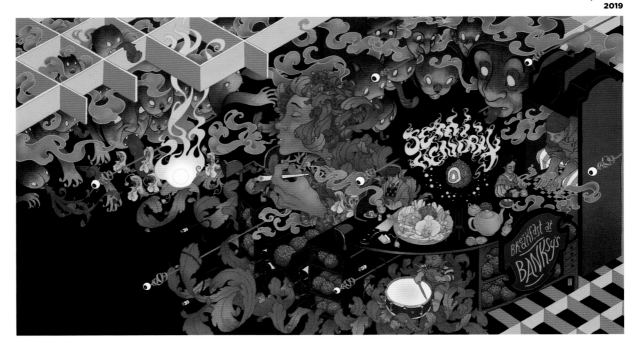

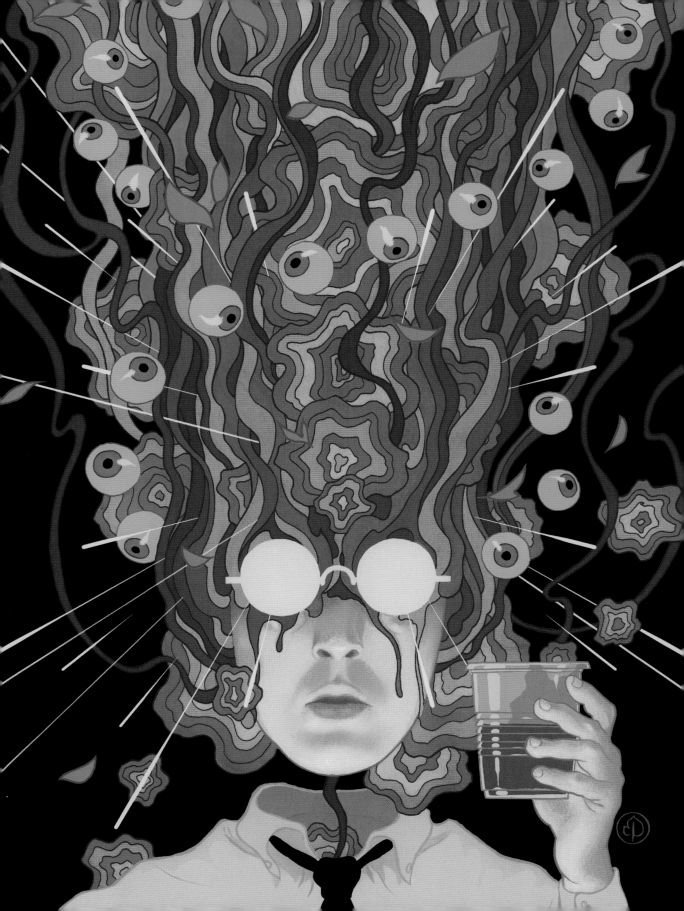

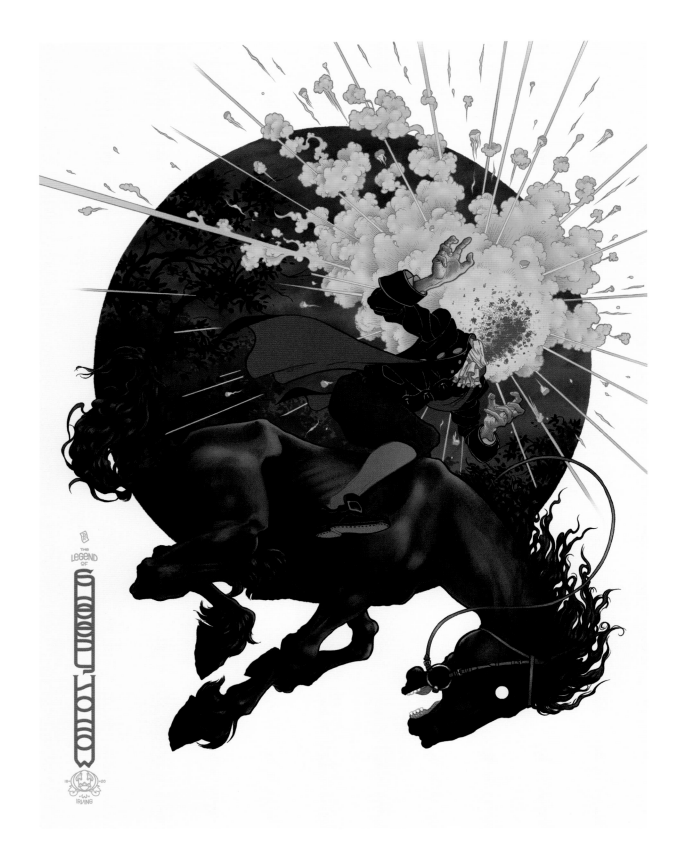

THE LEGEND OF SLEEPY HOLLOW

1820 W. IRVING

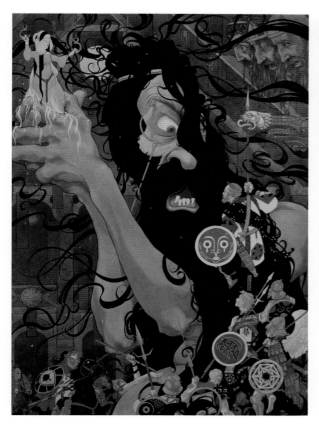

In Penkawr's Hall
2017-2018

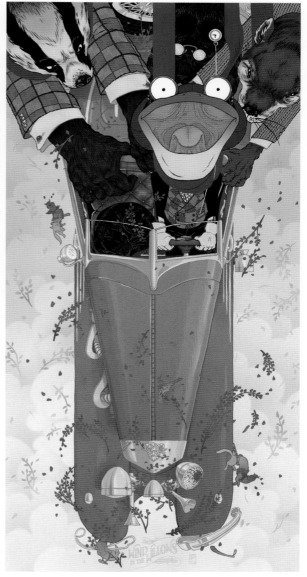

The Wind In The Willows
2017

The Legend Of Sleepy Hollow
2017

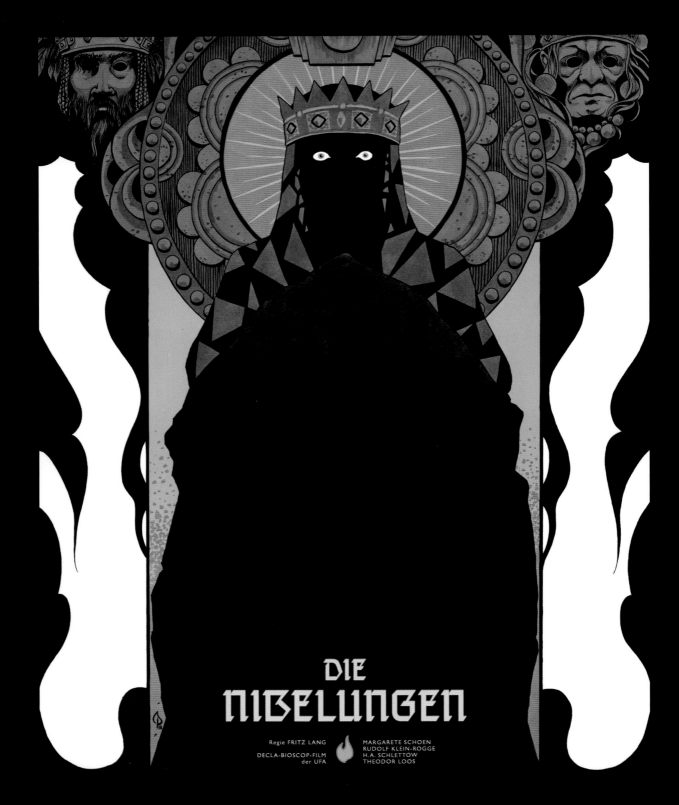

DIE
NIBELUNGEN

Regie FRITZ LANG   MARGARETE SCHOEN
                         RUDOLF KLEIN-ROGGE
DECLA-BIOSCOP-FILM   H.A. SCHLETTOW
        der UFA   THEODOR LOOS

Die Nibelungen
2018

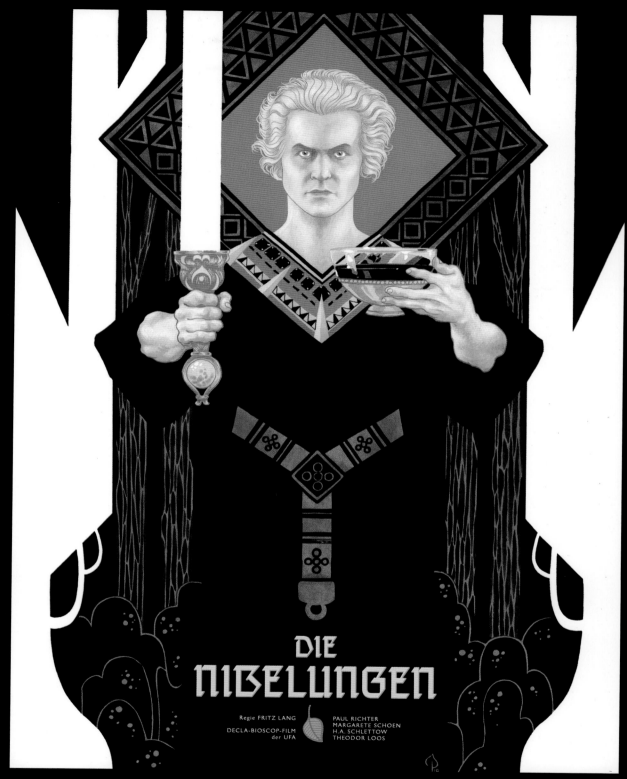

DIE
NIBELUNGEN

Regie FRITZ LANG   PAUL RICHTER
                         MARGARETE SCHOEN
DECLA-BIOSCOP-FILM   H.A. SCHLETTOW
      der UFA   THEODOR LOOS

Die Nibelungen
2018

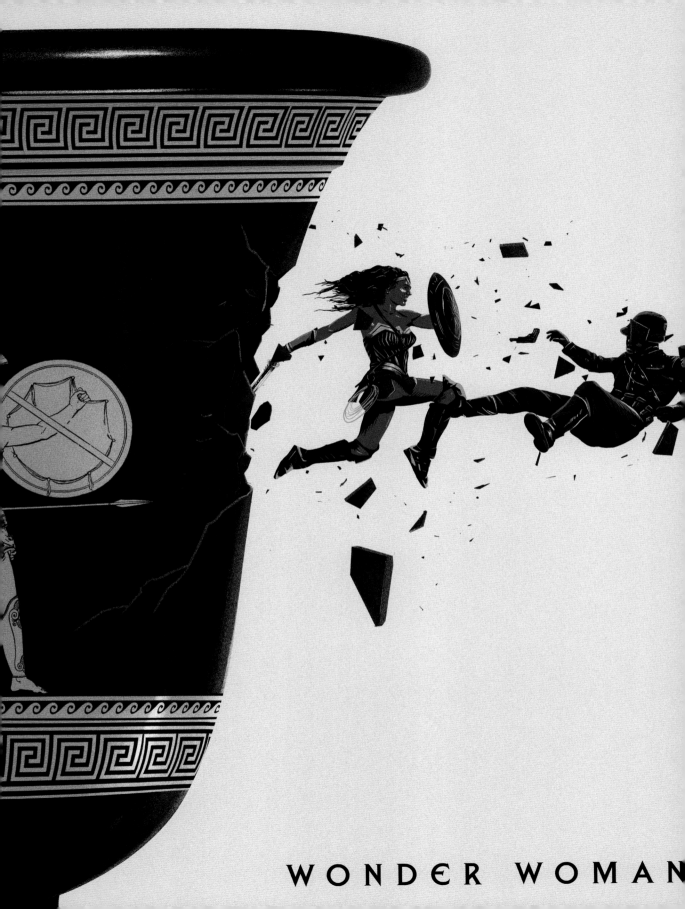

WONDER WOMAN

DOALY

Doaly is a UK-based graphic designer and digital illustrator with a passion for storytelling. His work is characterized by his conceptual approach to illustration and his ability to adapt his style to be sympathetic to the subject matter.

Over the years he has created artwork for a wide range of clients including the BBC, Disney, Pixar, Marvel, Lucasfilm, Warner Bros., 20th Century Fox, Sony Pictures, *Wired* magazine, and Sony PlayStation. He is also active in the pop-culture gallery scene and has created official artwork for properties including Spider-Man, Wonder Woman, Superman, the Flash, *South Park*, *Rick and Morty*, and *Star Wars*.

WEBSITE: www.doaly.com
INSTAGRAM: @_doaly
TWITTER: @Doaly

" I enjoy the art of storytelling and finding new ways to tell those stories."

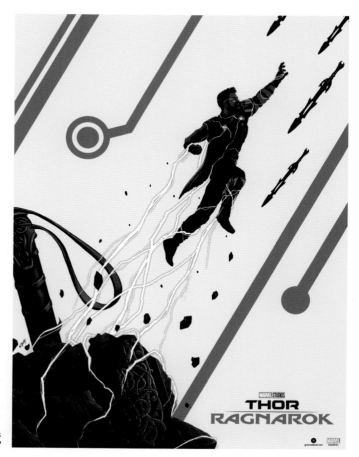

Wonder Woman
2017

Thor Ragnarok
2017

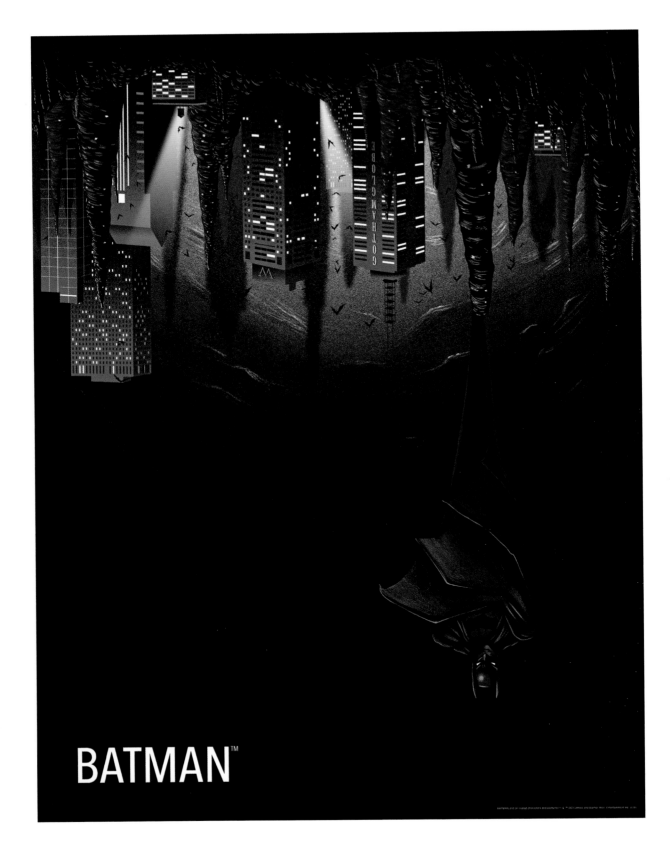

BATMAN™

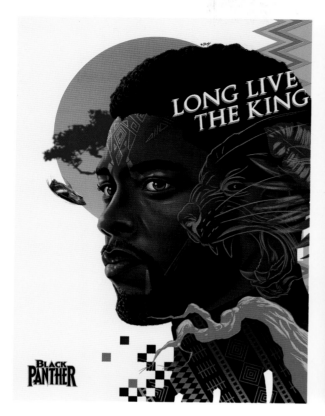

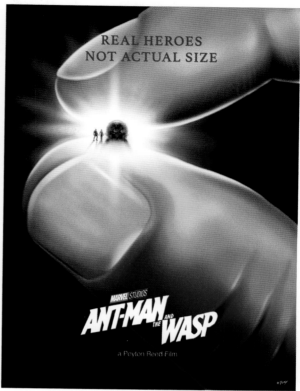

Black Panther
2018

Ant-Man and the Wasp
2018

Captain Marvel - Cover for
Empire magazine
2019

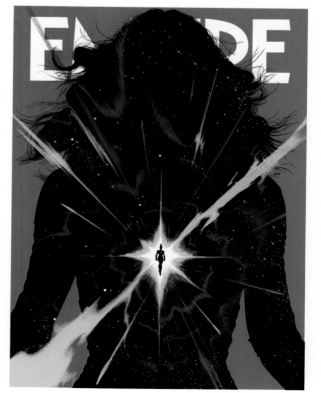

Batman
2019

LAURENT DURIEUX

L aurent Durieux doesn't actually live in a retro-futuristic world imagined by H. G. Wells and designed by Raymond Loewy. In Durieux's world, gigantic robots tower over forests populated by mythical beasts such as Bigfoot and King Kong; city skies are thick with airships shaped like Snoopy, while Buck Rogers–like vehicles whiz by on slender monorails; and movie monsters are portrayed as sensitive creatures, victims of their grotesqueries rather than revenge-fueled fiends.

Though he's spent two decades as a designer and teacher, the forty-two-year-old Brussels illustrator and graphic artist was only recently discovered in the United States, thanks to a number of high-profile awards and marquee commissions, including a 2013 screenprint for *Jaws*, which caught the eye of the film's director, Steven Spielberg. The climb from relative obscurity began in 2011, when Durieux was named one of the world's 200 Best Illustrators by the influential international advertising magazine *Lürzer's Archive*.

WEBSITE: www.laurentdurieux.com
ONLINE STORE: www.retropolis.bigcartel.com
CONTACT: jackdurieux70@gmail.com
INSTAGRAM: @laurent_durieuxillustration
FACEBOOK: /LaurentDurieuxIllustration
TWITTER: @laurentdurieux4

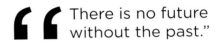

" There is no future without the past."

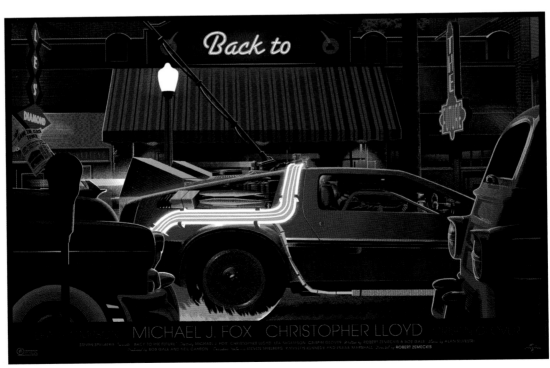

Back to the Future
2014

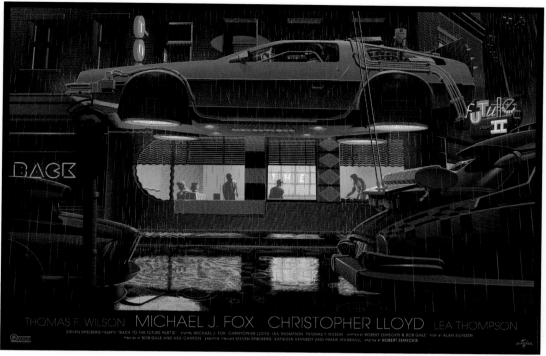

Back to the Future
2014

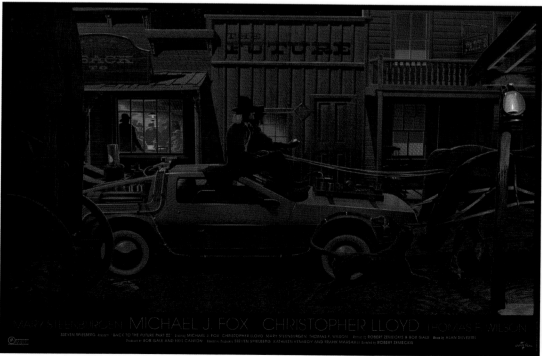

Back to the Future
2014

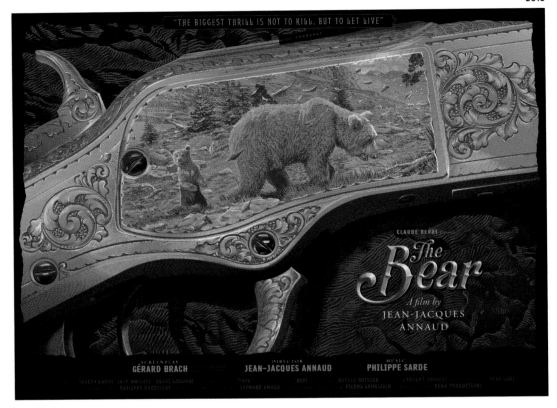

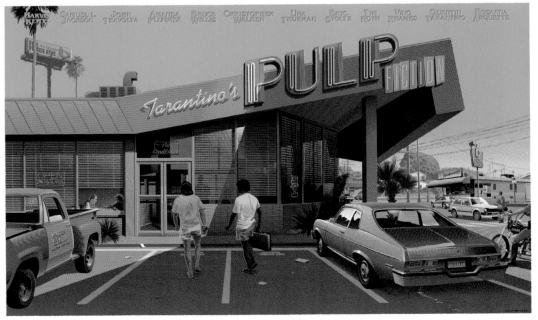

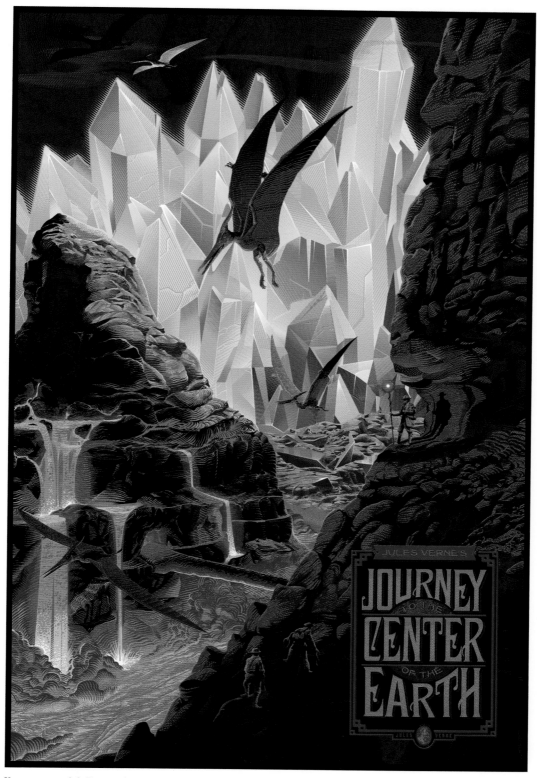

Voyage au centre de la Terre
2014

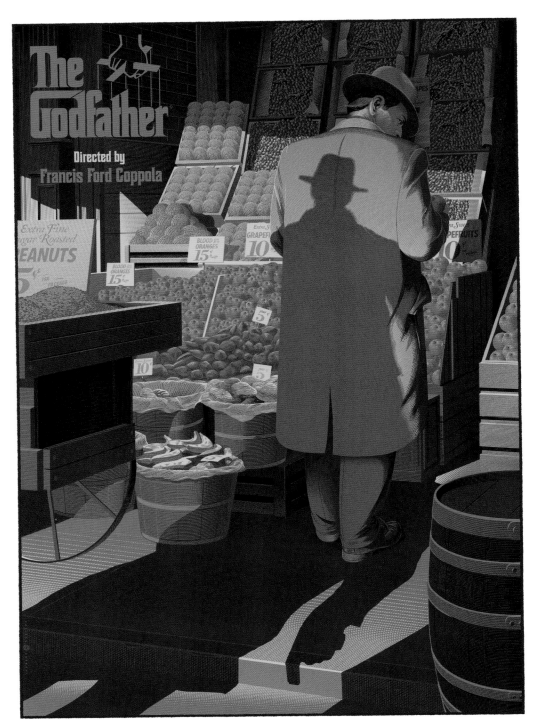

The Godfather part I
2014

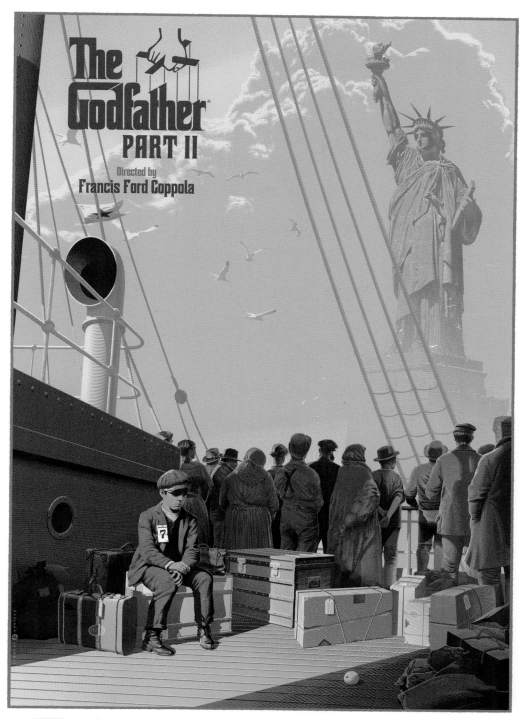

The Godfather part II
2014

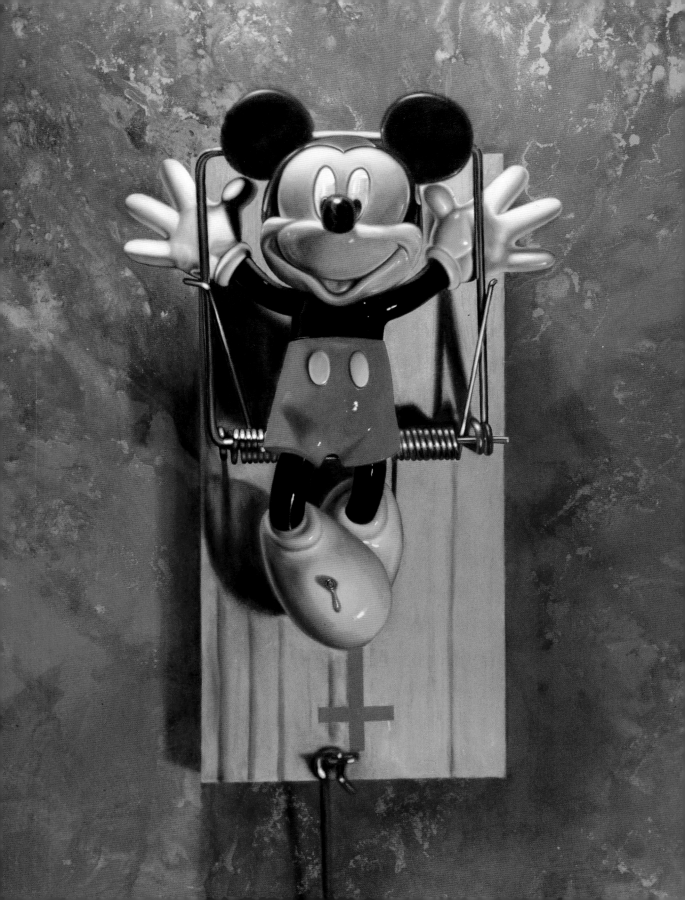

RON ENGLISH

One of the most prolific and recognizable artists alive today, Ron English has bombed the global landscape with unforgettable images—on the street, in museums, in movies, books, and television. English coined the term POPaganda to describe his signature mash-up of high and low cultural touchstones, from superhero mythology to totems of art history, populated with his vast and constantly growing arsenal of original characters, including MC Supersized, the obese fast-food mascot featured in the hit movie *Supersize Me* (English also appears as an on-camera interview subject in the film) and Abraham Obama, the fusion of America's sixteenth and forty-fourth presidents, an image widely discussed in the media as directly impacting the 2008 election.

Other characters carousing through English's art, in paintings, billboards, and sculpture include three-eyed rabbits, udderly delicious cowgirls, and grinning skulls, blending stunning visuals with the bitingly humorous undertones of America's premier pop iconoclast.

WEBSITE: www.popaganda.com
TWITTER: @ronenglishart
INSTAGRAM: @ronenglish

Mousetrap
2000

Super Supper
2010

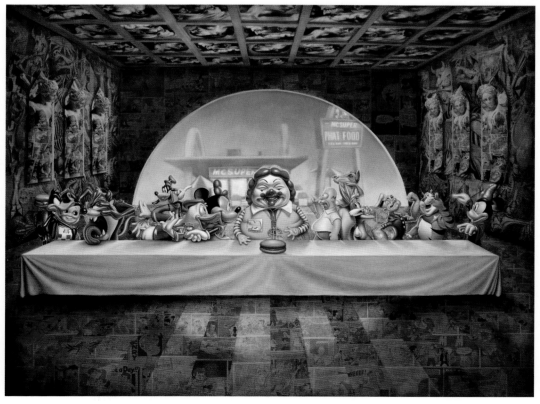

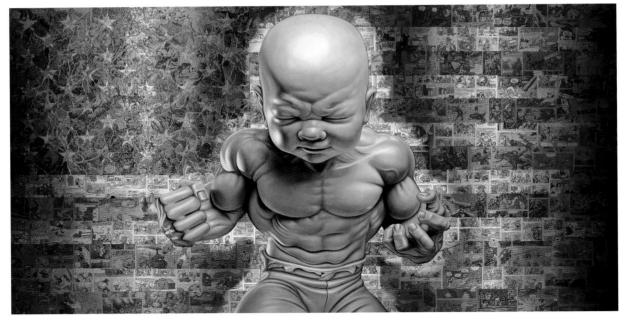

The American Infantile
2010

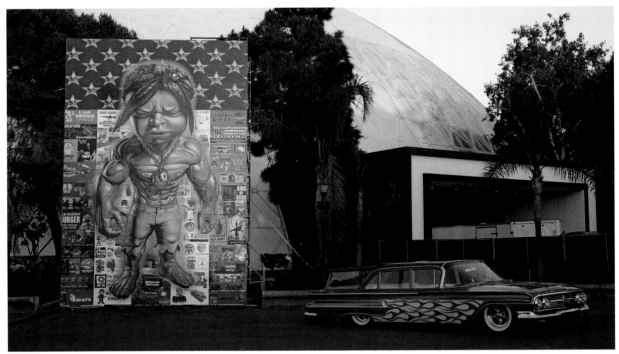

Temper Tupac mural
2016

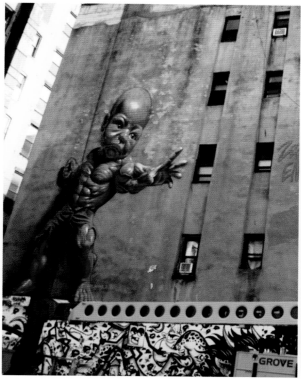

Pink temper tot mural
2016

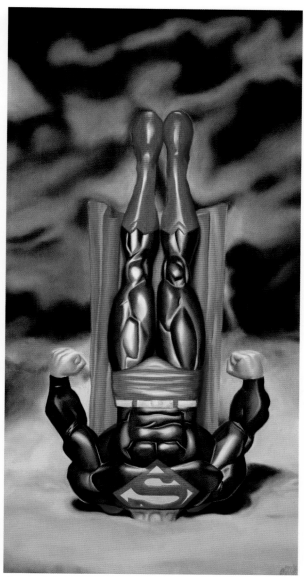

Descension of Superman
2017

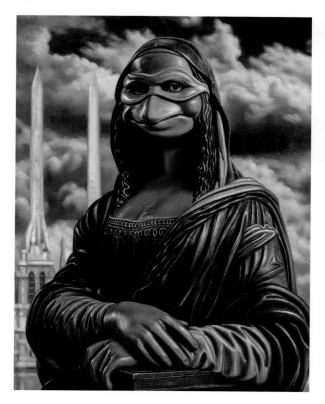

TMNT Da Vinci
2012

Telegrinnies
2011

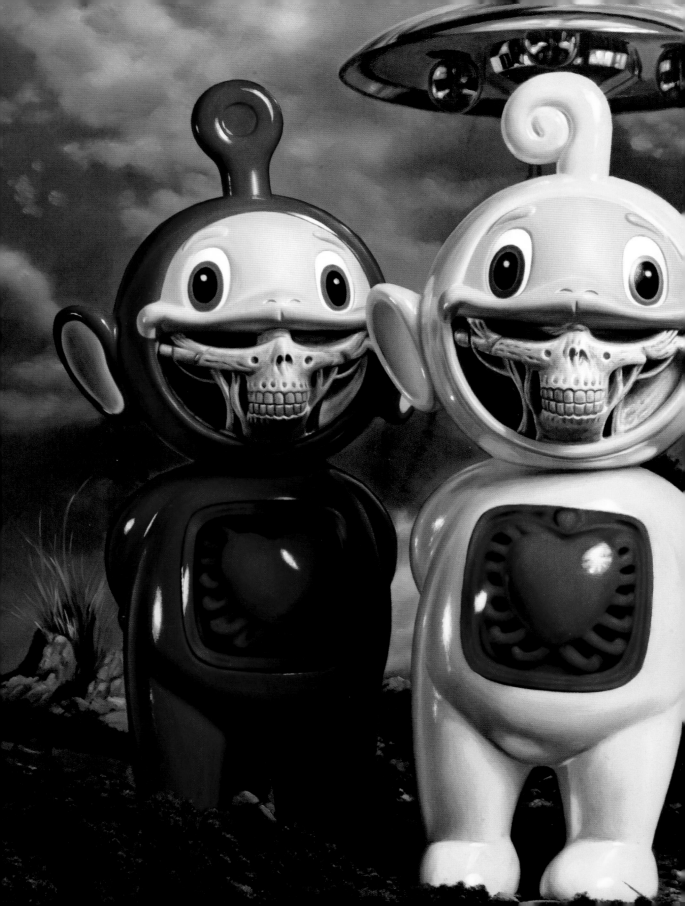

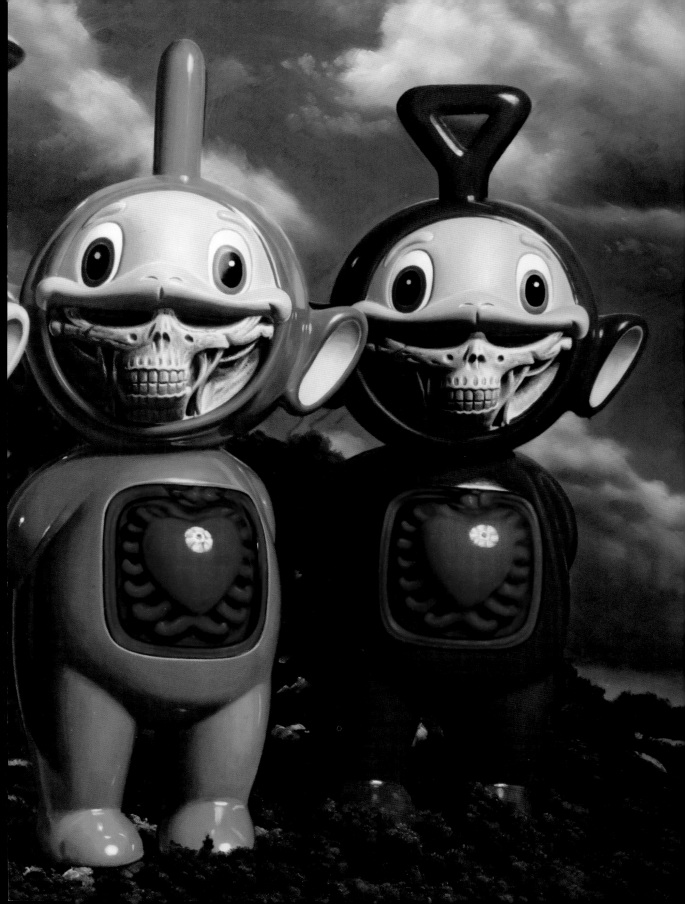

CRISTIAN ERES

Cristian Eres is a sci-fi and fantasy illustrator born in Valencia, Spain, in 1990. He finished his graphic design degree in 2012 and, since then, he has dedicated himself to creating fantasy worlds in his studio. His work is influenced by numerous European sci-fi artists, such as Roger Dean, Kilian Eng, Philippe Druillet, and Philippe Caza; although his main reference is the master of masters, Moebius. And one shouldn't forget to mention the Japanese influences of Katsuhiro Otomo and Hayao Miyazaki. Cristian Eres works digitally, but he does so using the traditional ink drawing technique. He enjoys making large landscapes where his knowledge of perspective plays a fundamental role and he challenges himself with complex compositions in which scale changes become the highlight. He spends entire days adding each detail and exploring new ranges of colors.

He's a cinema and music lover; Cristian works in the world of alternative film posters making limited edition serigraphs of his favorite sci-fi, fantasy, and animated films. In them, he does not settle for copying scenes or faces of actors, but rather he uses his imagination to show his own perspective of the film. He has also worked for the music industry creating graphic material for well-known groups and musicians.

WEBSITE: www.cristianeres.com
CONTACT: contact@cristianeres.com

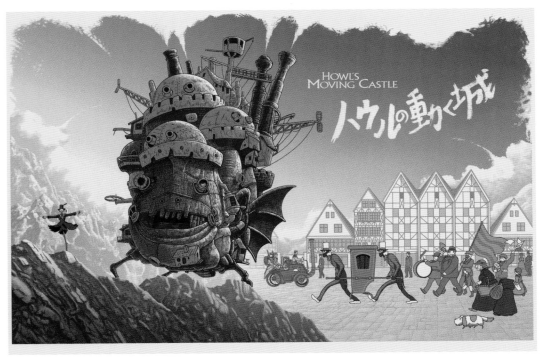

Howl's Moving Castle
2018

Planet of the Apes
2018

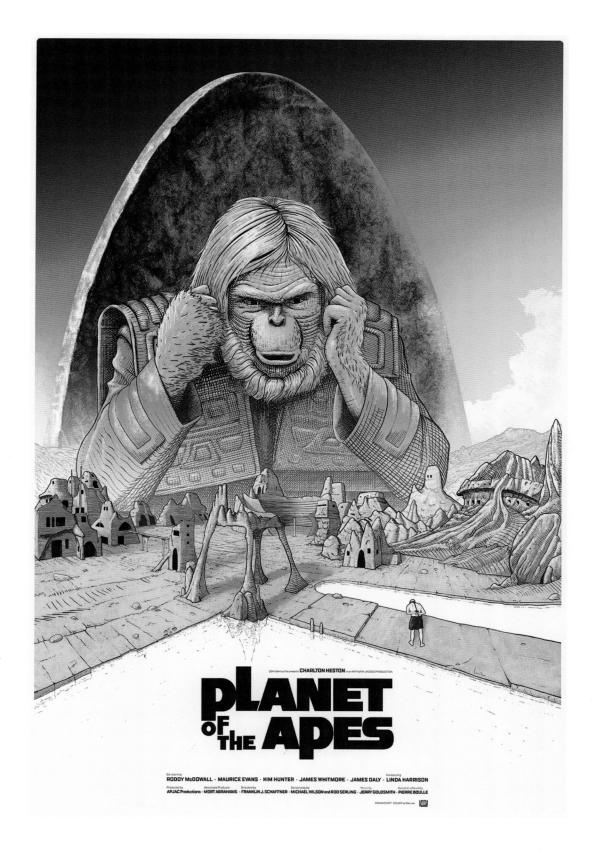

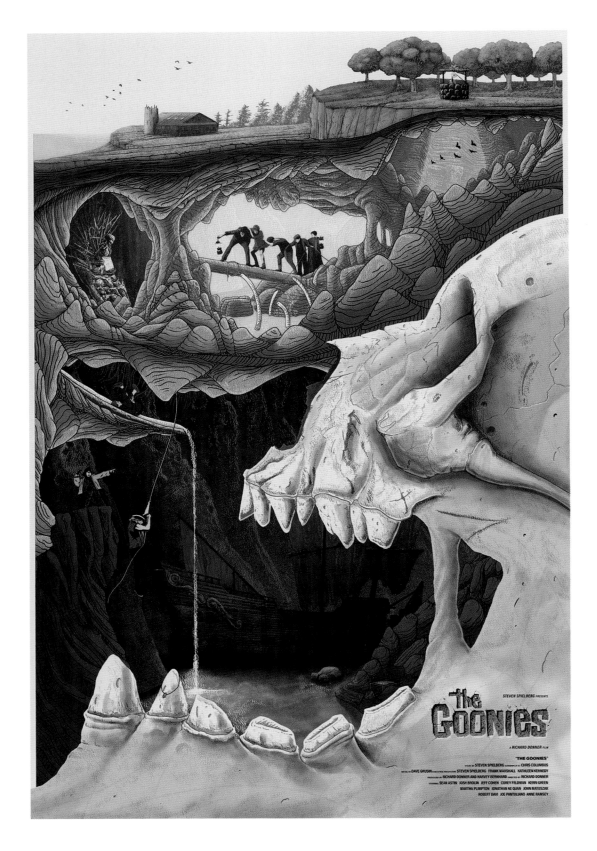

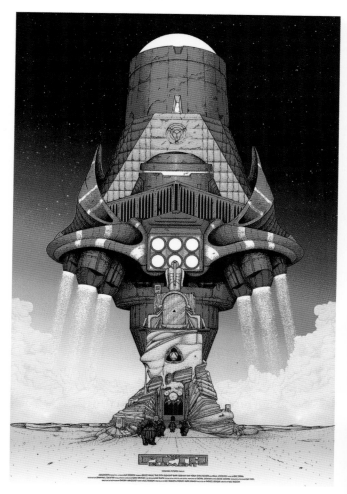

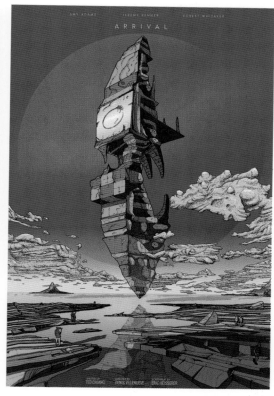

The Fifth Element
2017

Arrival
2017

Alien
2017

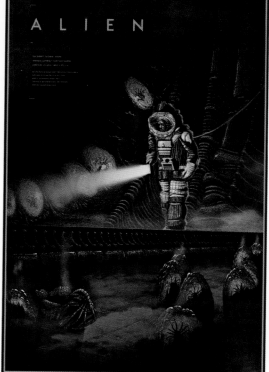

The Goonies
2018

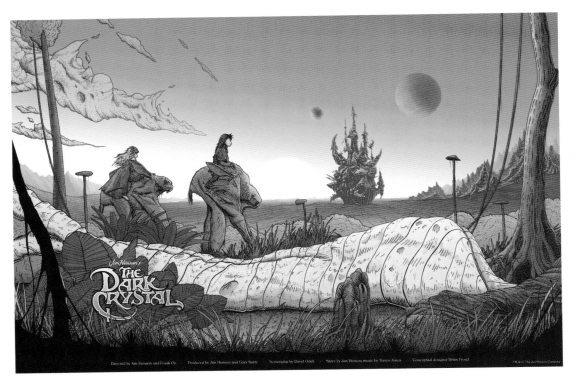

The Dark Crystal
2018

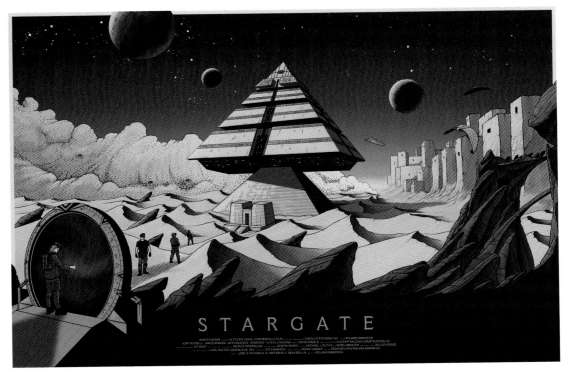

Stargate
2017

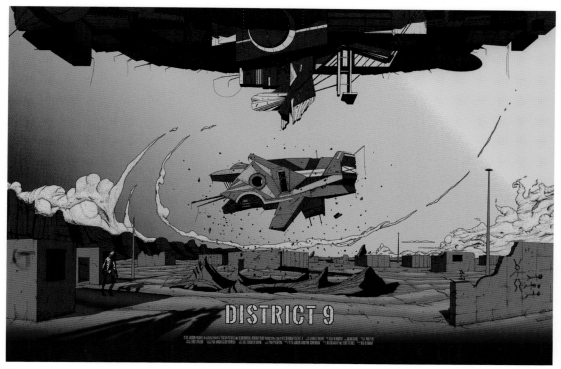

District 9
2017

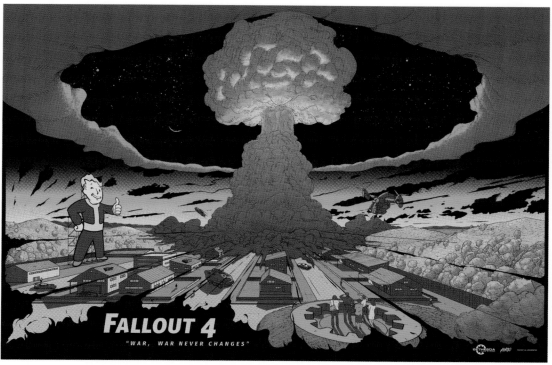

Fallout 4
2018

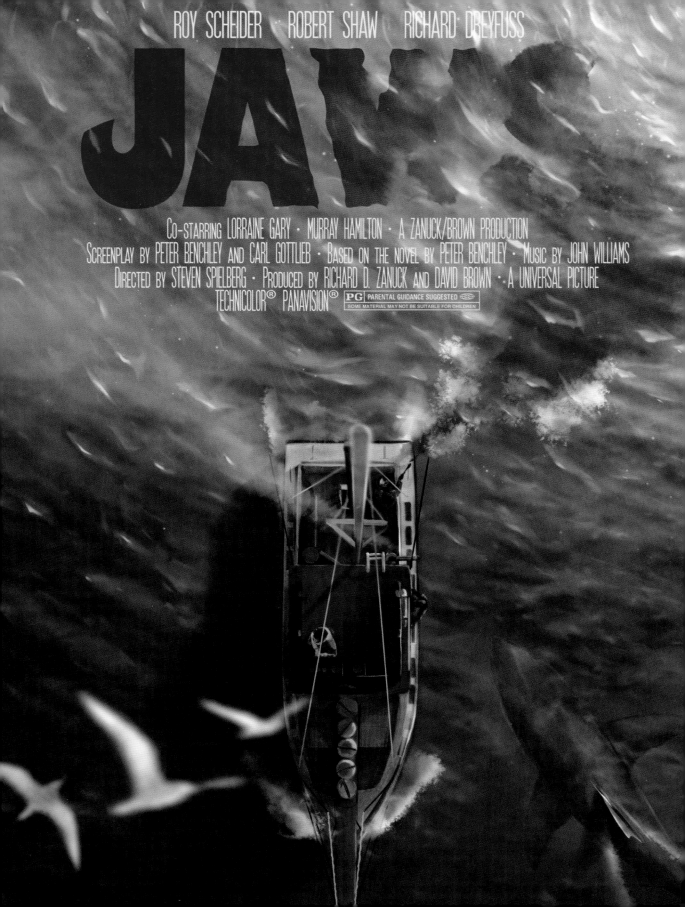

ANDY FAIRHURST

Andy Fairhurst is a digital painter, currently living in North Wales. He specializes in alternative movie posters and pop culture art prints. Clients include Marvel, Lucasfilm, Disney, 20th Century Fox, Pixar, DC Comics, and the BBC. He is also a part of a collective of artists known as the Poster Posse and regularly sells licensed limited-edition artwork.

WEBSITE: www.andyfairhurstart.com
INSTAGRAM: @andyfairhurst72
FACEBOOK: /AndyFairhurstArt
TWITTER: @andy_fairhurst

" Doing what I do is my way of never growing up."

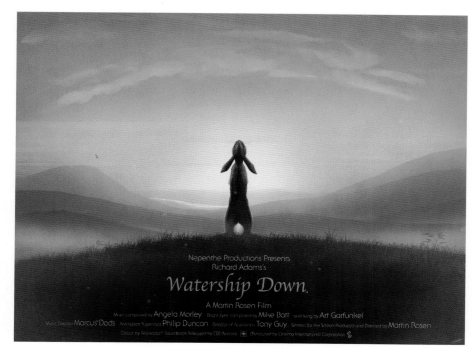

Jaws
2014

Watership Down
2014

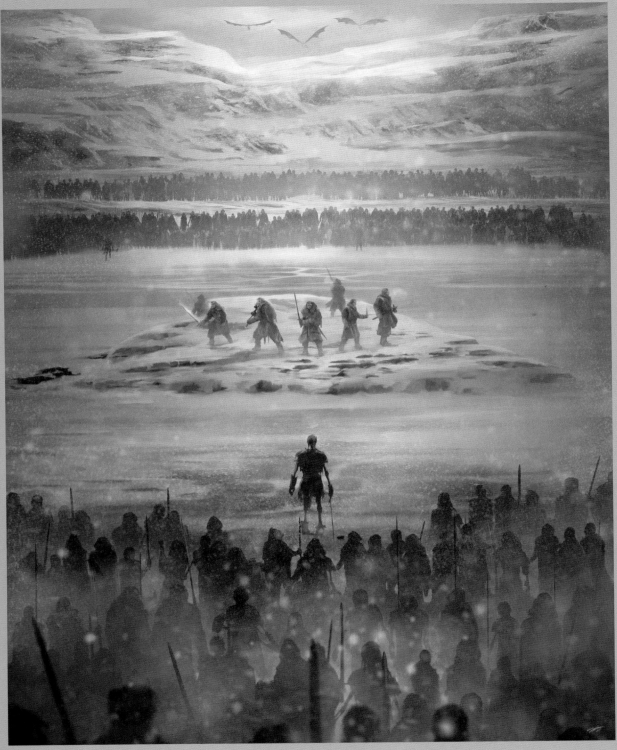

Beyond the Wall
2017

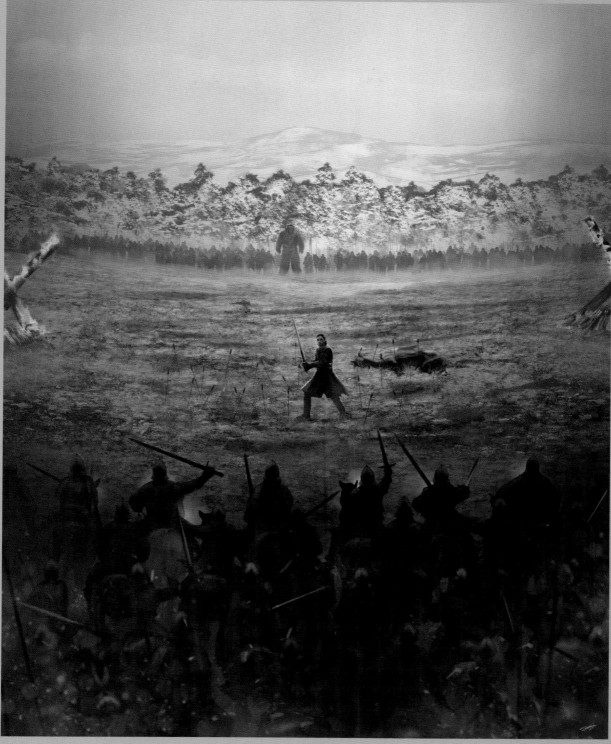

Battle of the Bastards
2016

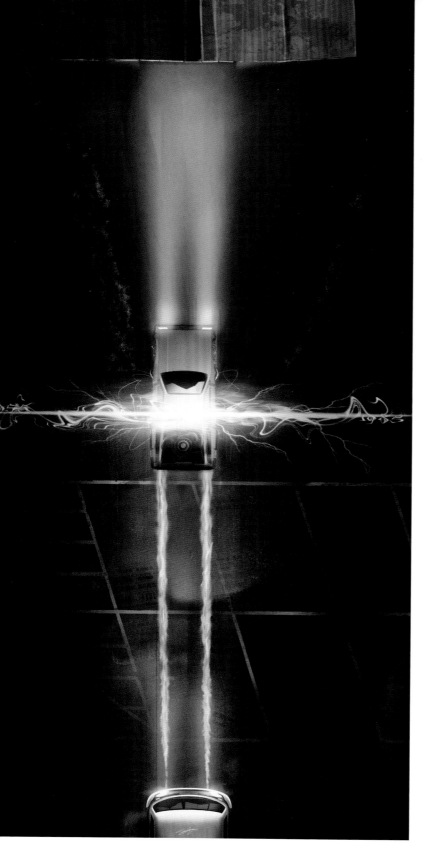
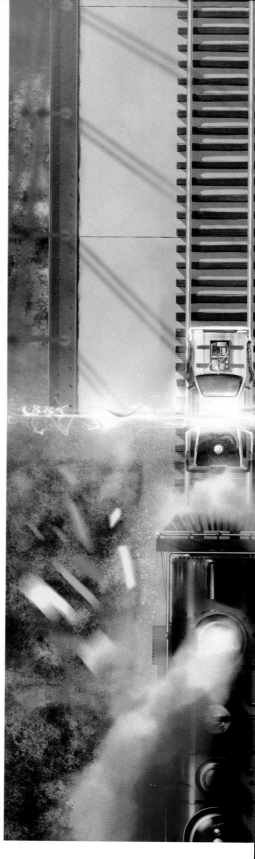

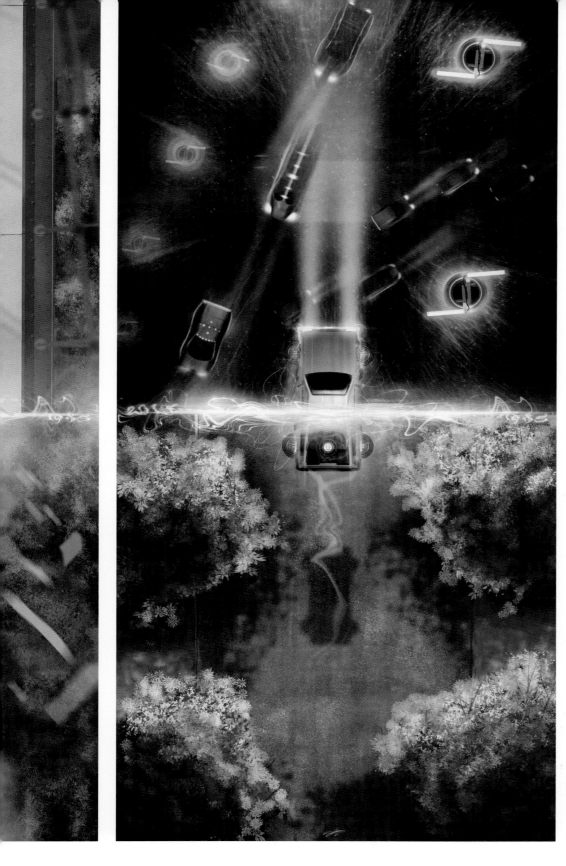

CORY FREEMAN

Cory Freeman is a freelance graphic designer/illustrator and a proud life-long geek. Always finding inspiration in games, movies and television, and books, he's had a pretty varied career so far, including creating officially licensed designs for some of the coolest pop-culture brands out there.

WEBSITE: www.coryfreemandesign.threadless.com

> " I've always loved stories. Pop culture is filled with stories about superheroes, dragons, and space pirates, and they all have one thing in common: they bring people together. Those stories allow fans to connect to each other as we cheer on our heroes or boo the villains we love to hate."

Happy Bantha
2016

Goron Ruby Rock Candy
2015

Iceberg Lounge
2015

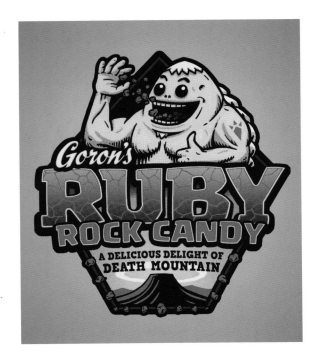

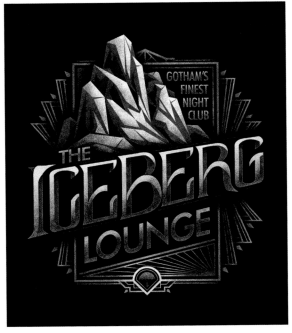

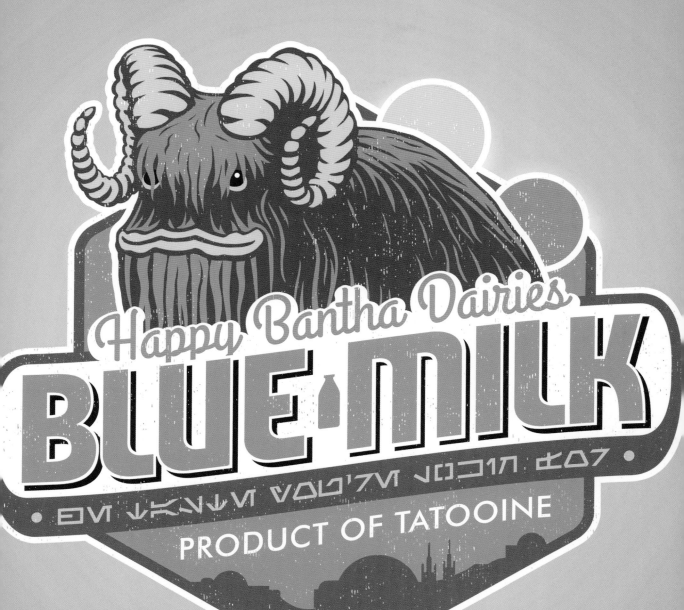

Happy Bantha Dairies

BLUE·MILK

PRODUCT OF TATOOINE

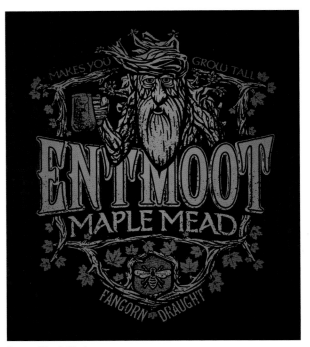

Entmoot Mapple Mead
2015

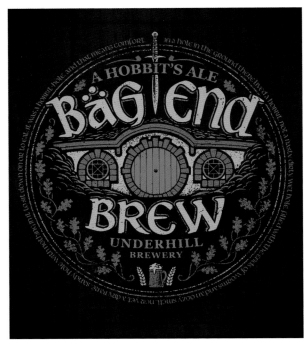

Bag End Brew
2014

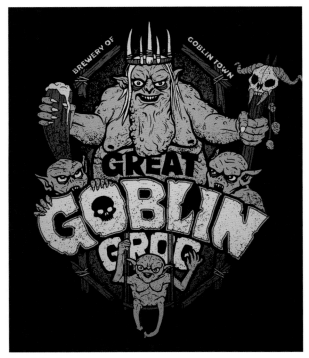

Great Goblin Grog
2016

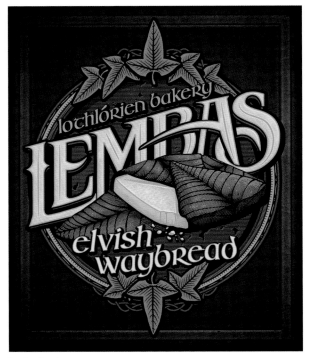

Lembas Bread
2016

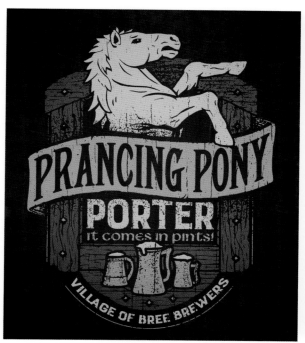

Prancing Pony
2015

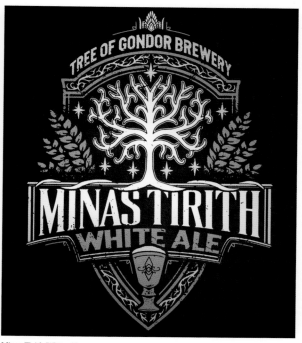

Minas Tirith White Ale
2015

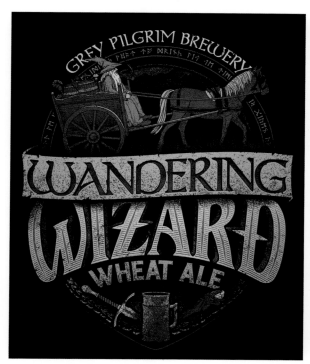

Wandering Wizard
2017

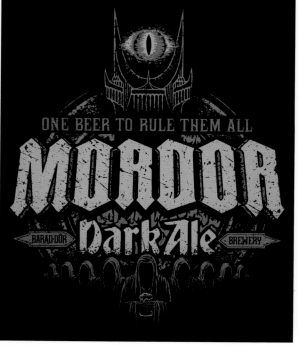

Mordor Dark Ale
2014

GAX

Guy-Pascal Vallez, a.k.a. Gax, is a passionate illustrator/author of role-playing games and video games. The ultimate D&D fan of *Baldur's Gate* and the post-apocalyptic world of *Fallout*, he is Inspired by artists like Hieronymus Bosch, Mike Mignola and, Ashley Wood. Usually Gax stays cloistered in his laboratory with a large cup of coffee, busy blackening the leaf, but he occasionally takes his watercolors and draws on his terrace, warmed by the Nîmes sun. A follower of media mix, he works on a traditional basis (paper) before working on colors and textures digitally.

INSTAGRAM: @guyvallez
FACEBOOK: /vallezgax
TWITTER: @Gaxix
TUMBLR: www.gaxix.tumblr.com
CONTACT: gaxixx@gmail.com

> ❝ I have entered the world of pop culture through Dungeons & Dragons, which made me want to become an illustrator. I have never looked back since.❞

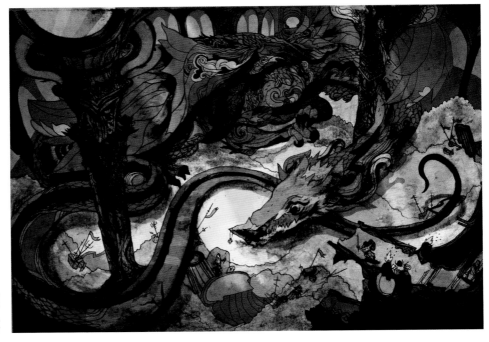

Smaug
2014

Lord of the Rings
2017

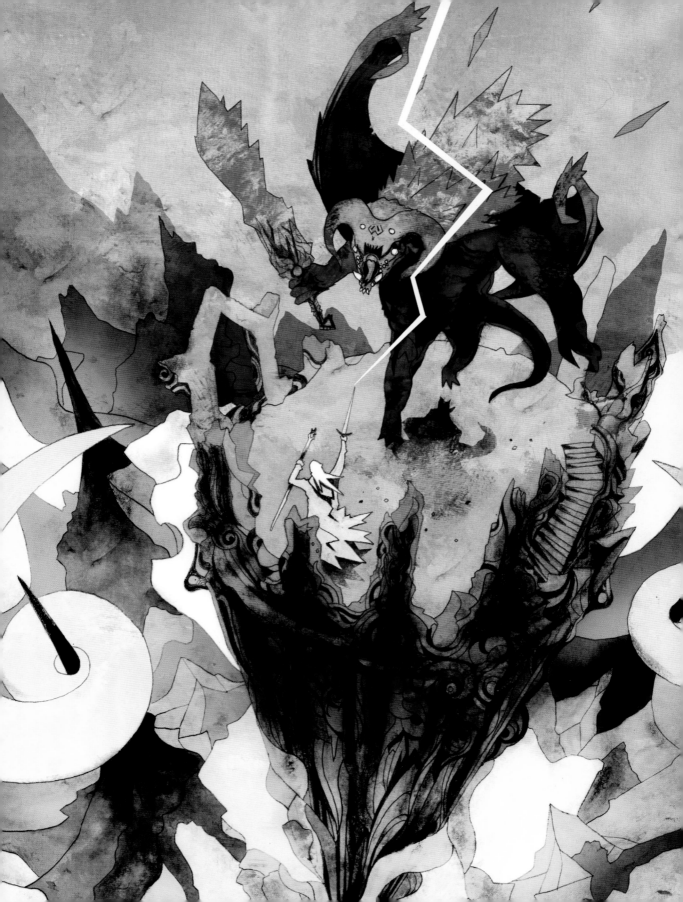

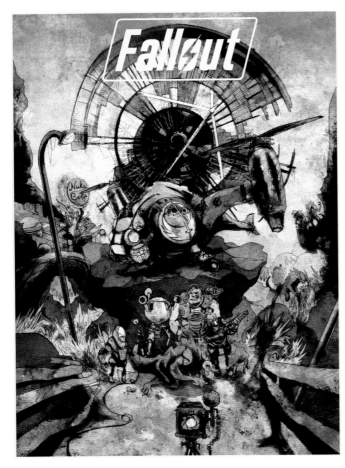

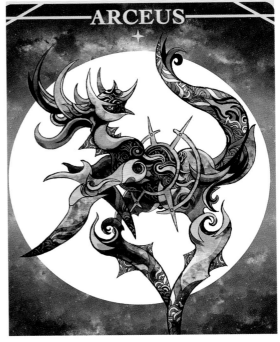

Fallout
2015

Pokemon Arceus
2019

Farcry
2018

Death Stranding
2019

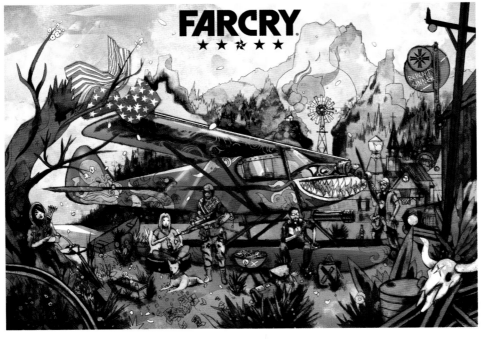

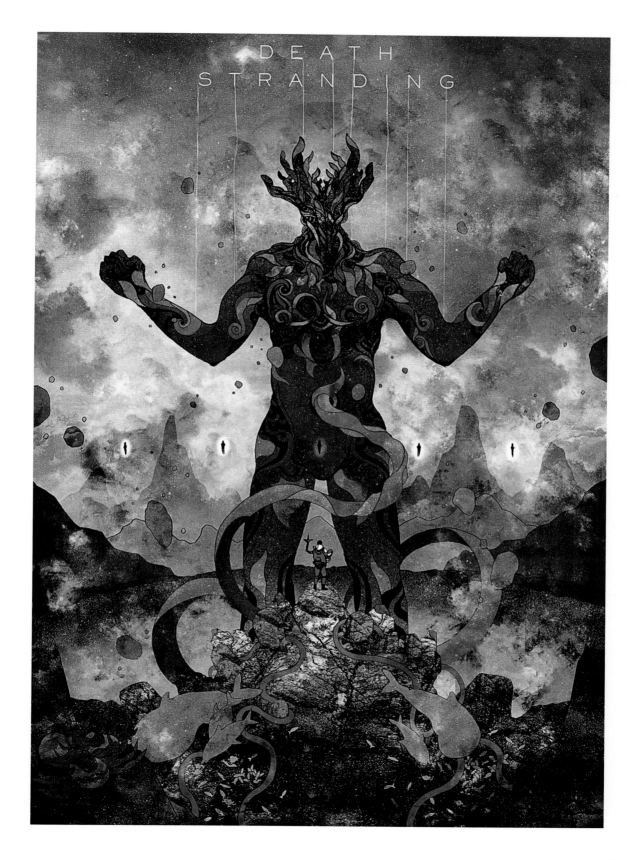

JAMES GILLEARD

James Gilleard is an illustrator and animator from the United Kingdom, currently residing in New York with his wife and son, working (for now) as a designer in the animated film industry. His work is inspired by glitch art, impressionism, and retro CGI.

WEBSITE: www.jamesgilleard.com

Red Dead Redemption 2
2018

Tomb Raider
2014

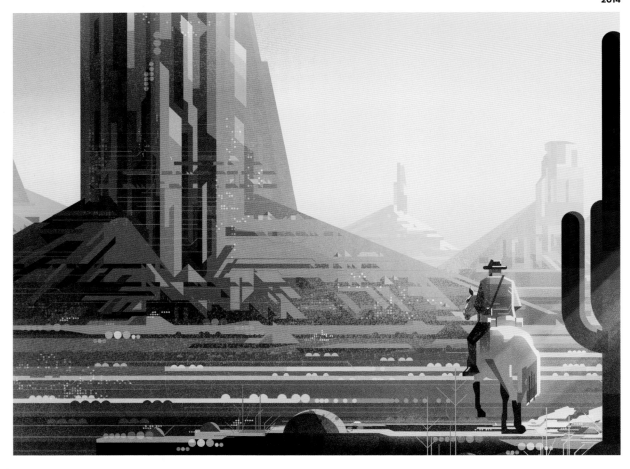

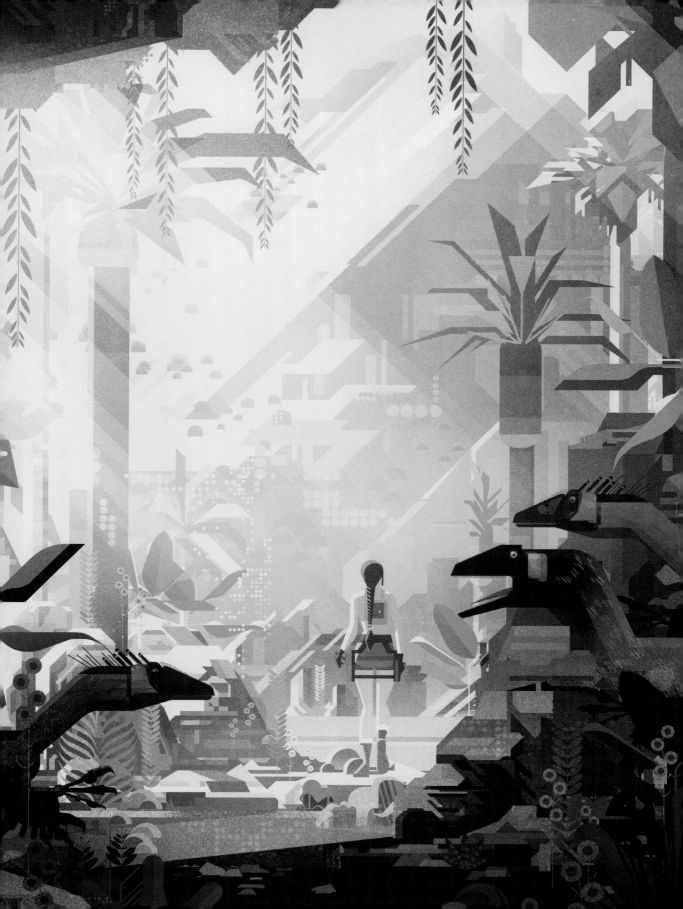

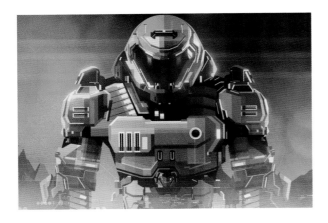

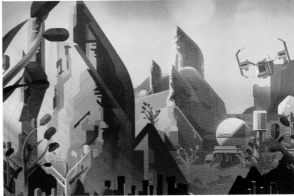

Doom Guy
2018

No Man's Sky 4
2018

No Man's Sky 1
2018

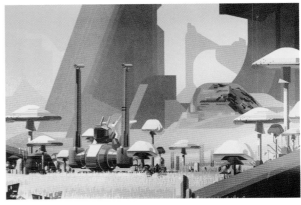

Metal Gear
2018

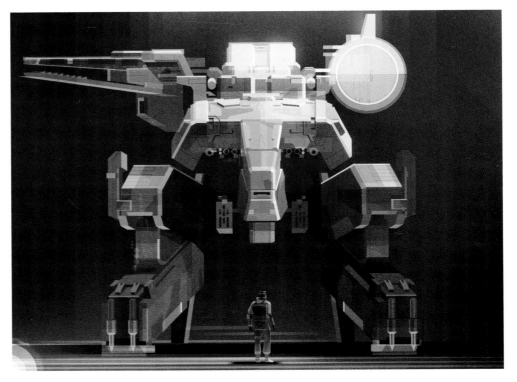

> " The first image I remember creating
was an image of Knight Rider—I did
a kind of map of an episode when I was five."

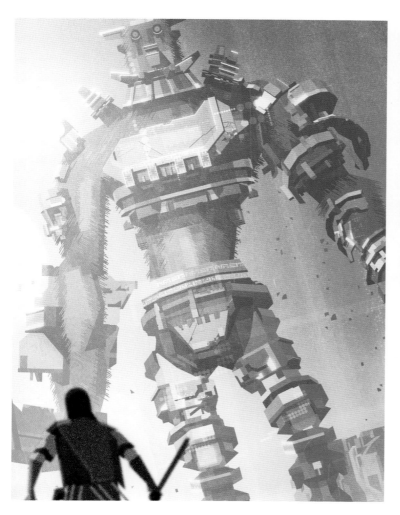

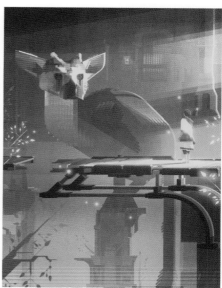

The Last Guardian
2018

Shadow of the Colossus
2018

ALE GIORGINI

An Italy-based artist working for several brands (Jeep, Puma, Warner Bros., Foot Locker, Sony Pictures, Fandango, Kinder), Giorgini has had shows all around the world (Milan, New York, Rome, Los Angeles, San Francisco, Vienna, Paris). His works are displayed at Hero Complex Gallery (Los Angeles), Bottleneck Gallery (New York), and Galerie Sakura (Paris).

WEBSITE: www.alegiorgini.com
BLOG: www.aaargh.it
CONTACT: ale@alegiorgini.com
INSTAGRAM: @alegiorgini
FACEBOOK: /alegiorgini.fanpage
TWITTER: @alegiorgini_

May the Love be with you
2014

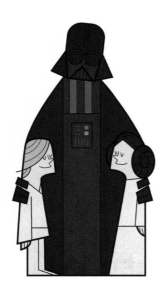

> **" "** Someone called my style 'geometric retro style.' I agree—it takes a lot from cartoons and comics of my childhood. Every one of us is joined to others and to the world in an invisible way. Nothing in life is made randomly. That's why characters and things on my artworks are always connected."

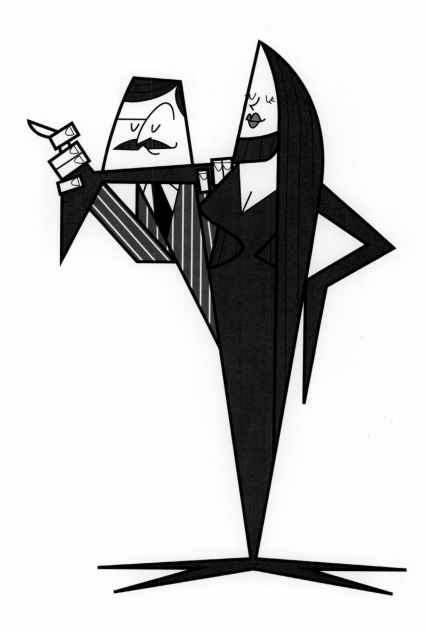

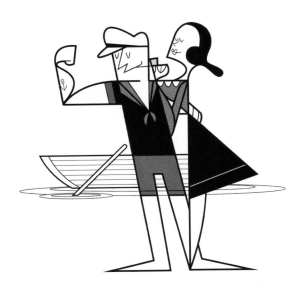

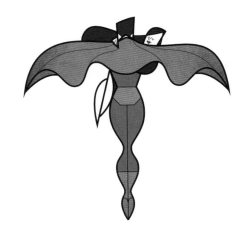

We will sail away   Fly me to the moon
2005   **2014**

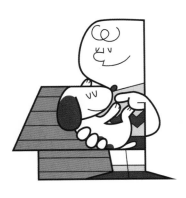

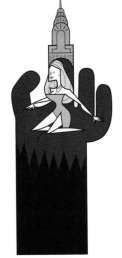

Home is where you are   You are my Queen
2006   **2014**

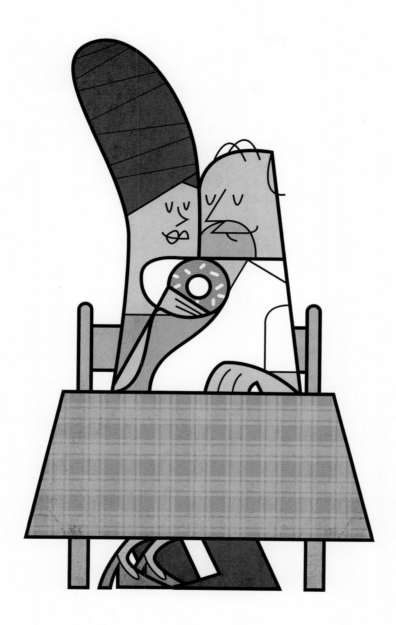

You are the sweetest thing
2014

GODMACHINE

Godmachine was born in Cardiff, South Wales. He grew up on a steady diet of nothing, 2000 AD comics, and Santa Cruz skateboards. He uses a Wacom, Photoshop, and coffee to achieve his detailed images that have made quite an impact on band merch, skateboards, and clothing companies today. He has two cats: Bear and Miss Boo Boo Kitty Fuck II, and has a worrying amount of coffee mugs with cats on them. Although a vegetarian and a devout antitheist, he collects animal skulls, animal horns, and crucifixes, along with old discarded black-and-white photos.

WEBSITE: www.godmachine.co.uk
INSTAGRAM: @godmachine
FACEBOOK: /theoriginalgodmachine

> " My art is born of Jim Philips, raised by Simon Bisley, and adopted by my everyday influences: film, literature, and music."

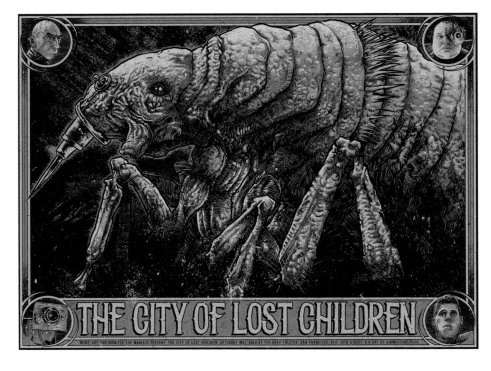

The City of Lost Children
2015

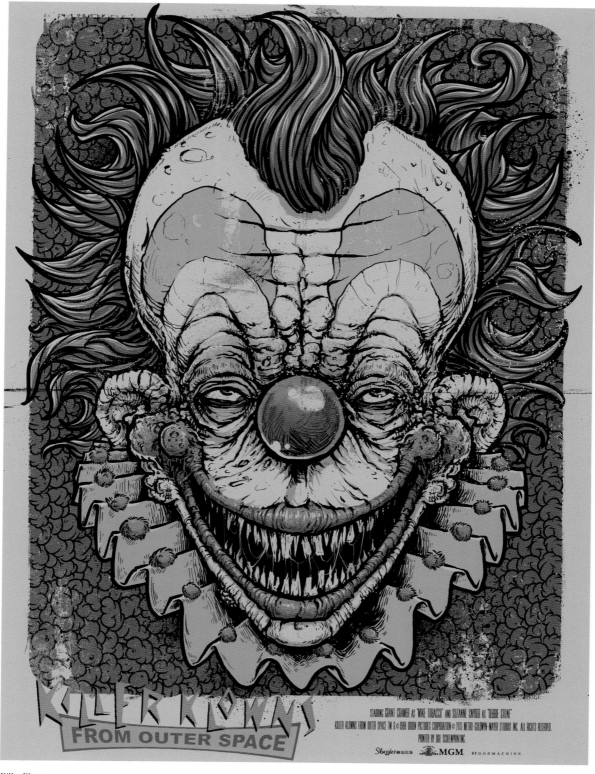

Killer Klowns
2014

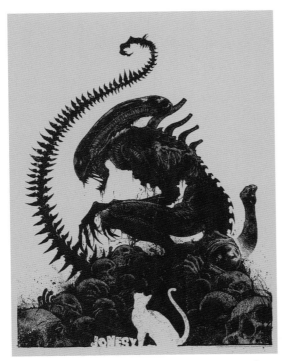

70s Jonesy
2016

90s Jonesy
2016

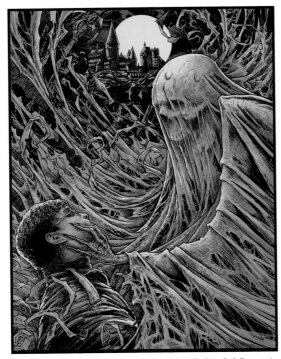

Soul Sucking Jerk Downstairs
2015

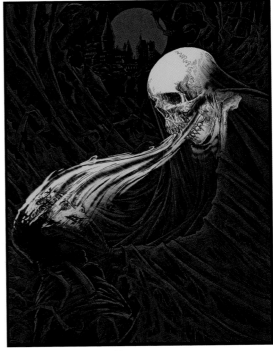

Soul Sucking Jerk Downstairs Glows
2015

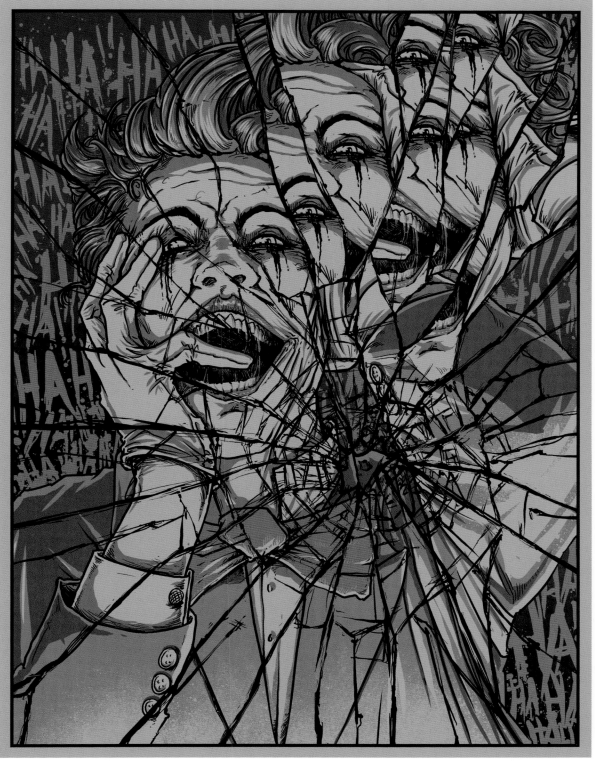

The Joker
2014

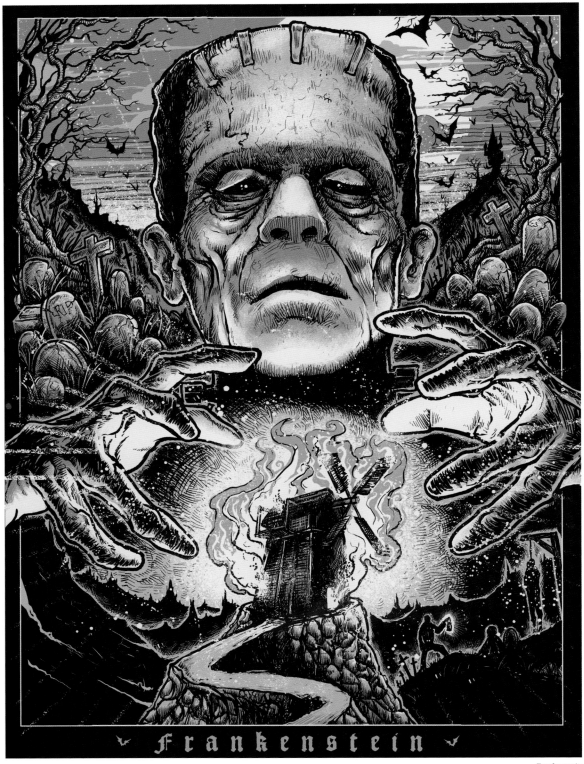

Frankenstein
2014

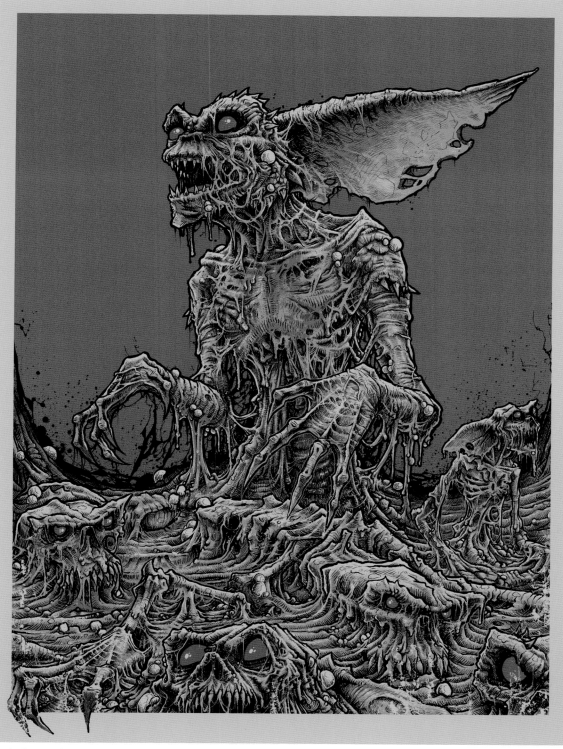

Another Reason to Hate Xmas
2014

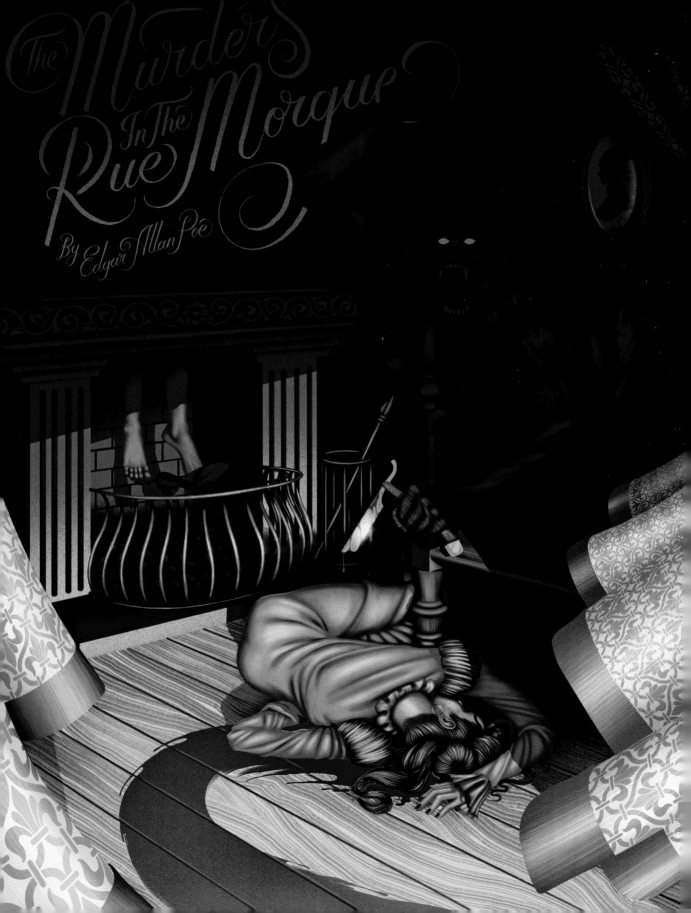

JAY GORDON

Jay Gordon is a Cape Town, South Africa–based illustrator with a love for drawing, film, graphic novels, golden-age illustration, and weird fiction. Jay's influences range from the classic pulp art to the cinematography of Roger Deakins, John Alcott, and Stanley Kubrick. His tools of choice are Photoshop, a Wacom Cintiq, and a Bialetti coffeepot.

WEBSITE: www.jaygordondraws.com
CONTACT: hello@jaygordondraws.com
INSTAGRAM: @jaygordondraws

" I see pop culture as a universal language using iconography and storytelling to bridge gaps in society and help us discover and connect with people where verbiage, grammar, and diction may fall short. It allows us to connect over a nostalgic movie or story moment irrespective of creed or culture."

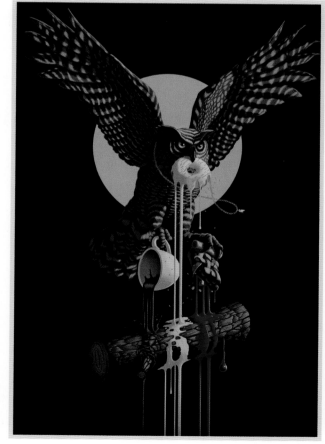

The Murders In The Rue Morgue
2018

The Owls Are Not
What They Seem
2017

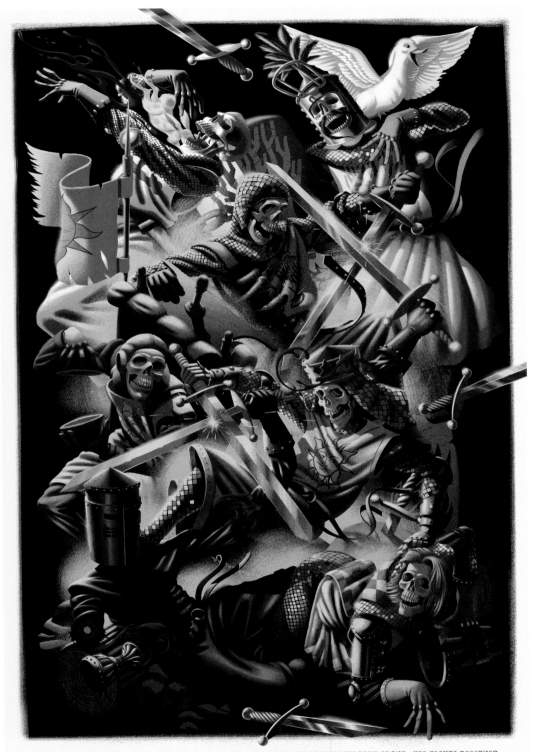

Brave Knights
2018

The Life Aquatic
2018

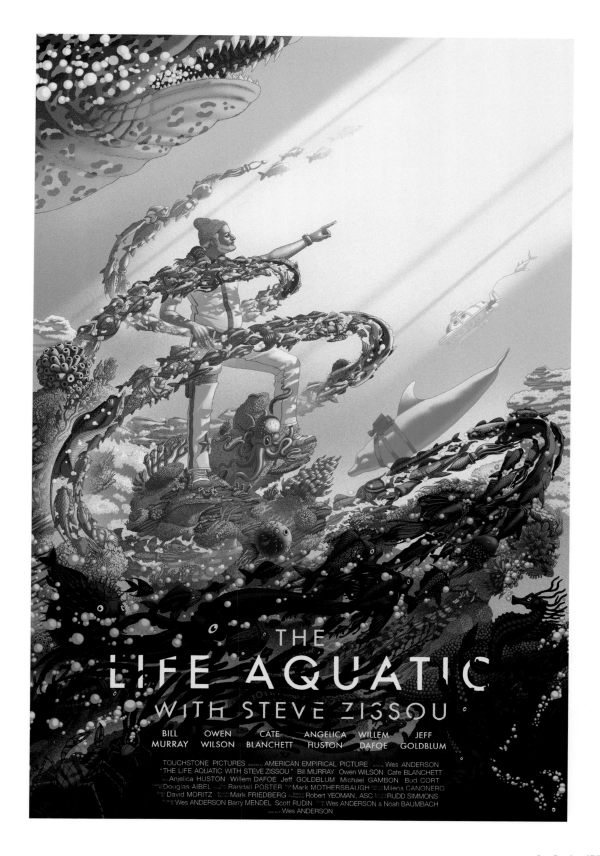

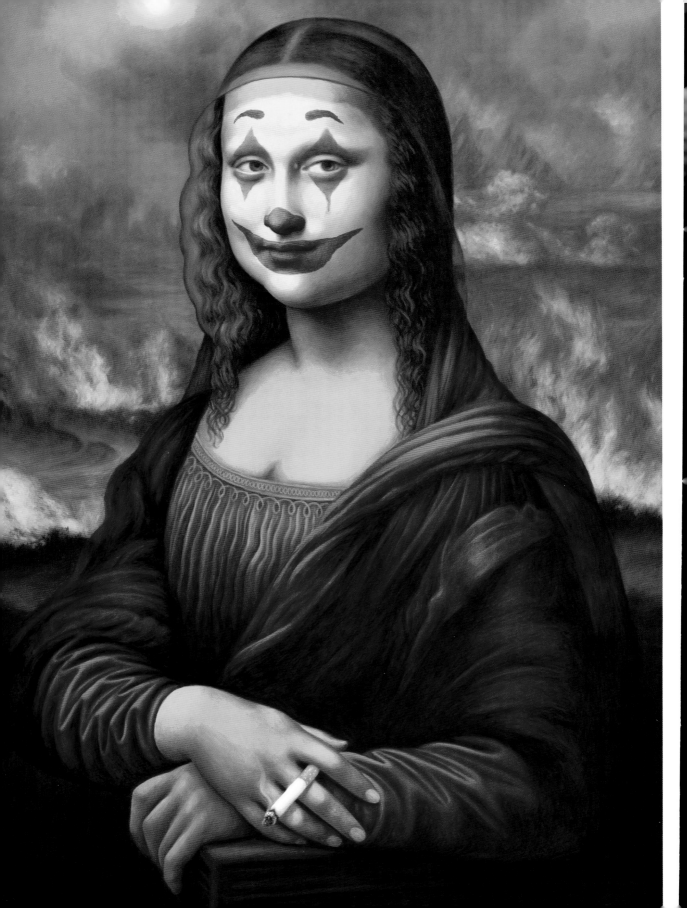

ALEX GROSS

Alex Gross was born in 1968 in Roslyn Heights, New York, and is currently based in Los Angeles, California. In 1990, he received a bachelor of fine arts with honors from the ArtCenter College of Design in Pasadena. In 2007, Gross' work was the subject of a solo exhibition at the Grand Central Art Center in Santa Ana, California. Gross is a recipient of the prestigious Artist's Fellowship from the Japan Foundation, and several faculty grants from ArtCenter College of Design.

WEBSITE: www.alexgross.com
INSTAGRAM: @artofalexgross
FACEBOOK: /the-art-of-alex-gross

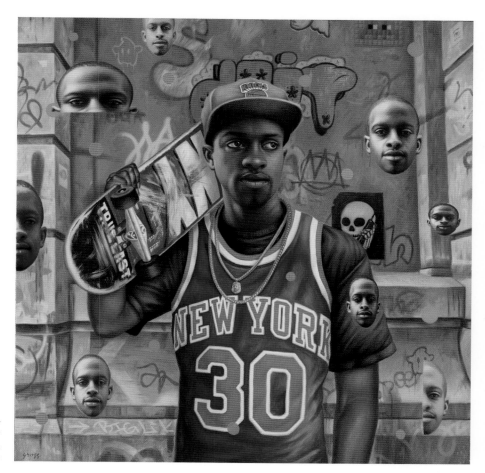

Mona Lisa Joker
2019

Dave Willis
2013

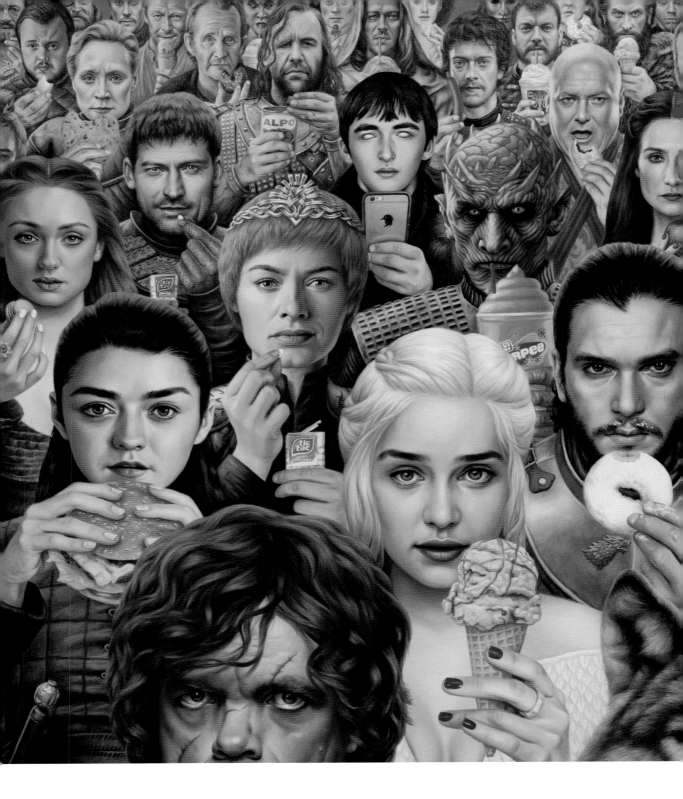

Obsession
2019

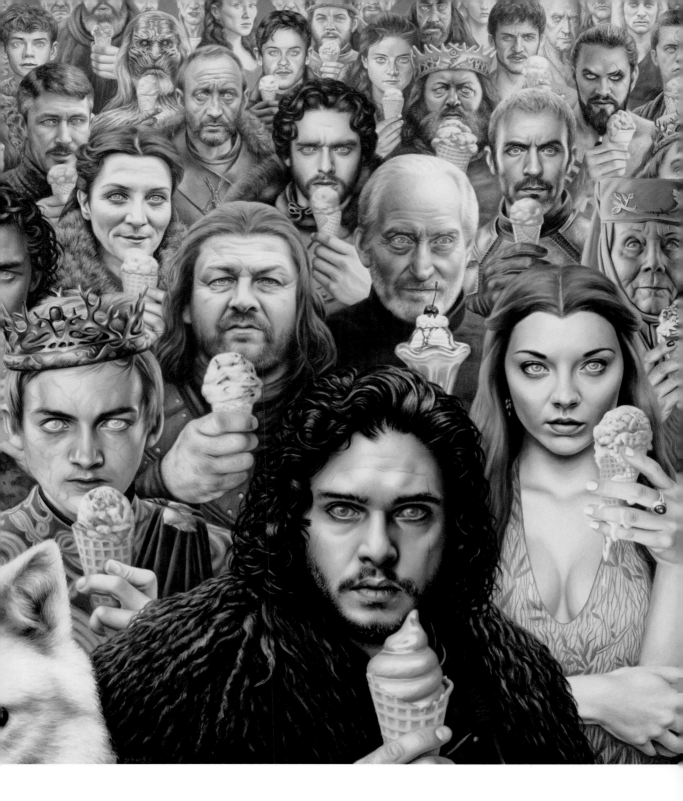

Valar Morghulis
2019

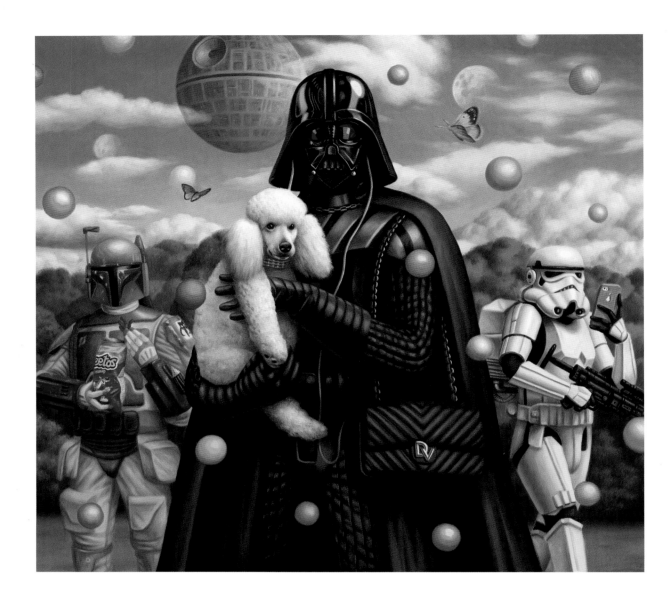

DV Posse
2017

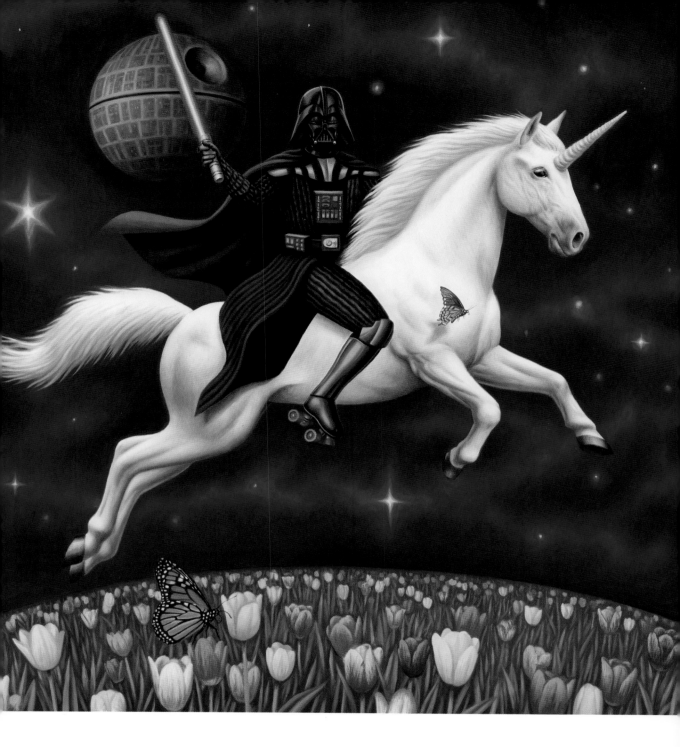

DV Unicorn
2017

JORGE R. GUTIERREZ

Jorge R. Gutierrez is a Mexican animator, painter, writer, and director who, along with his wife, Sandra Equihua, created the multiple Annie and Emmy Award–winning animated television series *El Tigre: The Adventures of Manny Rivera* for Nickelodeon. Born in Mexico City and raised in Tijuana, Gutierrez has completed various films, cartoons, illustrations, and paintings exploring his love affair with Mexican pop and folk culture. He won two Annie Awards (Best Animated Show for Children — TV and Best Character Design — TV) and one Daytime Emmy Award (Outstanding Individual Achievement in Character Design) for *El Tigre*. He was also nominated for an Annie for Disney's *The Buzz on Maggie*. Most recently, he co-wrote and directed the animated feature *The Book of Life*, which earned him a 2014 Golden Globe Award nomination for Best Animated Feature Film. In 2018, he opened his first paintings in a solo show in Los Angeles. He is currently working on an animated TV show for Netflix.

FACEBOOK: /Jorge-R-Gutierrez
TWITTER: @mexopolis
INSTAGRAM: @mexopolis

Ese Mi Bob
2016

El Morro Simpson
2016

Estar Guars
2016

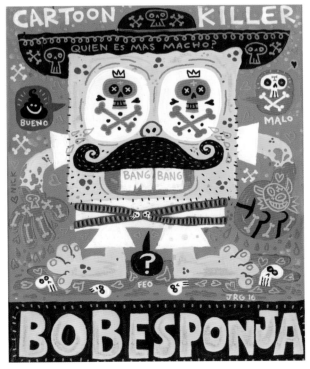

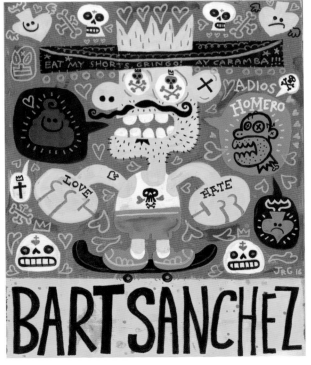

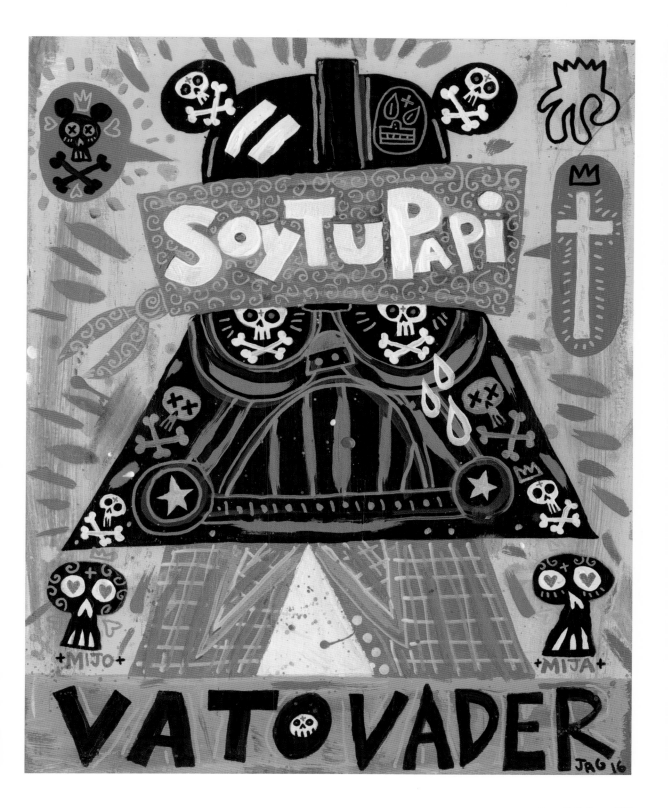

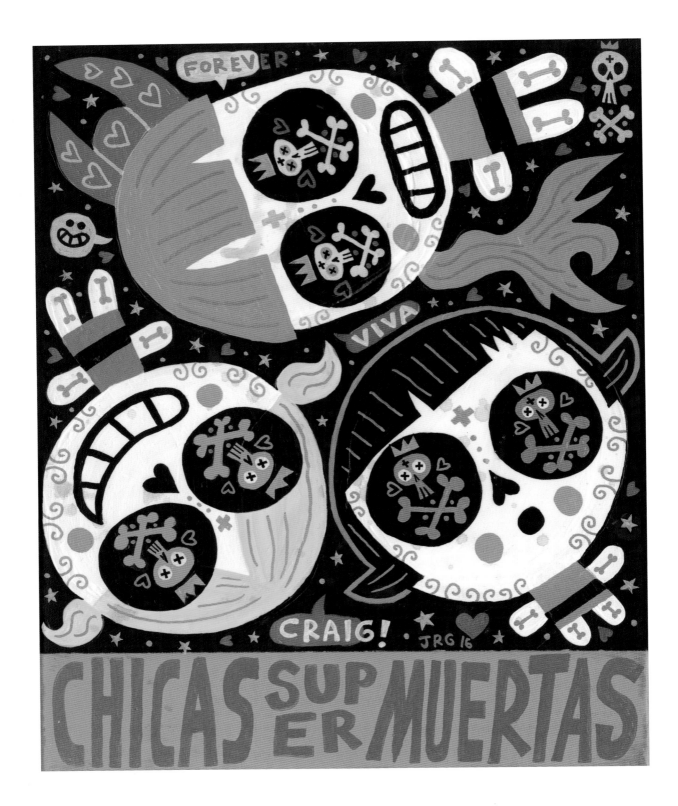

The Holy Trinity
2016

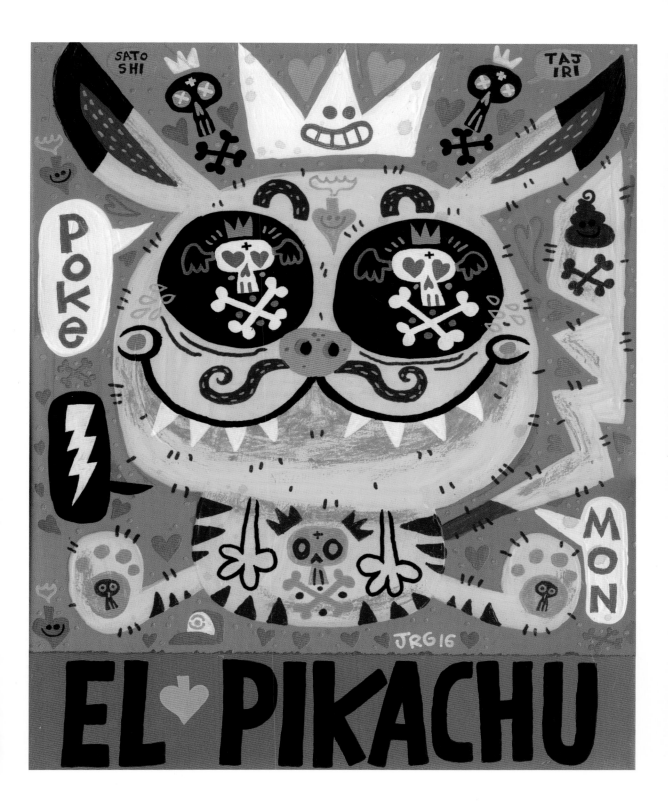

Magic Japanese Cockfighting
2016

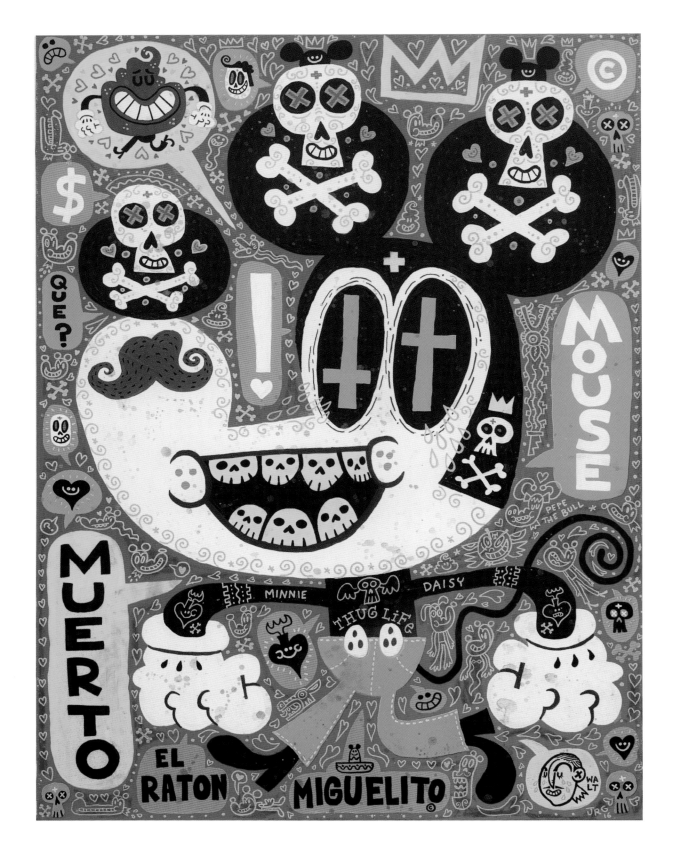

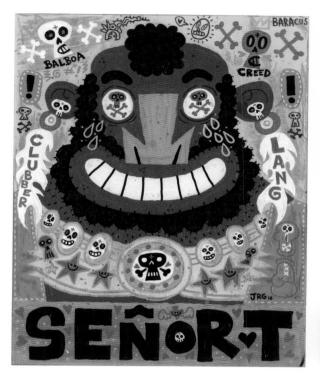

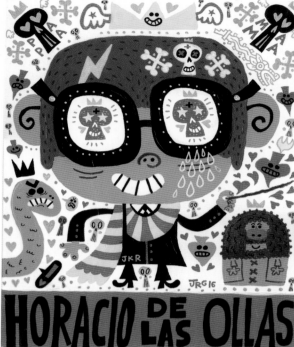

Idolo
2016

La del Niñito Brujo
2016

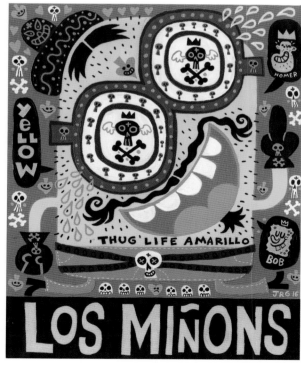

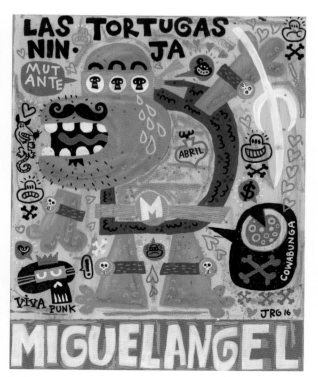

Super Muerto Mouse
2016

Los Monitos Amarillos
2016

Los Mutantes
2016

ERIN HUNTING

Erin Hunting is an Australian illustrator who works in children's publishing, comics, and visual development in animation. She has drawn comic covers for *Adventure Time, Rick and Morty*, and *Jughead*, as well as authored and illustrated a short comic for *Garfield*. She has also worked numerous times with Sesame Workshop, Nickelodeon, *Stranger Things*, Netflix, and Will Smith. She is currently illustrating a picture book series, *The Tooth Fairy vs Santa,* with Penguin Workshop (USA).

WEBSITE: www.erinhunting.com
CONTACT: erin@erinhunting.com
TWITTER: @ErinHunting
INSTAGRAM: @erinhunting

" I am surrounded by pop culture in the form of figurines and artwork in my studio every day and I love to create different spins on pop-culture figures in the form of fan art. To me fan art has made me a better artist as it has taught me how to see shapes, break them down, and then build them back up in my own unique way."

McDonalds Mascots
2017
Muppet Babies
2018

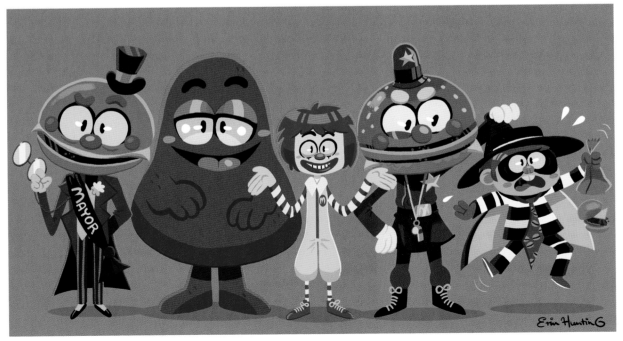

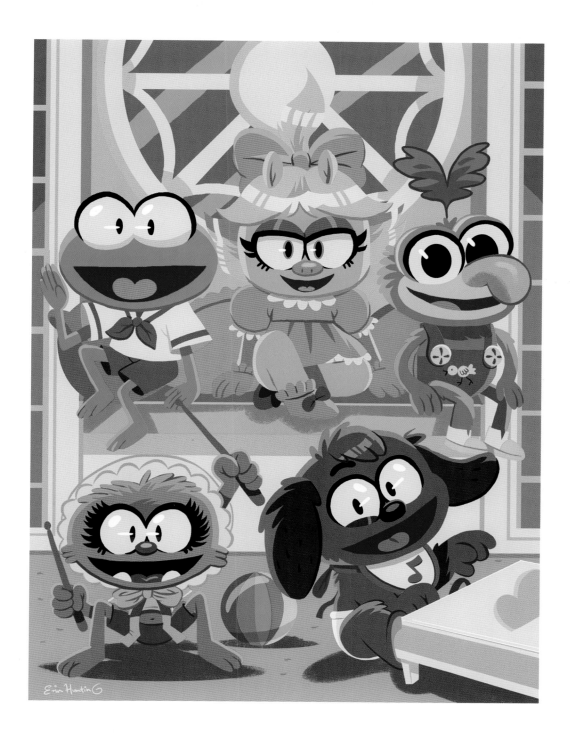

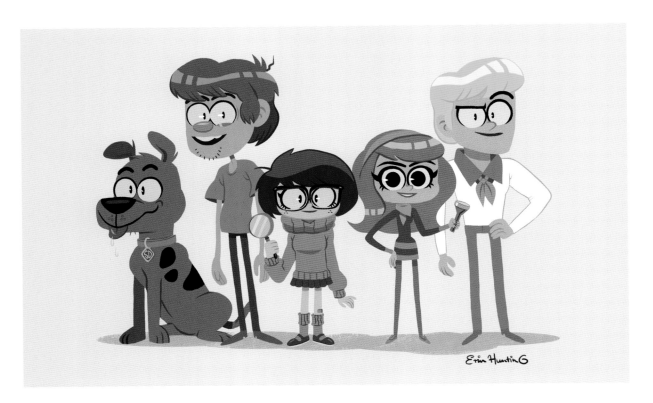

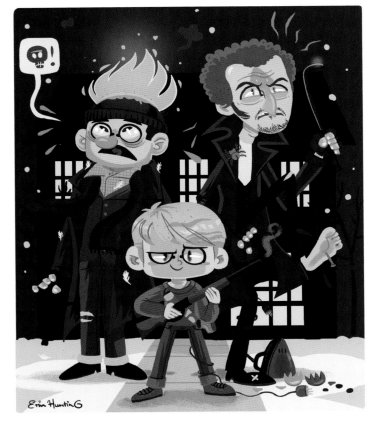

Home Alone
2013

Scooby Doo
2017

Garfield and Pooky
2018

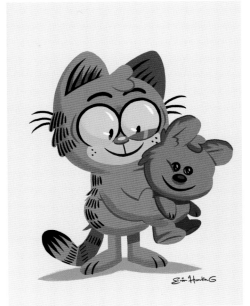

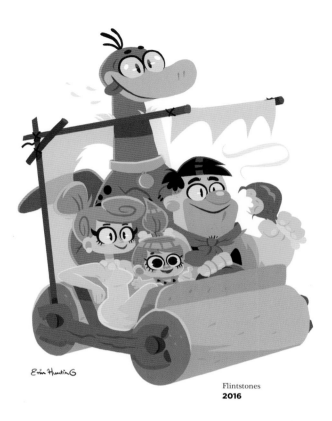

Flintstones
2016

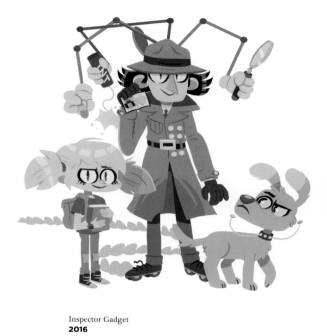

Inspector Gadget
2016

Daria and Jane
2015

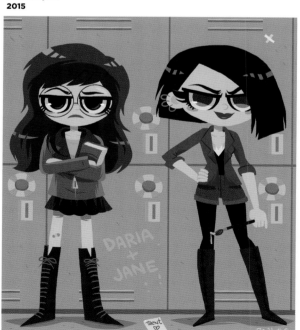

Rugrats
2017

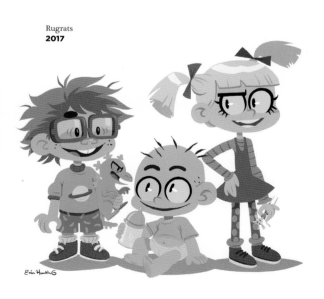

KILLER BOOTLEGS

orn in the 1980s, Killer Bootlegs artist Peter Goral's childhood was saturated with action figures, Saturday morning cartoons, and classic movies. When he was four years old, his father showed him a bootleg VHS of *The Empire Strikes Back*. Little did he know that this would start Peter on a path that would lead to him being at the forefront of the bootleg action figure movement. Today, Peter's artwork is highly sought after by collectors and has been in galleries worldwide. He has inspired countless other artists to follow in his footsteps. What started as a hobby collecting toys has grown into a full-time career for Peter, letting him do what he loves best every day, play with toys. Peter resides in Rockford, Illinois with his wife Heather and his two children.

WEBSITE: www.killerbootlegs.com

" If good artists copy and great artists steal, then only the very best artists bootleg."

Mini Draco Knuckleduster
2018

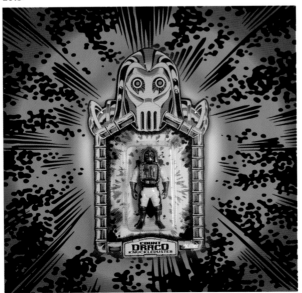

Phantom Starkiller
2018

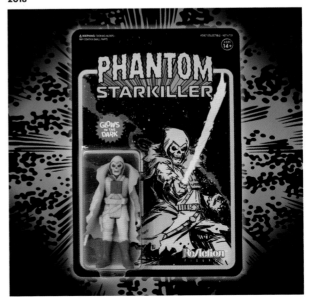

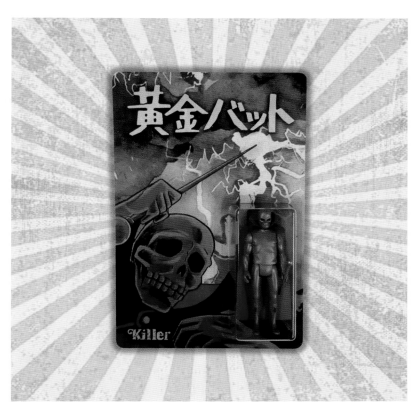

1966 Ōgon Bat
2019

Ōgon Bat
2018

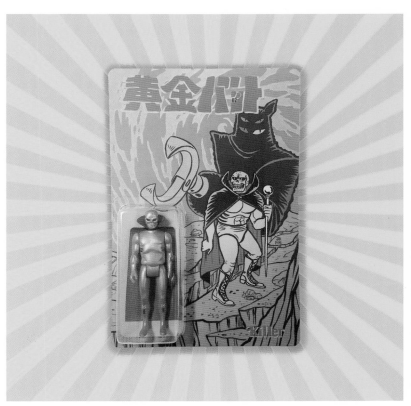

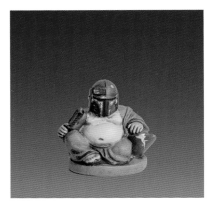

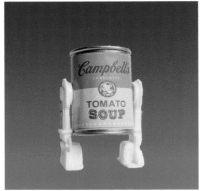

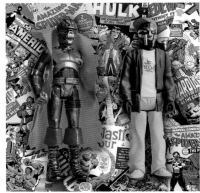

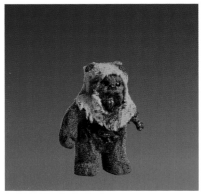

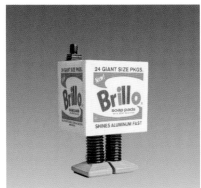

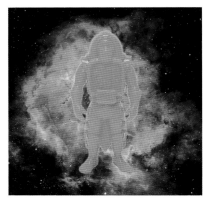

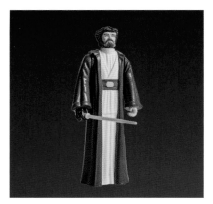

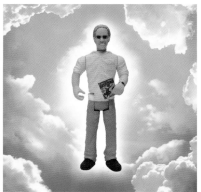

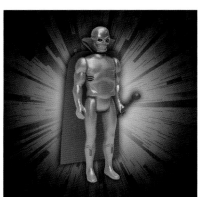

Buddha Fett
2016

The Ewoking Dead
2016

Luke Skywalker
2016

Star Warhol
2016

Star Warhol 2
2016

Stan Lee
2018

Czarface Meets Metal Face
2018

Plutonium Pink Count Draco Knuckelduster
2018

Ōgon Bat
2018

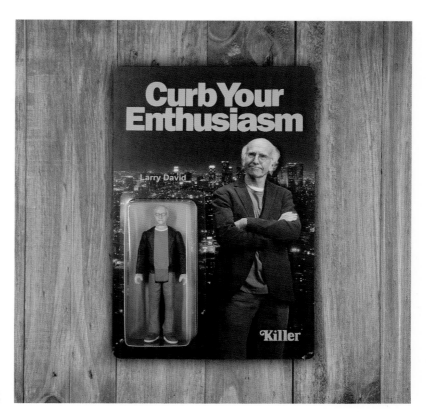

Curb Your Enthusiasm
2018

The Curse of The Werewolf
2018

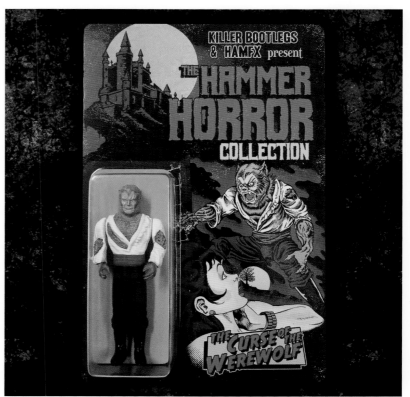

KOBUSHER

Kobusher (Jeck Ebreo) describes himself as a "newbie" to the art world, but as always having had a keen interest in painting. He began to produce sketches of popular cartoon characters during his time working as a creative director for the advertising agency BBDO Guerrero in Manilla.

Kobusher gave up his job to focus on what he loved, painting. This allowed what had been drawings of cartoon characters to be transformed into eye-catching acrylic pieces, work that showed well-known characters such as Homer Simpson and Popeye in a completely different way.

His artistic skills were developed during his time studying fine arts at the University of the Philippines. His work combines artistic flair with a childhood fascination with pop culture. This stemmed from exposure at a young age to influences from both eighties Western and Japanese sources, ranging from MTV to manga.

Indeed Kobusher has taken a lot from manga, including his name, which is derived from a character in *Mazinger Z*, Koji Kabuto, and also his artistic style.

INSTAGRAM: @kobusher
FACEBOOK: /jeck.ebreo

God
2019

Armour
2019

Soldier
2019

Monster
2019

" Pop culture is
a generation's
metaphorical tattoo."

Adventure Dog
2017

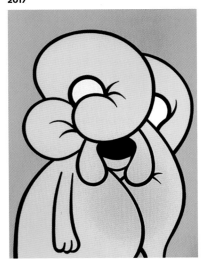

Pikatsu
2017

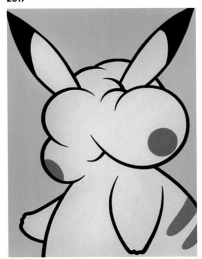

Pludoh
2017

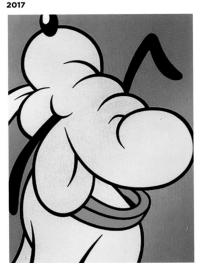

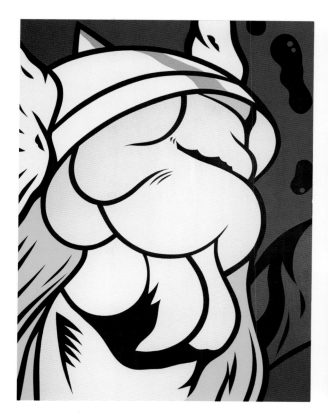
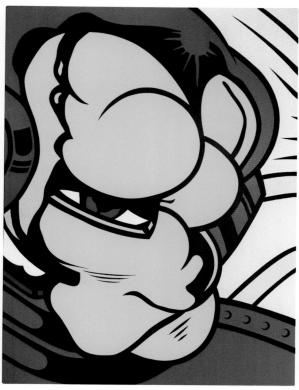
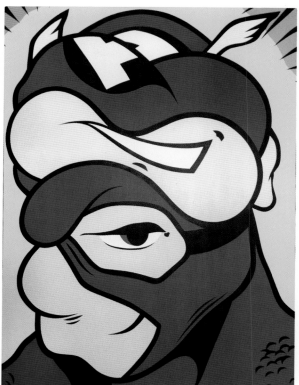
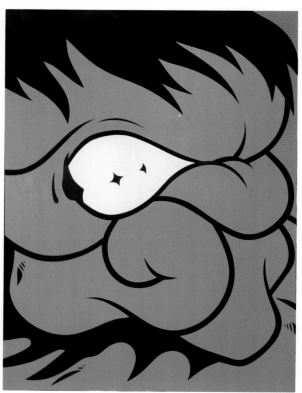

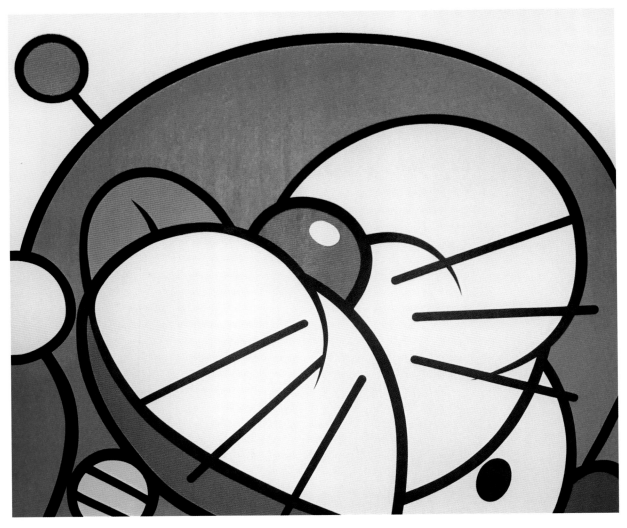

Doraemon
2018

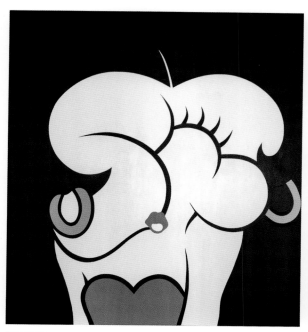

Betty Bloop
2018

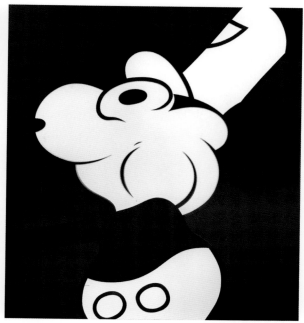

Enter The Void
2019

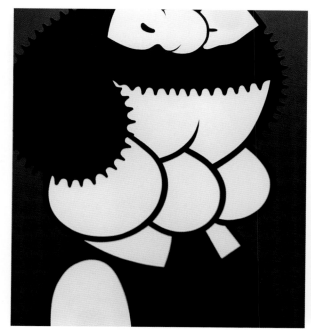

Nonesee
2019

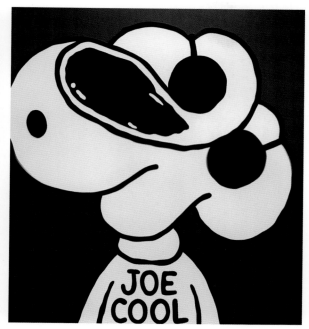

Spoopy
2019

BARTOSZ KOSOWSKI

Bartosz Kosowski is an illustrator and poster artist based in Lodz, Poland. He was educated at Strzeminski Academy of Art. Working mostly with posters, portraits, and editorial illustrations, he has created award winning posters for numerous films and cooperated with such clients as Apple, Legendary Pictures, Canal+, Orange, ING, *The New Yorker*, *The Economist*, *The New Republic*, the *Hollywood Reporter*, *Smithsonian*, *Chicago* magazine, and *Newsweek*. He has received three gold medals from Society of Illustrators (in New York) and Society of Illustrators of Los Angeles and his works have been selected and awarded by American Illustration, World Illustration Awards, Spectrum, 3x3 Design, Graphis, European Design Awards, Lahti Poster Biennial, Ecuador Poster Bienal, and New York Festival Awards. They have also been published in Taschen's *Illustration Now!* Vol.4, Bloomsbury's *Illustration: A Theoretical and Contextual Perspective*, and Flesk's *Spectrum 23* and *Spectrum 25*. For the last four years Kosowski has been an Adobe Design Achievement Awards mentor.

WEBSITE: www.bartoszkosowski.com/
INSTAGRAM: @bartoszkosowski
FACEBOOK: /bartosz.kosowski
TWITTER: @BartoszKosowski
BEHANCE: /BartoszKosowski

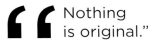

" Nothing is original."

The Shining
2018

Jaws
2015

Lolita
2014

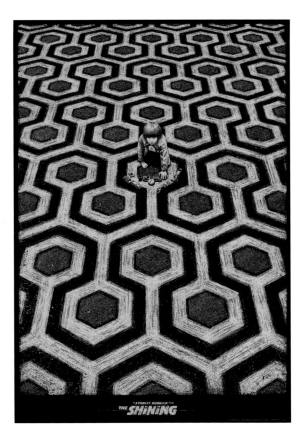

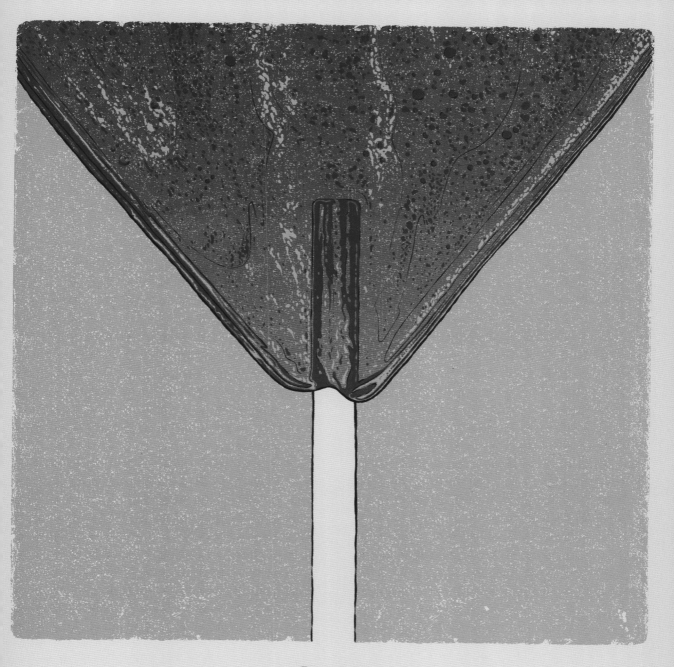

Lolita

A STANLEY KUBRICK FILM

METRO-GOLDWYN-MAYER IN ASSOCIATION WITH SEVEN ARTS PRODUCTIONS PRESENT JAMES B. HARRIS AND STANLEY KUBRICK'S "LOLITA"

STARRING JAMES MASON · SHELLEY WINTERS · PETER SELLERS AS "QUILTY" AND INTRODUCING SUE LYON AS LOLITA

MUSIC BY NELSON RIDDLE   FILM EDITOR ANTHONY HARVEY   DIRECTOR OF PHOTOGRAPHY OSWALD MORRIS

SCREENPLAY BY VLADIMIR NABOKOV   BASED ON HIS NOVEL LOLITA   DIRECTED BY STANLEY KUBRICK

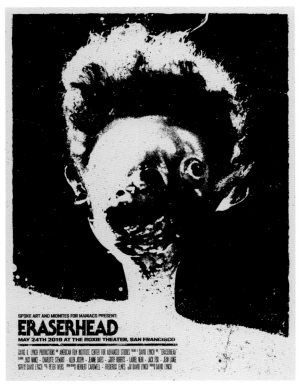

Eraserhead
2017

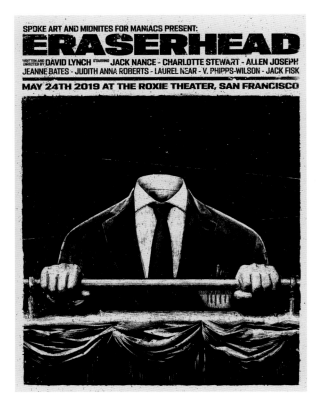

Eraserhead
2017

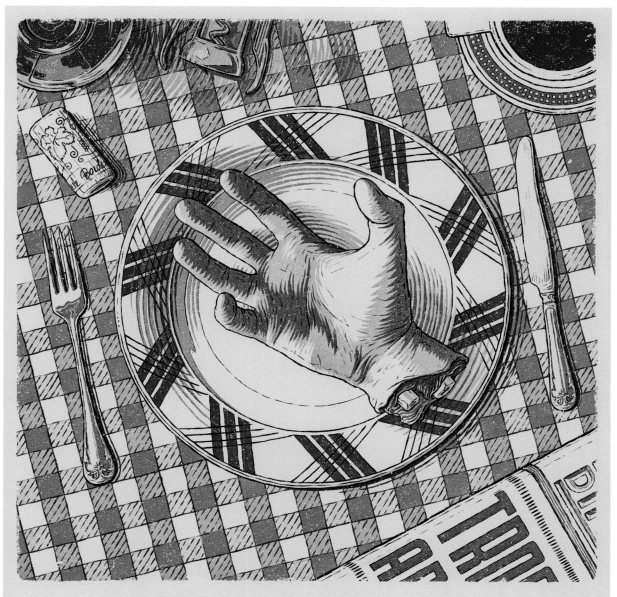

Delicatessen

AVEC DOMINIQUE PINON · MARIE-LAURE DOUGNAC · JEAN-CLAUDE DREYFUS · KARIN VIARD · TICKY HOLGADO · ANNE-MARIE PISANI

SILVIE LAGUNA · RUFUS · JACQUES MATHOU · JEAN-FRANÇOIS PERRIER · HOWARD VERNON · CHICK ORTEGA

MUSIQUE ORIGINALE CARLOS D'ALESSIO SON JÉRÔME THIAULT ET VINCENT ARNARDI CRÉATION DES COSTUMES VALÉRIE POZZO DI BORGO MONTAGE HERVÉ SCHNEID

SCÉNARIO DE JEAN-PIERRE JEUNET · MARC CARO · GILLES ADRIEN DIRECTEUR DE LA PHOTOGRAPHIE DARIUS KHONDJI DIRECTEUR DE PRODUCTION MICHÈLE ARNOULD

UN FILM DE JEAN-PIERRE JEUNET ET MARC CARO

RORY KURTZ

Rory Kurtz is an illustrator and artist living on the shore of Lake Michigan in America's Midwest. Focusing in pencil, ink, and digital paint, Rory has carved out his niche as a unique voice in the illustration community. Each of his pieces are individualistic yet share a sense of fantasy in a modern reality. His work can be seen regularly in publishing, editorial, and advertising around the world.

WEBSITE: www.rorykurtz.com/
INSTAGRAM: @rorykurtz
FACEBOOK: /rorykurtzillustration

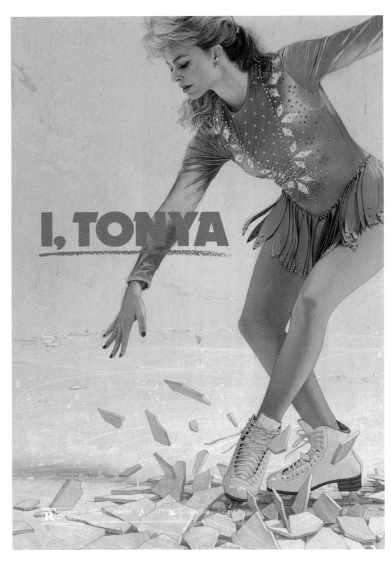

I, Tonya
2017

Annihilation
2018

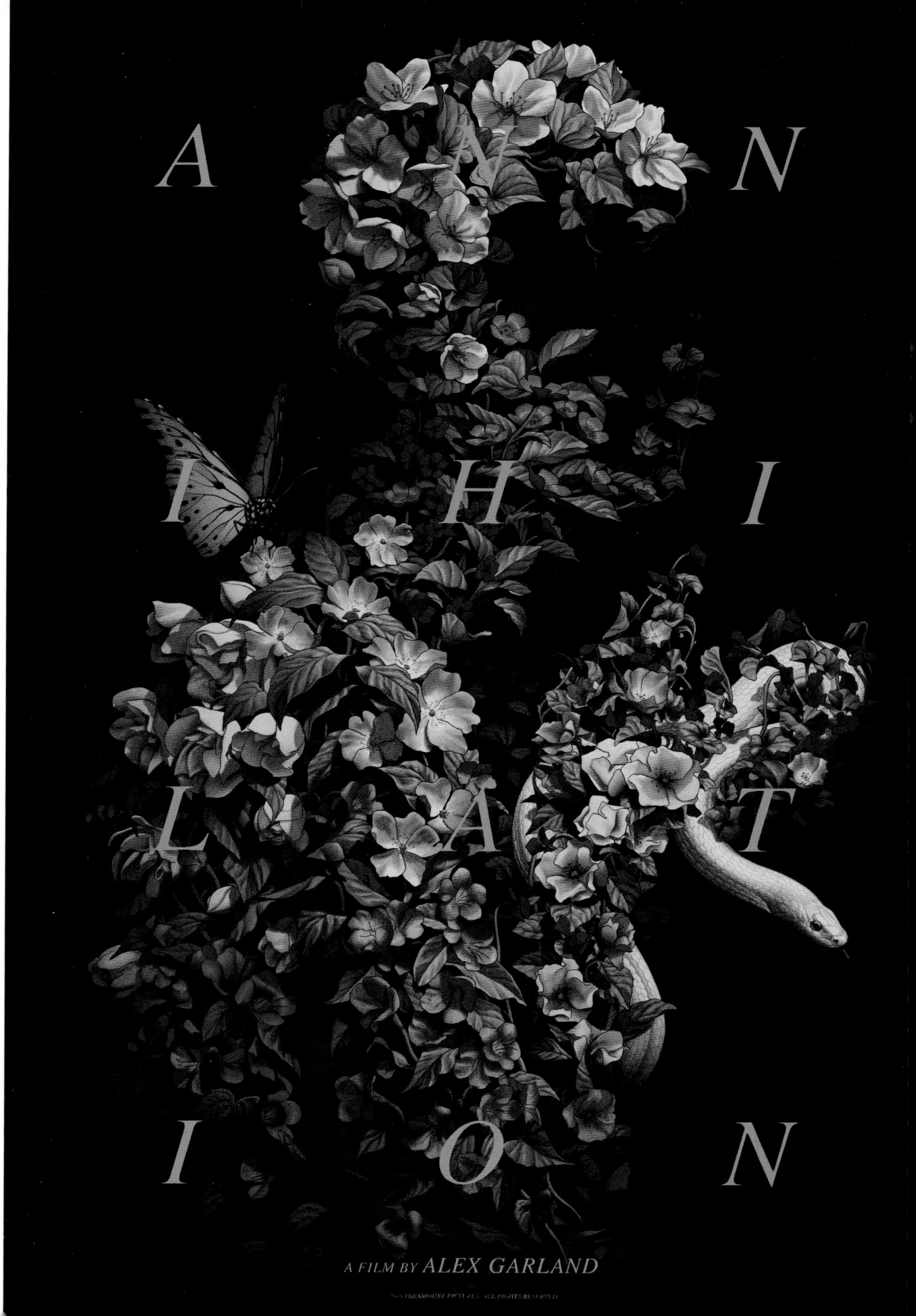

A N N
I H I
L A T
I O N

A FILM BY ALEX GARLAND

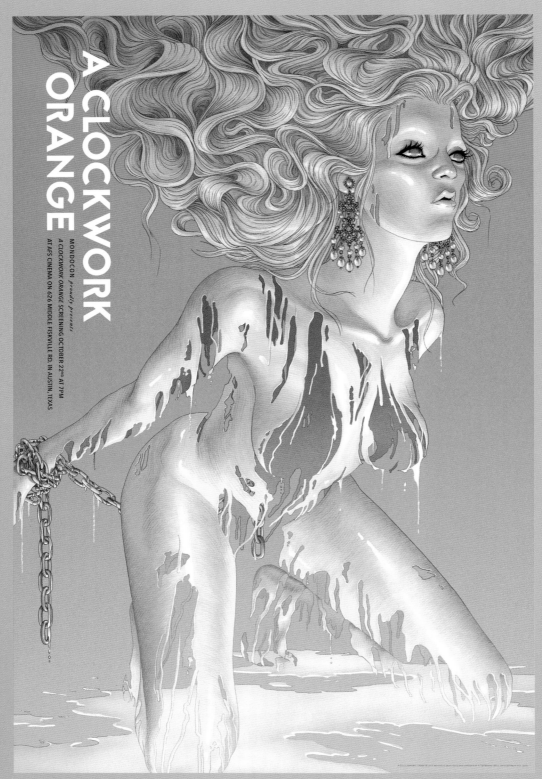

A CLOCKWORK ORANGE

MONDOCON proudly presents
A CLOCKWORK ORANGE SCREENING OCTOBER 22ND AT 7PM
AT AFS CINEMA ON 626 MIDDLE FISKVILLE RD. IN AUSTIN, TEXAS

A Clockwork Orange
2016

The Graduate
2016

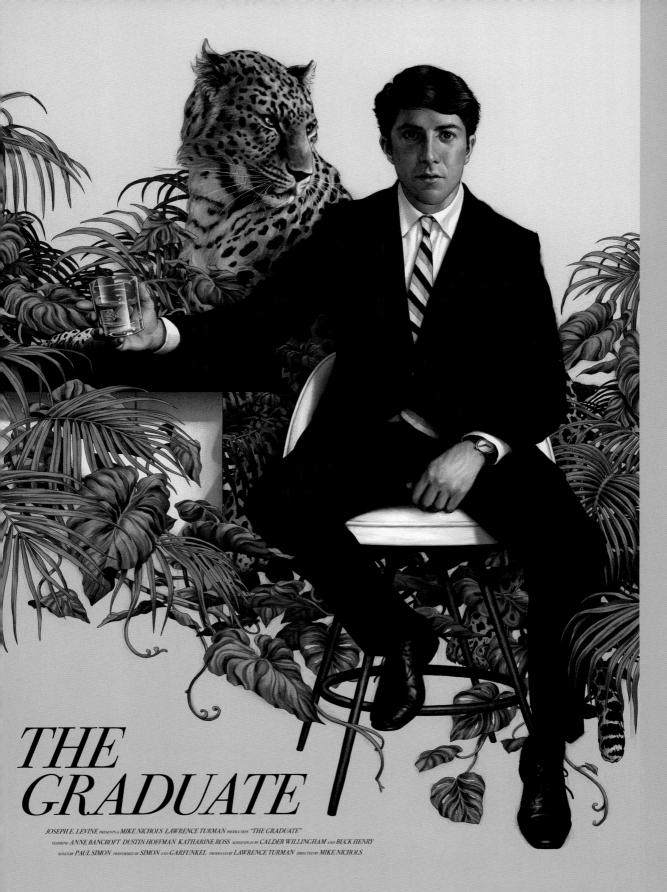

THE GRADUATE

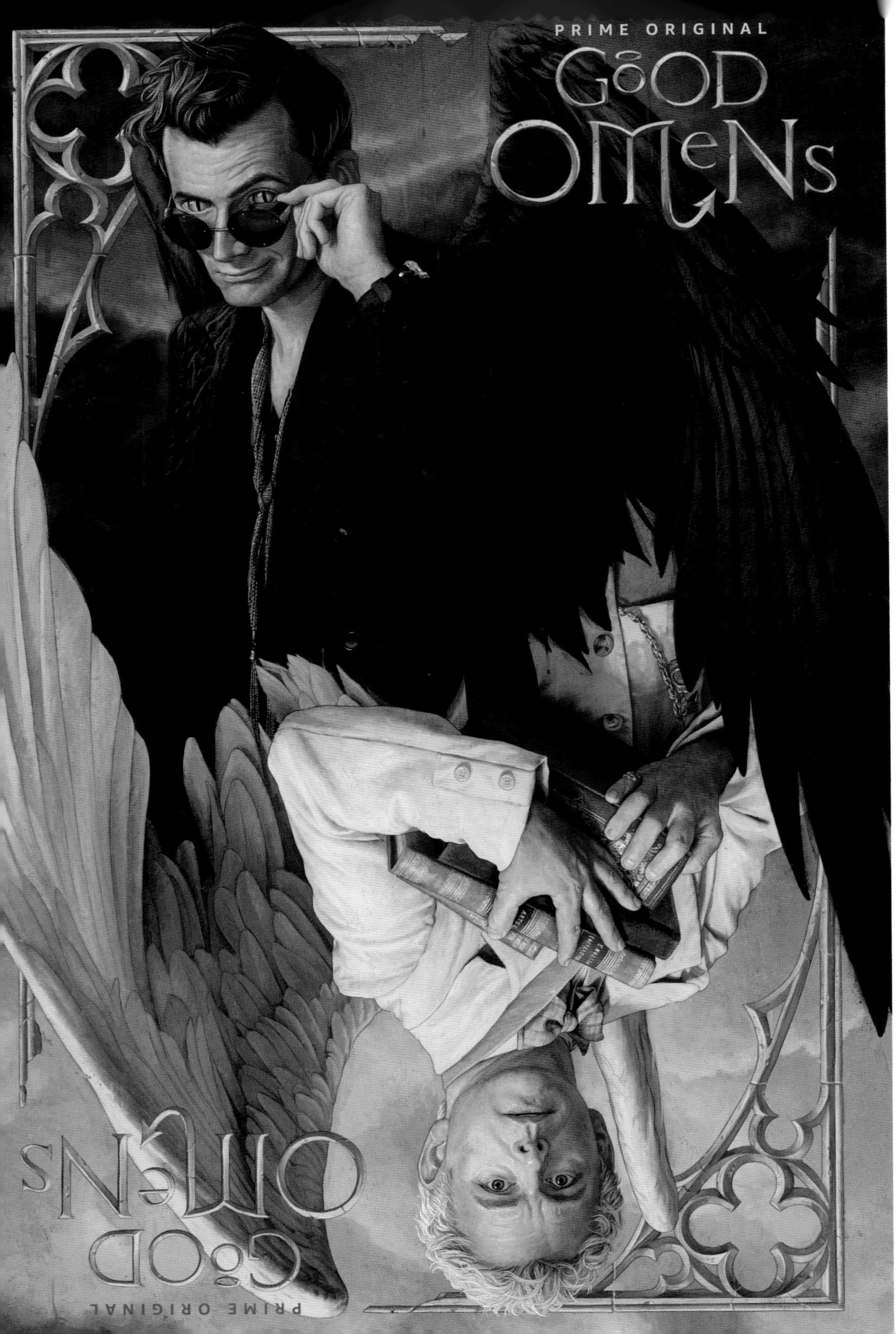
PRIME ORIGINAL
GOOD OMENS

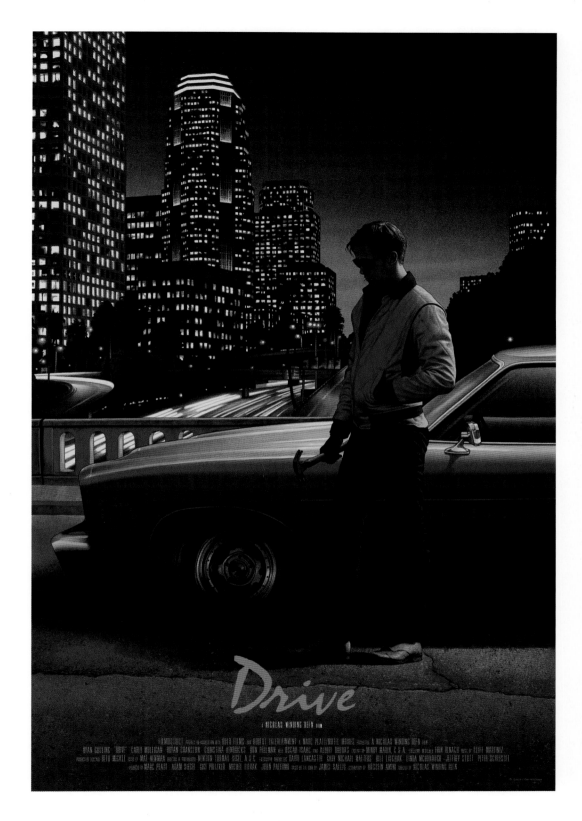

Good Omens
2018

Drive
2017

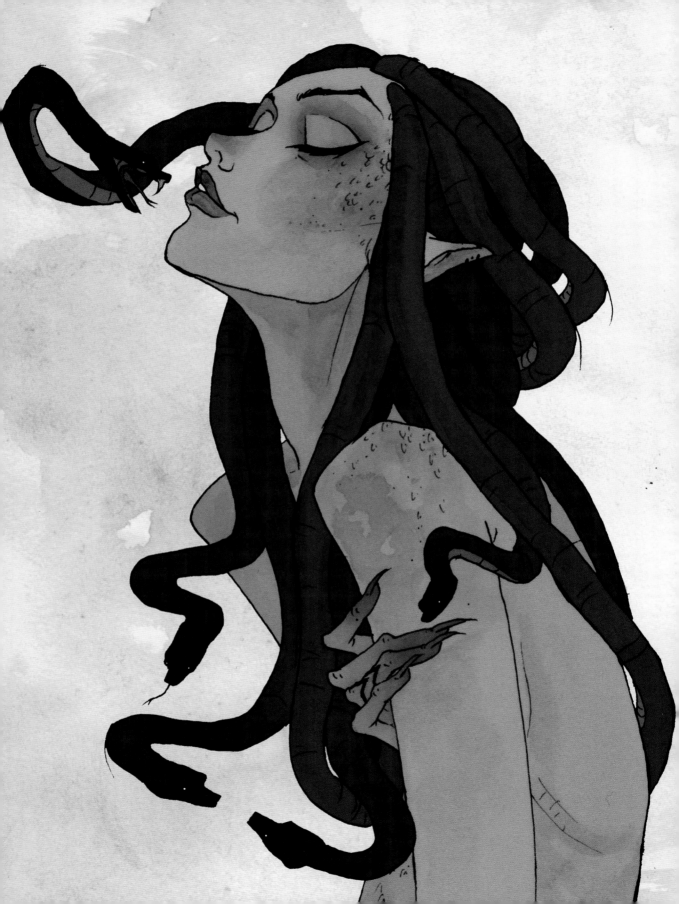

ABIGAIL LARSON

Abigail's strange and macabre illustrations have been shown in galleries throughout the United States and Europe, including New York City, Los Angeles, London, and Paris. She's worked with DC Vertigo, IDW Publishing, Titan Comics, Image Comics, Pelican Publishing, 3dtotal, the SyFy channel, and Sideshow Collectibles. In 2016 Abigail won the Hugo Award for Best Professional Artist.

WEBSITE: www.abigaillarson.com
INSTAGRAM: @abigail_larson
TWITTER: @Abigail_Larson
CONTACT: abigail@abigaillarson.com

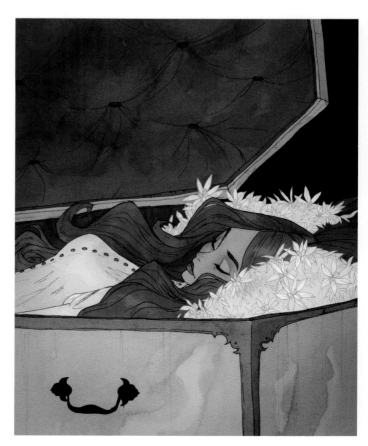

Medusa
2018

Lucy's Funeral
2018

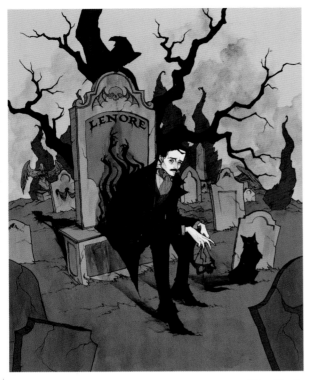

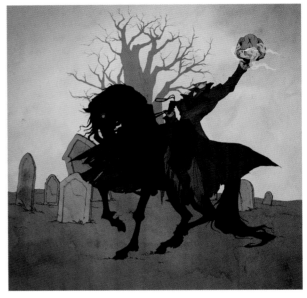

Edgar Allan Poe
2015

Legends of Sleepy Hollow
2017

Mary Shelley and Her Creation
2018

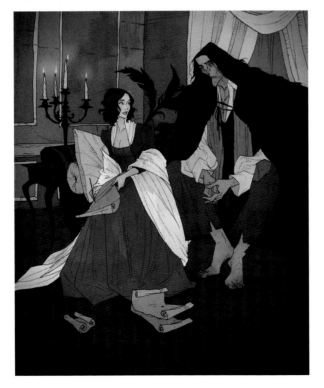

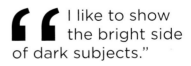

> ❝❝ I like to show
> the bright side
> of dark subjects."

Blood of my Blood
2018

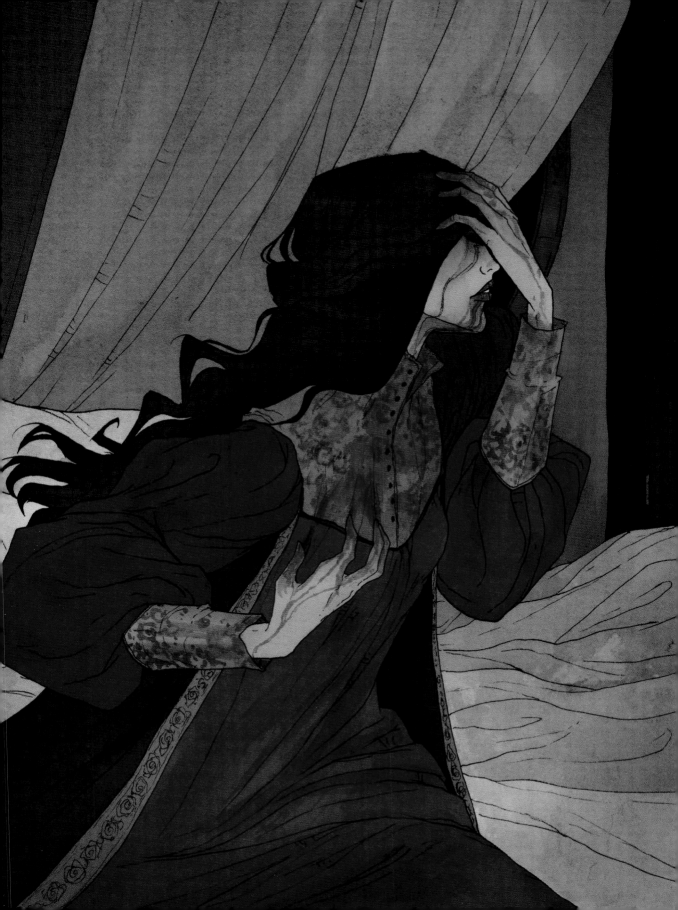

MIKE LEAVITT

Michael Leavitt is best known for his "Art Army" series, a collection of handmade action figures of well-known artists, including James Turrell, Andy Warhol, Banksy, and Ai Weiwei, which reference the signature practice of the subject's work. Sculpted in clay and finished with paint and mixed media, the figures satirize the relationship between consumer and celebrity cultures and contemporary art, reducing art figures to caricatures. Working under the name Kitchen Productions, Leavitt has produced a variety of conceptual art projects, performance works, animations, and curio-kitsch objects; "The Penny Places" is an ongoing series of pennies found in the street, which Leavitt paints with miniature landscapes that depict the locations where they were found. He has also experimented with architectural structures, such as his set of "*Portable Homeless Shelters,*" built from recycled materials and deployed in Seattle since 1999.

WEBSITE: www.mikeleavittart.com
FACEBOOK: /MikeLeavittArt

Hitchcock
2016

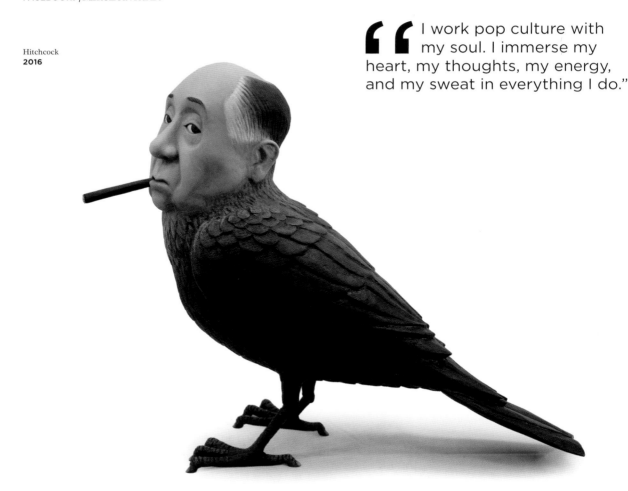

"" I work pop culture with my soul. I immerse my heart, my thoughts, my energy, and my sweat in everything I do."

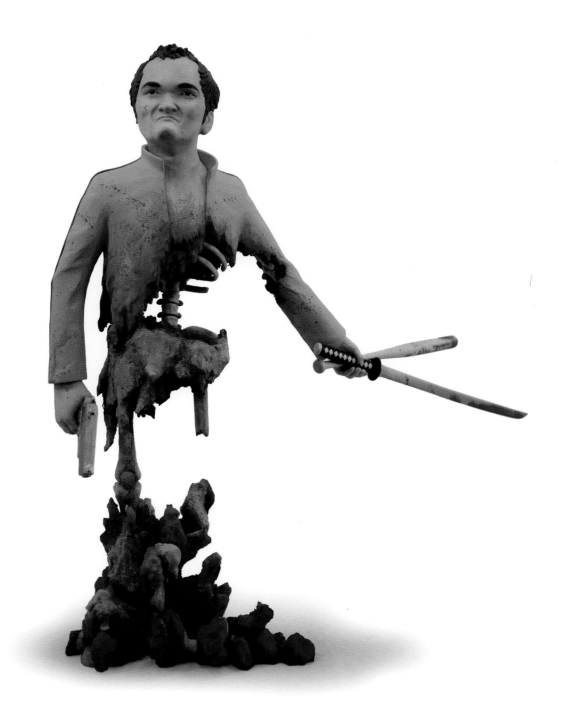

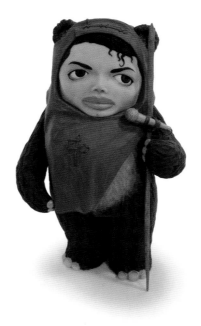

A Mirror Entrance in the Secret
2013

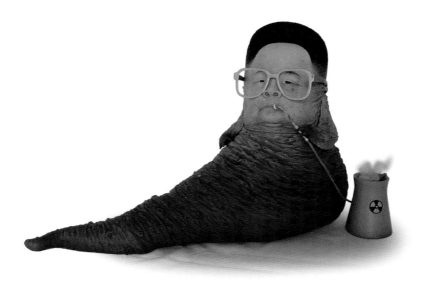

Dear Mind Powers Work our Leader
2013

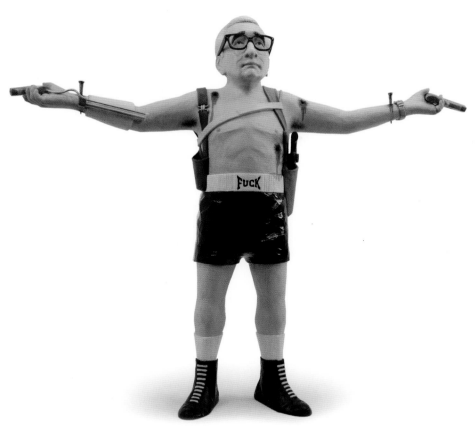

Scorsese
2016

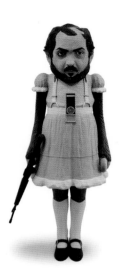

Kubrick
2016

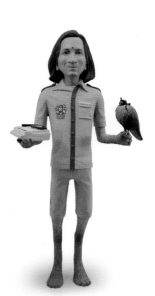

Wes Anderson
2016

FRÉDÉRIC LE MARTELOT

A graduate of the southern axis of a Marseillaise graphic arts school and after a stint in advertising as well as in role playing, Frédéric Le Martelot lives and currently works in video games in Paris as an illustrator/concept artist. Having grown up in the nineties, his visual culture was based on post-apocalyptic worlds, futuristic cities, choreographed fusions, and light sabers.

INSTAGRAM: @flemartelot
FACEBOOK: /LeMartelotFrederic
TWITTER: @flemartelot
BEHANCE: /flemartelot

> " Born with a pencil in my hand, my visual culture has been shaped by films *like Star Wars*, *Rambo*, and *Blade Runner*. I like to explain and reinterpret these universes through my compositions."

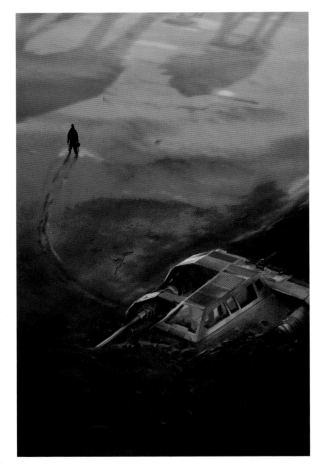

In the Middle of Nowhere
2014

Immortan's Land
2015

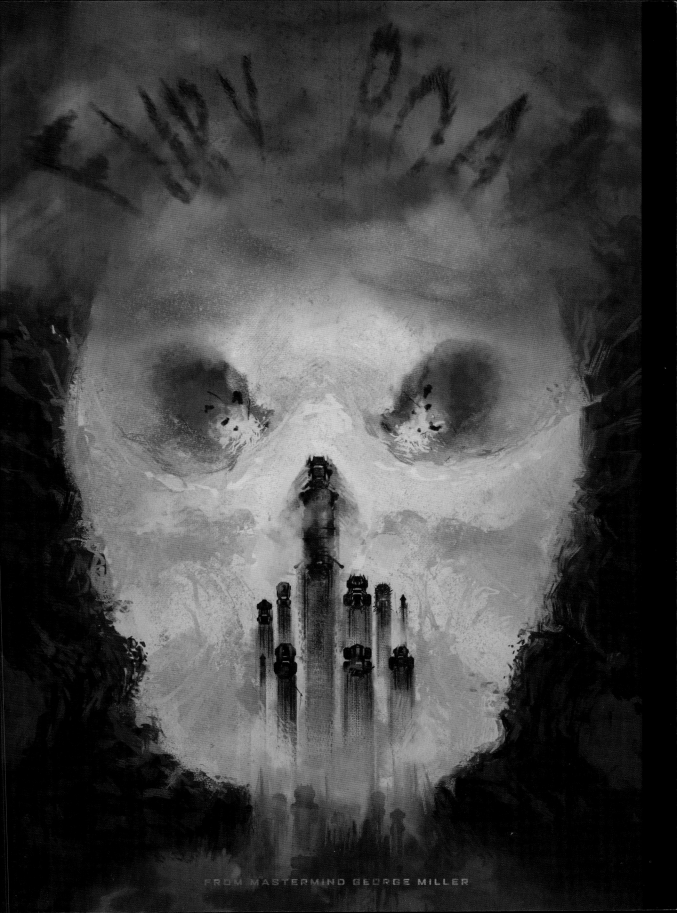

FROM MASTERMIND GEORGE MILLER

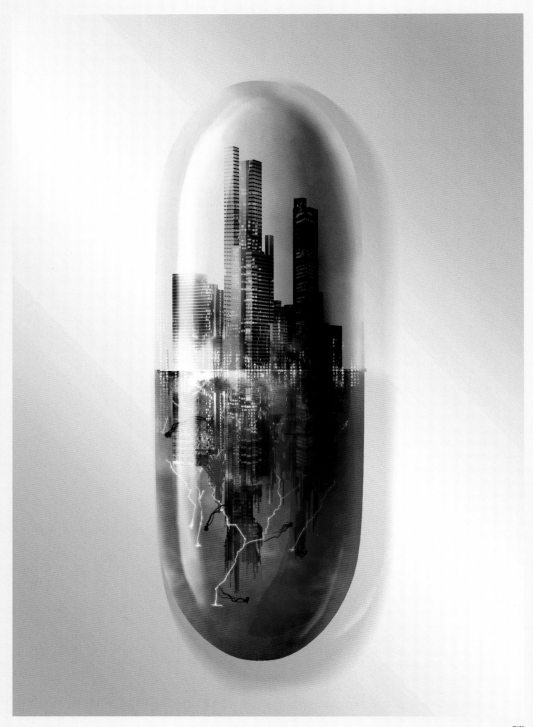

Pill
2015

Miss Peregrine
2016

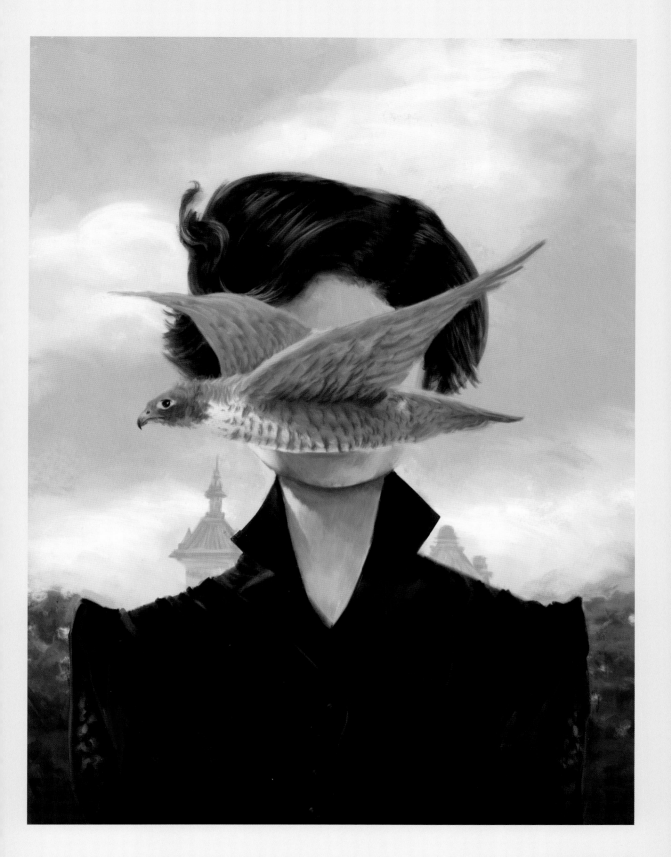

MATHEUS LOPES

Matheus Lopes is a thirty-two-year-old designer/illustrator based in Belo Horizonte, a city in the southeast of Brazil. He has been working with art since he was fourteen. His job is his passion and he can't see himself doing any other thing for a living. He uses this passion to communicate with others in a way words can't reach. When it comes to style, it's hard for him to define what he does in one or two categories. He experiments with different techniques, from watercolor to collage, and explores different themes, from pop culture to art nouveau. He likes to say he has no specific style is his style.

He strongly believes that art has the power to touch people's minds and change their perceptions, so he likes to incorporate positive, playful, and optimistic concepts into his creations. He likes to think he is helping people—even if it's small scale—making them feel better about themselves and about the world that surrounds us.

WEBSITE: www.mathiole.com
INSTAGRAM: @mathiole

> " I strongly believe that art has the power to touch people's minds and change their perceptions, so I like to incorporate positive, playful, and optimistic concepts into my creations. I like to think I'm helping people—even on a small scale—feel better about themselves and about the world that surrounds us."

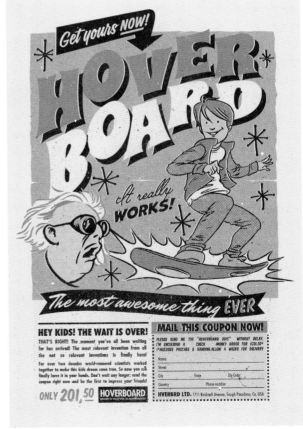

Hoverboard
2016

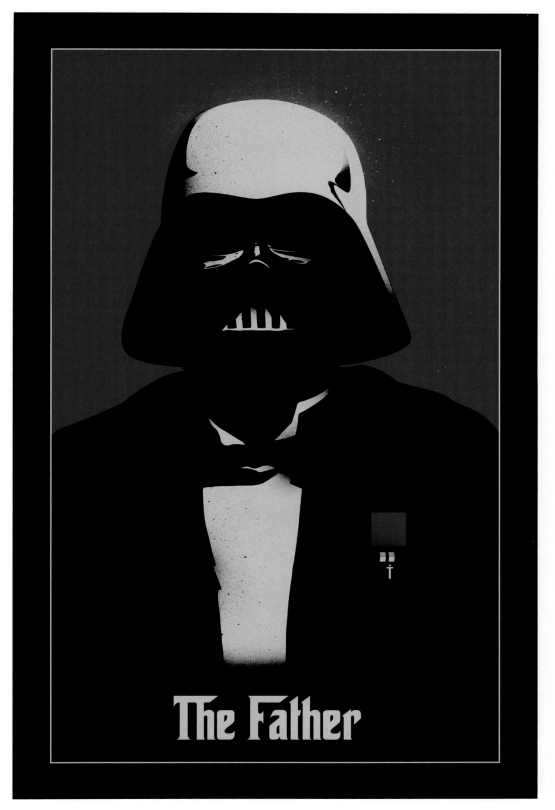

The Father
2011

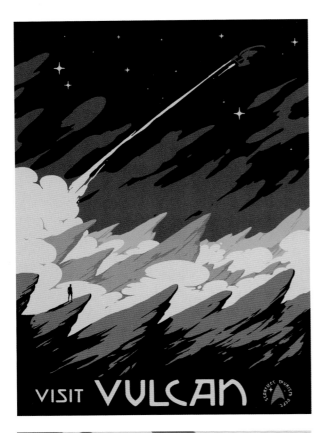

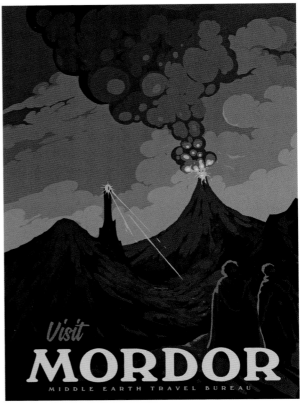

Visit Vulcan
2018

Visit Mordor
2018

Visit Hogwarts
2018

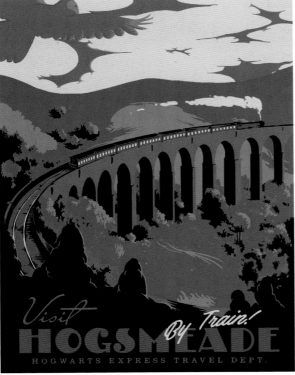

Visit Zebes
2018

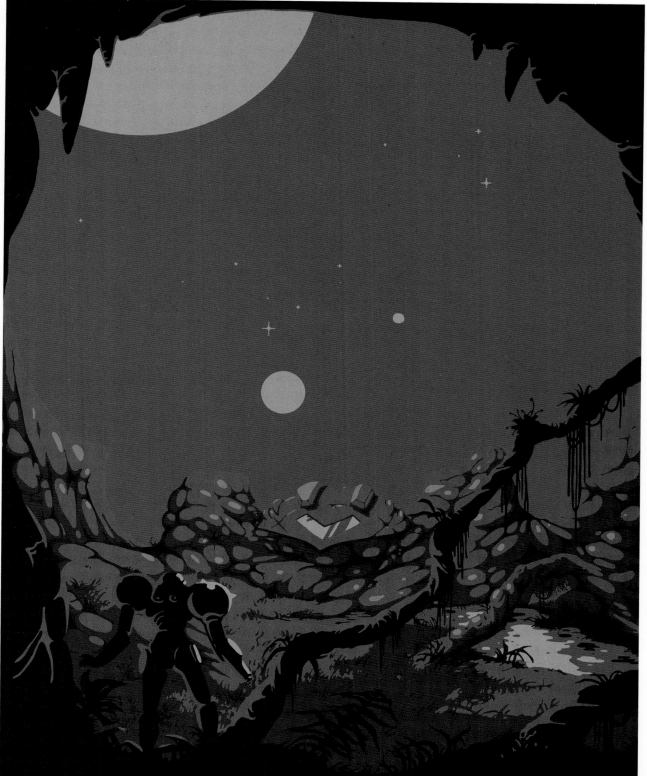

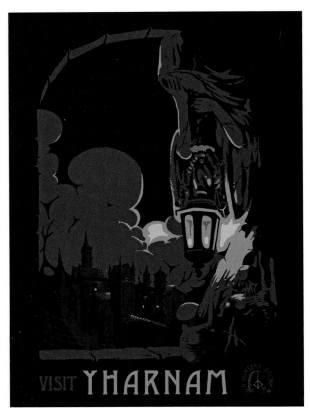

Visit Yharnam
2018

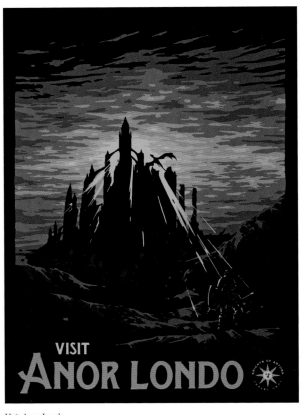

Visit Anor Londo
2018

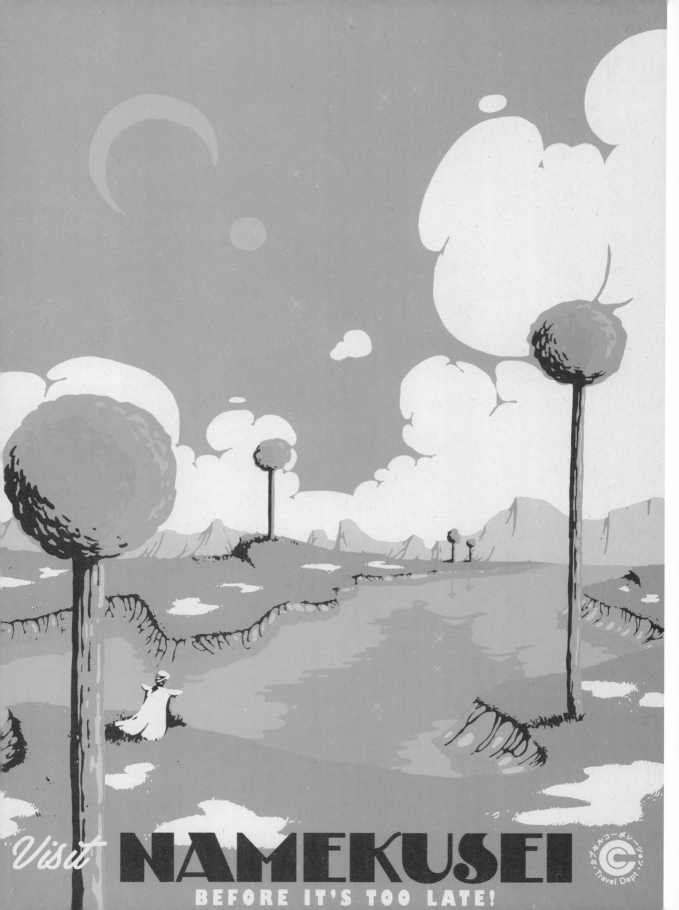

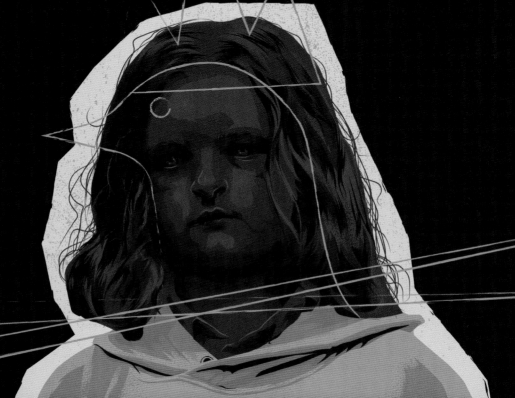

TIBOR LOVAS

Tibor Lovas has been working as a graphic designer in Budapest, Hungary, for nearly ten years. About five years ago he started making alternative movie posters. He wanted to create something that was relaxing and inspirational at the same time. He thinks he found it.

Everyone sees and loves different things in a movie. What he is trying to show is his point of view. His style is constantly evolving, but it has certain characteristics: contrasting figures, minimalist geometric shapes, neon colors, glitch, and interesting typography.

BEHANCE: /lovastibor

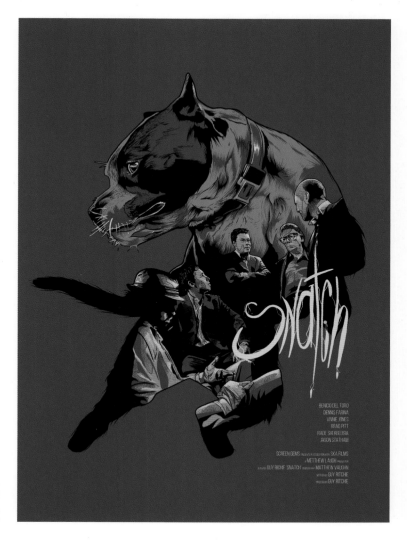

Hereditary
2018

Snatch
2019

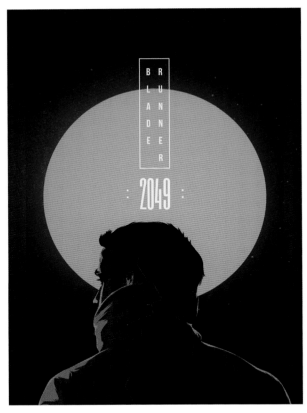

Blade Runner 2049
2017

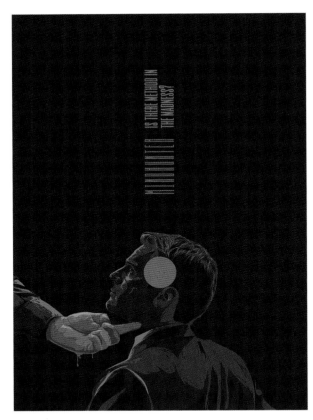

Mindhunter
2018

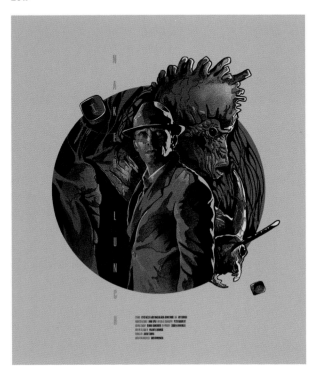

Naked Lunch
2019

Joker
2019

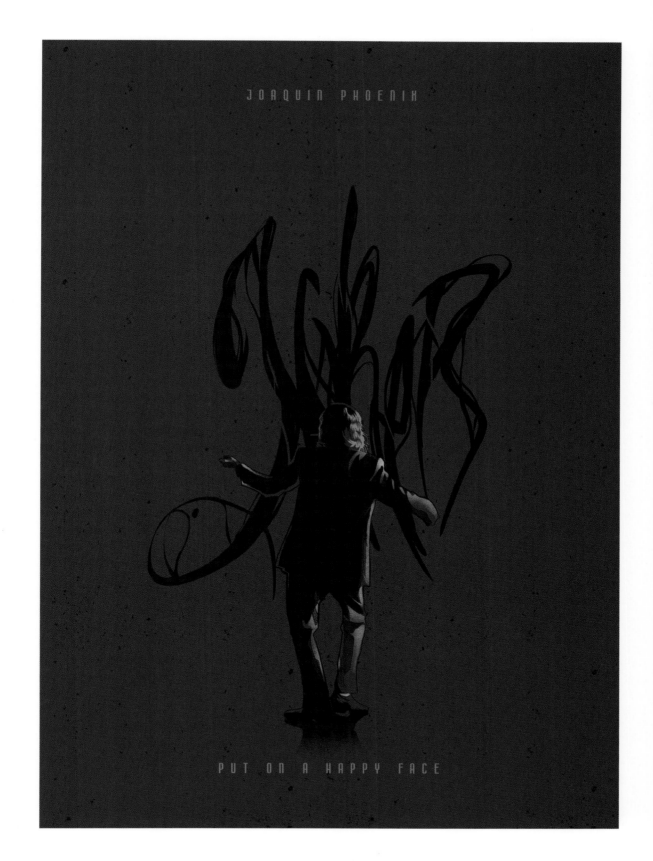

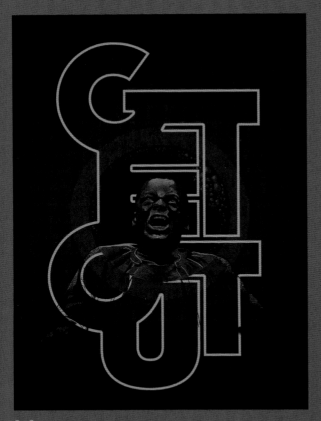

Get Out
2019

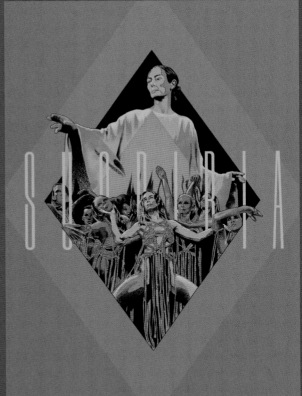

Suspiria
2019

" . . . You probably never gave it a thought, but all great films, without exception, contain an important element of no reason. And you know why? Because life itself is filled with no reason."

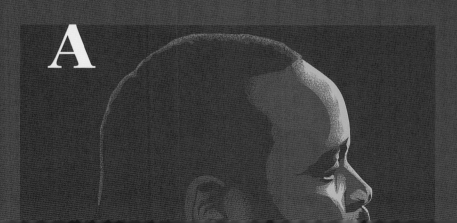

A T L A N T A

Donald Glover
Brian Tyree
Lakeith Stanfield
Zazie Beetz

ZEB LOVE

Zeb Love is from a small cornfield town in Illinois. In 2009 he moved out to the city of Pittsburgh to pursue being a roadie for his friend's band and creating art. Since making his first screenprint in his living room a year later, Zeb got incredibly interested in the medium. After many years of figuring out the process, he has made gig posters for national touring acts such as Pearl Jam, Foo Fighters, the Avett Brothers, Dead & Company, and many more. He had his first art show in London in 2015, and more recently had a solo show full of new paintings in West Virginia.

He is currently working as freelance illustrator and screenprinter. When work isn't all consuming, he finds time to ride his bike and paint.

WEBSITE: www.zeblove.com
INSTAGRAM: @zeb_love

Fantastic Mr. Fox
2014

Big Lebowski
2018

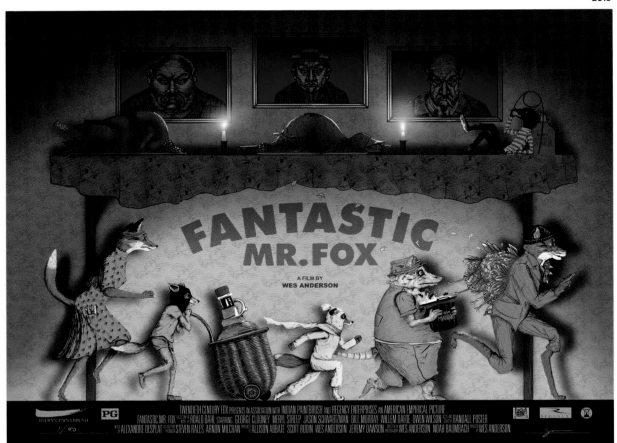

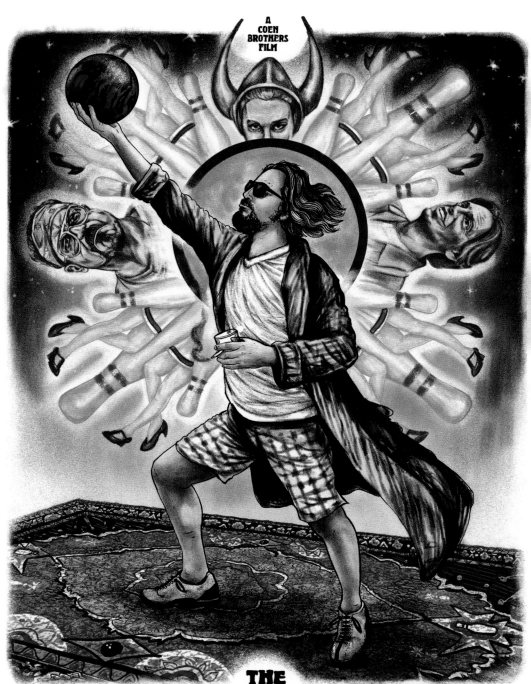

THE **BIG LEBOWSKI**

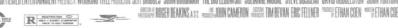

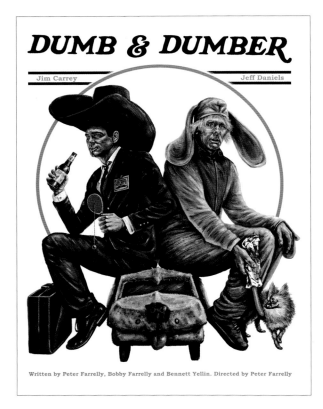

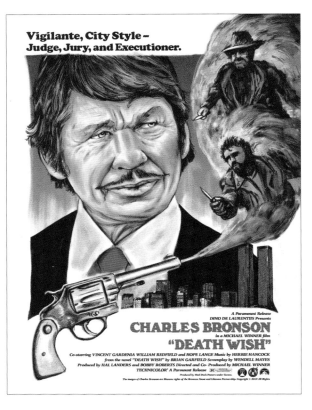

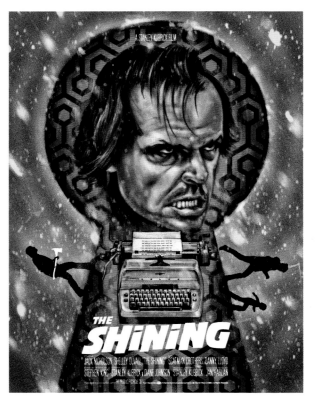

Dumb & Dumber
2018

Death Wish
2018

The Shining
2018

Reefer Madness
2018

❝❝ I feel like good pop culture reflects the state of where we are as human beings. It either makes light of a situation, or reflects on heavy ideas. It connects all of us in some way.”

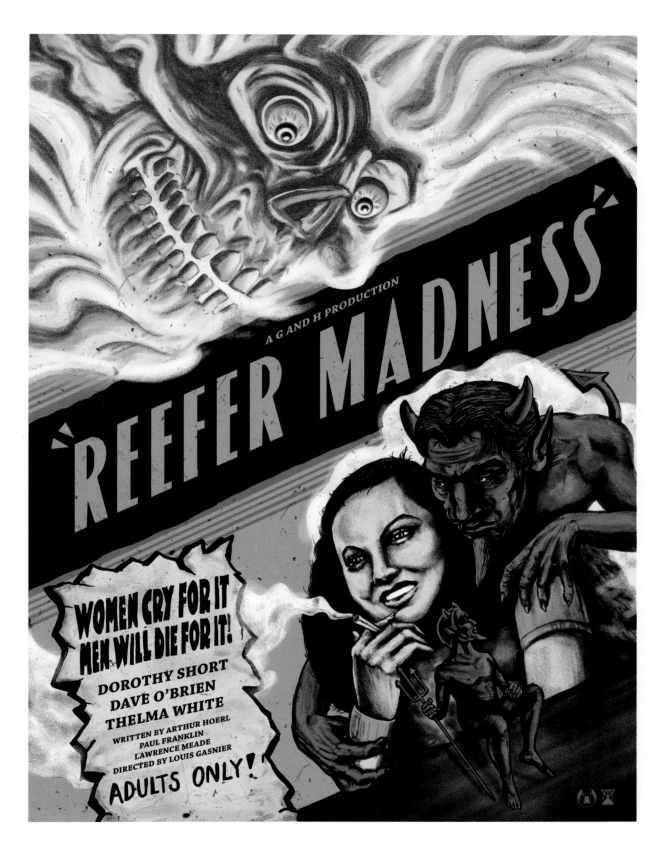

JIM MAHFOOD

Jim Mahfood, a.k.a. Food One, has been working as a professional freelance artist since 1997, amassing an impressive cult following across the globe. Highlights of his career include art chores on Kevin Smith's *Clerks* comics, his creator-owned titles *Grrl Scouts, Los Angeles Ink Stains*, and *Carl, the Cat That Makes Peanut Butter Sandwiches*. Recent projects include *Miami Vice: Remix, Tank Girl All-Stars*, the *Supernaut Sketchbook*, character design work on the *Into the Spider-Verse* feature film, and the *Grrl Scouts: Magic Socks* TPB, available from Image Comics. Jim's brand-new project is the upcoming *Grrl Scouts: Stone Ghost* miniseries. His popular music podcast is available for free at SkullFunkRadio.Fireside.FM.

WEBSITE: www.jimmahfood.com
INSTAGRAM: @jimmahfood

Tank Girl 2
2012

Tank Girl 1
2012

Tank Helmet
2011

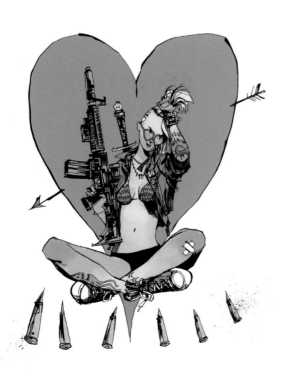

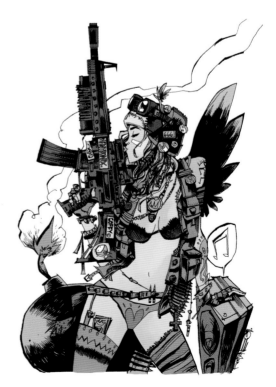

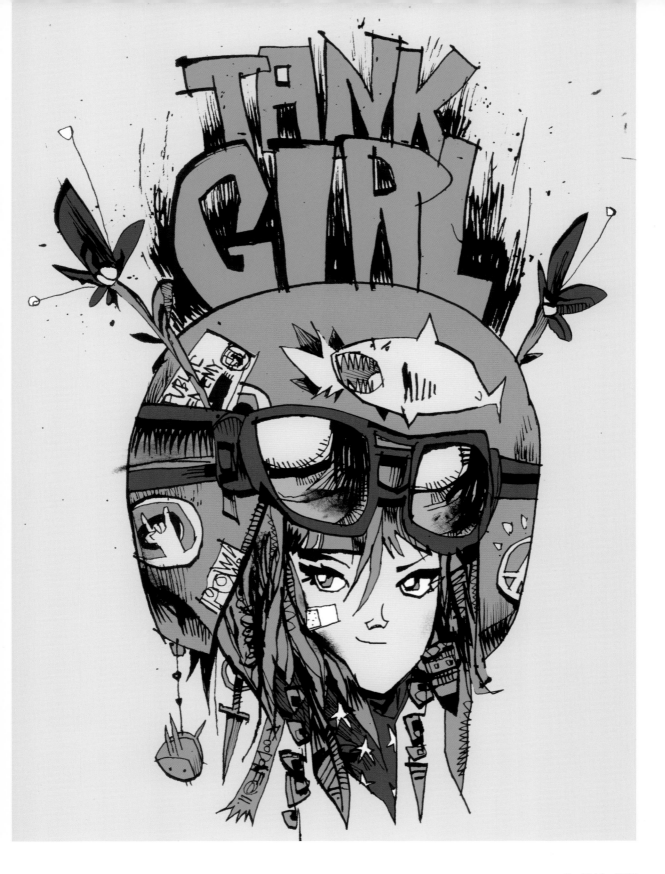

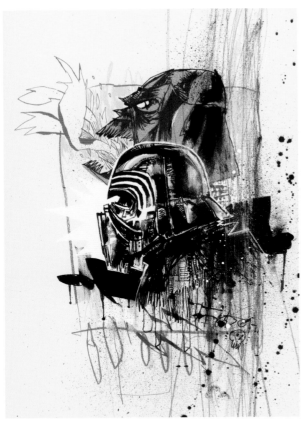

Dark Side Rules
2019

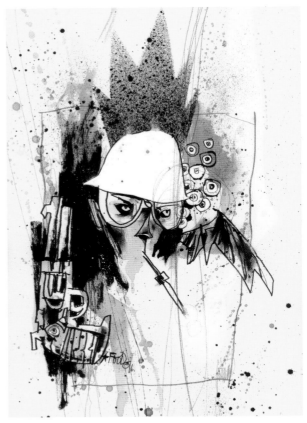

Fear and Loathing in Las Vegas n° 1
2016

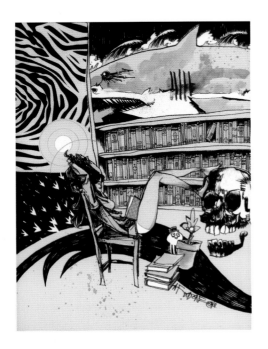

❝❝ I've been obsessed with pop
culture since I was a little
kid. I'm thrilled to be an artist, a
person responsible for putting a
creative vision out into the world,
and hopefully making this place a
more interesting, fun, bugged-out,
psychedelic experience."

Shark Attack Library
2018

Pan's Labyrinth
2018

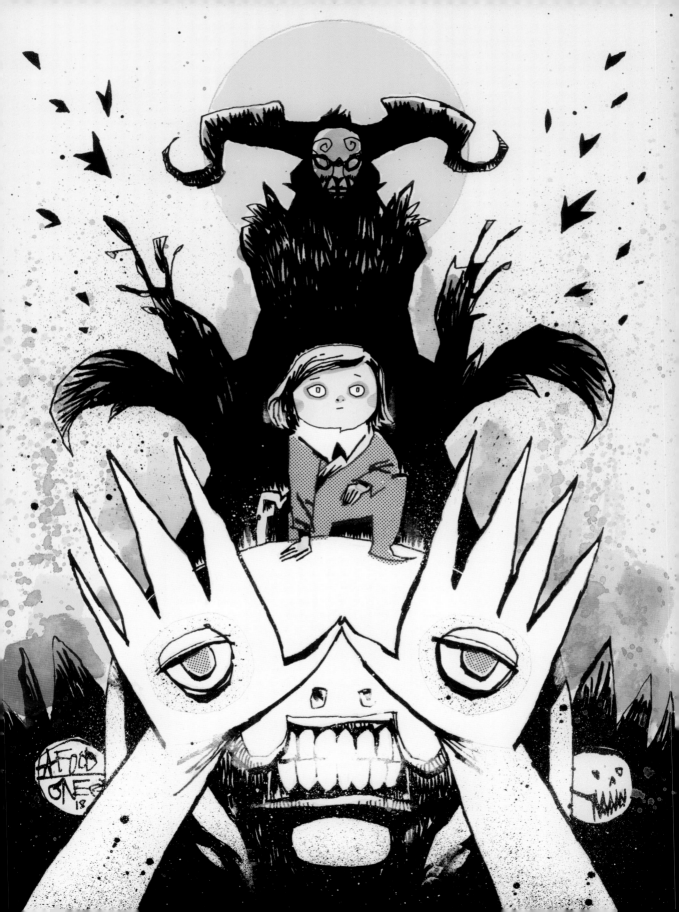

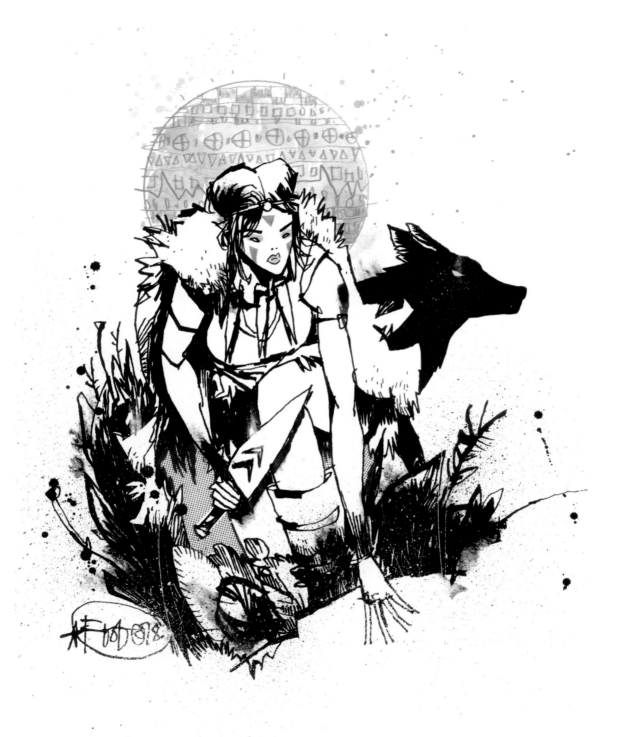

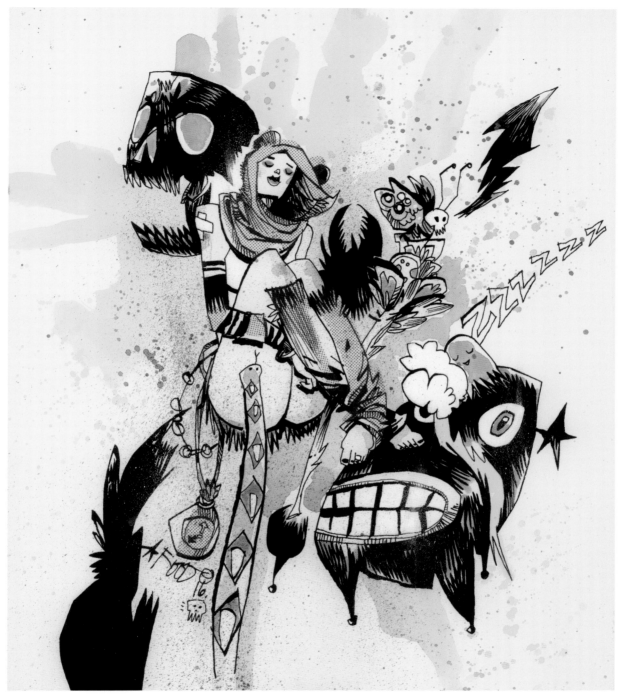

Sacred Protectors of the ZZZs
2016

Princess Mononoke
2018

Funky Beats, Sir?
2011

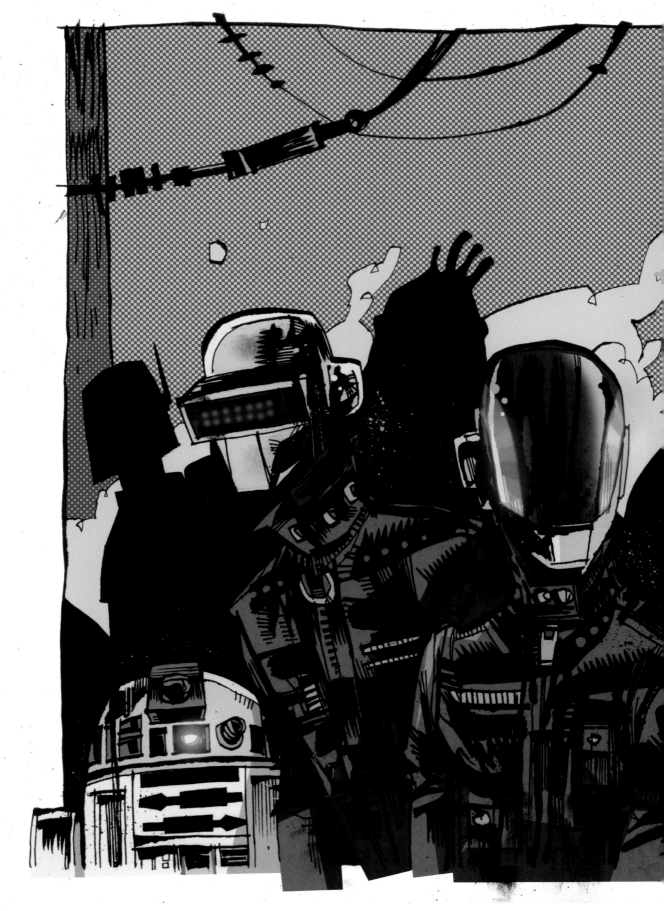

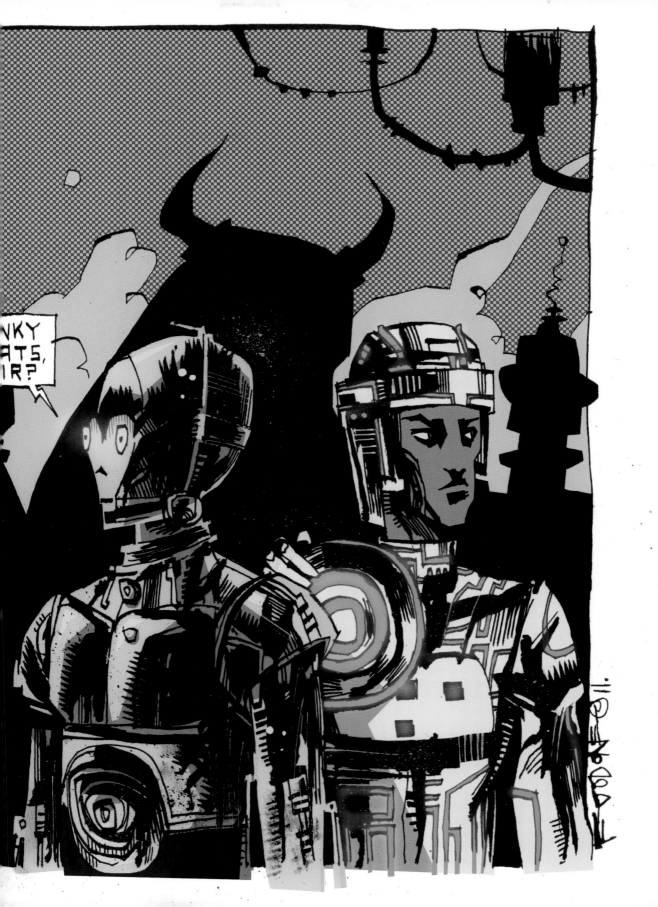

CHRIS MALBON

Based in Bristol, England, Chris Malbon classes himself as a creative all-rounder, comfortable designing on the side of a matchbox or large murals, be it with pencil, pen, paint, or pixel, he's happy using them all. A hardworking and prolific contributor, Chris has created work for an array of clients and agencies over the past seventeen years. He has worked on campaigns for Marvel, Netflix, Nike, Coca-Cola, Sony, London 2012, Unilever, Carhartt, and MTV.

WEBSITE: www.cmalbon.com

> " Pop culture is escapism, I love to spend time in this far far away land as much as I can, I do this through my art, it's a fast track ticket to Neverland or Tatooine or Gotham or the Spider-Verse—wherever I like and for that I'm eternally grateful!"

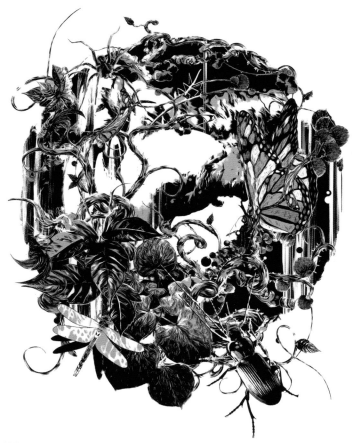

Once
2014

Little Shop of Horrors /
Out To Lunch
2015

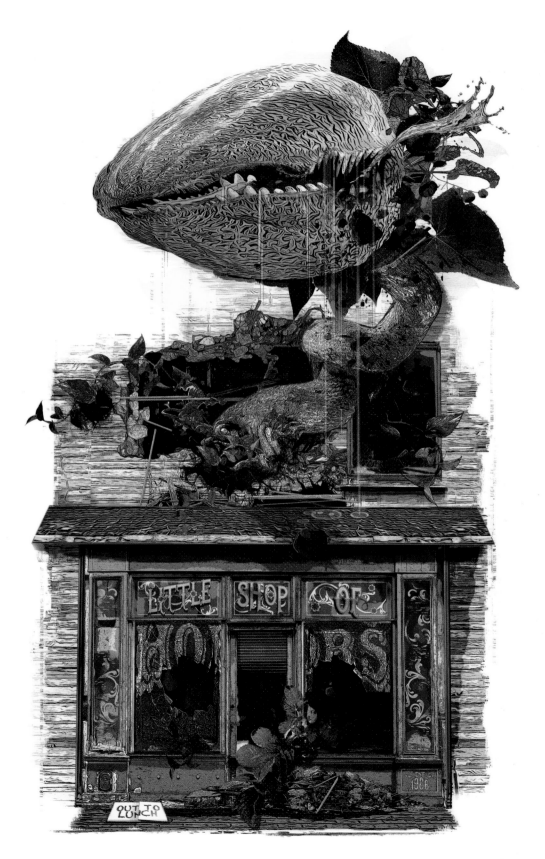

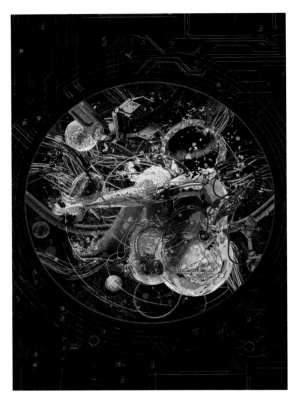

Ghost in the Shell
2017

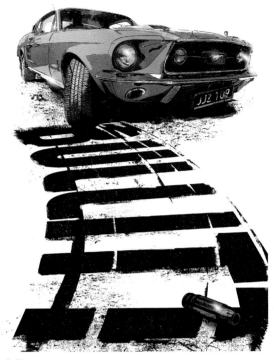

Bullitt
2015

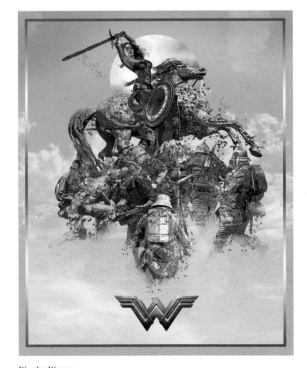

Wonder Woman
2017

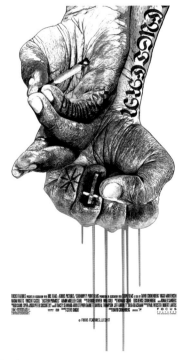

Eastern Promises
2017

House Keeping
2019

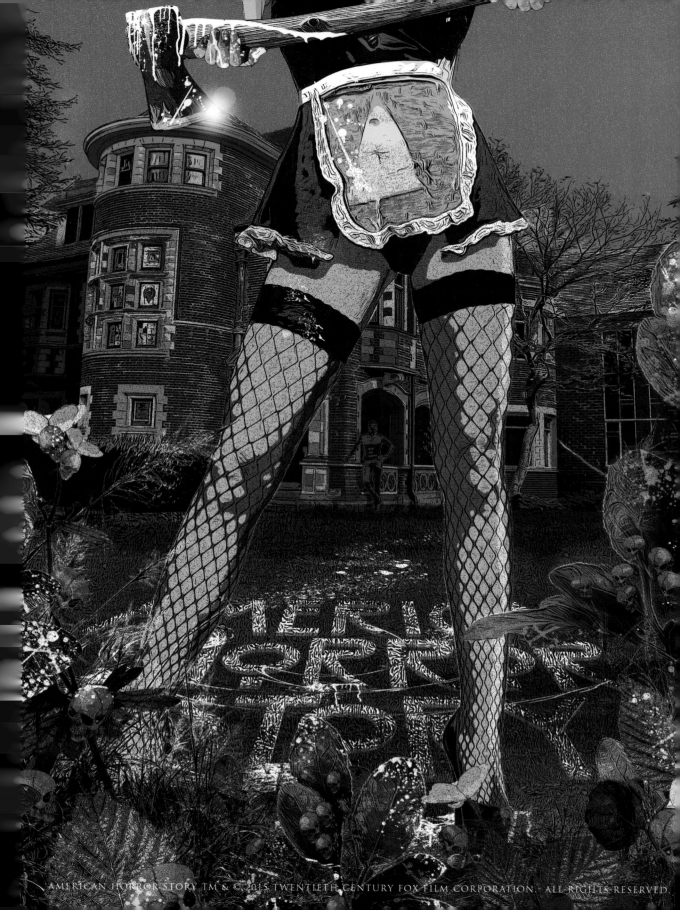

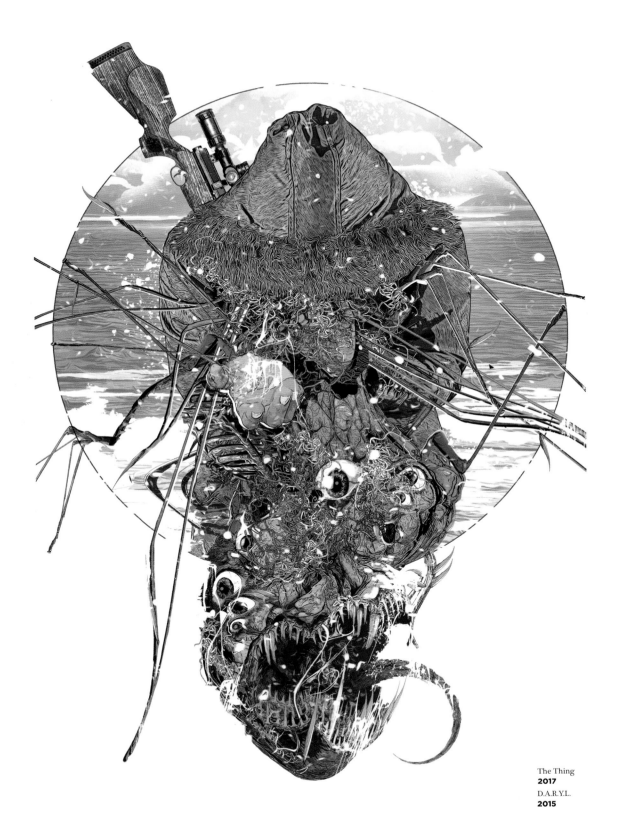

The Thing
2017
D.A.R.Y.L.
2015

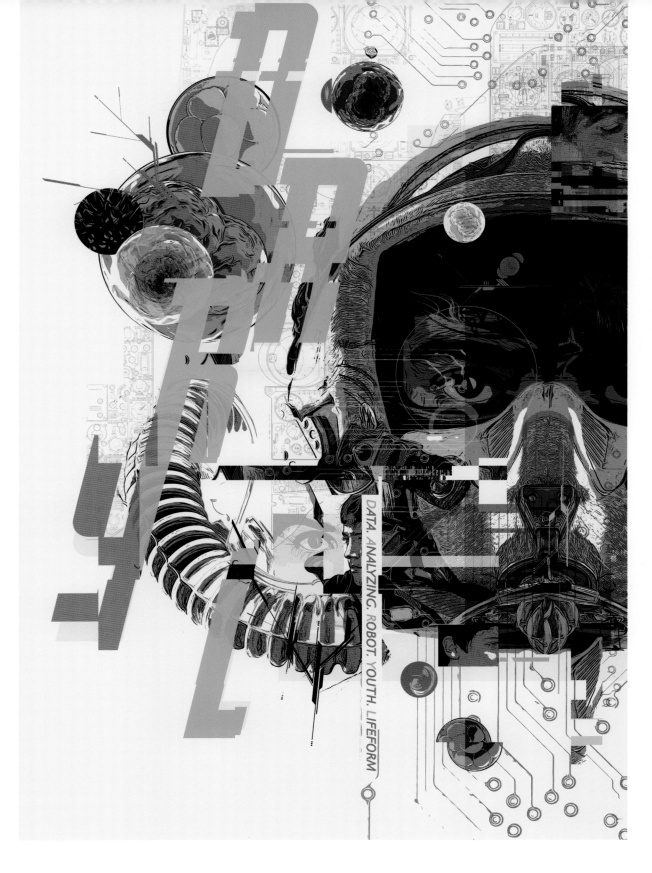

DATA. ANALYZING. ROBOT. YOUTH. LIFEFORM

GAUVAIN MANHATTAN

Gauvain Massé Apéré, a.k.a. Gauvain Manhattan, is about to complete his studies and embrace the life of a comic book author in Angoulême. He spent his adolescence in the countryside of France, where the houses were covered with canvas, playing video games and assembling and painting his Warhammer figurines. During his studies at ÉESI Angoulême — Poitiers, while working on kitsch, he wanted to bring together the two worlds of his childhood, which seemed to him both fundamentally opposite and appreciably close. He searches old canvas in flea markets and garage sales, and then takes a malicious pleasure in "unbridling" them before embedding his favorite characters from video games.

WEBSITE: www.gauvainmanhattan.com
INSTAGRAM: @gauvainmanhattan

❝ I was born three years too late to watch *Dragon Ball Z*, *Teenage Mutant Ninja Turtles*, and *Sailor Moon* on TV. But our generation had *Pokémon*!"

Homer Donuts
2016

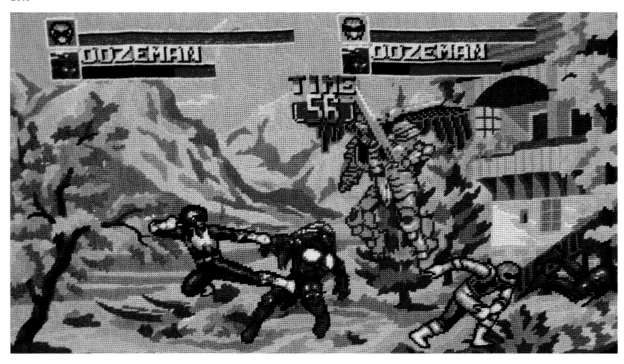

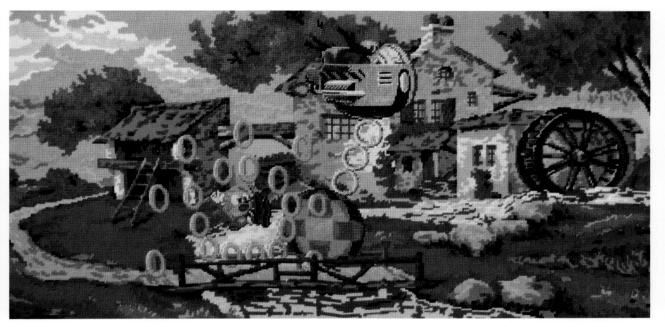

Sonic
2015

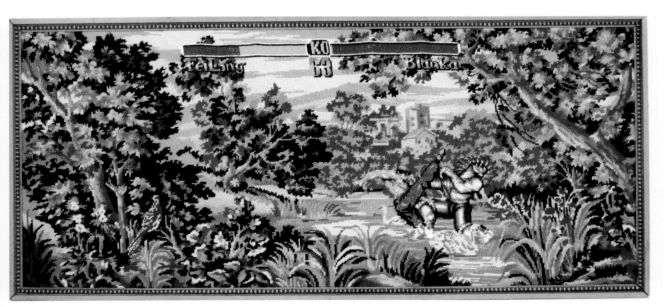

Sonic Street Fighter
2015

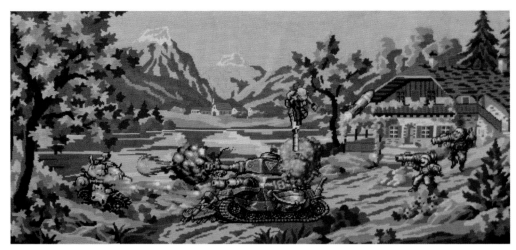

Metal Sug 1
2015

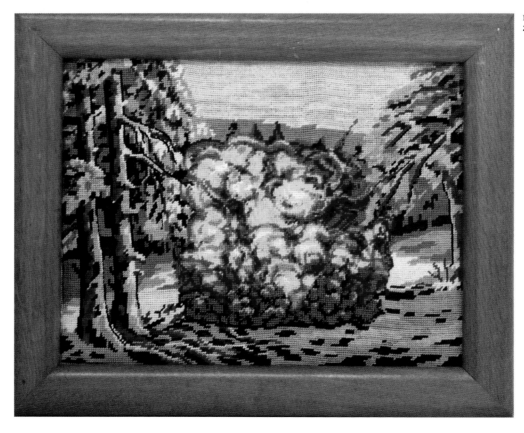

Metal Sug 2
2015

Metal Sug 3
2015

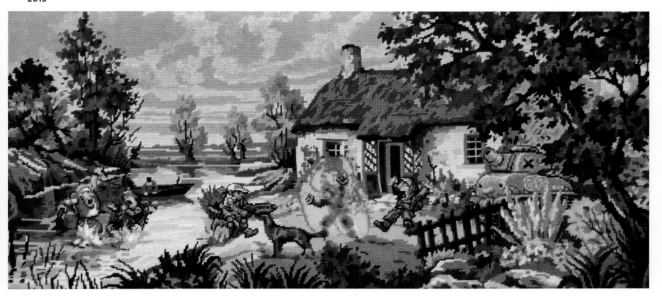

Duck Hunt
2015

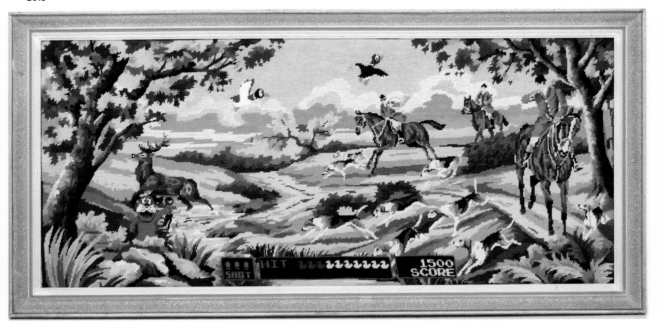

Mario Kart
2015

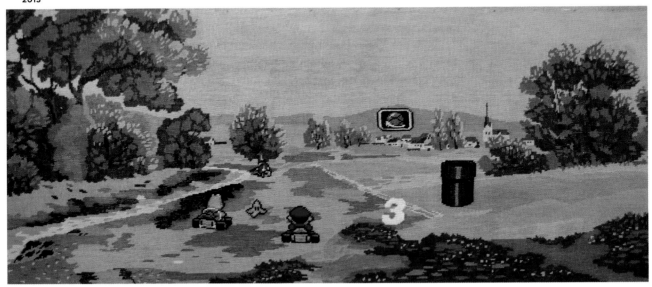

Castlevania
2015

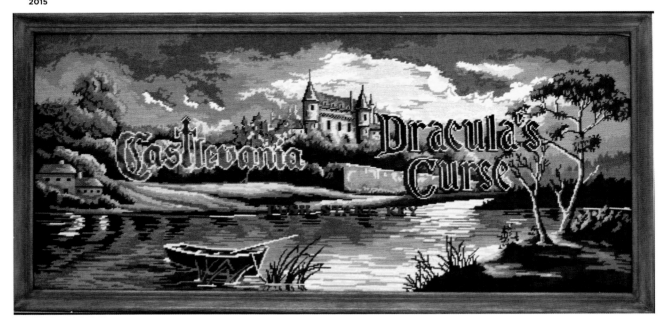

Pokémon
2015

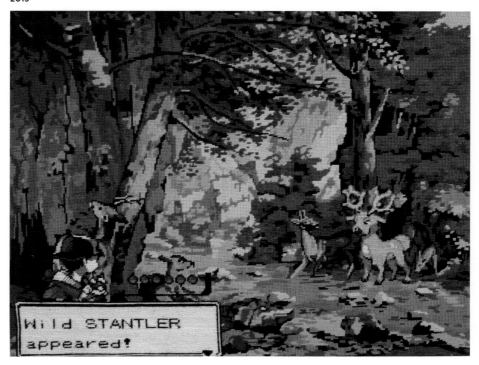

Golden Axe
2015

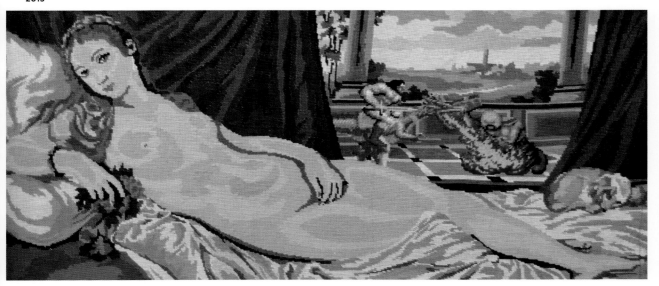

STAN MANOUKIAN

S tan Manoukian is a French graphic artist born in 1969 in Paris. He has had a passion for drawing since his childhood and most of his inspiration comes from retro sci-fi, classic monster movies, as well as the novels of authors such as Edgar Allan Poe, H. P. Lovecraft, Mary Shelley, and Jules Verne.

In 1988, after he graduated from École Estienne, he started to work in France and the United States as a cartoonist, designer, and storyboarder for the movie industry and in advertising. In 2007, Manoukian issued himself an artistic challenge: Draw one monster a day for one year. This large-scale initiative gave birth to the book called *Diary of Inhuman Species*. Since then, the exploration of his phantasmagoric world pushes him toward bigger and more ambitious projects, where he tests diverse techniques in both drawing and sculpture. An heir of Gustave Doré, Franklin Booth, and Bernie Wrightson, Stan Manoukian refines a unique visual scripture through hatching and dimming, which employs ink or graphite to mimic an engraving. Currently, his works are internationally recognized and have been displayed in several exhibitions and books in the United States, Japan, Australia, France, and Europe.

FACEBOOK: /stan.manoukian
INSTAGRAM: @grograou

Freddie Mercury
2018

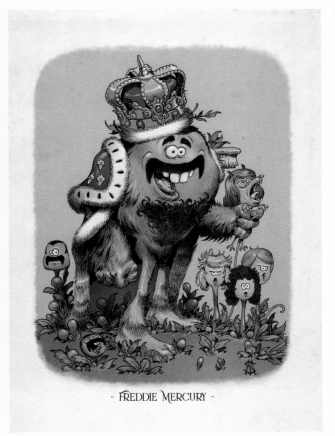

- FREDDIE MERCURY -

Kiss
2019

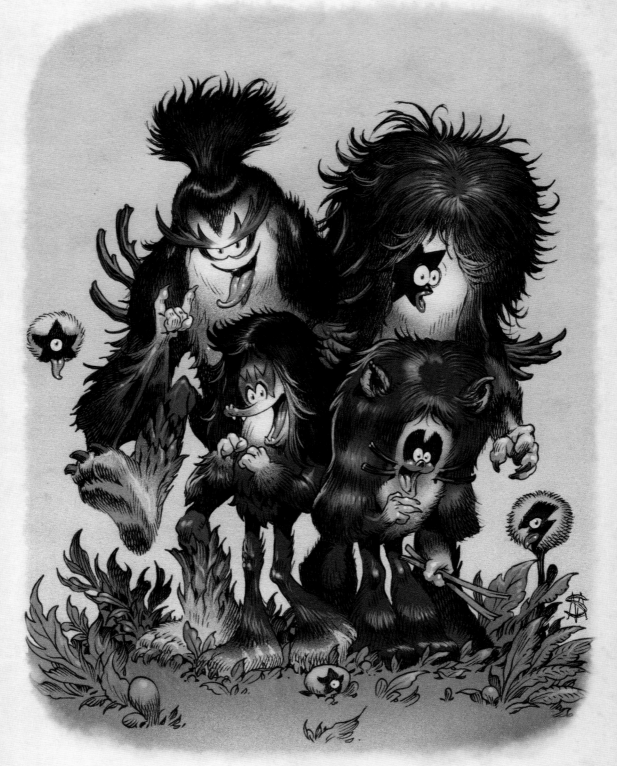

- KISS -

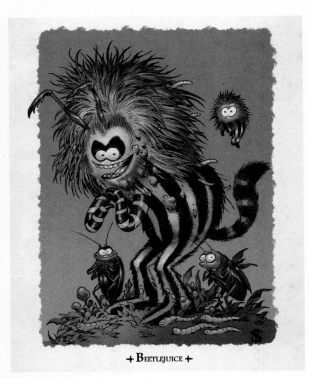

+ BEETLEJUICE +

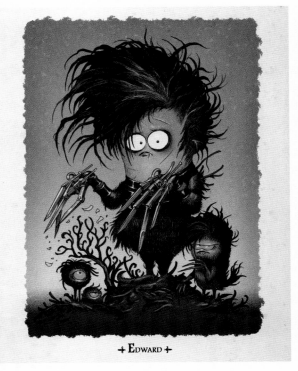

+ EDWARD +

Beetlejuice
2018

Edward
2018

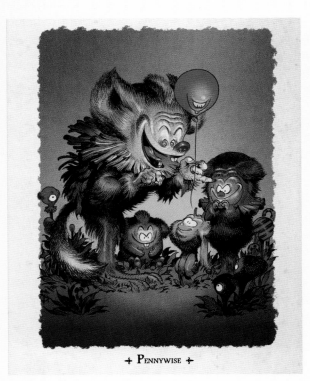

+ PENNYWISE +

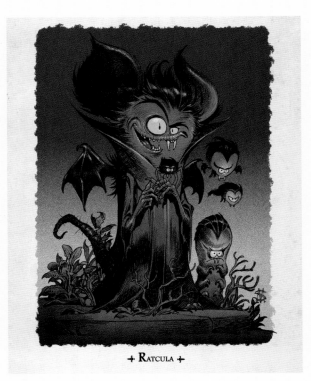

+ RATCULA +

Pennywise
2018

Ratcula
2018

The Addams Family
2018

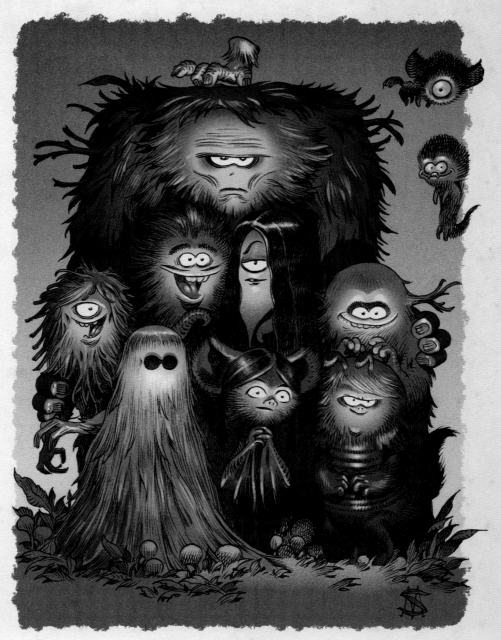

✦ THE ADDAMS FAMILY ✦

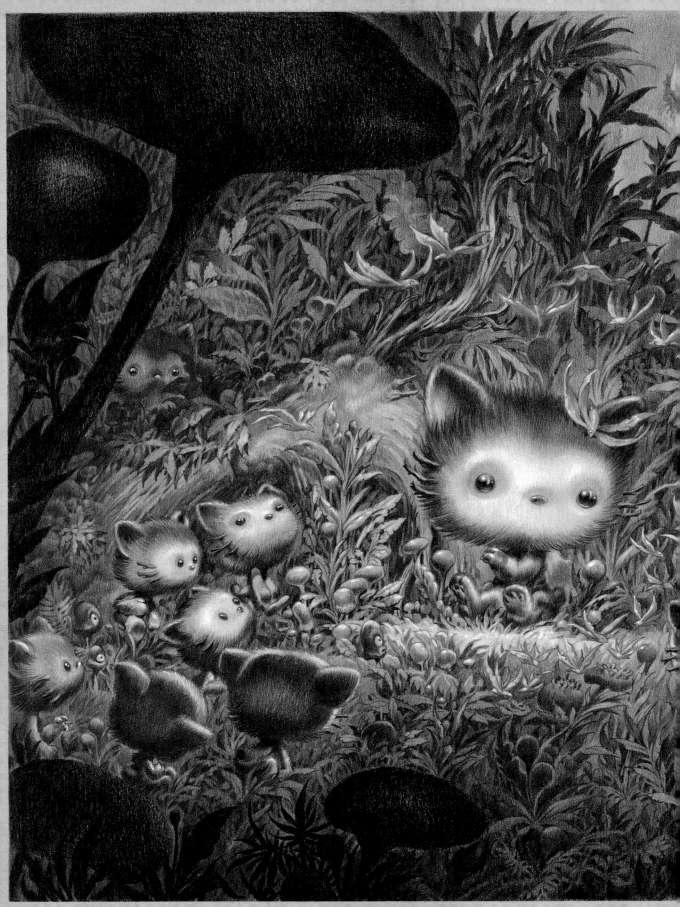

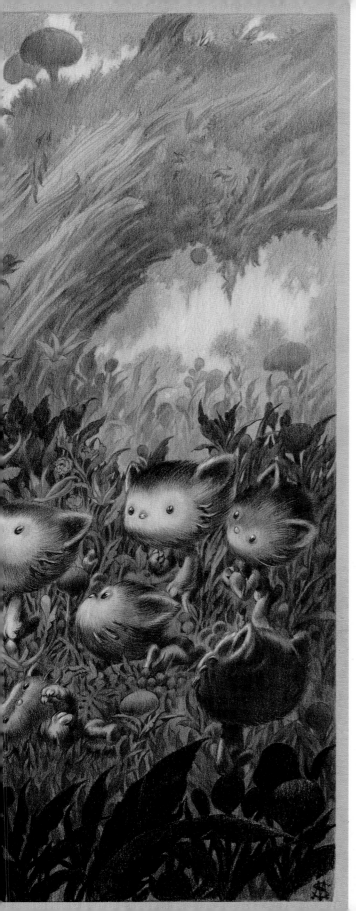

Fly Of The Butterflies (Hello Kitty)
2019

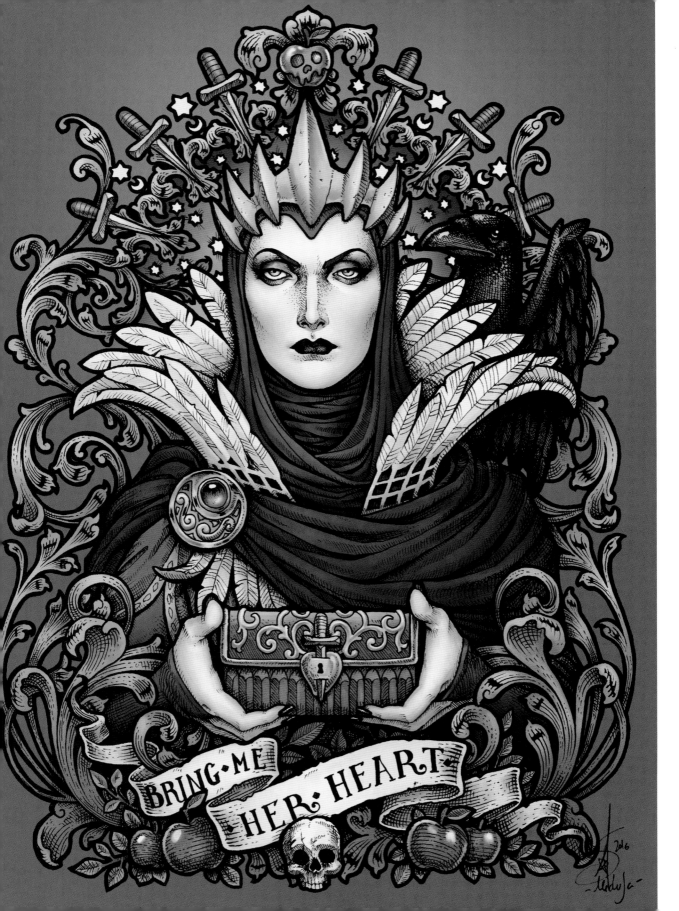

MEDUSA DOLLMAKER

Medusa Dollmaker (Asunción Macián Ruiz, born 1983—Valencia) is a self-taught digital and traditional illustrator, mercenary, curly stuff designer, and part-time gorgon.

WEBSITE: www.medusathedollmaker.com
CONTACT: medusadollmaker@gmail.com

> ❝ ARS LONGA,
> VITA BREVIS.❞
> (Life is short, art prevails.)

Bring me her heart. —Evil Queen
2016

Gamer Girl Nouveau
2015

Ave Furiosa
2015

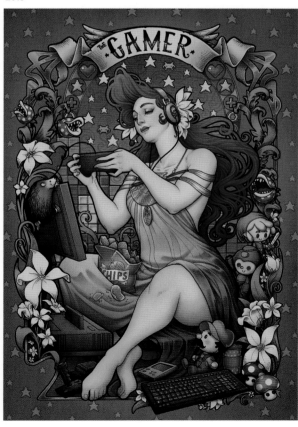

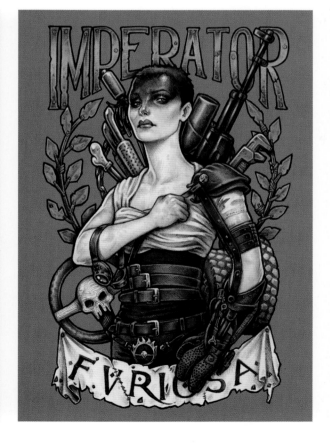

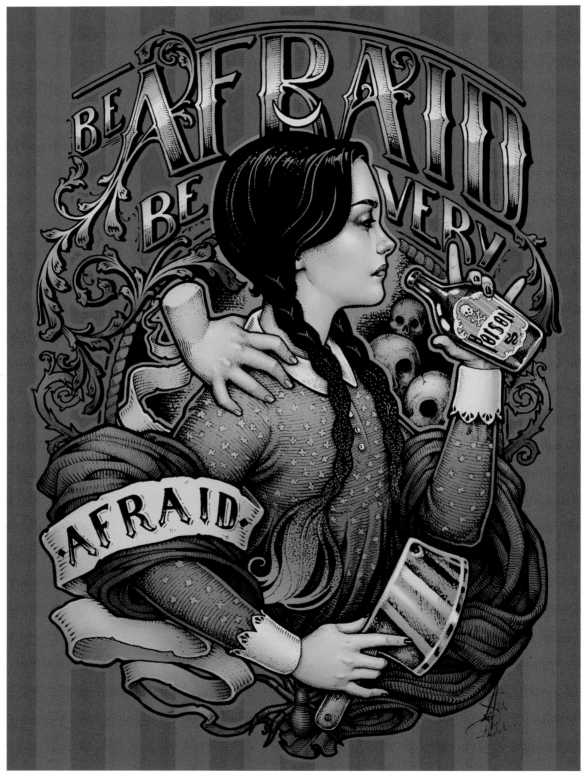

Be Afraid. —Wednesday
2016

Don't torture yourself, Gomez. That's my job. —Morticia
2016

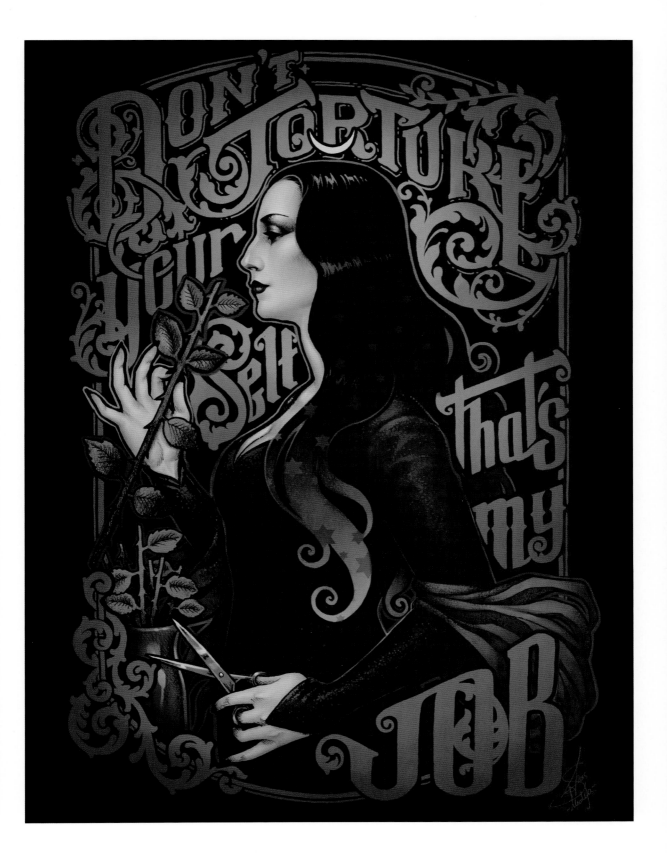

MISTER HOPE

M ister Hope is a freelance illustrator from the north of England. His love of pop-culture icons is only outweighed by his love of creating art based on his favorite heroes and villains. When not drawing, Mister Hope can be found watching movies, reading comics, or playing with Lego.

WEBSITE: www.misterhope.wordpress.com
INSTAGRAM: @misterhope
TWITTER: @misterhpe

" Creating the art I make is my way of paying homage to the things I love . . . I just love a lot of things!"

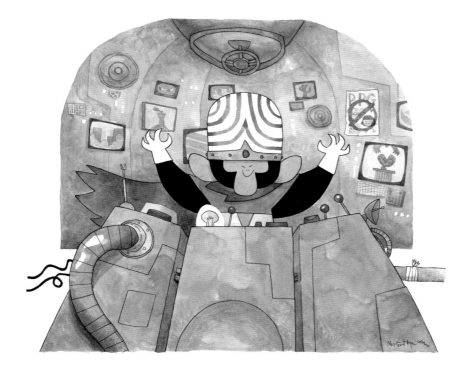

Mojo Jojo
2019

Monsters Inc.
2018

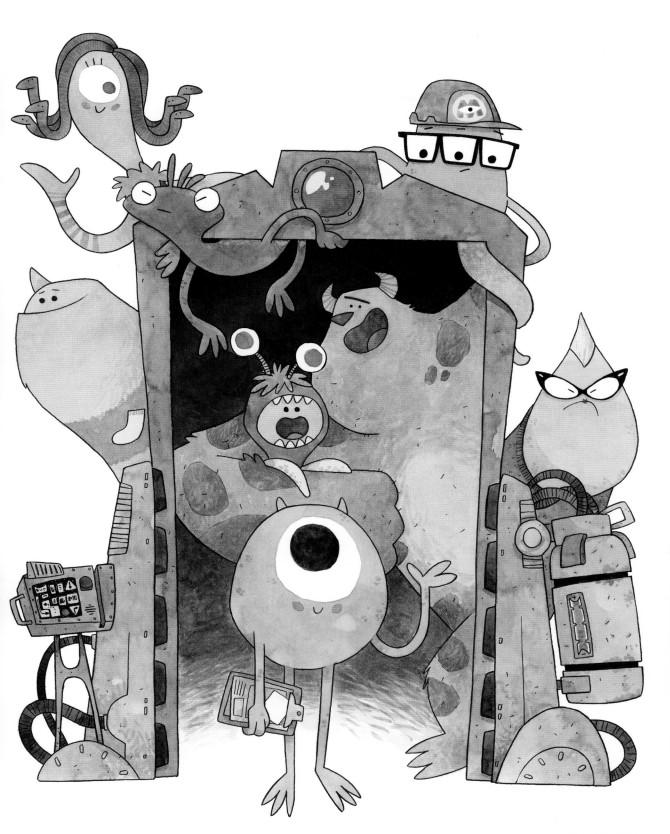

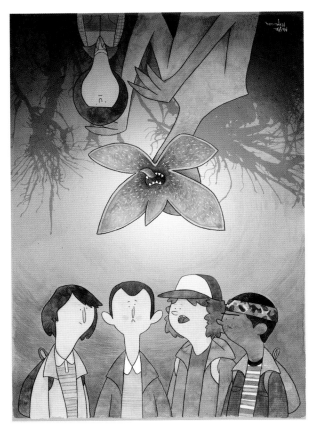

Stranger Things
2017

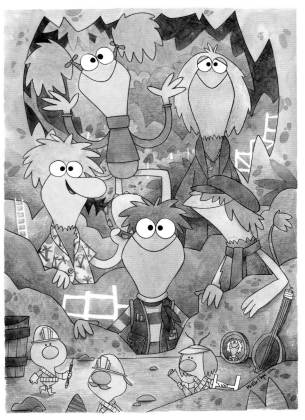

Down at Fraggle Rock
2019

Hogwarts Founders
2017

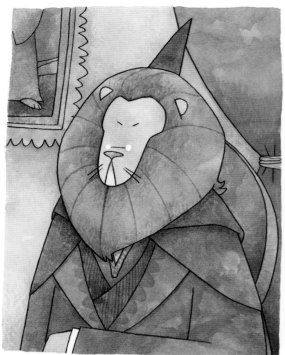

Godric Gryffindor

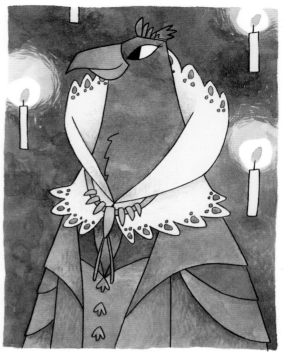

Rowena Ravenclaw

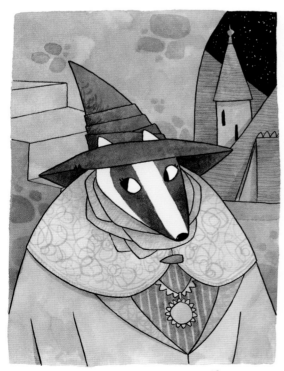

Helga Hufflepuff

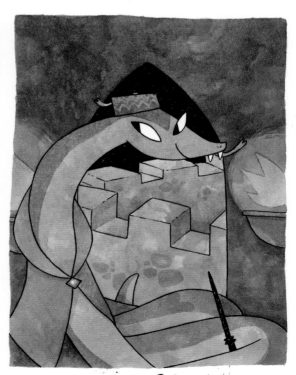

Salazar Slytherin

MARK MORRIS

L os Angeles–based artist Mark Morris is a graphic designer and illustrator with a passion in paper and dimensional art. His influences include pop culture and synth wave.

WEBSITE: www.squaredco.org

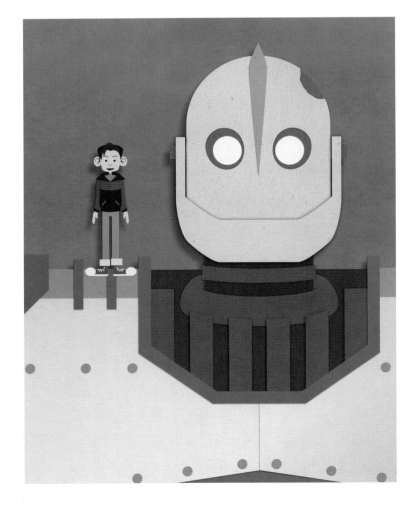

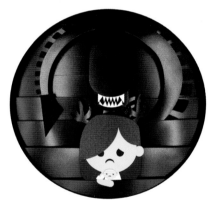

My Bestfriend Is A Giant Robot
2018

Aliens - Don't Look Back
2016

E.T.
2018

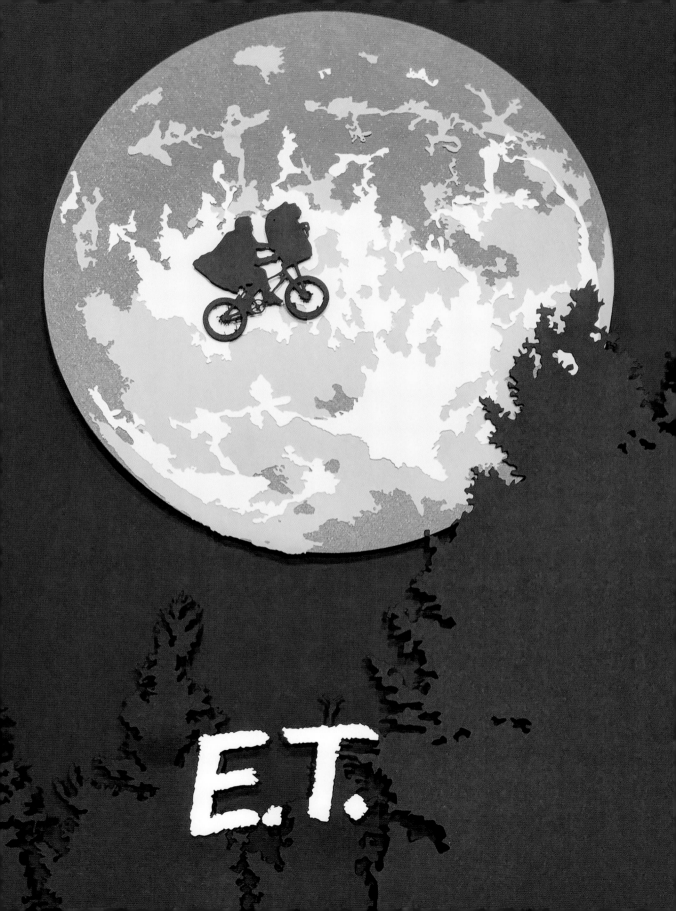

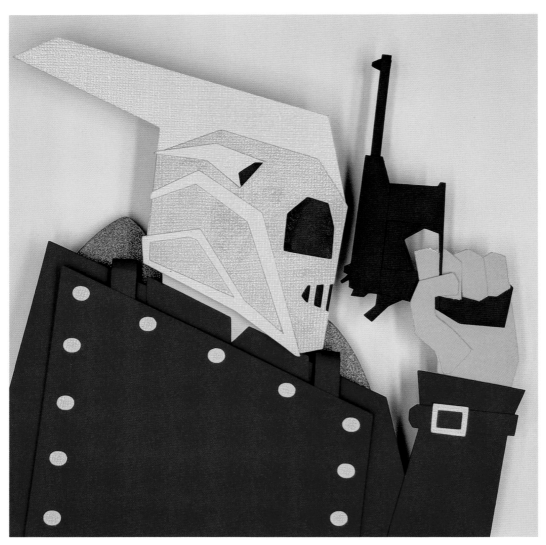

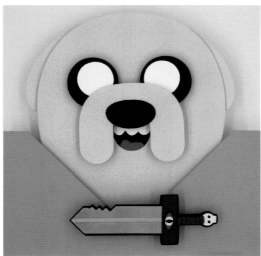

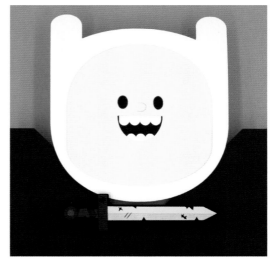

Rocketeer
2018

Jake
2016

Finn
2016

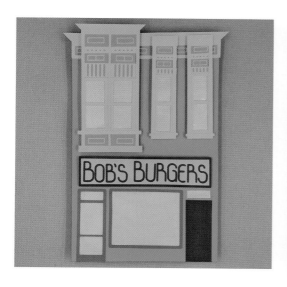

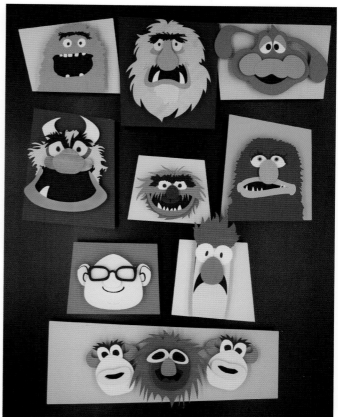

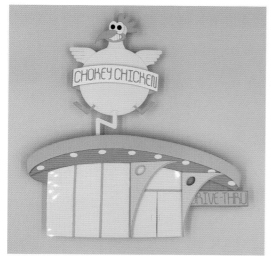

Bob's Burgers
2019

Muppets
2017

Chockey Chicken
2019

Krang
2016

" I love TMNT
and pizza."

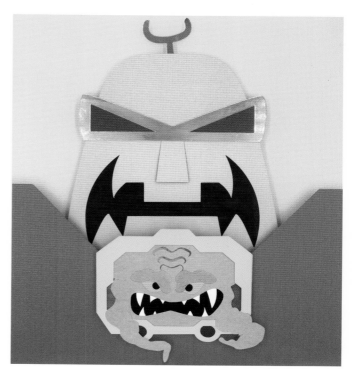

DAN MUMFORD

Dan Mumford is a freelance illustrator based in central London, mainly working within the lowbrow pop-culture scene creating screenprints, posters, album covers, and more. Clients include Disney, Sony, Iron Maiden, Wizards of the Coast, Icon Motosports, CBS, and many, many bands and record labels from around the world.

WEBSITE: www.dan-mumford.com
INSTAGRAM: @danmumforddraws
TWITTER: @Danmumforddraws

Blue Team Stand Down
2016

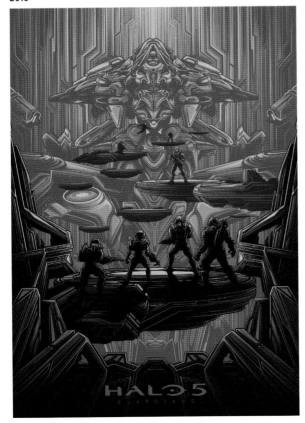

❝ ❝ I try to take any subject matter and make it beautiful, that's the main aim with all of my artwork."

Return of the King
2016

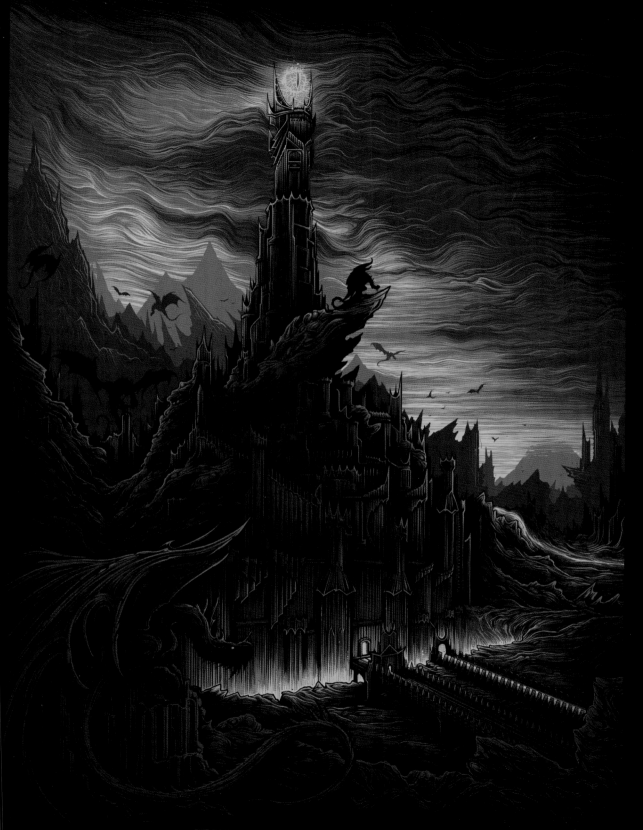

Protect the Innocent Uphold the Law
2016

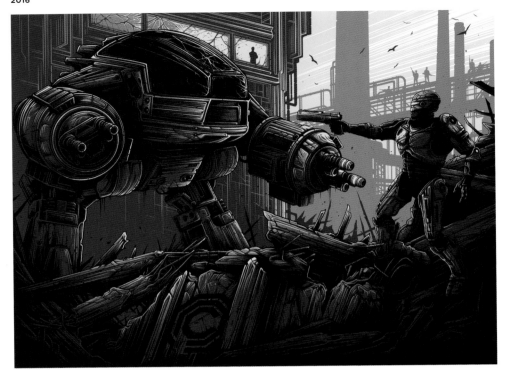

Never Tell me The Odds
2016

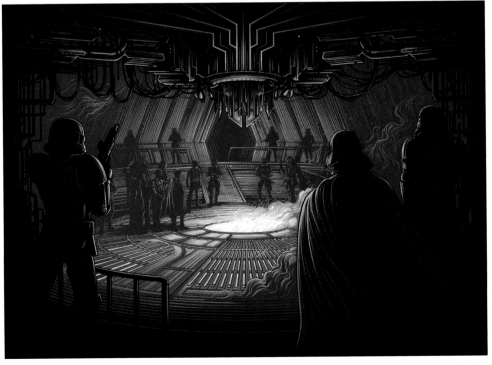

The Empire Strikes Back - © & ™ Lucasfilm Ltd. SWESB457SS

258 Dan Mumford

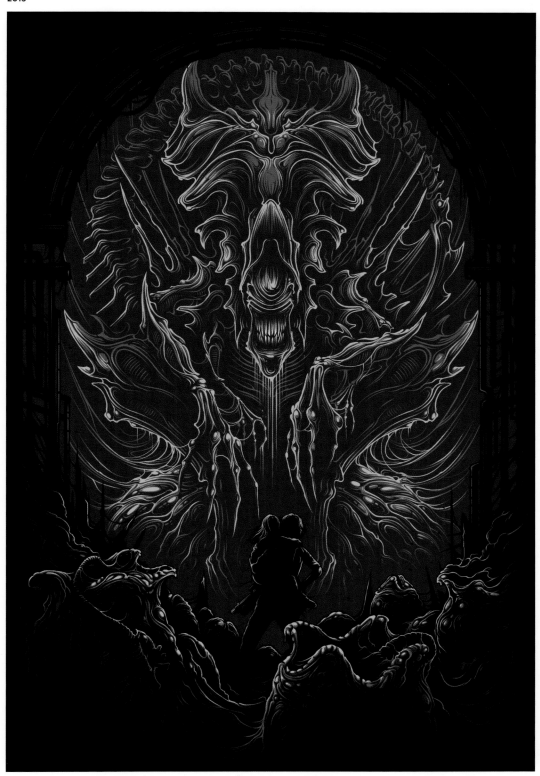

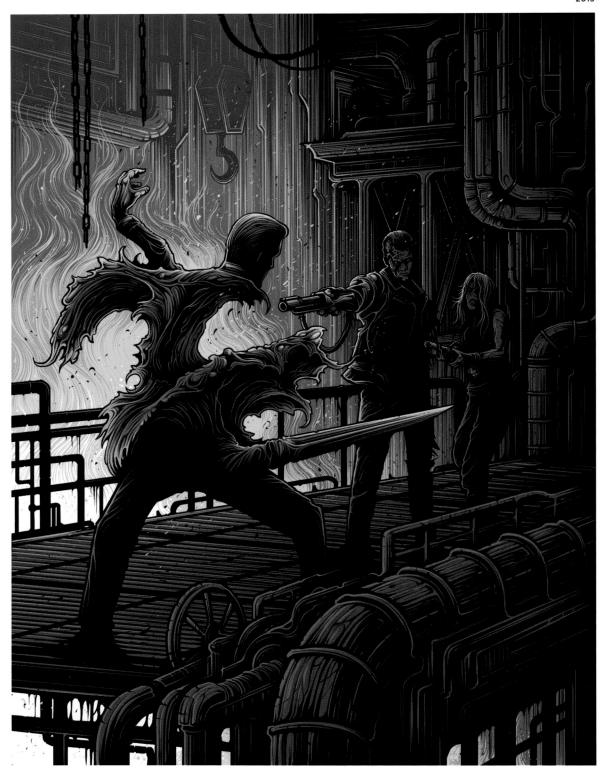

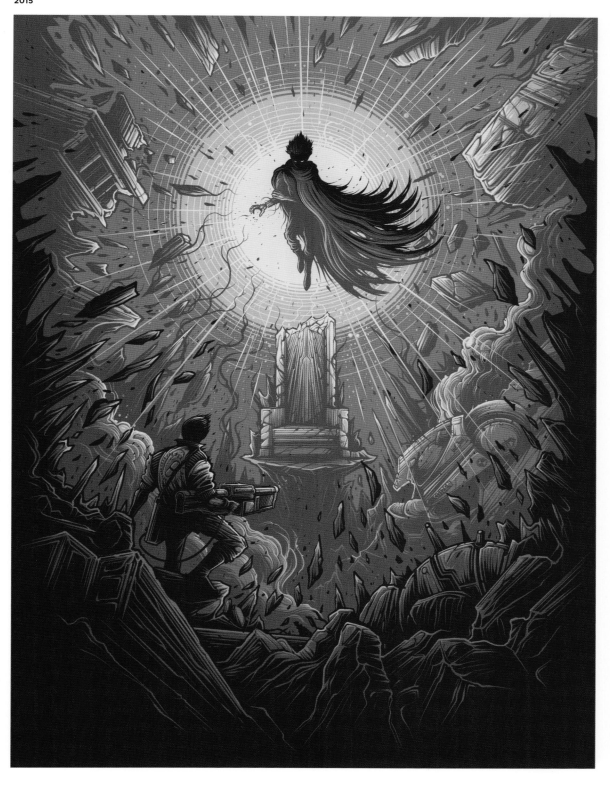

JARED MURALT

To engage with the vivid drawings of Bern-based illustrator Jared Muralt is to be transported to a particular time in history, place in nature, or captivating imaginative world. Muralt is largely inspired by the quotidian: His sketchbooks, which he carries with him at all times, are filled with fascinating studies of people, scientific inventions, and the animal kingdom. Indeed, it is via these primary, diaristic sketches that Muralt's vast imagination takes shape—delightful, energetic caricatures; sci-fi experiments; and both alternate and future worlds are all boldly rendered in pen on paper. As such, Muralt's curious and adventurous spirit manifests in wholly idiosyncratic illustrations and ultimately underpins his artistic practice.

Muralt was born in 1982 in Bern, Switzerland. Though he attended art school for one year in Bern, Muralt is primarily self-taught, and he developed his precision and skill through the careful study of books as diverse as those pertaining to anatomy, art history, and comics. Muralt is currently working on his postapocalyptic comic series *The Fall*. Among others he has illustrated for *The New York Times* and Pottermore.

Jared is a part of BlackYard with Christian Calame. BlackYard consists of four graphic designers/illustrators in their best age who acquired their abilities through different professional careers. In 2009 they teamed up and settled their business location in the picturesque part of the small neighborhood Matte in downtown Bern. Their primary area of focus is illustration and graphic design, executed with much care for detail. BlackYard likes to sketch, draw, and ink by hand, before utilizing machines to merge together all textures and layers preparing the artwork for the offset and screenprinting process. Posters, illustrations, logos, cover artwork, as well as original art and customized objects have found a broad audience in and outside of Switzerland and applied leverage to BlackYard's aspiring career.

WEBSITE: www.jaredillustrations.ch
INSTAGRAM: @jaredmuralt
TWITTER: @JaredMuralt

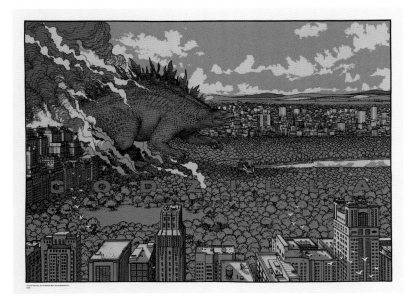

Godzilla
2015

Babyboom
2013

❝❝ Pop culture is both the creativity and weakness of our society."

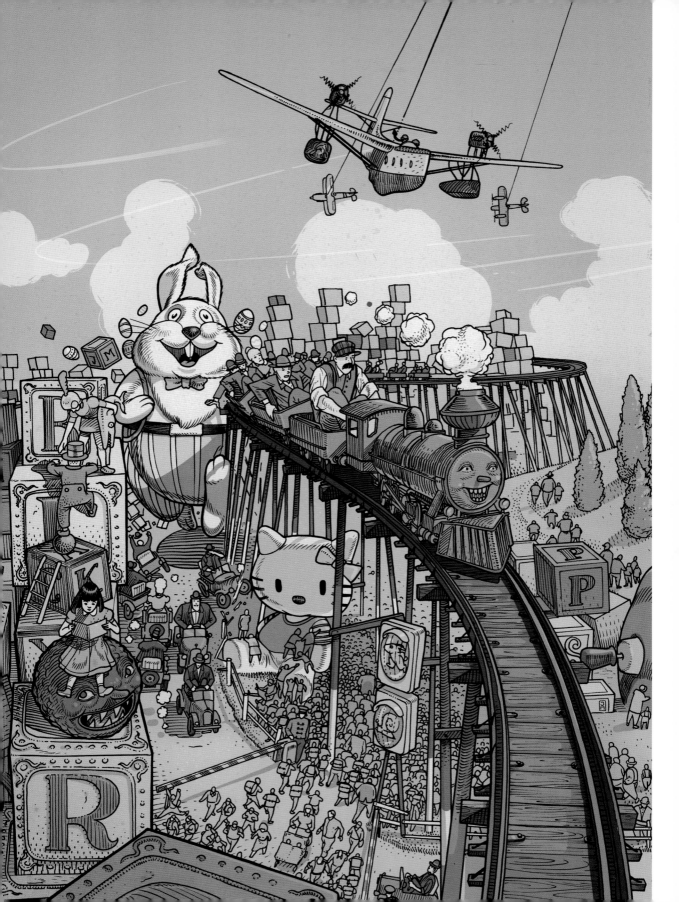

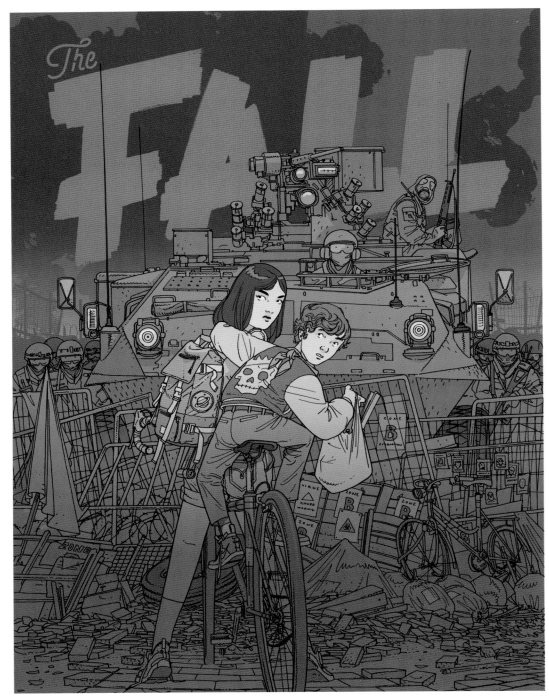

The Fall
2018

Tarkin
2017

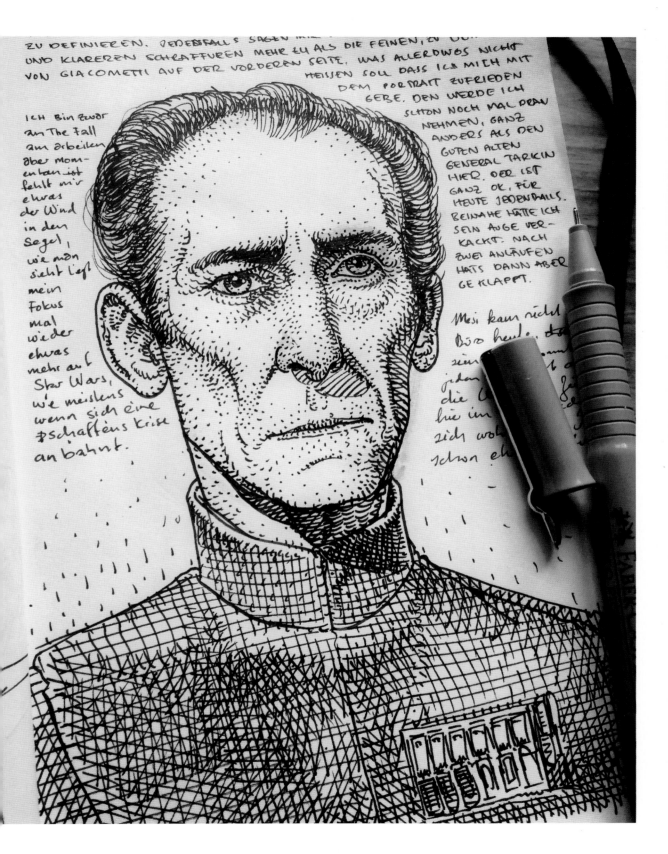

ZU DEFINIEREN. JEDENFALLS SAGEN MIR [...] DIE FEINEN, ZU DÜ [...]
UND KLARERN SCHRAFFUREN MEHR ZU ALS DIE FEINEN, ZU DÜ [...]
VON GIACOMETTI AUF DER VORDEREN SEITE, WAS ALLERDWOS NICHT
HEISSEN SOLL DASS ICH MICH MIT
DEM PORTRAIT ZUFRIEDEN
GEBE, DEN WERDE ICH
SCHON NOCH MAL DRAN
NEHMEN, GANZ
ANDERS ALS DEN
GUTEN ALTEN
GENERAL TARKIN
HIER, DER IST
GANZ OK, FÜR
HEUTE JEDENFALLS.
BEINAHE HÄTTE ICH
SEIN AUGE VER-
KACKT. NACH
ZWEI ANLÄUFEN
HATS DANN ABER
GEKLAPPT.

ICH BIN ZWAR
AM THE FALL
AM ARBEITEN
ABER MOM-
ENTAN IST
FEHLT MIR
ETWAS
DER WIND
IN DEN
SEGEL,
WIE MAN
SIEHT LIEß
MEIN
FOKUS
MAL
WIEDER
ETWAS
MEHR AUF
STAR WARS,
WIE MEISTENS
WENN SICH EINE
SCHAFFENS KRISE
ANBAHNT.

Mei kann nicht
Büro heute, da
sein [...]
[...]
die U [...]
hie im [...]
sich wohl [...]
schon eh [...]

MATT NEEDLE

Matt is a Cardiff, Wales, based freelance designer/illustrator and art director specializing in editorial illustration and key art for films and TV. Over the last decade he has exhibited artwork globally and worked for clients worldwide including Disney, Pixar, Marvel, Sony Pictures, 20th Century Fox, *Men's Health*, *Wired*, *GQ*, and many more.

"I have been inspired by films, TV, music, and pop culture in general since quite a young age. When I was a kid, I would draw my own film posters and album covers and that has somehow transformed into my full-time job now. Every project I work on is influenced in some way by pop culture, mainly cinema."

WEBSITE: www.mattneedle.co.uk
INSTAGRAM: @needledesign
TWITTER: @needledesign
CONTACT: matt.needle@hotmail.co.uk

Mary Poppins Returns
2018

Vertigo
2018

Star Wars - The Last Jedi
2017

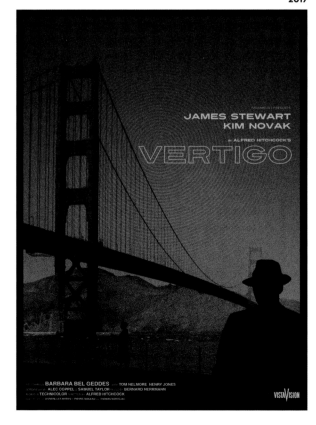

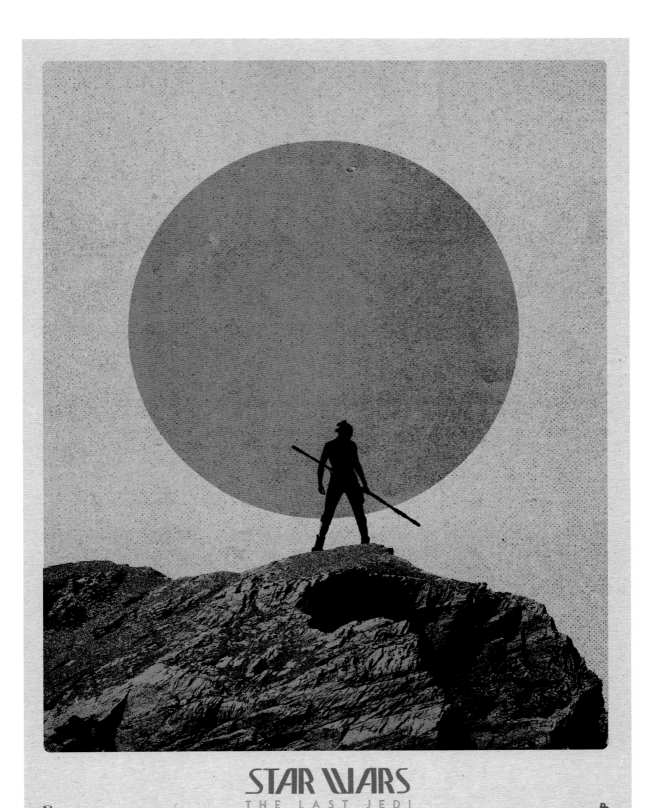

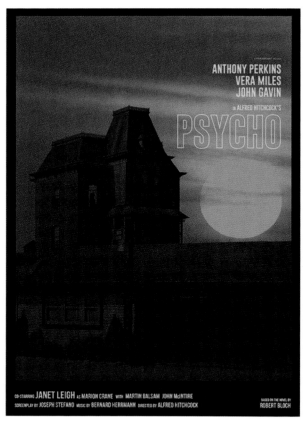

Psycho
2018

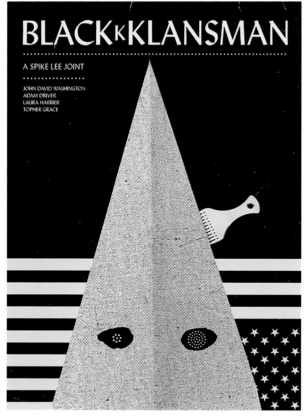

Blackkklansman
2019

“ I have been inspired by films, TV, music, and pop culture in general since quite a young age. When I was a kid I would draw my own film posters and album covers and that has somehow transformed into my fulltime job now. Every project I work on is influenced in some way by pop culture, mainly cinema.”

One Flew Over The Cuckoo's Nest
2017

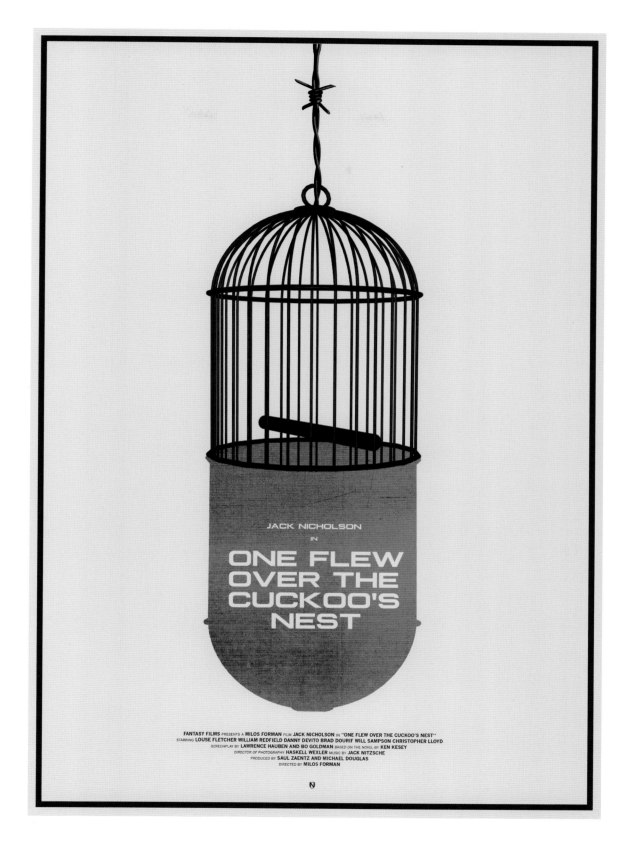

JACK NICHOLSON

IN

ONE FLEW OVER THE CUCKOO'S NEST

FANTASY FILMS PRESENTS A MILOS FORMAN FILM JACK NICHOLSON IN "ONE FLEW OVER THE CUCKOO'S NEST"
STARRING LOUSE FLETCHER WILLIAM REDFIELD DANNY DEVITO BRAD DOURIF WILL SAMPSON CHRISTOPHER LLOYD
SCREENPLAY BY LAWRENCE HAUBEN AND BO GOLDMAN BASED ON THE NOVEL BY KEN KESEY
DIRECTOR OF PHOTOGRAPHY HASKELL WEXLER MUSIC BY JACK NITZSCHE
PRODUCED BY SAUL ZAENTZ AND MICHAEL DOUGLAS
DIRECTED BY MILOS FORMAN

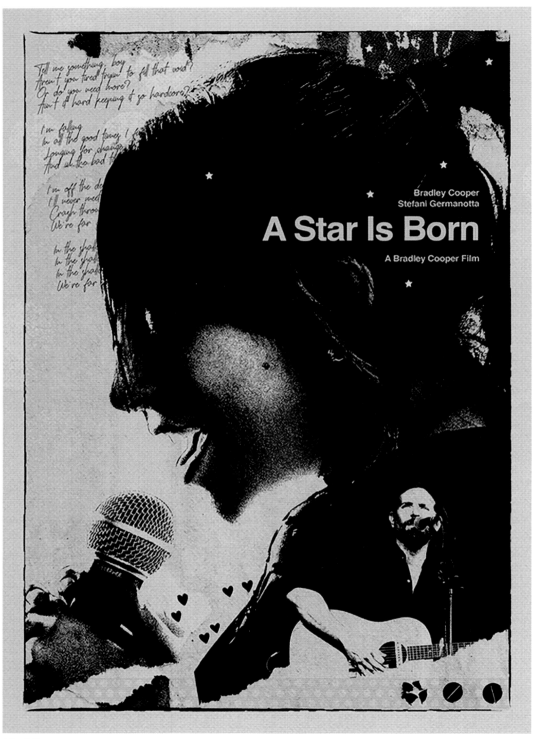

A Star Is Born
2019

The Elephant Man
2017

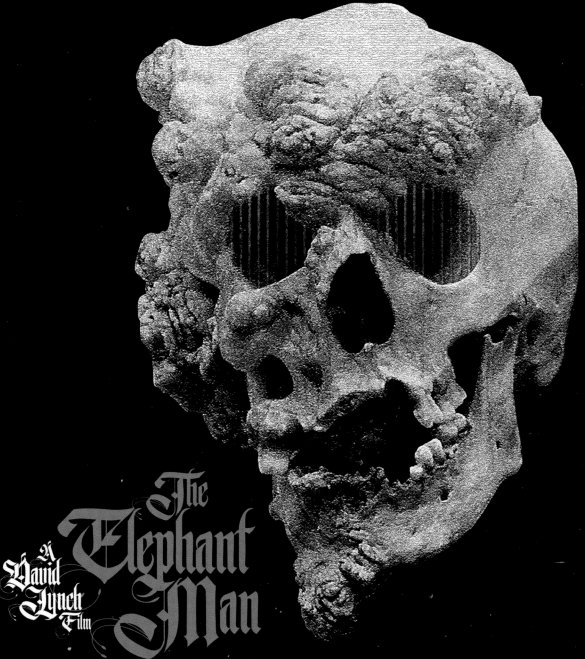

A David Lynch Film
The Elephant Man

PARAMOUNT PICTURES PRESENTS
A BROOKSFILMS PRODUCTION
STARRING JOHN HURT ANTHONY HOPKINS
ANNE BANCROFT SIR JOHN GIELGUD WENDY HILLER
EXECUTIVE PRODUCER STUART CORNFELD
SCREENPLAY BY CHRISTOPHER DEVORE
ERIC BERGREN & DAVID LYNCH
PRODUCED BY JONATHAN SANGER
DIRECTED BY DAVID LYNCH

NYCHOS

The Austrian urban art and graffiti illustrator Nychos was born in 1982 in Styria, Austria, where he grew up in a hunting family. Getting confronted by the anatomy of dead animals at an early age and being an eighties kid with an interest in cartoons and heavy metal ended up being some of the ingredients that inspired him when he started graffiti and painting at the age of eighteen. Over the years he developed a distinctive style which stands out—his dissections and cross sections of human and animal bodies are easily recognized. The focus and reinterpretation of dissected motives in a combination of colorful outlines can be seen as his branding. He is well known for his huge and technically outstanding art pieces in the urban environment as well as several gallery exhibitions all over the world.

WEBSITE: www.rabbiteyemovement.at
TUMBLR: www.nychos.tumblr.com
INSTRAGRAM: @rabbiteyemovement_official
FACEBOOK: /RABBITEYEMOVEMENT

Dissection of Batman
2016

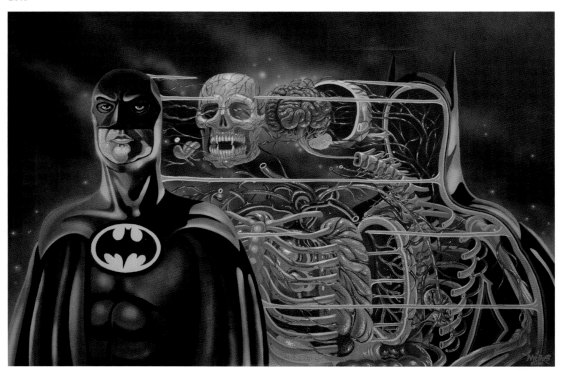

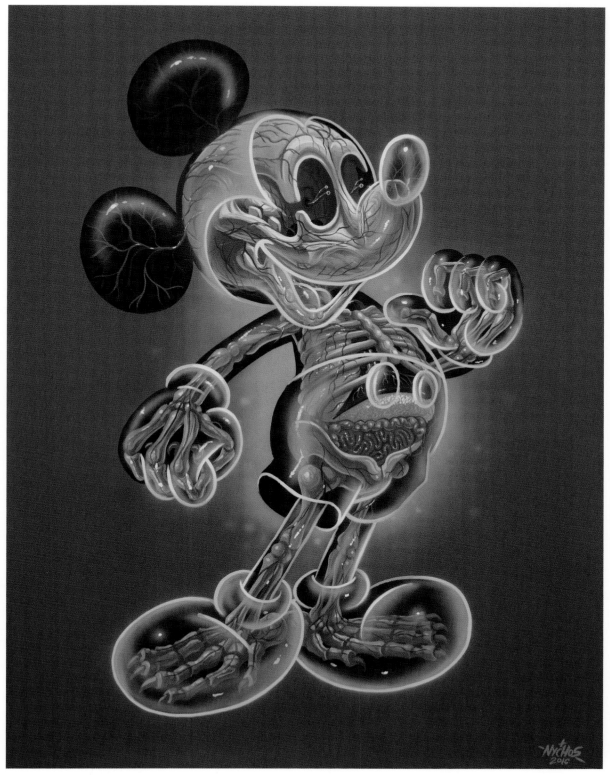

Translucent Mickey
2016

Dissection of Yoda
2016

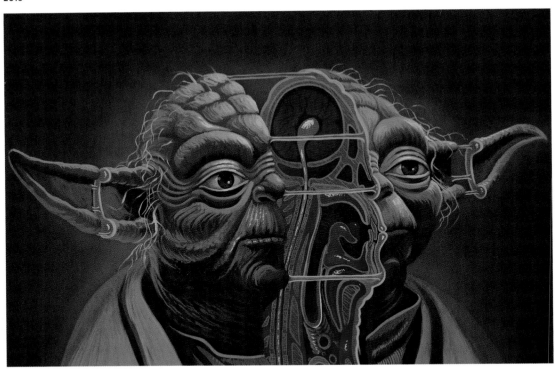

Dissection of Spock
2016

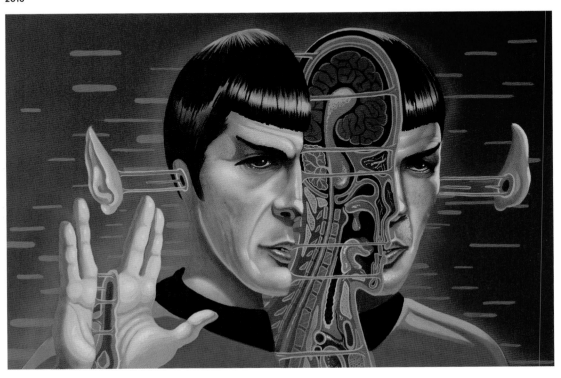

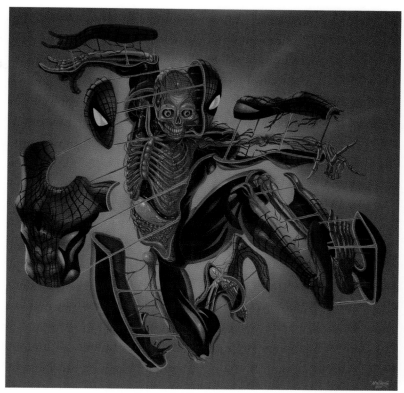

> **❝** I see the Rabbit Eye Movement as a way to connect all the 'Rabbits' from around the world who are participating in the growing evolution of urban art."

Dissection of Hasselhoff
2016

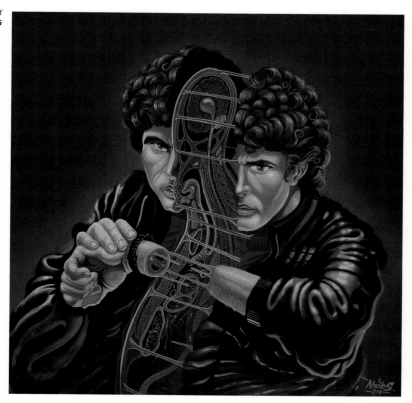

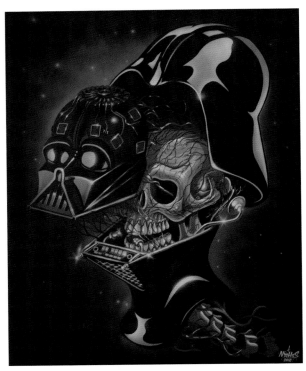

Dissection of Darth Vader
2016

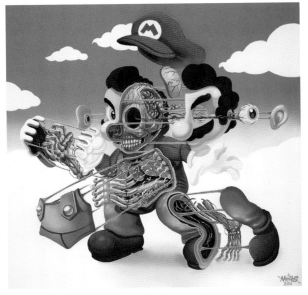

Dissection of Mario
2016

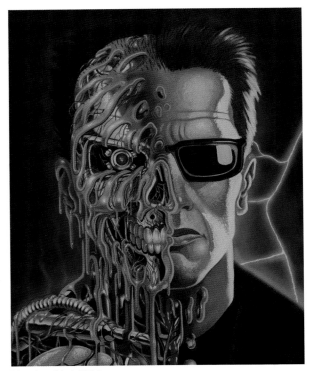

Dissection of Arnie Meltdown
2016

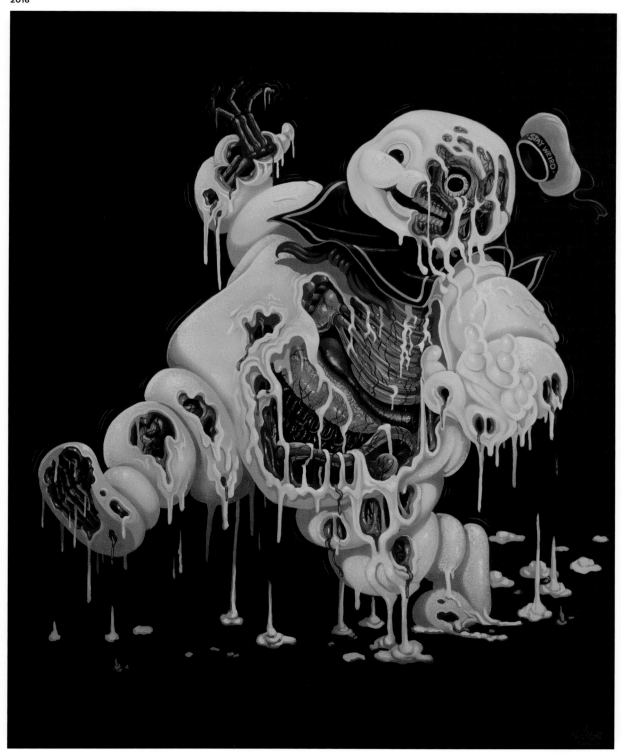

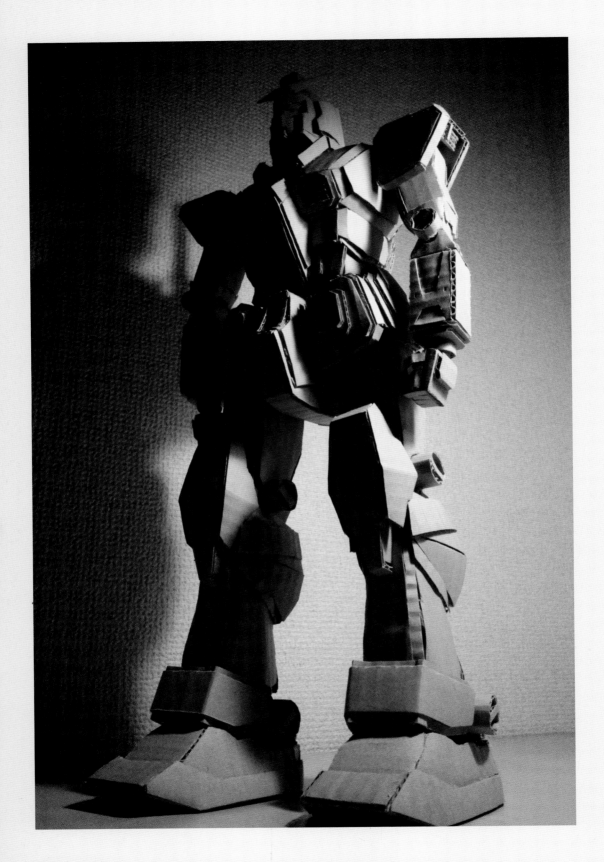

MONAMI OHNO

onami Ohno was born in Wakayama Prefecture in 1991 and graduated from the Osaka University of Arts. While still in university, Ohno started creative activities with cardboard and also worked as a lecturer of painting. She is primarily a cardboard artist and currently lives in Kichijōji, Tokyo. In 2016, she held a one-man exhibition at Cheepa's Gallery in Ginza, Tokyo. Ohno also participated in the ComplexCon in Los Angeles in 2018 and other exhibitions. She has published books, including *Making Funny Vending Machine with Cardboard* (Boutique-Sha), and has done commercial work for "au TRANSFORMERS PROJECT" in 2017, "Casio G-SHOCK" in 2018, and others.

WEBSITE: www.ameblo.jp/ohnomonami
INSTAGRAM: @monamincb

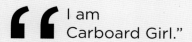

" I am
Carboard Girl."

Star Wars The Last Jedi
2017

Millenium Falcon
2016

Gundam
2015

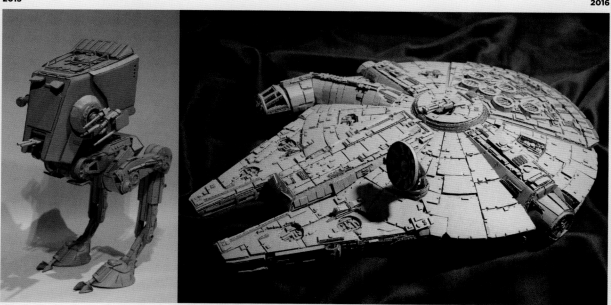

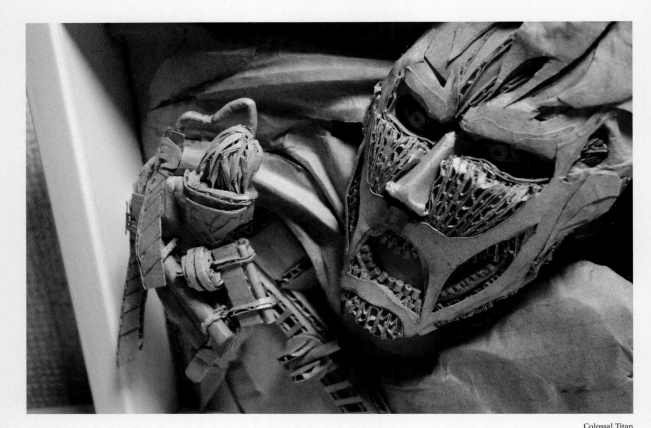

Colossal Titan
2015

Akira n° 1
2018

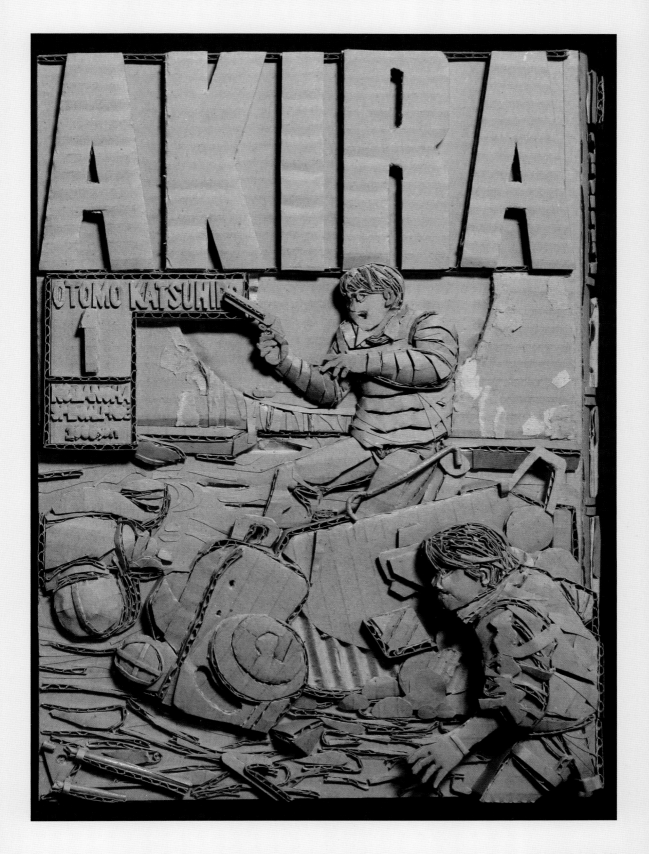

JUAN MANUEL OROZCO

Juan Manuel Orozco, known also as JML2ART, is a young graphic designer and illustrator from Costa Rica currently working as a freelancer in the clothing design industry, for several companies that sell products and designs inspired by pop culture and the geek and gaming world, and also for musicians and bands. He grew up with crayons and brushes with a passion for the world of art and illustration and above all a great passion about the geek world and the world of comics. He graduated with a degree in graphic design with a focus on illustration. His works are characterized by the vectorial style, complexity, and detail.

He has worked with a variety of international clients and with renowned brands, companies, and bands such as Threadless, TeeFury, Design by Humans, RageOn, Juniper Networks, ZeroTurnaround, Luxoft, LinkedIn, Excision, Stick Figure, Cartoon Theory, and Affinity, among others. His projects have also been exhibited at Game Art And Music (GAAM) and San Diego Comic-Con 2015 and 2016 in collaboration with Nindja Gear.

INSTAGRAM: @jml2art_studio
FACEBOOK: /Jml2art
TWITTER: @jml2art
BEHANCE: /jml2art

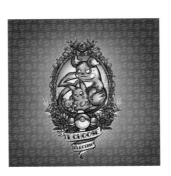
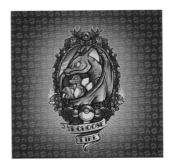
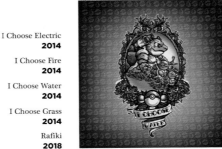
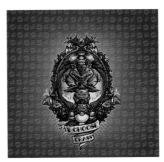

I Choose Electric
2014

I Choose Fire
2014

I Choose Water
2014

I Choose Grass
2014

Rafiki
2018

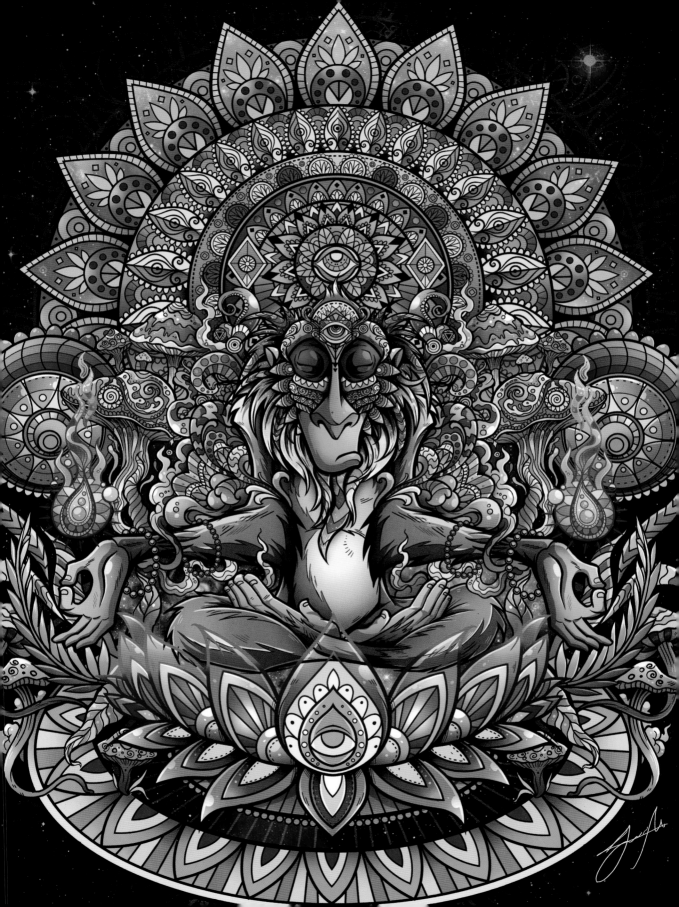

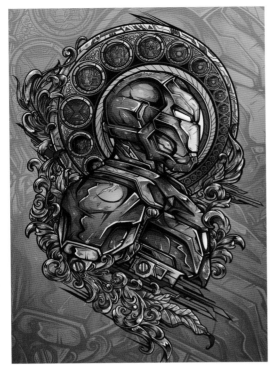

Iron Man
2016

Captain America
2016

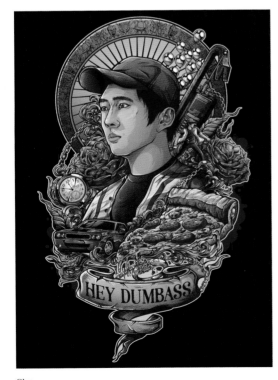

Glen
2016

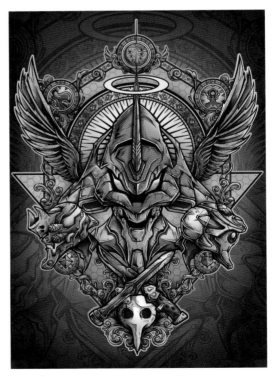

Evas against angels
2015

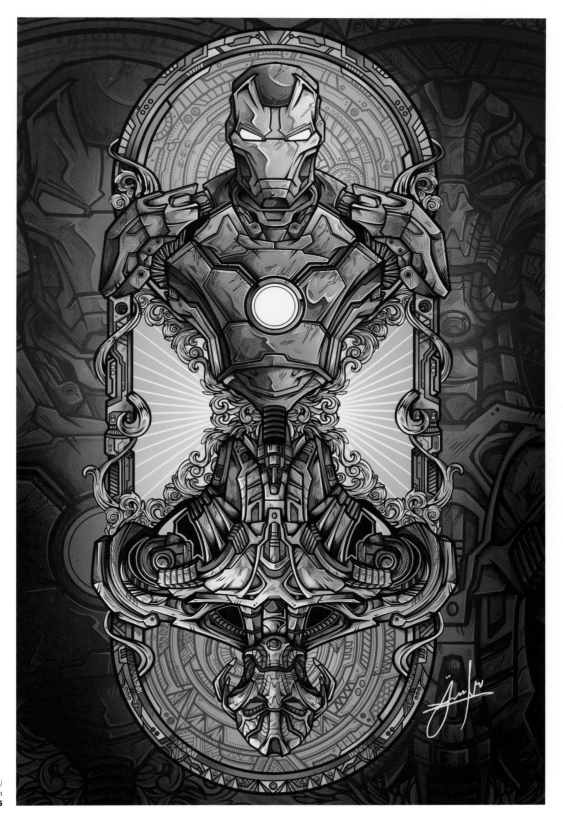

Two Sides of Power /
Iron Man vs Ultron
2015

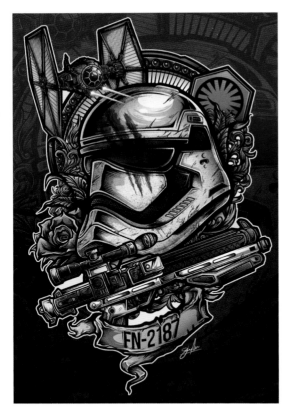

Warrior 2187
2016

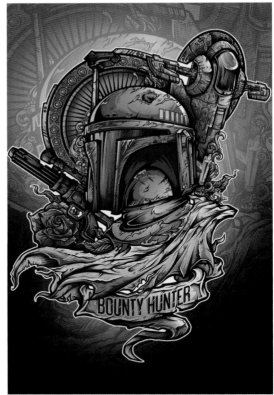

Bounty Hunter
2015

" With my drawings I felt that a way
to show my love for television series
and video games besides playing with action
figures was through drawing. I like clean lines,
saturated colors—placing many elements and
details in the composition so that the viewer
can take a moment to appreciate every detail
and every element important to the theme."

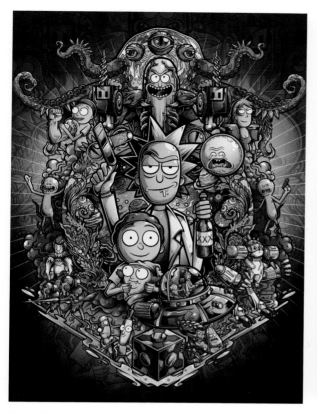

Rick and Morty
2017

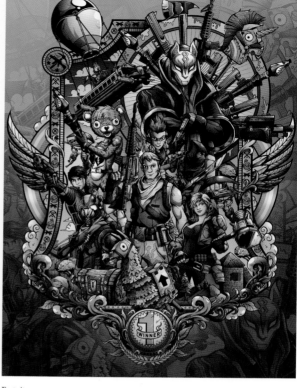

Fortnite
2018

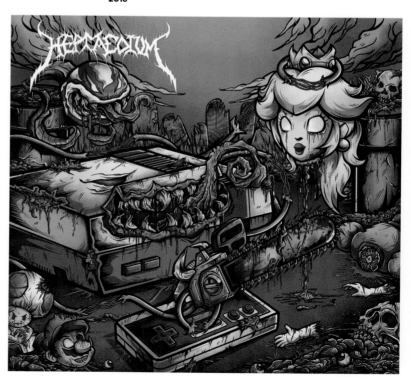

Heptaedium
2015

OSKUNK

Ozcan, alias Oskunk, started drawing at an early age and is now an illustrator and customizer. The world of video games, manga, comics, and graffiti have always occupied an important place in his life and are also a great source of inspiration. After visiting an exhibition dedicated to customs, he decided to try customizing an NES, which quickly attracted attention on social networks and resulted in a hundred custom consoles! Today he mainly paints on canvas in a style he calls "word cloud" (several chosen words form a character), but he also customizes some vinyl collectibles and even sneakers.

WEBSITE: www.oskunk.com
INSTAGRAM: @oskunk_

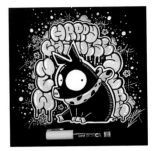

Ranma
2019

Bulma
2018

Lamu
2018

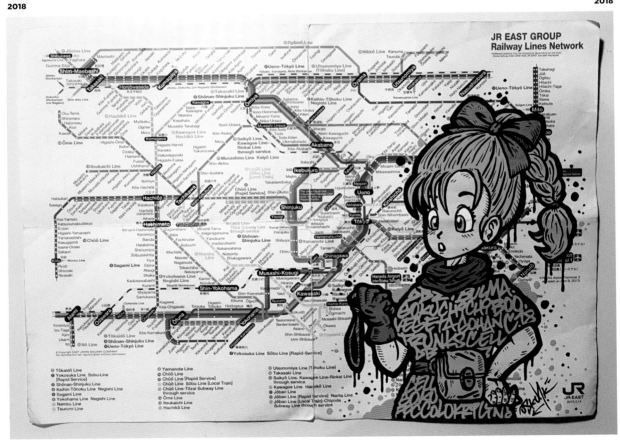

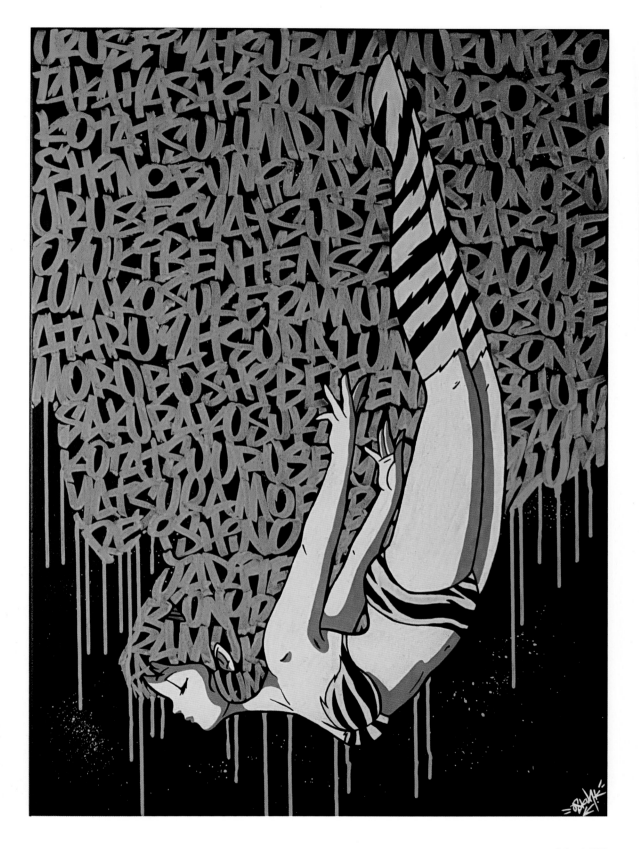

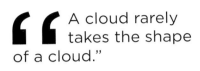

" A cloud rarely
takes the shape
of a cloud."

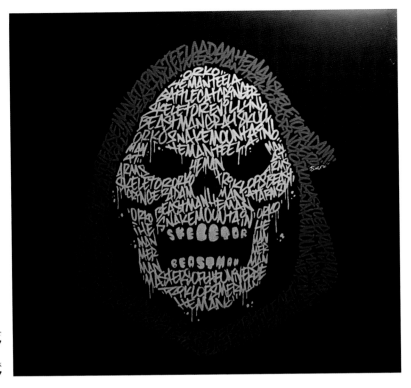

Skeletor
2017

Goldorak
2017

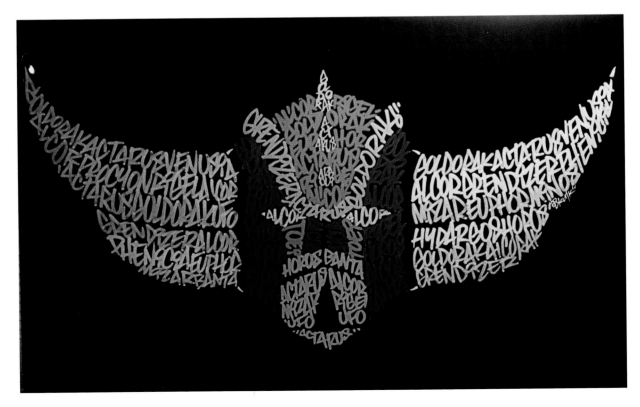

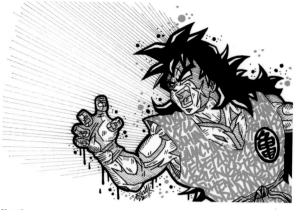

Yamcha
2018

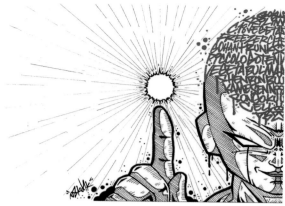

Freezer
2018

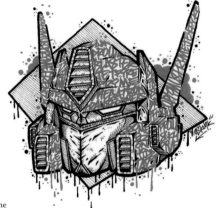

Optimus Prime
2018

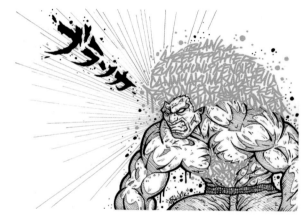

Blanka
2018

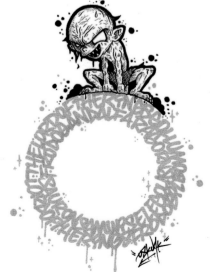

Gollum
2018

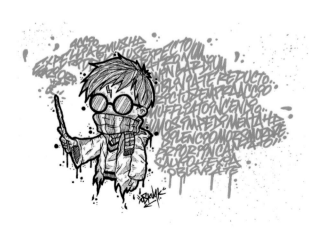

Harry Potter
2018

JÉRÉMY PAILLER

Jérémy Pailler practices watercolor and ink on paper. As an illustrator, he works on a variety of projects, from film posters to children's albums, video editing, and animated music videos. He also develops independent projects, notably in the framework of artist residencies abroad (Iceland, Thailand, etc.). Jérémy also wrote a thesis in visual arts on the practices of animation cinema. Collaborations include Warner Bros., Disney, Pixar, Lantana Publishing, Bach Films, and more.

WEBSITE: www.jeremypailler.com
CONTACT: paillerjeremy@gmail.com
INSTAGRAM: @jeremy_pailler
TWITTER: @jeremy_pailler

> " I discovered the movie posters via the covers of *Télé K7*. My appetite for cinema was born in these pages, decorated with this funny yellow and pink logo."

Hannibal -
The Silence of
the Lambs
2017

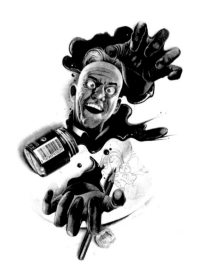

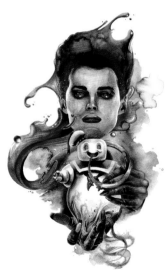

Judge Doom
2016

Gremlins
2015

Gozer
2016

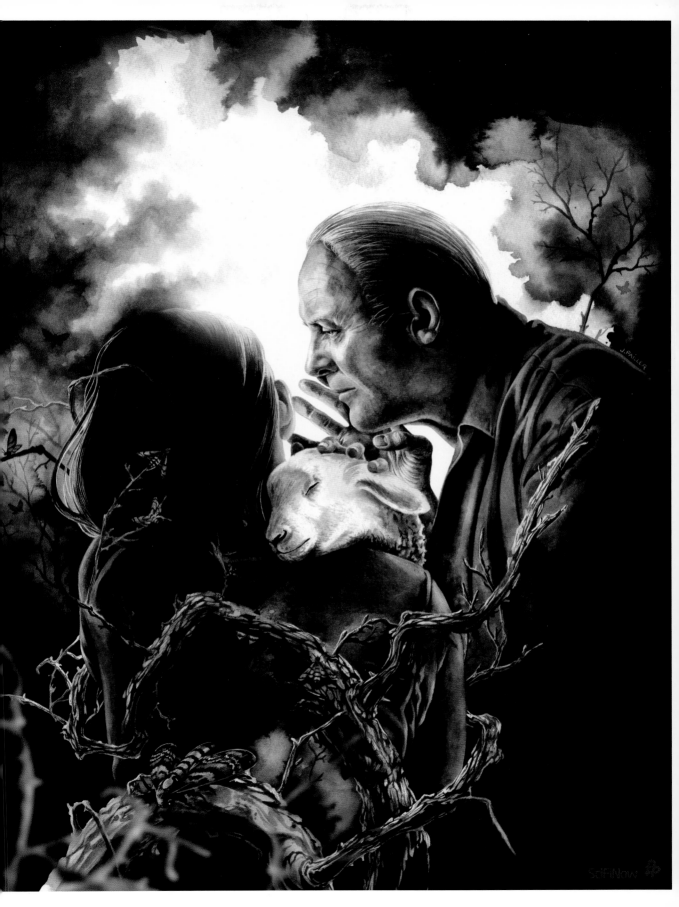

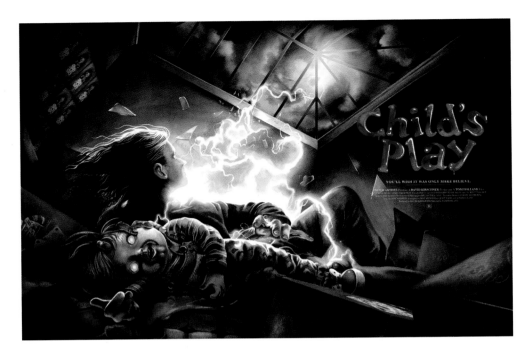

Child's Play
2018

It Follows
2019

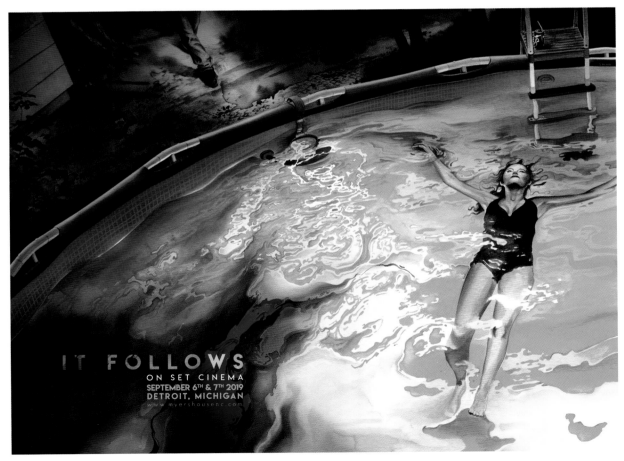

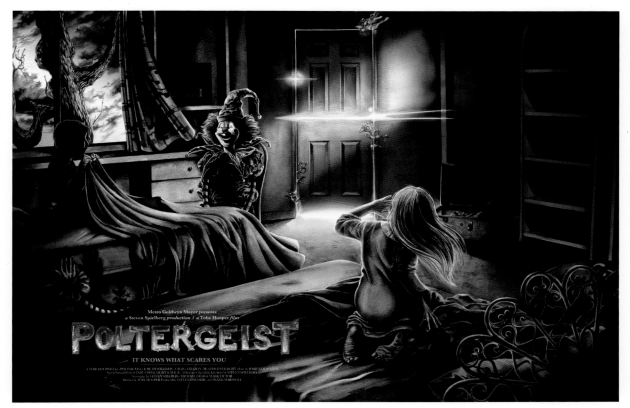

Poltergeist
2017

ANTHONY PETRIE

Anthony Petrie's portfolio includes work across a broad range of mediums. He likes creating good design for good people and has an unhealthy obsession with zombies. His headquarters are located in New York City, and he regularly displays work in Gallery1988 in Los Angeles. Anthony has more than twelve years of experience working with some of the largest brands in the world. His graphic design, illustration, and product designs can be seen everywhere from the entertainment and broadcasting industries to athletic brands.

WEBSITE: www.anthonypetrie.com
INSTAGRAM: @zombiebacons
TWITTER: @zombiebacons
CONTACT: anthony@anthonypetrie.com

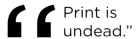

"Print is undead."

Chum Chart
2014

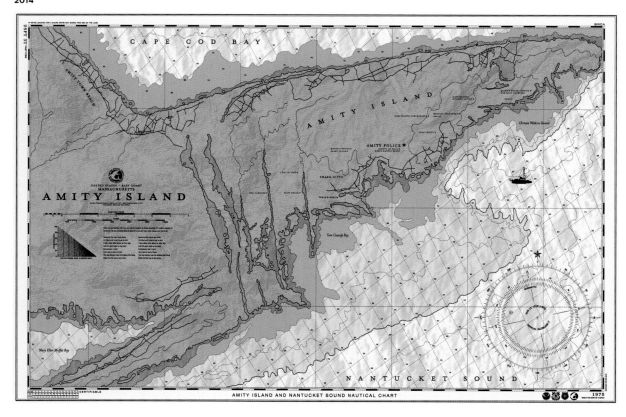

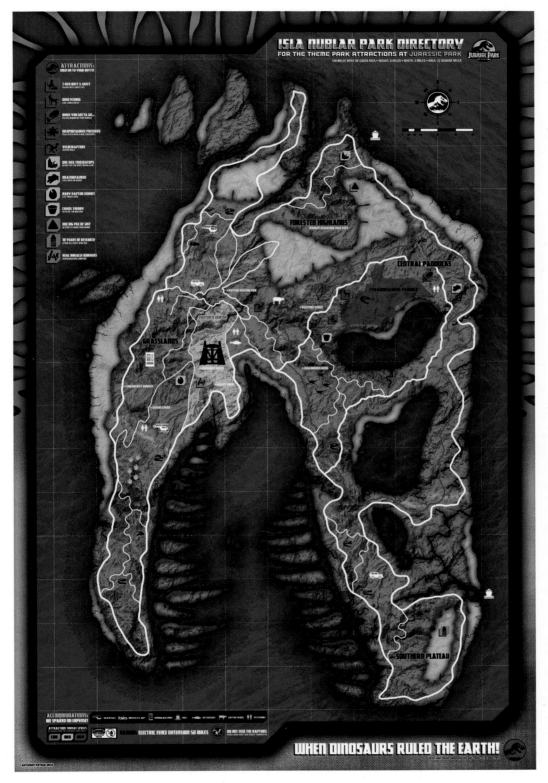

Dino Directory
2014

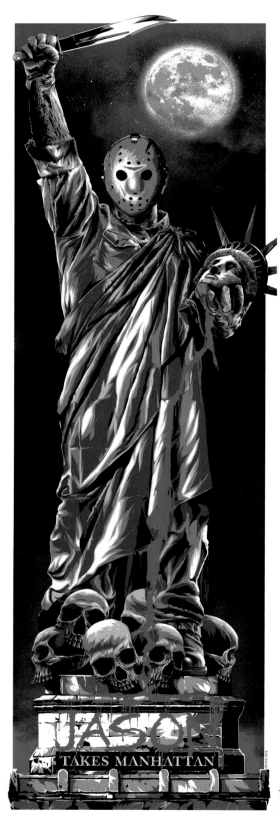

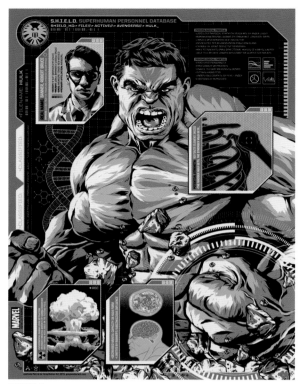

S.H.I.E.L.D.
Files: Hulk
2015

Jason Takes Manhattan
(Friday The 13th VIII)
2015

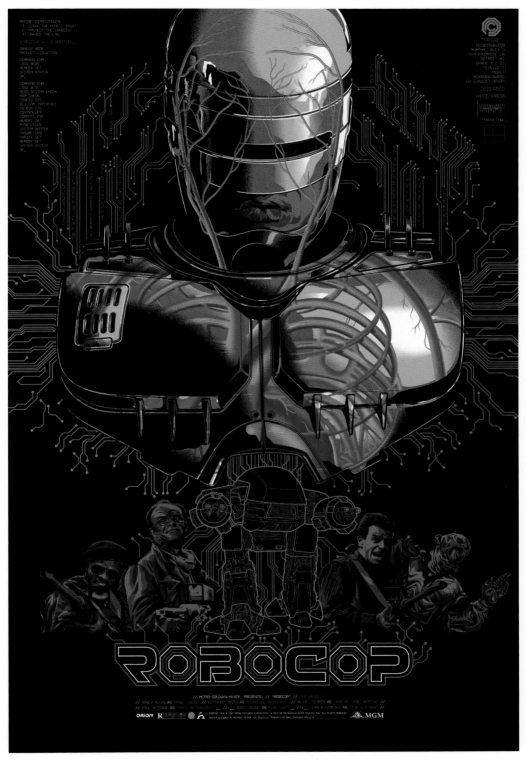

Robocop
2015

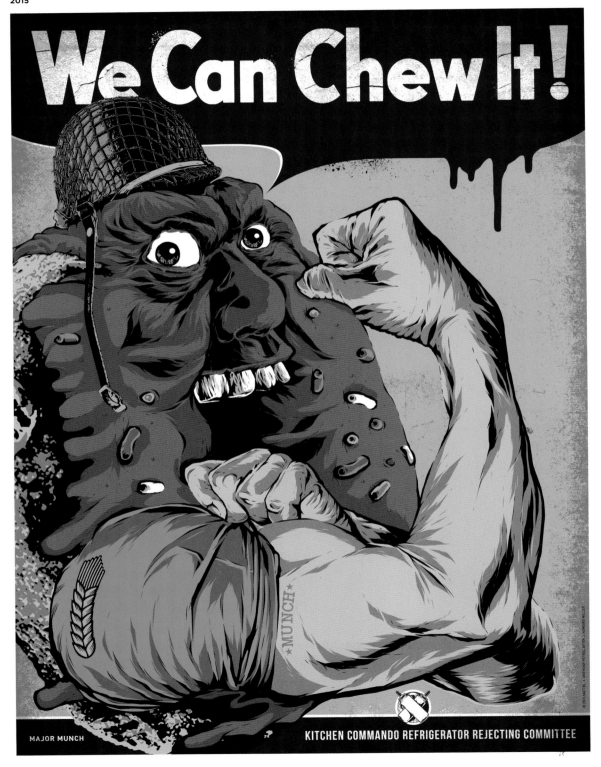

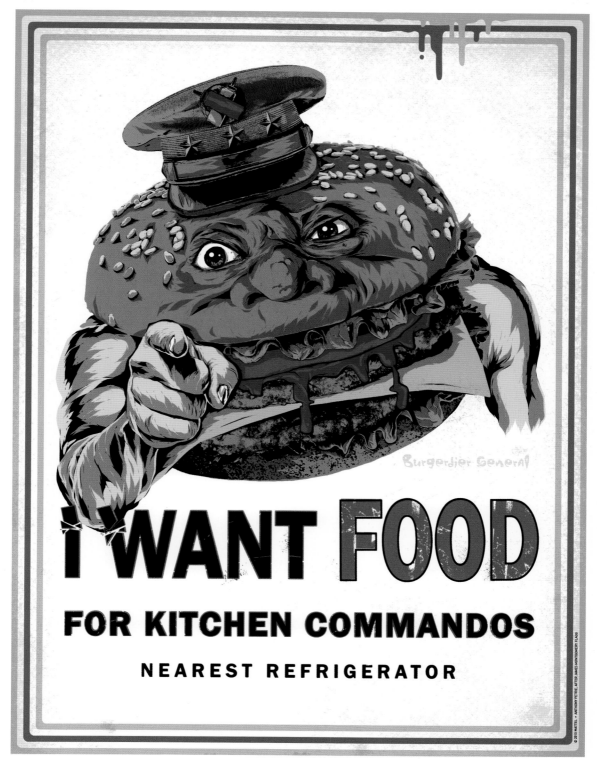

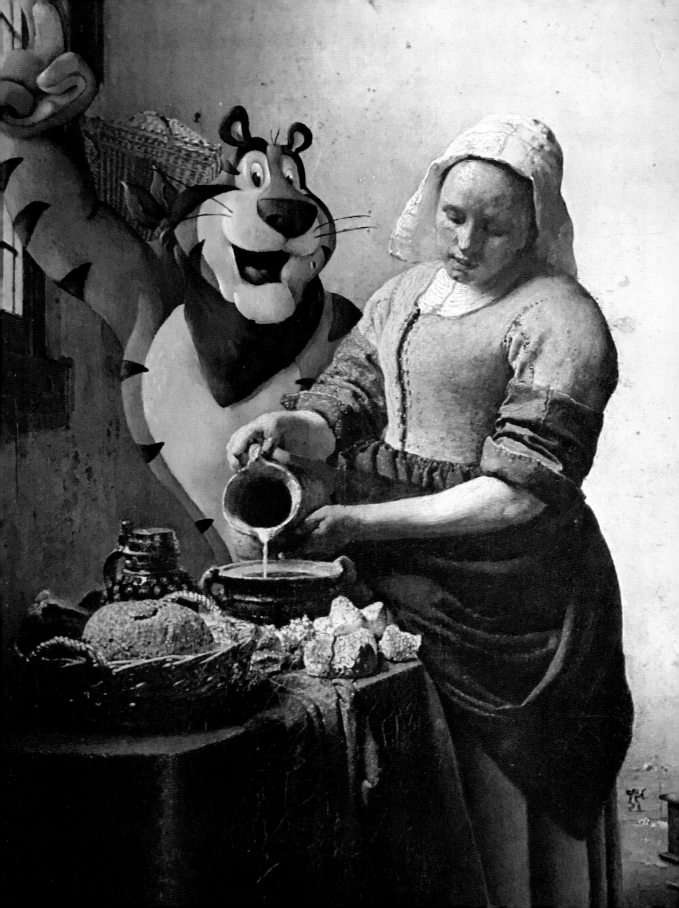

DAVE POLLOT

Dave Pollot's creative process begins inside thrift shops where he finds abandoned and forgotten artworks. He uses oil paints to alter these pieces and blend his additions, transforming them into new works with new meaning. His work challenges the idea that any one generation can claim sole custody of a particular bit of pop culture, and questions the rubric by which we as a community of consumers and critics decide what artwork will remain relevant and what will ultimately find its way to the forgotten stacks on thrift shop floors. His art is the confluence of time periods, zeitgeists, styles, and meaning. By integrating distinct elements of pop culture from one generation into the abandoned artwork of another, cultural property lines are blurred, and forgotten art is reintroduced into a more communal world where things like "modern nostalgia" and "classical pop art" make sense.

His work has been displayed and found homes in galleries, businesses, and private collections in all fifty states and in over forty countries around the globe. His work has attracted attention from the media both in the United States and abroad, including *Business Insider*, Instagram, and the SyFy Channel, and his corporate clients include Sony, Instagram, and Tröegs Brewing Company, among others.

WEBSITE: www.davepollot.com
INSTAGRAM: @davepollotart
FACEBOOK: /davepollotart

Old Market Expansion VII
2018

Product Placement
2019

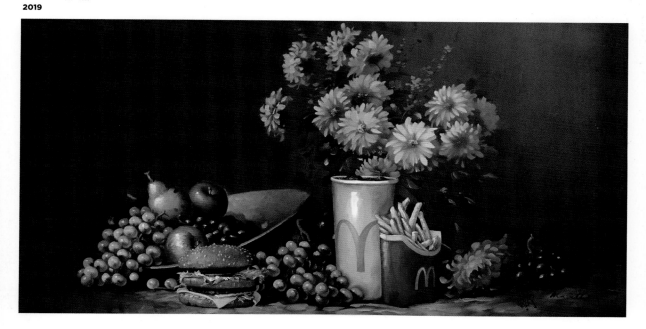

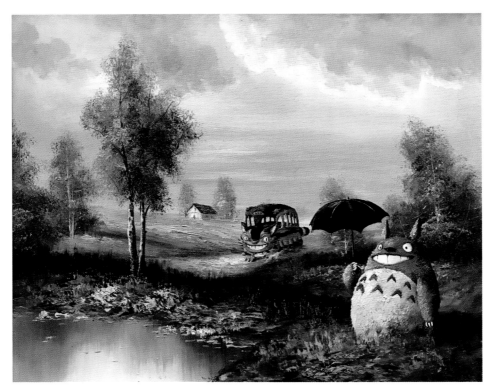

Bus Stop
2018

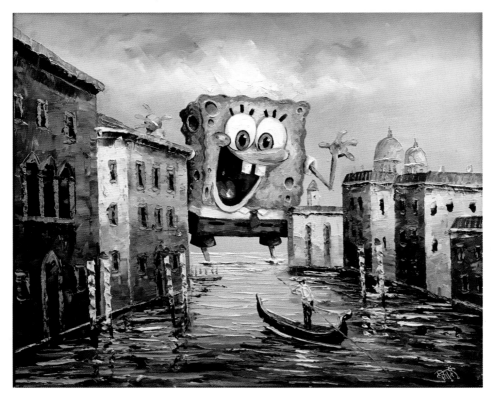

Fully Absorbed
2019

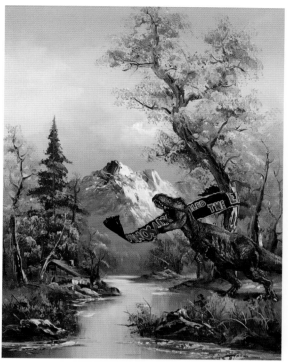

Second Chances
2019

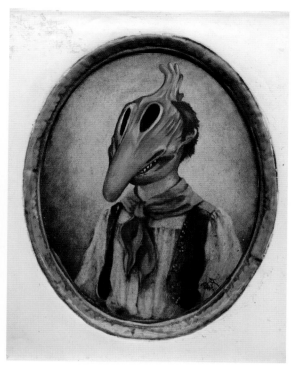

Parlor Trick I
2018

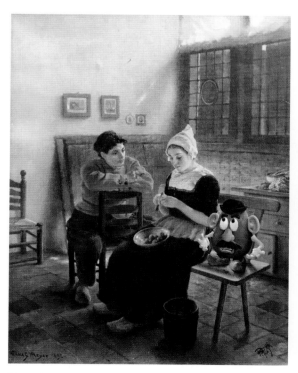

Intervention
2018

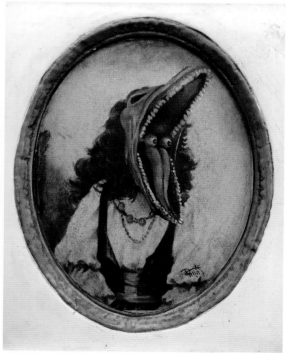

Parlor Trick II
2018

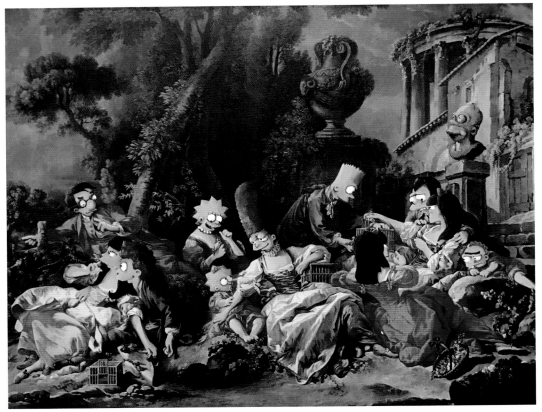

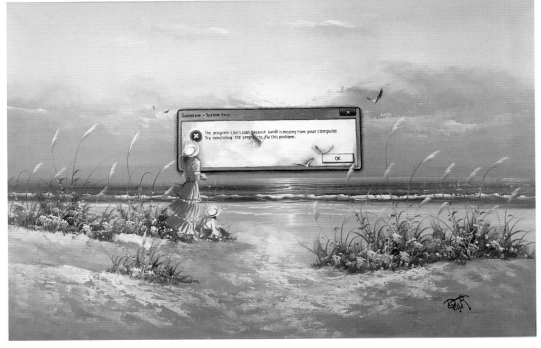

> "My art is the confluence of time periods, zeitgeists, styles, and meaning."

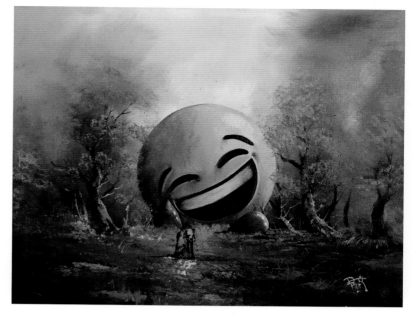

Breakdown
2018

The Birth of Dubstep
2018

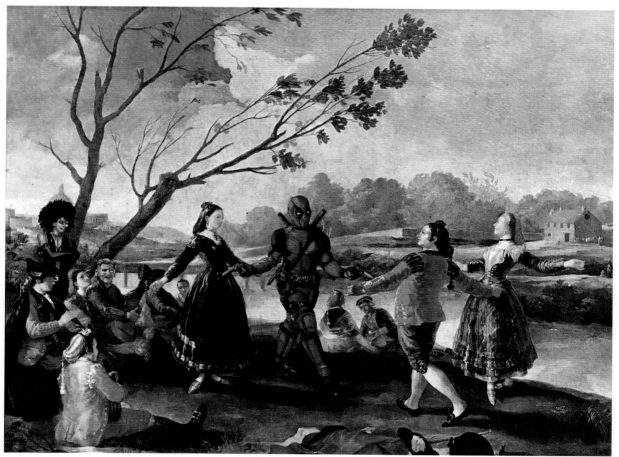

LUKE PREECE

A child of the eighties raised on a mixture of sci-fi, fantasy, comics, movies, and metal music, Luke Preece is an illustrator based out of the West Midlands in the United Kingdom. His clients include 2000 AD comics, Marvel, Lucas Film, Metallica, Sony Music, Music for Nations, Santa Cruz Skateboards, *Metal Hammer*, Xbox, Rebellion, Topps, and more. He also collaborates with various galleries on limited screenprints for various exhibitions, gig posters, and events around the globe.

WEBSITE: www.lukepreece.com
INSTAGRAM: @lukepreeceart
FACEBOOK: /lukepreeceart
TWITTER: @luke_preece

They Live
2018

Ghost
2019

Ozzy
2019

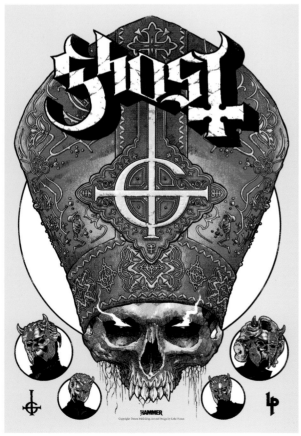

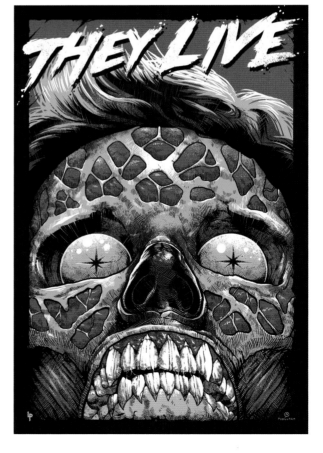

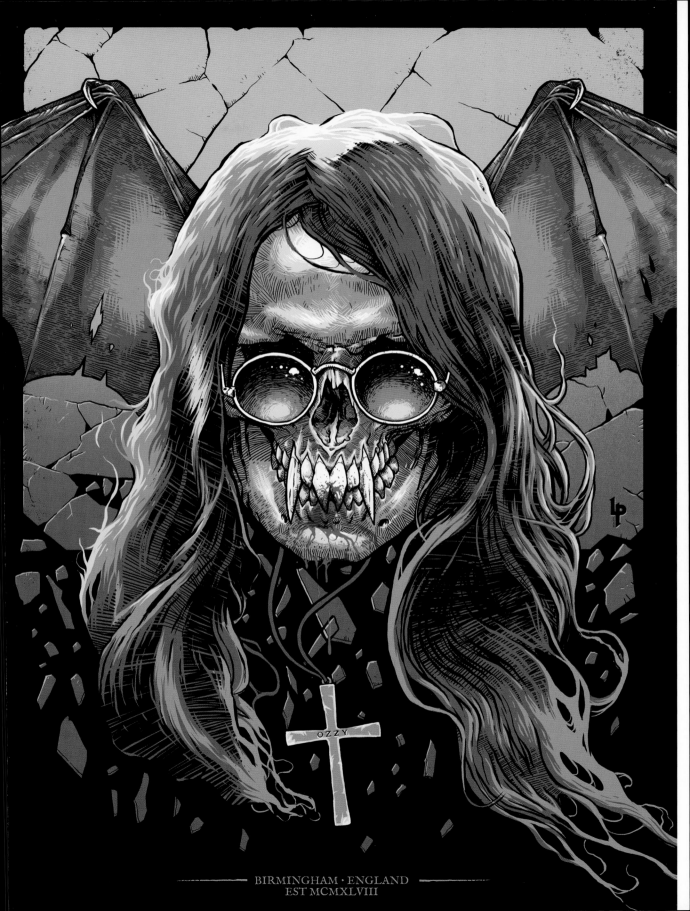

BIRMINGHAM · ENGLAND
EST MCMXLVIII

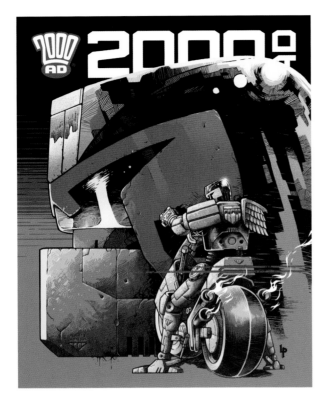

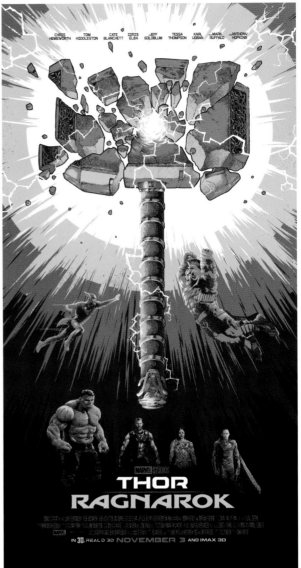

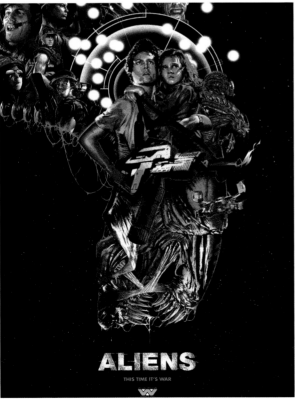

Mechanismo
2019

Thor Ragnarok
2017

Aliens / THEY MOSTLY COME
AT NIGHT... MOSTLY
2018

"Be patient. If your work is good, something WILL happen."

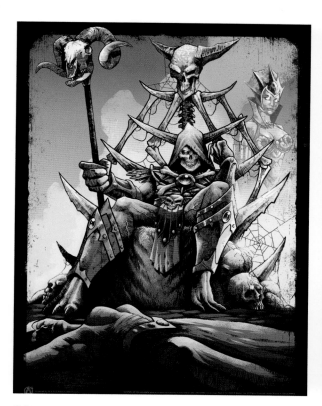

Skeletor
2018

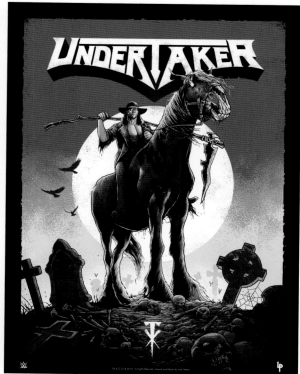

Undertaker
2018

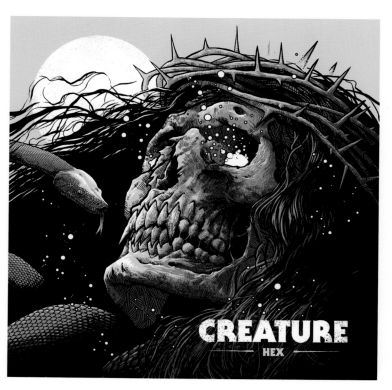

Creature
2018

QETZA

Jorge Garza, a.k.a. Qetza, is an artist from northwest Indiana. With major influences from comic book art, horror illustration, ancient cultural art of the Americas and screenprinting, his work ranges from simple to highly detailed pen and ink.

WEBSITE: www.qetza.com
INSTAGRAM: @qetzaart
FACEBOOK: /QetzaArt
TWITTER: @qetza

Aztec Dredd
2019

Aztec Alien
2017

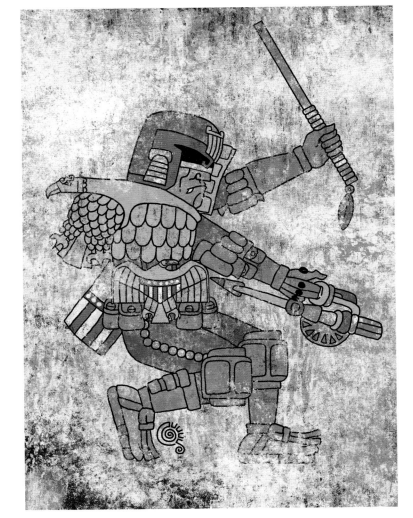

" Pop culture creates new worlds, icons, symbols, and provides an experience which at its best brings people together who enjoy it."

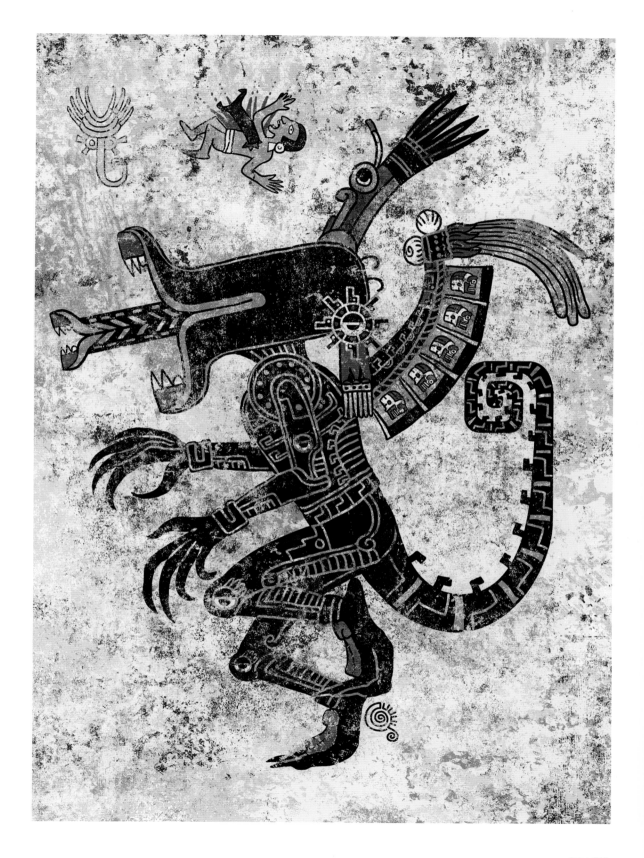

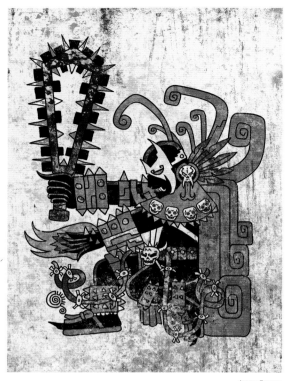

Aztec Spawn
2017

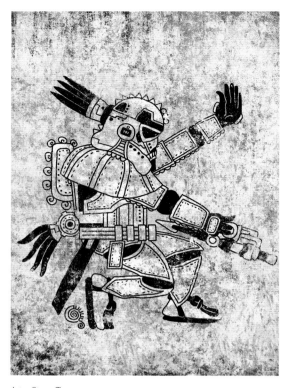

Aztec Storm Trooper
2018

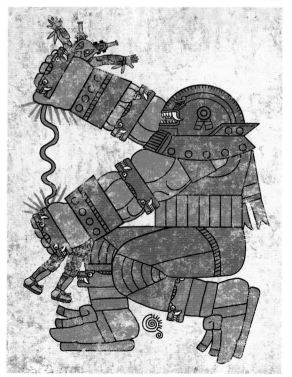

Aztec Juggernaut
2018

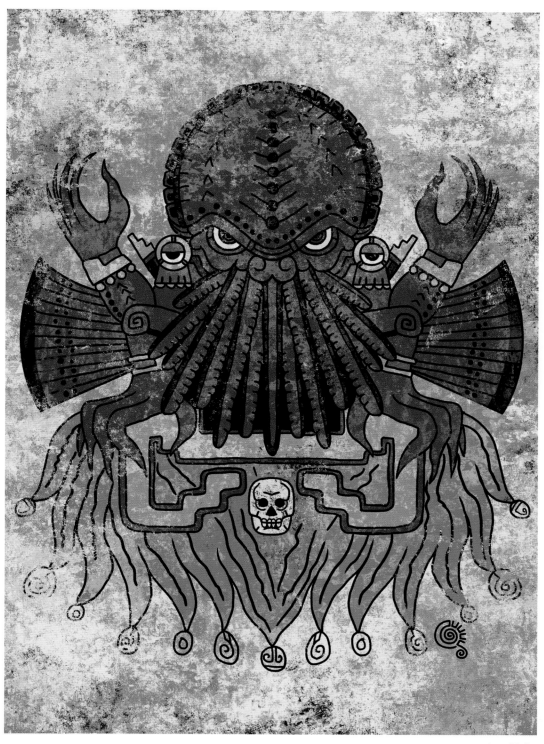

Aztec Cthulhu
2017

One Last Spin
2019

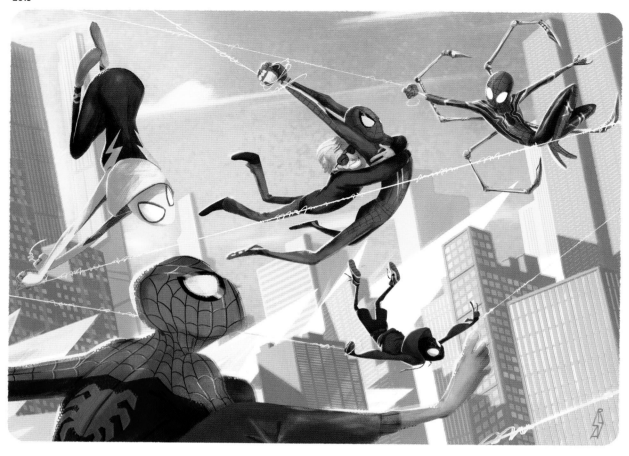

Papa Geek
2016

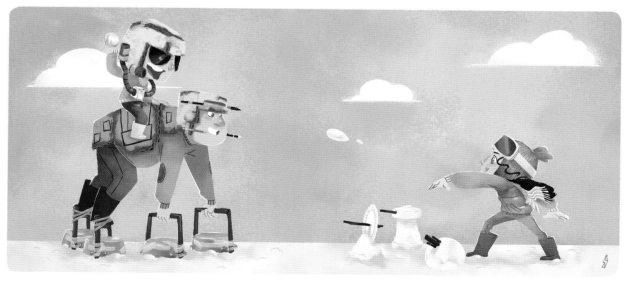

ANDRY RAJOELINA

Andry Rajoelina is a thirty-three-year-old child, character designer, and colorist for animation series who, between family life, work, cinema sessions, and video games, still finds time to pay tribute to the characters and universes that rocked his childhood.

INSTAGRAM: @andryshango
TWITTER: @AndryShango
FACEBOOK: /AndryShango
TUMBLR: www.el-shango-drew-and-shot.tumblr.com

" In the very first movie that I saw at the cinema, there were anthropomorphic turtles eating pizzas, followers of ninjutsu and who had for father a rat. But it's okay, since I live it pretty well."

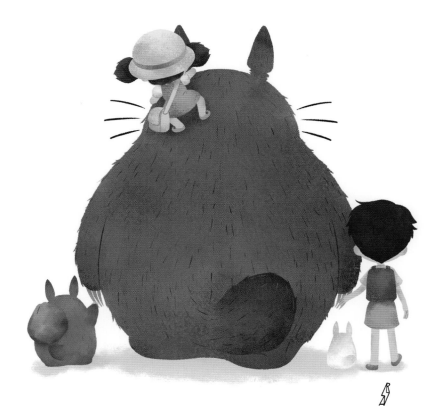

Neighbour Family
2018

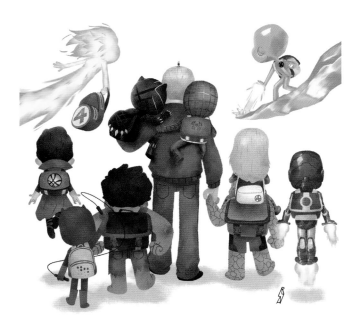

Excelsior Family
2019

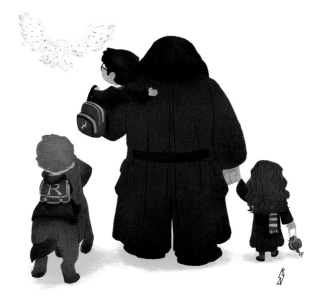

Wizards Family
2016

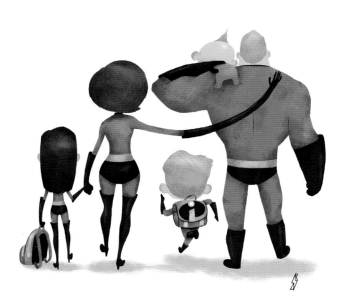

Incredible Family
2018

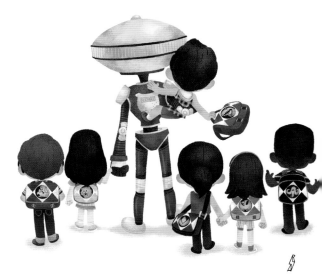

Rangers Family
2017

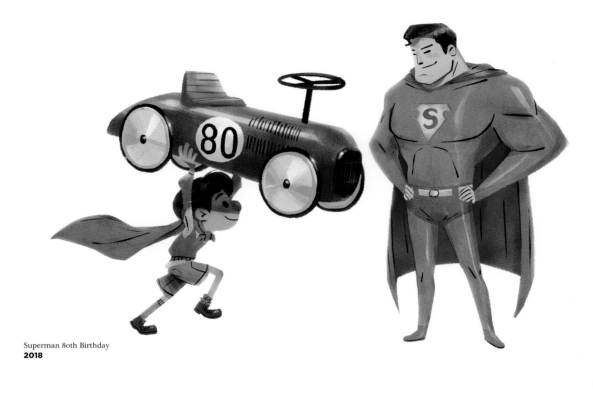

Superman 80th Birthday
2018

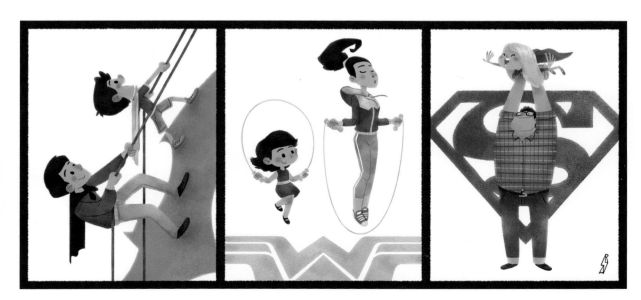

Trinity Family
2018

JÉRÔME RASTO

Born in 1978 in Perpignan, France, Jérome was introduced to painting by his father, an artist. His story begins when he was a child with the discovery of books like *The Very Rich Hours of the Duke of Berry*. The drawings, the characters, the buildings, the animals . . . the decorative aspect of the illumination, and especially its symbols, will leave a lasting mark on him. The stained glass that fascinates him will influence the thickness of his line, his play on transparencies, his colors. After a brief stint at the Arts Deco (ENAD) in Limoges, he continued painting in the studio before starting to work in the street three years ago. He paints on different supports, canvases, walls, bulky, a universe mixing medieval iconography with more contemporary references like that of the video games with which he grew up.

WEBSITE: www.jeromerasto.com
INSTAGRAM: @jeromerasto
FACEBOOK: /jeromerasto

> ❝ Pop culture . . . this is ours; we grew up with these references. They shaped us. I admit to being somewhat obsessive about the Mario Bros. universe, this is my 'madeleine de Proust'.❞

Buccina
2019

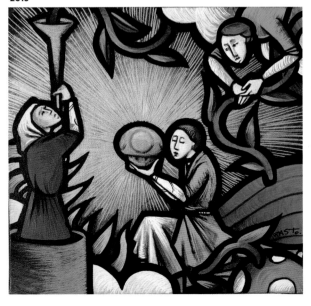

Printemps
2017

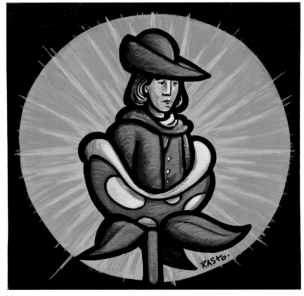

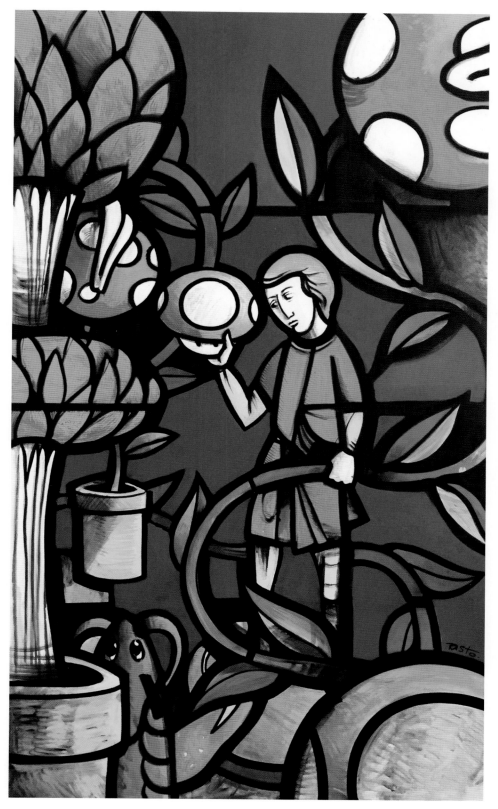

Jardin
2017

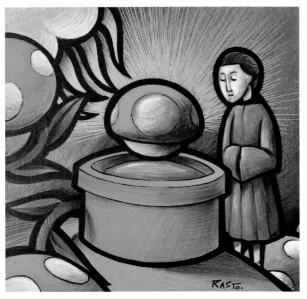

Le Champignon Magique
2019

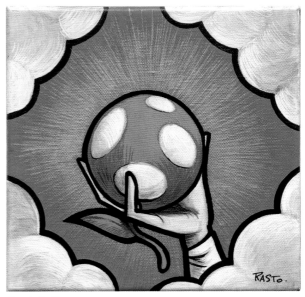

Glossaire La Plante
2019

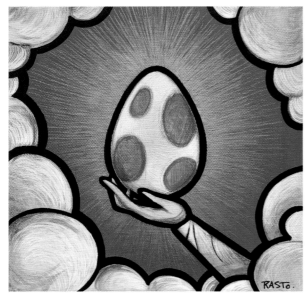

Glossaire L'Œuf
2019

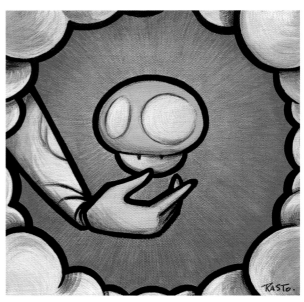

Glossaire Le Champignon
2019

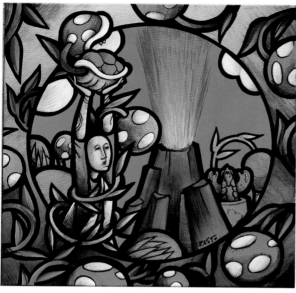

Le Volcan
2019

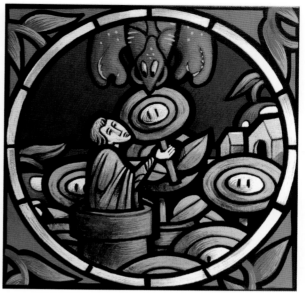

Courtil
2018

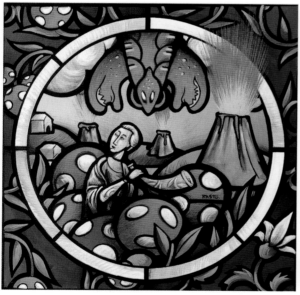

Olifant
2019

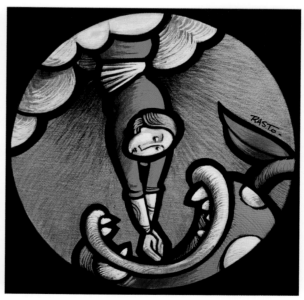

Le Plongeon
2019

STEVEN RHODES

Steven Rhodes is a graphic artist and illustrator best known for his offbeat reimagining of children's activity books from the seventies and eighties. With designs such as "Let's Summon Demons" and "Pyrokinesis For Beginners" you would be forgiven for thinking he has an affinity for the dark arts. In truth, Steven's iconic "Sinister Seventies" collection was born from his dual love of retro nostalgia and pitch-black humor.

Steven's collections are available in multiple clothing and merchandise retailers internationally, including Spencer's and Hot Topic. He has created exclusive designs for brands such as Threadless, Wicked Clothes, Loot Crate, Mambo, Killstar, Creepy Co., and Cavitycolors.

Based in Brisbane, Australia, Steven enjoys the quiet life of a freelancer. He spends his free time exploring vintage stores and not speaking to strangers.

WEBSITE: www.stevenrhodes.threadless.com
INSTAGRAM: @stevenrhodesart
FACEBOOK: /stevenrhodesart

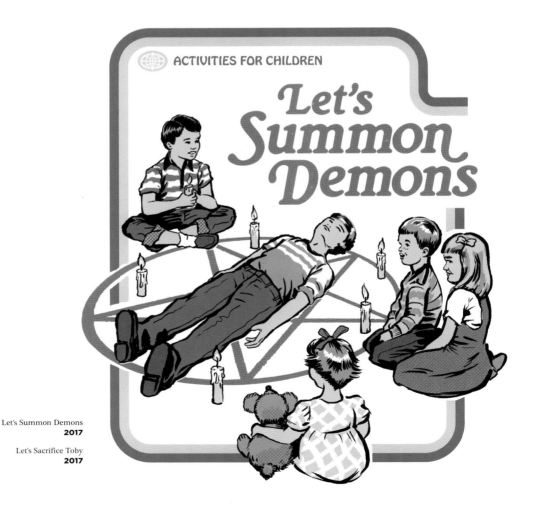

Let's Summon Demons
2017

Let's Sacrifice Toby
2017

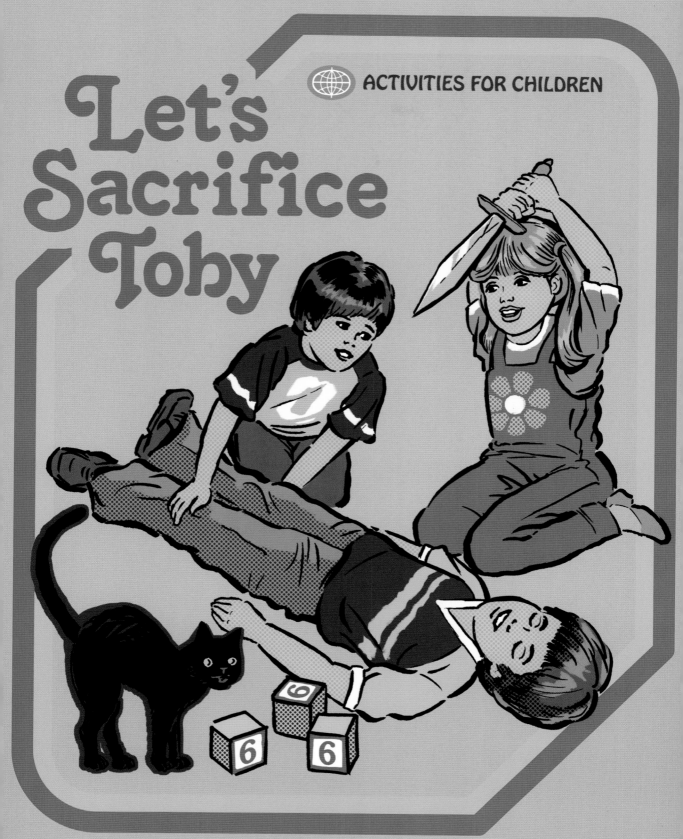

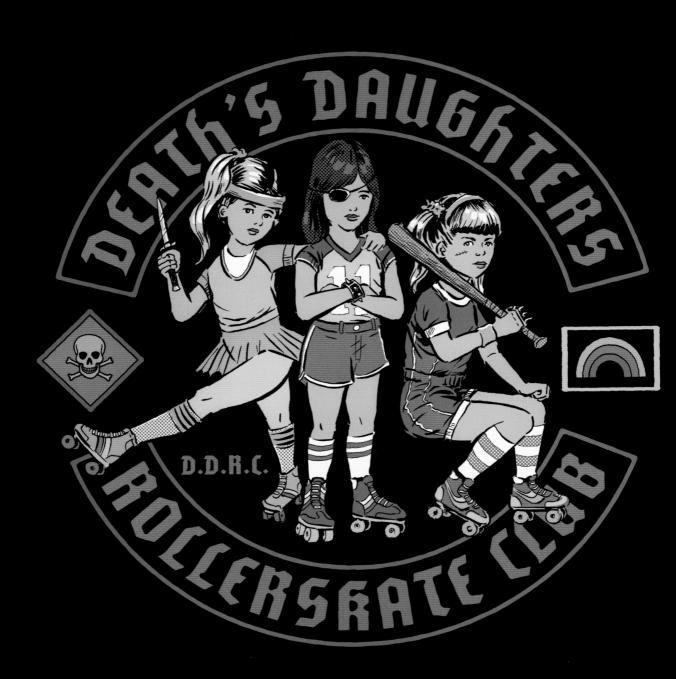

Death's Daughters Rollerskate Club
2018

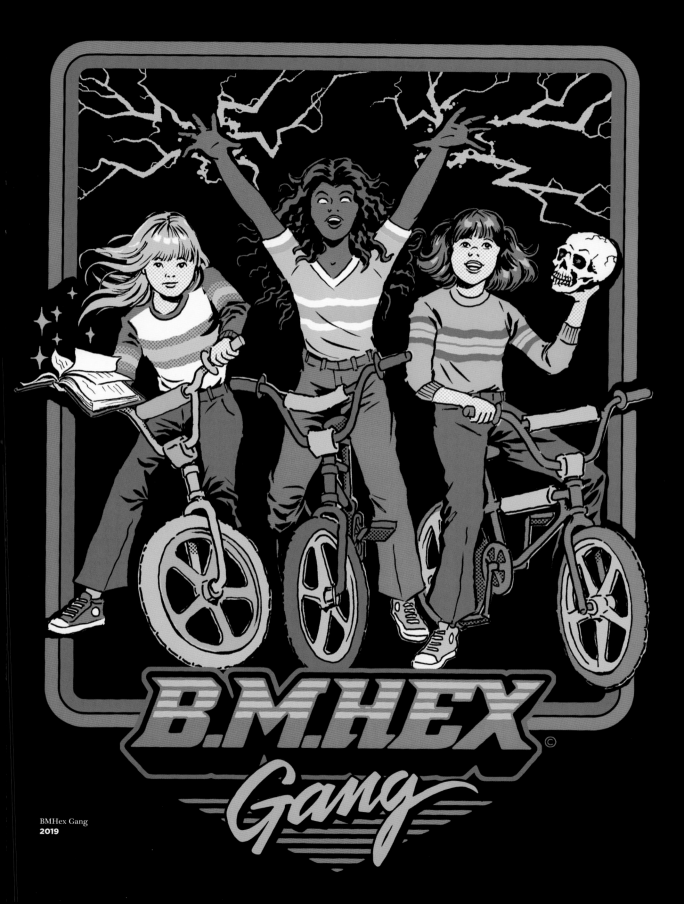

BMHex Gang
2019

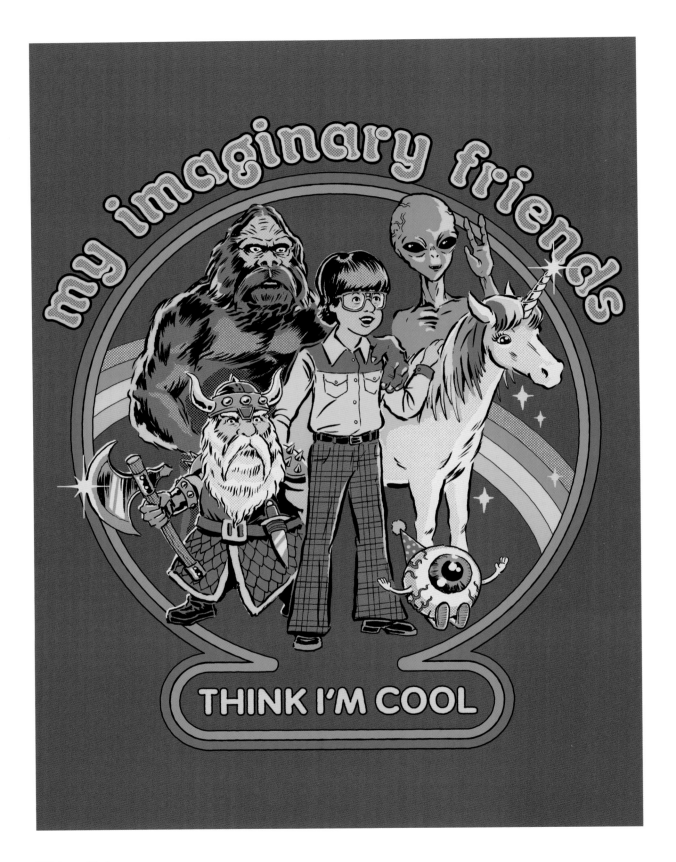

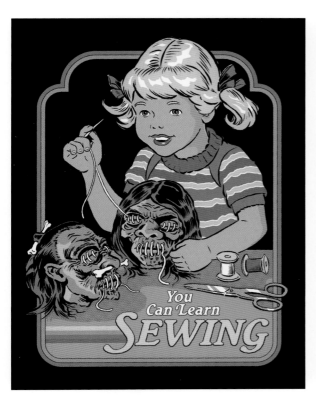

You Can Learn Sewing
2018

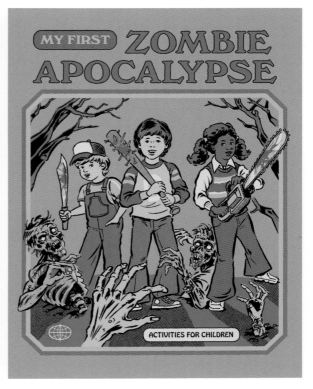

My First Zombie Apocalypse
2018

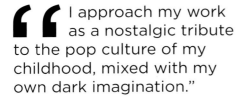

> I approach my work as a nostalgic tribute to the pop culture of my childhood, mixed with my own dark imagination."

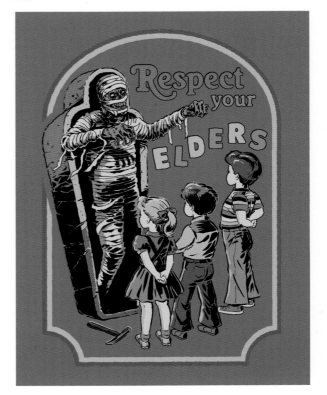

Respect Your Elders
2018

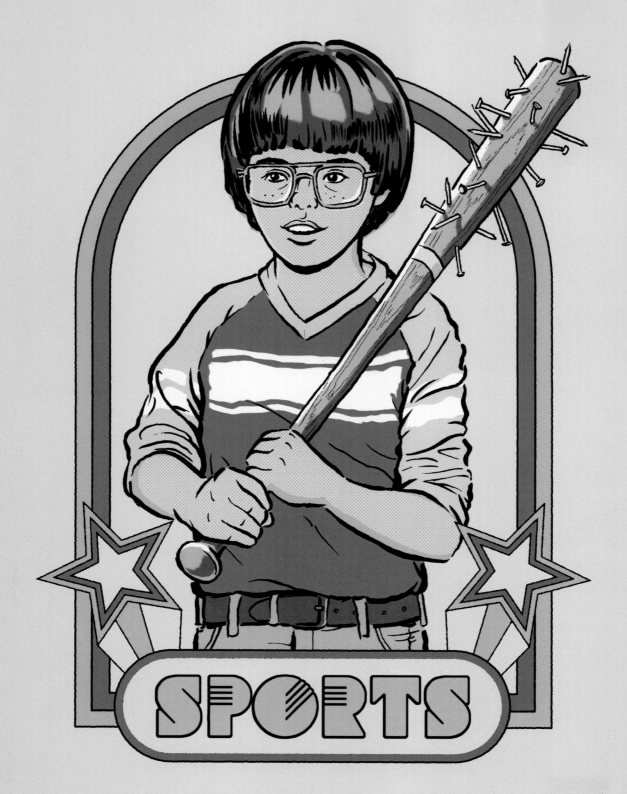

SPORTS

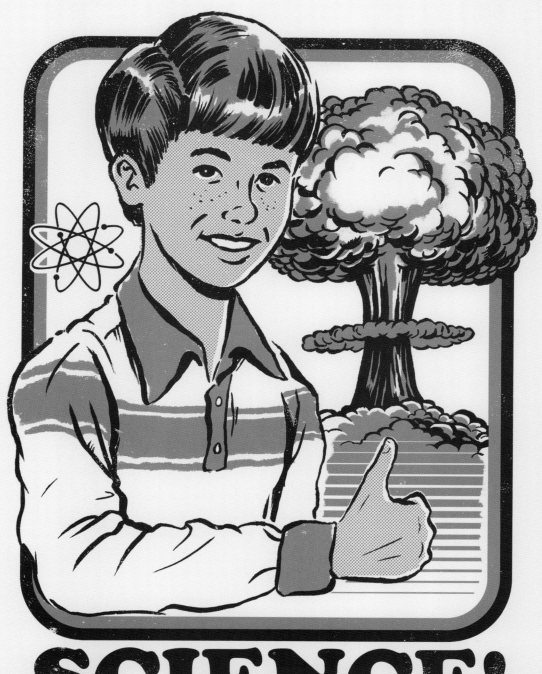

SCIENCE!

Science!
2016

EYAL ROSENTHAL

An engineer by day, Eyal Rosenthal is a self-taught designer at night. He likes to create, again and again. For him, design is a necessity, a way of exploring the world. According to him, a good design must make you think and feel. He applies this leitmotif for each achievement. His series of lamps inspired by *Star Wars*, in a very "Scandinavian design" universe, has toured the Internet.

WEBSITE: www.eyalrosenthal.wordpress.com

❝❝ Through my creations, I explore minimalism and sophistication, always with a touch of humor."

Vader
2016

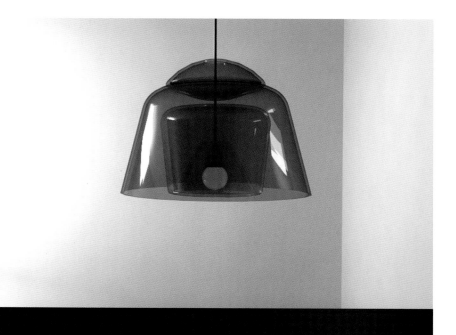

Vajdër

och att den första filmen var klart verkar under en alternativ berättelse där Vader var en separat karaktär

01

Fett
2016

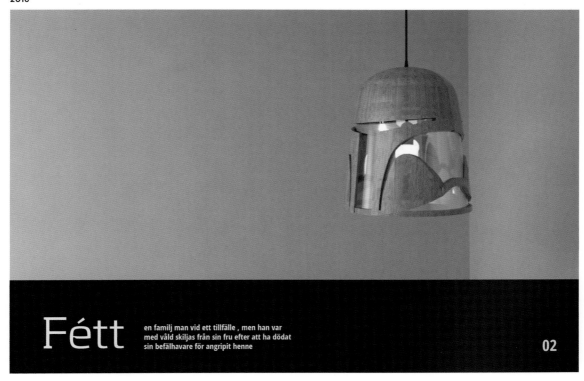

Fétt
en familj man vid ett tillfälle , men han var
med våld skiljas från sin fru efter att ha dödat
sin befälhavare för angripit henne

02

BB8
2016

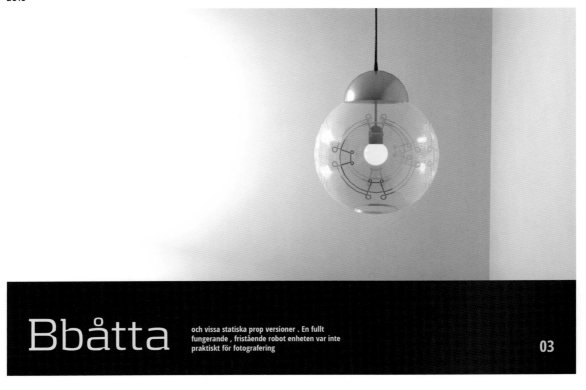

Bbåtta
och vissa statiska prop versioner . En fullt
fungerande , fristående robot enheten var inte
praktiskt för fotografering

03

Rey
2016

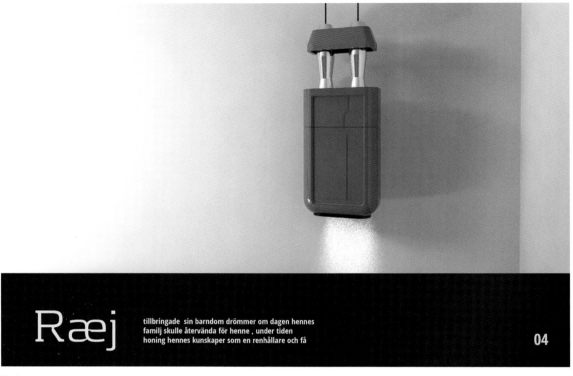

Ræj

tillbringade sin barndom drömmer om dagen hennes
familj skulle återvända för henne , under tiden
honing hennes kunskaper som en renhållare och få

04

Maul
2016

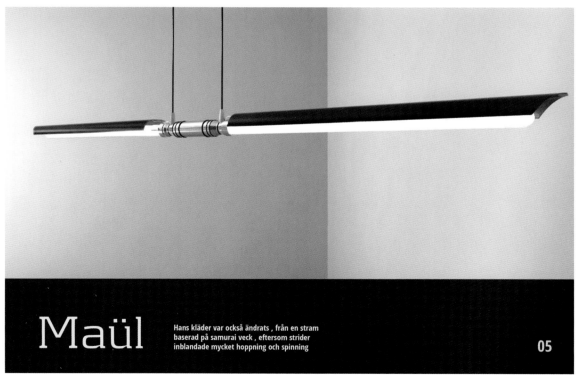

Maül

Hans kläder var också ändrats , från en stram
baserad på samurai veck , eftersom strider
inblandade mycket hoppning och spinning

05

Snowtrooper
2016

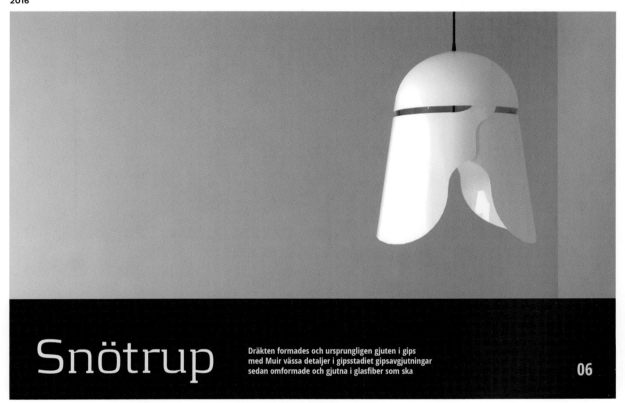

Snötrup

Dräkten formades och ursprungligen gjuten i gips
med Muir vässa detaljer i gipsstadiet gipsavgjutningar
sedan omformade och gjutna i glasfiber som ska

06

JEAN-SÉBASTIEN ROSSBACH

After seventeen years of a well-illustrated illustrator career, with clients as diverse as Gallimard, Pocket, Mondadori, Ubisoft, Microsoft, Marvel, and Dark Horse, Rossbach's illustrations on the cover of a novel or a comic book are probably familiar to you.

WEBSITE: www.artstation.com/jeansbastienrossbach
FACEBOOK: /jeansebastienrossbach

> " More than politics, economics, or the social sciences, popular culture shapes the society in which we live. The big decision-makers of today are the geeks we made fun of yesterday."

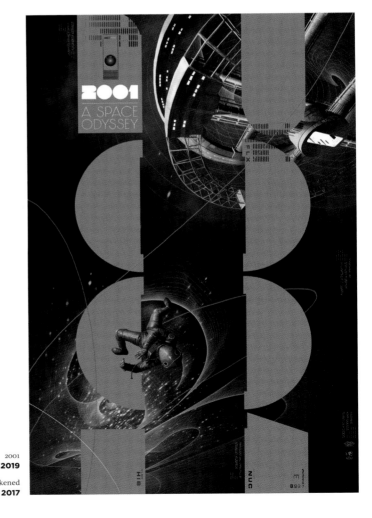

2001
2019

Dune, The Sleeper has Awakened
2017

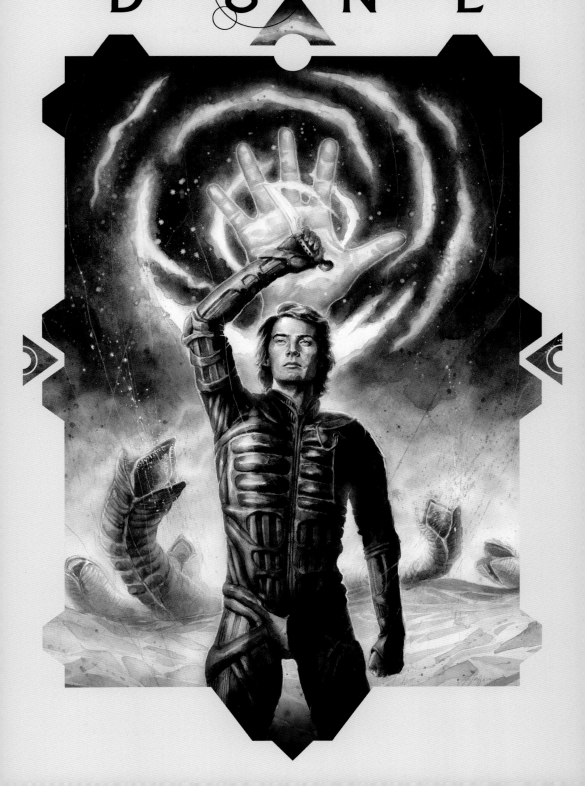

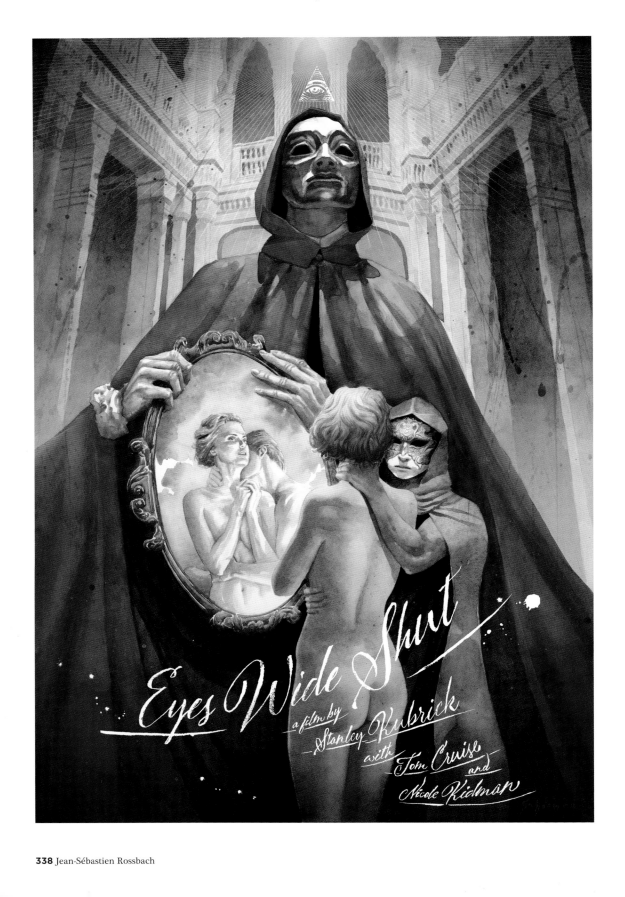

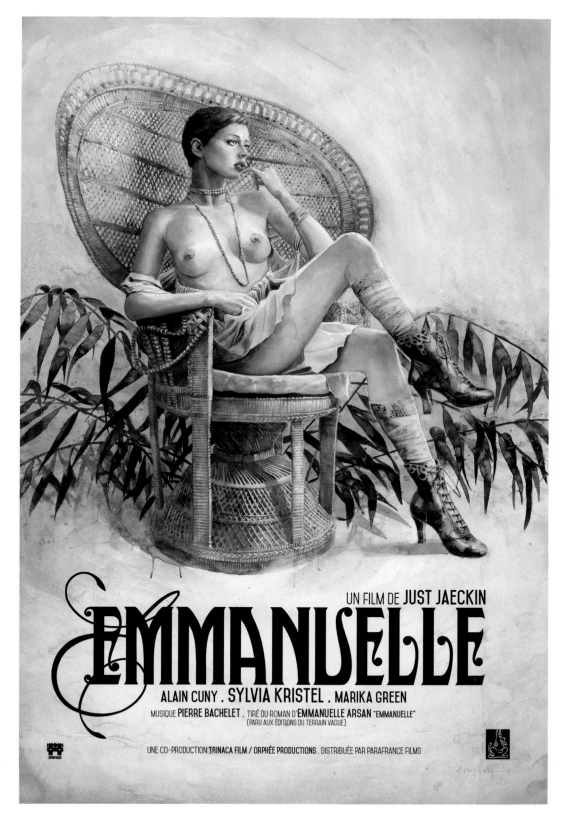

UN FILM DE **JUST JAECKIN**

EMMANUELLE

ALAIN CUNY . **SYLVIA KRISTEL** . **MARIKA GREEN**

MUSIQUE **PIERRE BACHELET** . TIRÉ DU ROMAN D'**EMMANUELLE ARSAN** "EMMANUELLE"
(PARU AUX ÉDITIONS DU TERRAIN VAGUE)

UNE CO-PRODUCTION **TRINACA FILM** / **ORPHÉE PRODUCTIONS** . DISTRIBUÉE PAR **PARAFRANCE FILMS**

Emmanuelle
2016

Eyes Wide Shut
2016

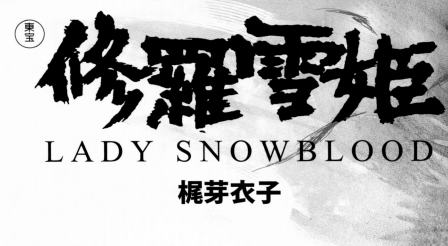

修羅雪姫

LADY SNOWBLOOD

梶芽衣子

Lady Snowblood
2016

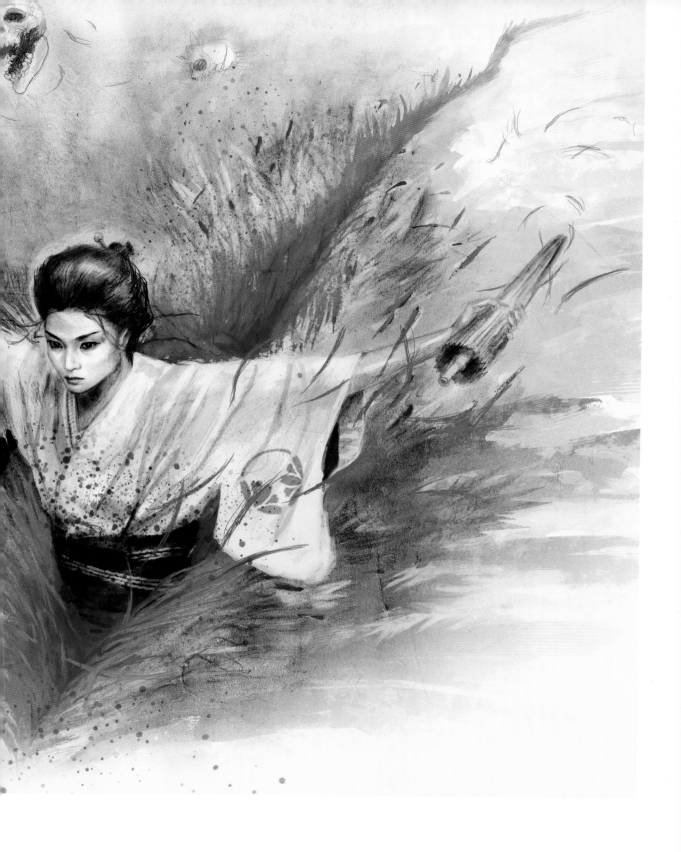

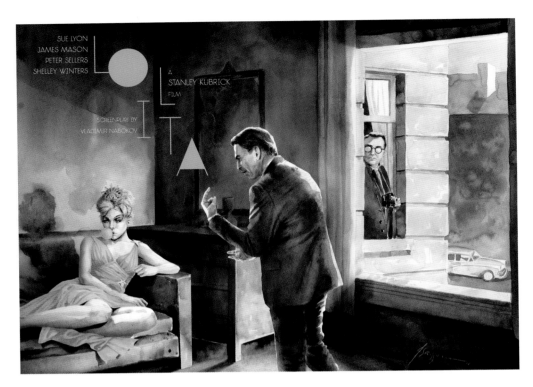

Lolita
2016

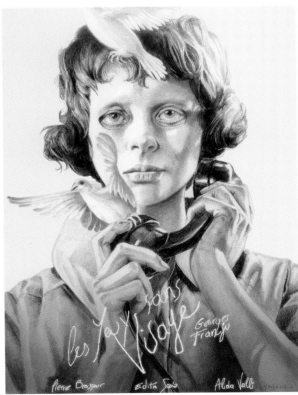

Les Yeux sans visage
2017

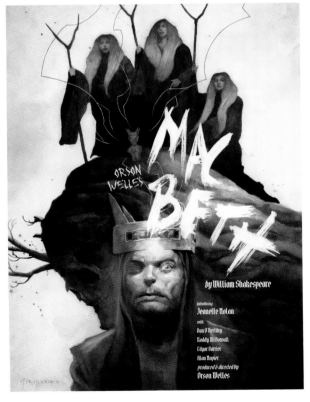

Orson Well's Macbeth
2016

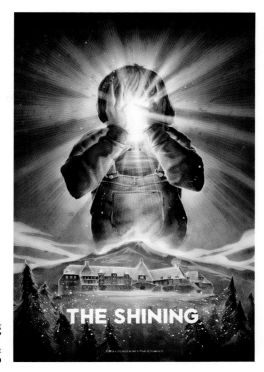

The Shining
2017

The Exorcist
2019

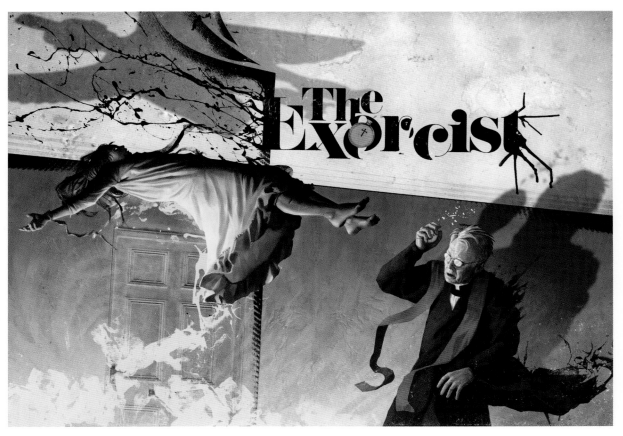

JAKUB ROZALSKI

Jakub Rozalski, also known as Mr. Werewolf, is a Polish visual artist, born in 1981, in Koszalin, professionally working as a concept artist, illustrator, and designer since 2002.

Best known as a creator of the World of 1920+ and his very evocative paintings full of dark storytelling. Starting in 2014, Rozalski began focusing only on personal projects.

WEBSITE: www.artstation.com/jakubrozalski

" As an artist, I always wanted to create my own original projects and worlds, rather than visualize other people's vision and ideas. I think this is exactly what artists should try to achieve: independence as a creator. It is a hard way but gives a lot more satisfaction and self-realization. Polish culture was always one of my main source[s] of inspiration. It's like a mix of everything that's cool and interesting: art, culture, history, creative vision, the past, and the future! I cannot imagine the world, and me as an artist, without pop culture. I grew up in the era of the first video games and VHS tapes. Movies and games have accompanied and inspired me all my life."

1920 - Before the storm
2014

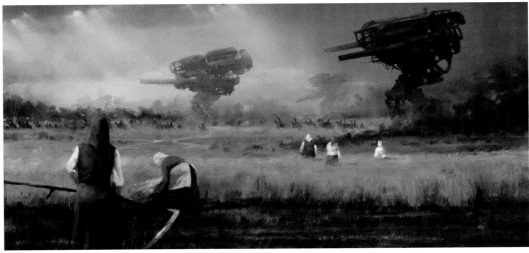

1920 - hussar
2015

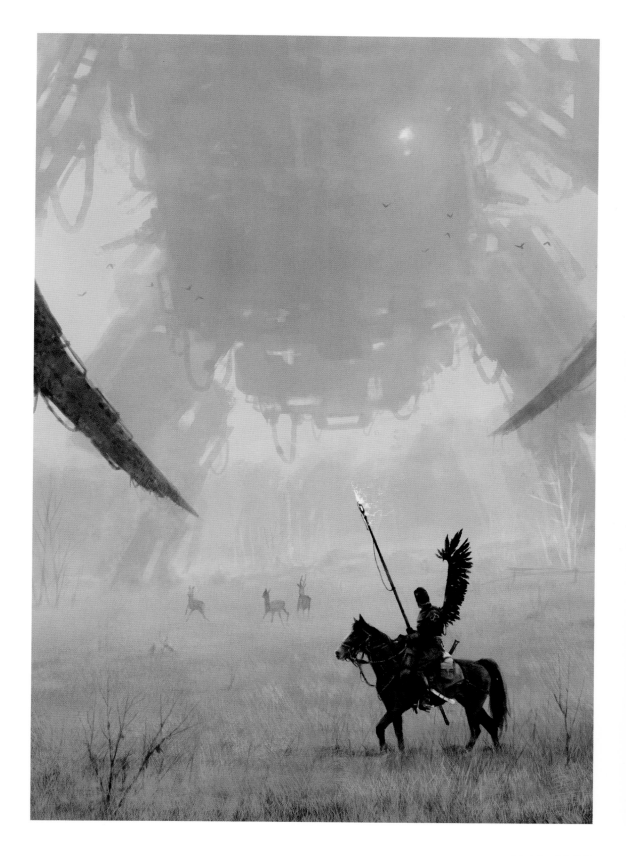

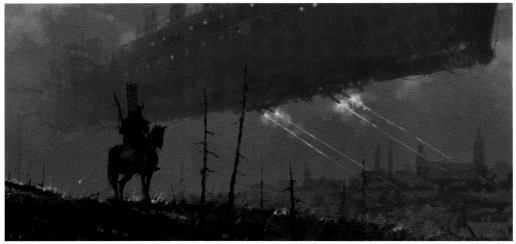

1920 - red dragon
2017

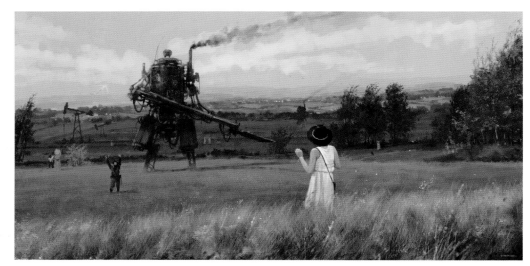

1920 - long time no see
2016

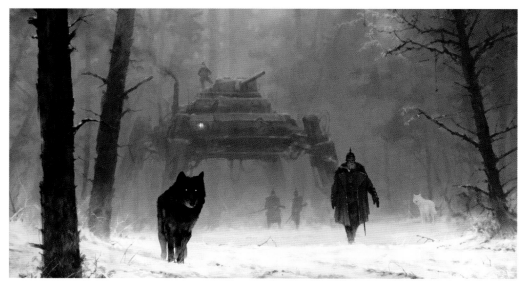

1920 - a walk through the woods
2017

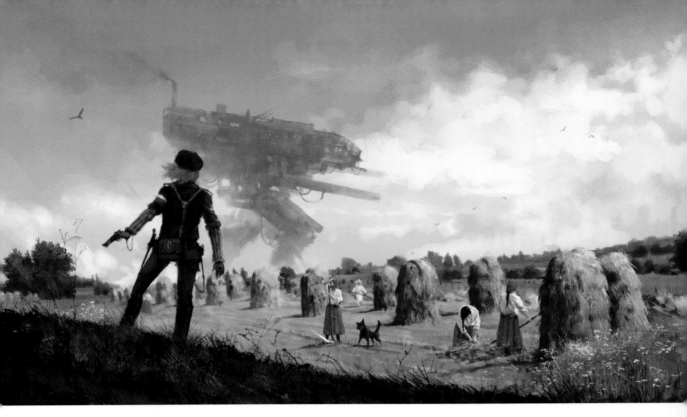

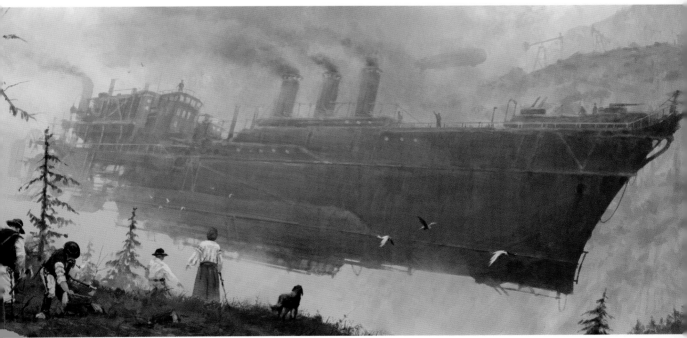

1920 - iron harvest
2016

1920 - wind gambit
2017

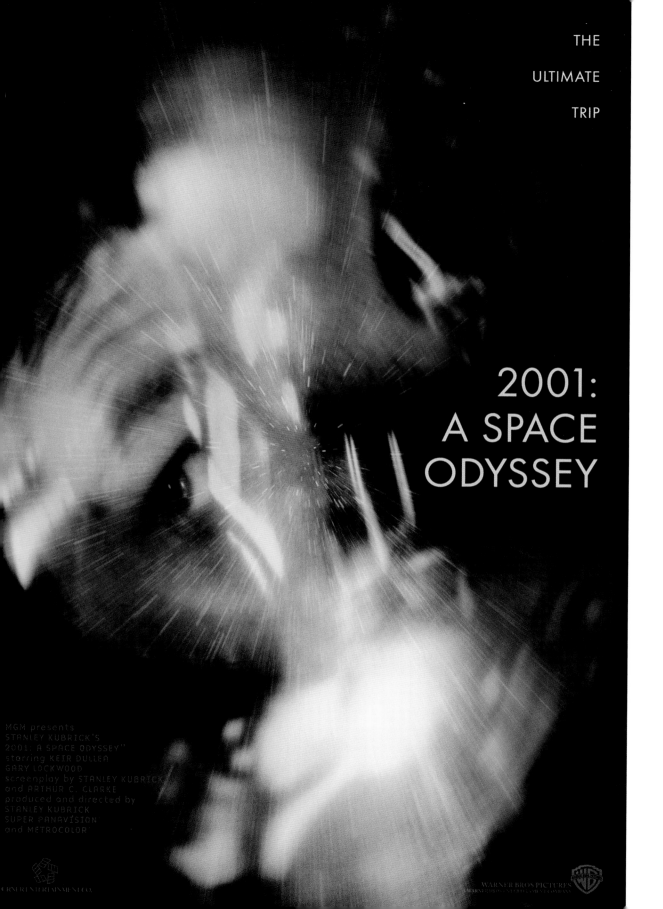

THE

ULTIMATE

TRIP

2001:
A SPACE
ODYSSEY

MGM presents
STANLEY KUBRICK'S
"2001: A SPACE ODYSSEY"
starring KEIR DULLEA
GARY LOCKWOOD
screenplay by STANLEY KUBRICK
and ARTHUR C. CLARKE
produced and directed by
STANLEY KUBRICK
SUPER PANAVISION
and METROCOLOR

SCOTT SASLOW

Scott Saslow is a freelance graphic designer based in Los Angeles specializing in alternative posters, theatrical key art, home video packaging, and assorted pop-culture geekery. Armed with a minimalist style and a need to always say more with less, Scott has created artwork for Blu-Ray releases and key art for many up-and-coming indie filmmakers plus an Oscar nominee. Oh, and he was once a test subject for NASA. Yes, really!

WEBSITE: www.scottsaslow.com
CONTACT: scott_saslow@yahoo.com
INSTAGRAM: @scottsaslow

2001: A Space Odyssey
2018

The Imitation Game
2016

Star Trek II: The Wrath of Khan
2016

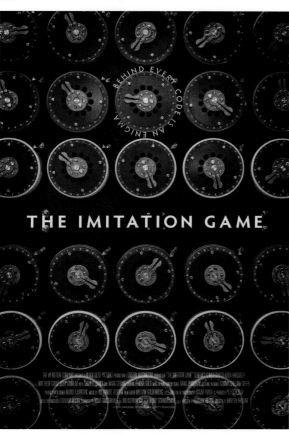

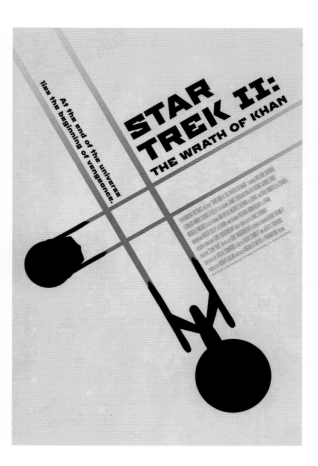

> "When I was a kid, I read *The Making of Star Trek: Deep Space Nine* by Judith and Garfield Reeves-Stevens and I couldn't believe people got paid to design such fantastical things. While my focus is on posters and not spaceships, I really believe the seed was planted right there: the idea of pursuing some kind of creative career, either in film or design. So I did both!"

Us
2019

Suspiria
2018

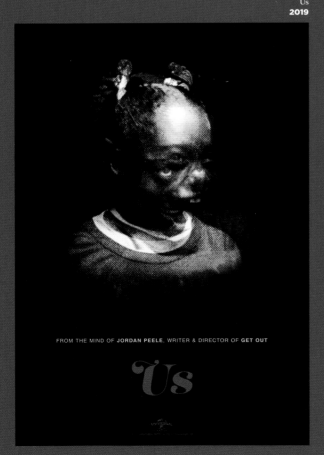

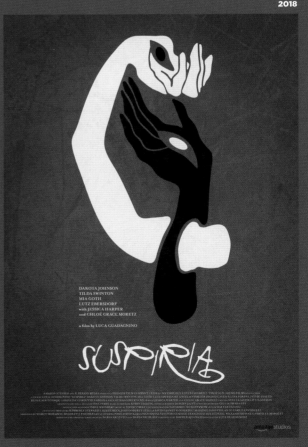

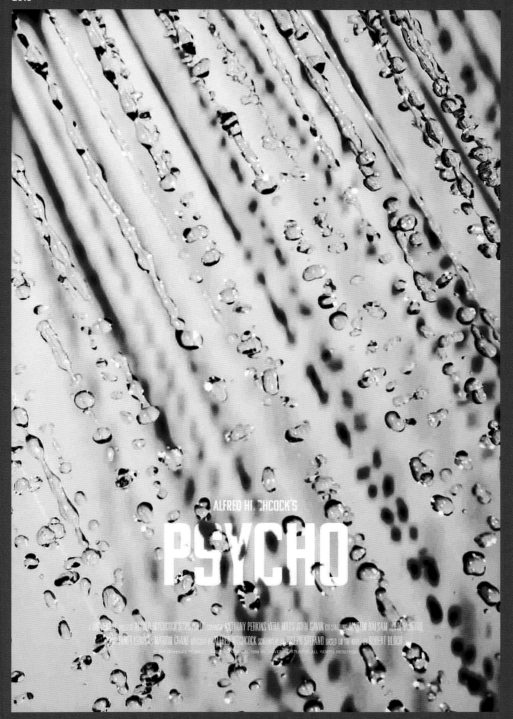

SCOTT SCHEIDLY

Scott Scheidly lives and works in Orlando, Florida. Known for his "pink series," which depicts notorious dictators, Hollywood celebrities, and contemporary politicians bathed in hues of pinks and purples, Scheidly's work presents a satirical analysis of power, corruption, celebrity, and masculinity. Through his exploration of color theory and sexual identity, Scheidly presents an important contemporary discussion of societal norms masked in a veil of humor and shock value.

WEBSITE: www.flounderart.com
INSTAGRAM: @scott_scheidly
FACEBOOK: /Scott-Scheidly

> " There is nothing more artistic than to evoke emotion."

Pretty in Pink
2013

Bobafett
2013

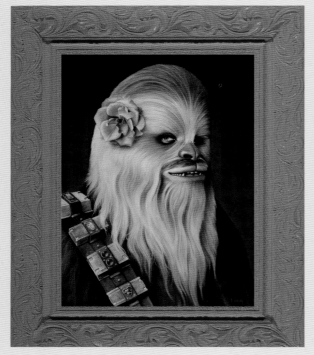

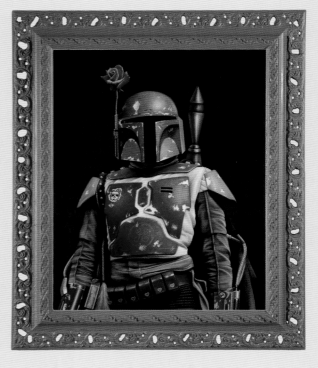

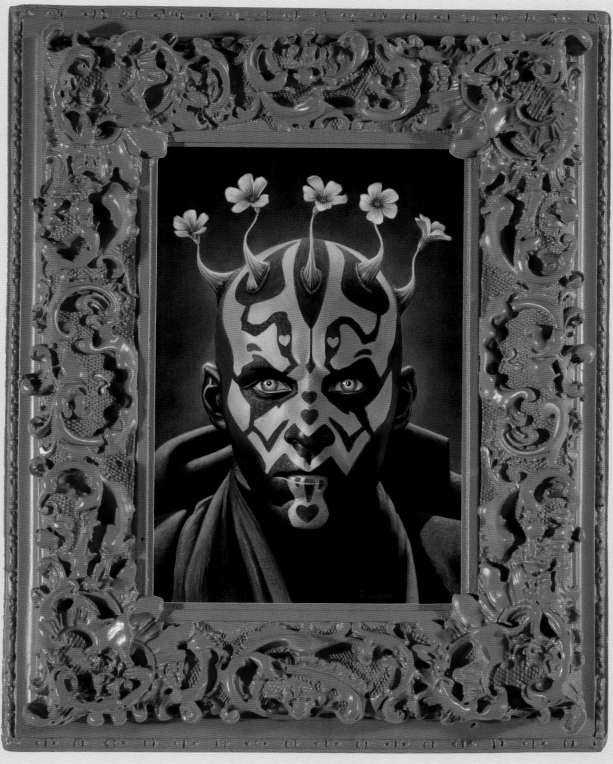

Darth Maul
2013

Frakenberry
2013

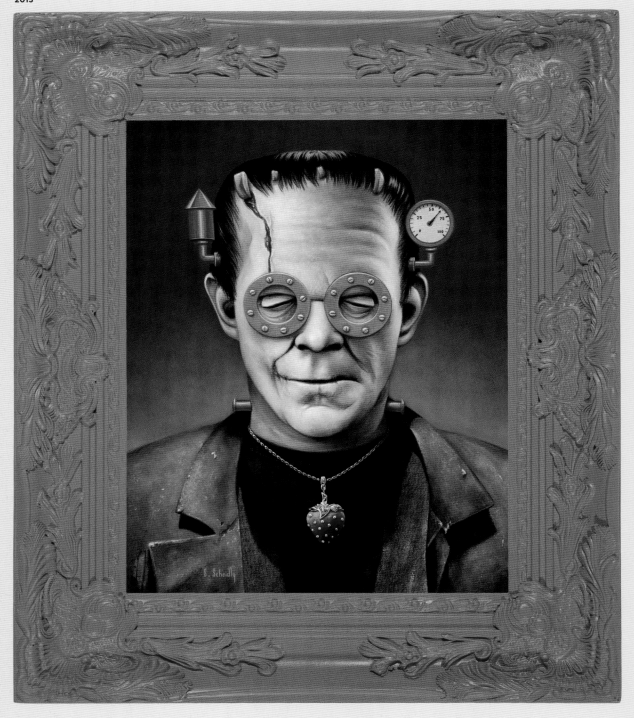

Mr. T for Teriffic
2013

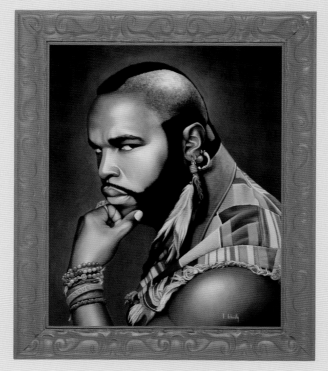

Rambo
2013

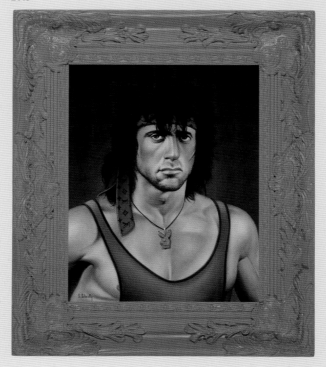

Clint
2013

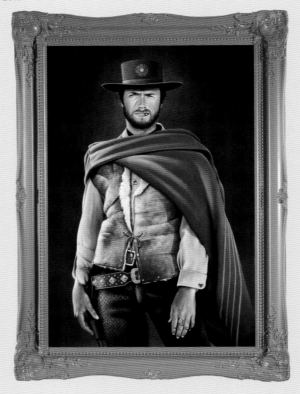

Chuck Norris
2013

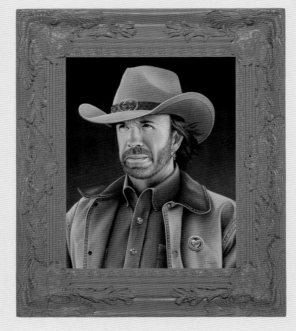

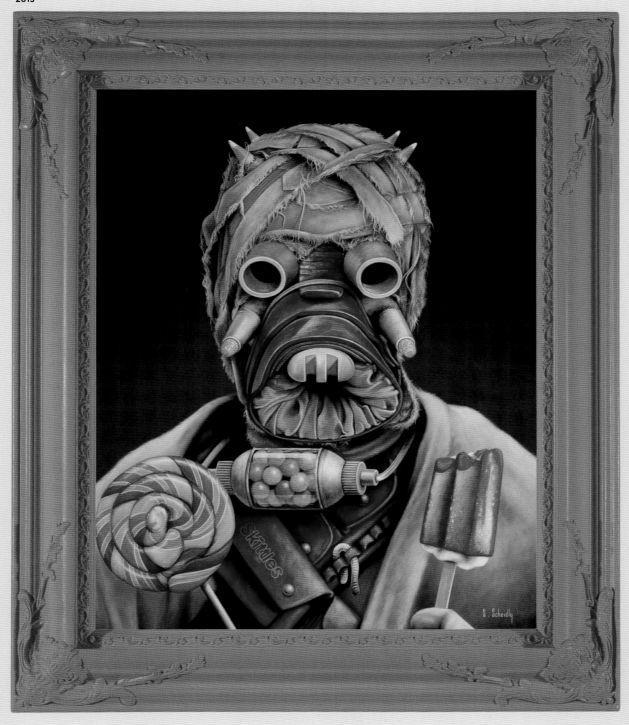

COLLIN SCHLICHT

Collin is a professional graphic designer and illustrator based out of the great Pacific Northwest. He's also an avid Batman enthusiast and rock drummer, enjoys a good laugh and a cold IPA, is constantly inspired by innovative filmmaking and pop-culture nostalgia, thrives in a mosh pit, rides his Schwinn into the sunset, and loves his beautiful wife Miriam—who gracefully puts up with his Lego building and other nerdery. He also thanks you wholeheartedly for your support.

WEBSITE: www.artbycollin.com
INSTAGRAM: @artbycollin
CONTACT: artbycollin@gmail.com

> " I believe that I'm a life-giving person, created to create life-giving art! If the illustration is vibrant, sharp, detailed, has a hint of nostalgia, and a positive message embedded within it—we've hit the bull's-eye."

The Head, The Tail
2017

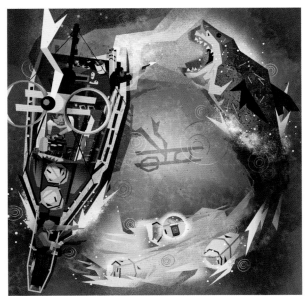

Forewarning
2018

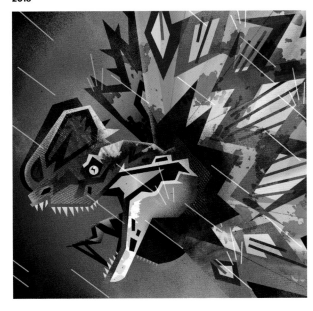

Heroic (Buzz Lightyear)
2018

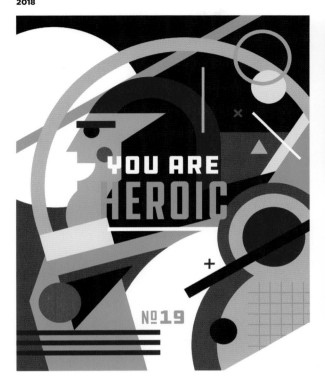

Valuable (Sheriff Woody)
2018

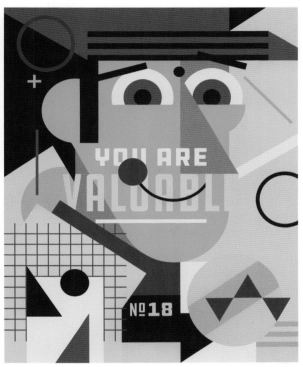

Deep Dish Action!
2018

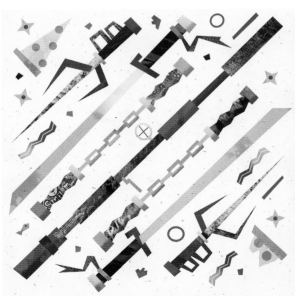

Blueprint
2018

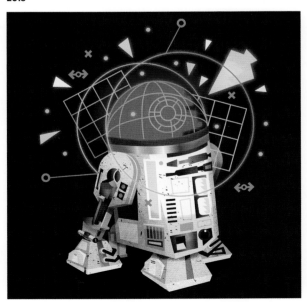

Collin Schlicht **359**

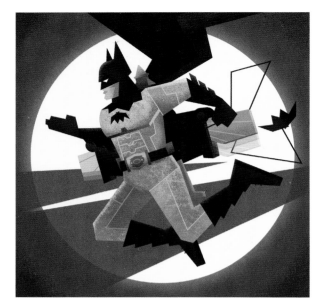

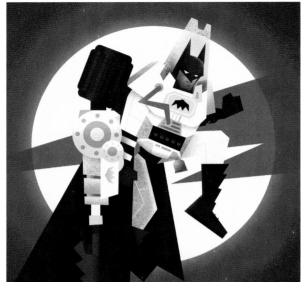

The Delux Knight - Tec-Shield Strike
2018

The Deluxe Knight - Arctic Armor Blast
2018

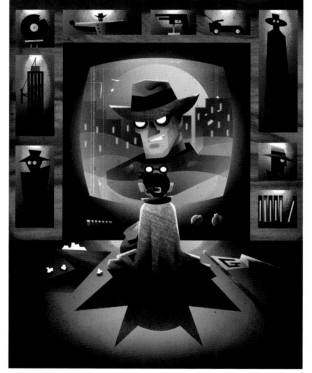

Ghosts
2018

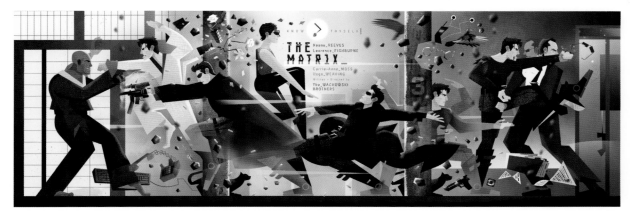

One
2019

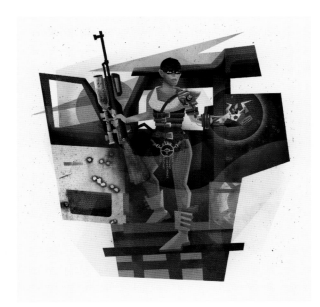

Warrior of Redemption
2018

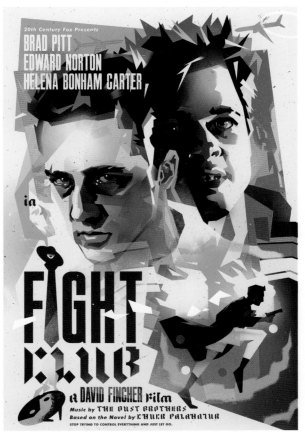

Without Sacrifice We Would Have Nothing
2019

STEVE SEELEY

After a childhood spent in Wisconsin watching cartoons, exploring the woods, and drawing comics, Steve Seeley graduated from the Ohio State University College of Arts and Sciences with a master's degree. His work encompasses his love for geekdom, nature, and heavy metal, the main sources of inspiration from his childhood. He now lives in Chicago amidst his comics and toys.

WEBSITE: www.linedoteditions.com/
INSTAGRAM: @steveseeleyart

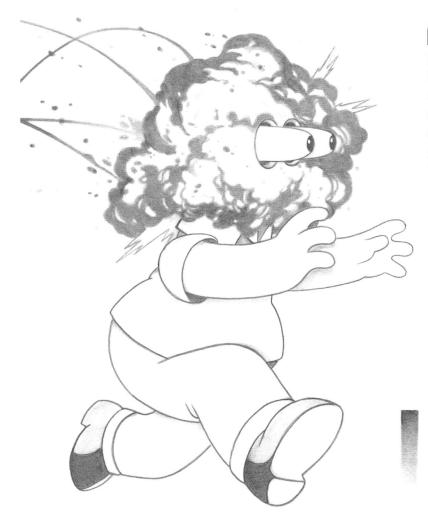

"My passion for geekdom probably started with He-Man. Then add comics, movies, and toys and this is the start of a long love affair with geekery. Which is far from over."

Untitled (Homersplosion)
2019

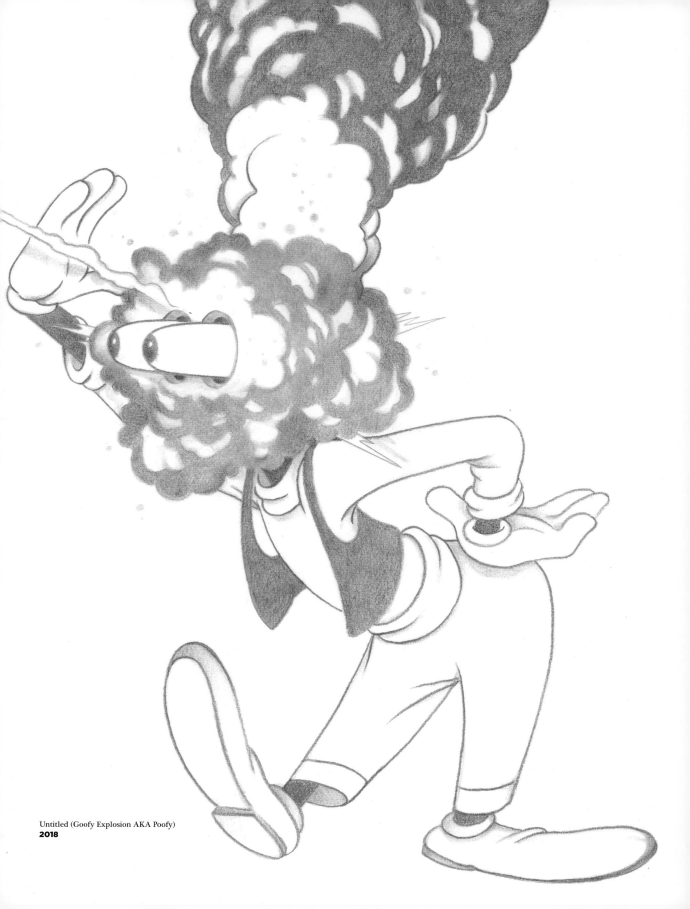

Untitled (Goofy Explosion AKA Poofy)
2018

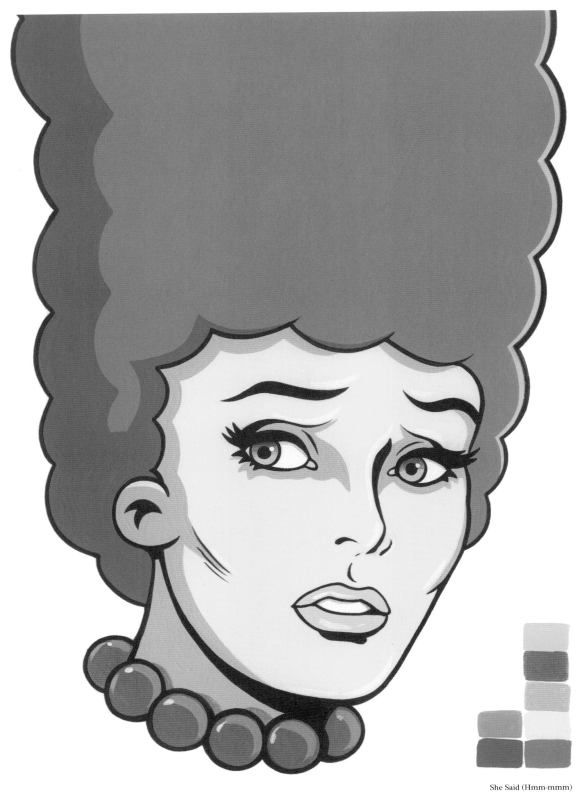

She Said (Hmm-mmm)
2018

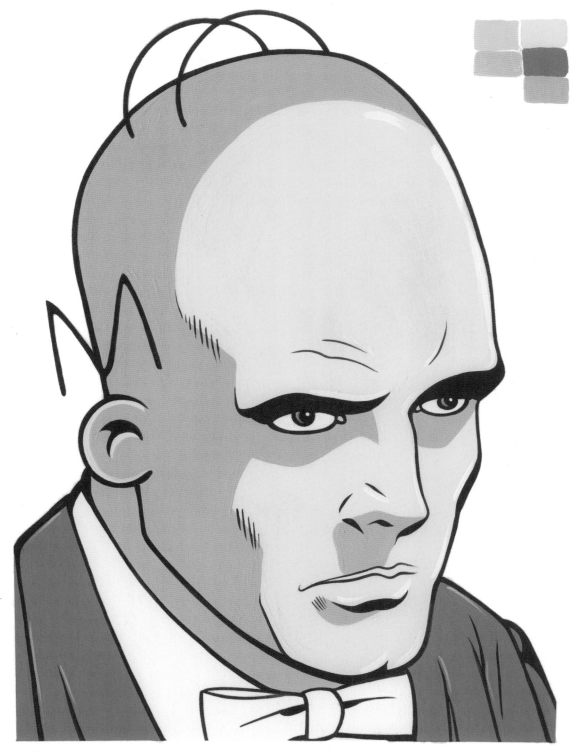

He Said (D'Oh)
2018

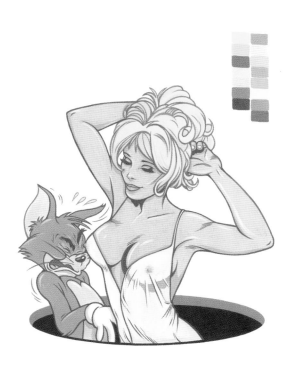

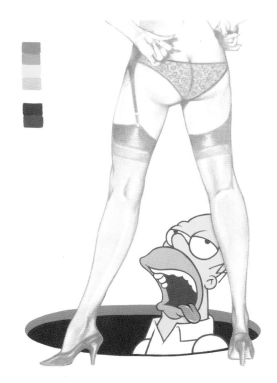

Hole Parade (Poke)
2019

Hole Parade (Pervert 2)
2019

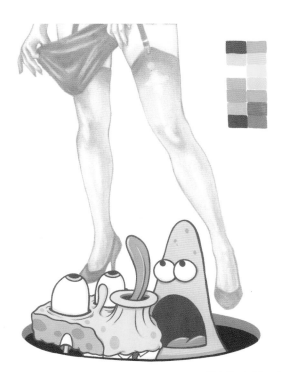

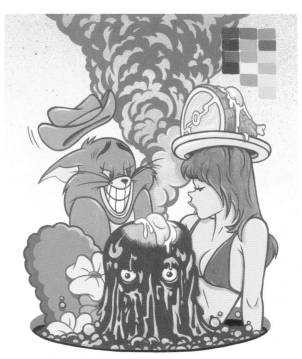

Hole Parade (Pervert 1)
2019

Hole Parade (Kitchen Sink/ The Hole Shebang)
2019

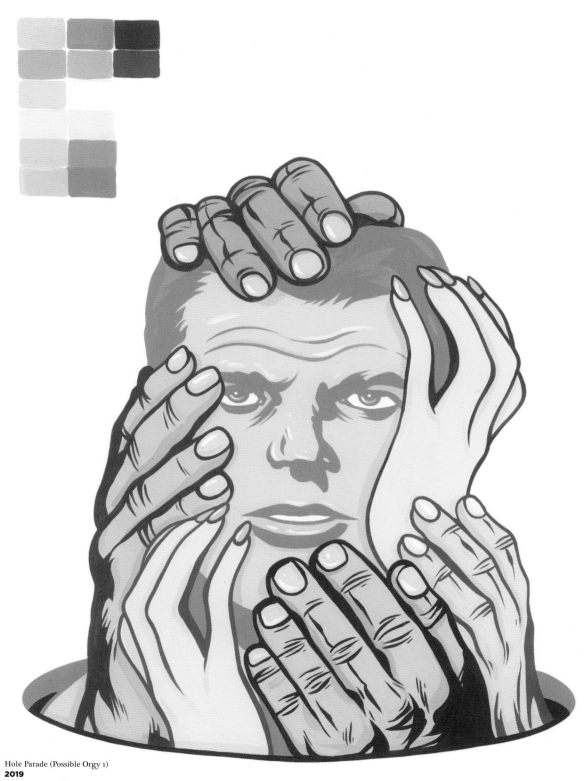

Hole Parade (Possible Orgy 1)
2019

YIN SHIAN

Shian is an independent illustrator based in Singapore. She has a myriad of influences and interests, ranging from classic Disney animation to Japanese woodblock prints and the Polish School of Posters, resulting in an eclectic mix of styles. She has produced art for Metallica, Weird Al Yankovic, and Pizza Hut.

WEBSITE: www.shiaaan.com
BEHANCE: /shiaaan
INSTAGRAM: @shiaaaan
FACEBOOK: /SHIANNNNN

> " I think of pop culture as a giant, ever fluctuating web of narratives, symbols, voices, and practices. I am both fly and spider in this web."

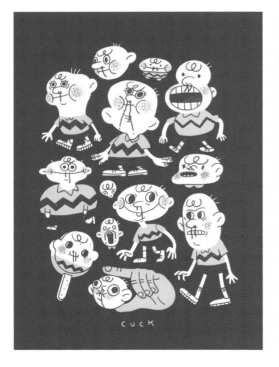

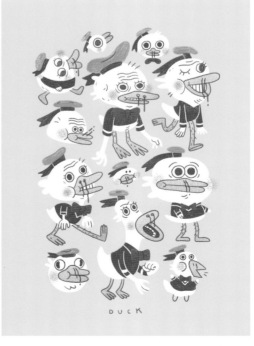

Charlie / The Cuck
2018

Donald / The Duck
2018

Mickey / Schmuck
2018

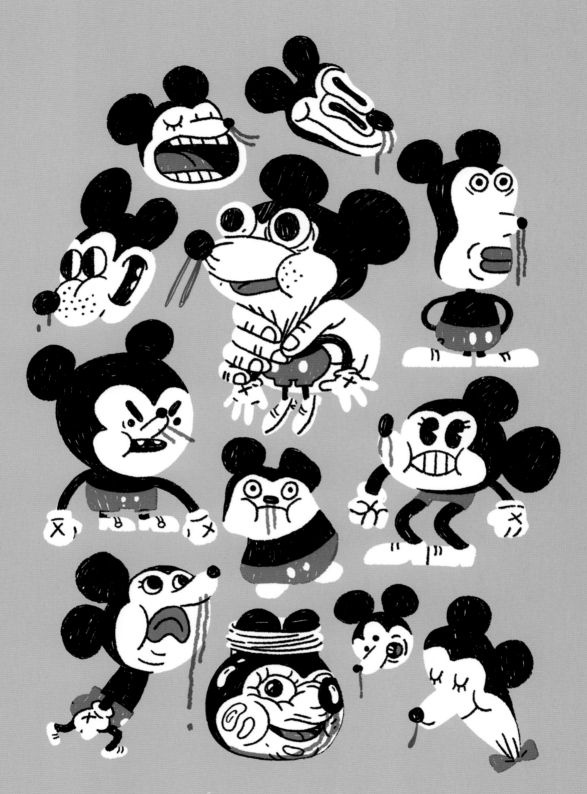

SCHMUCK

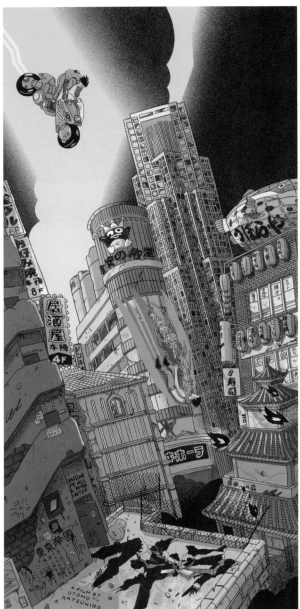

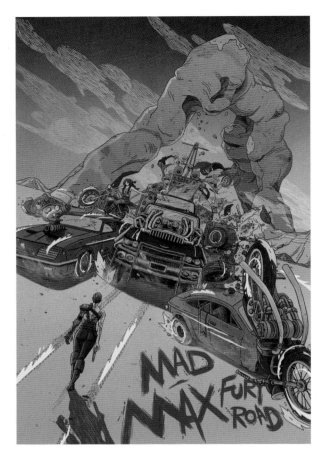

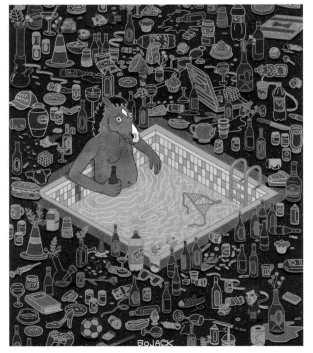

Akira
2016

Mad Max Fury Road
2017

BoJack Horseman
2018

Moulin Rouge!
2017

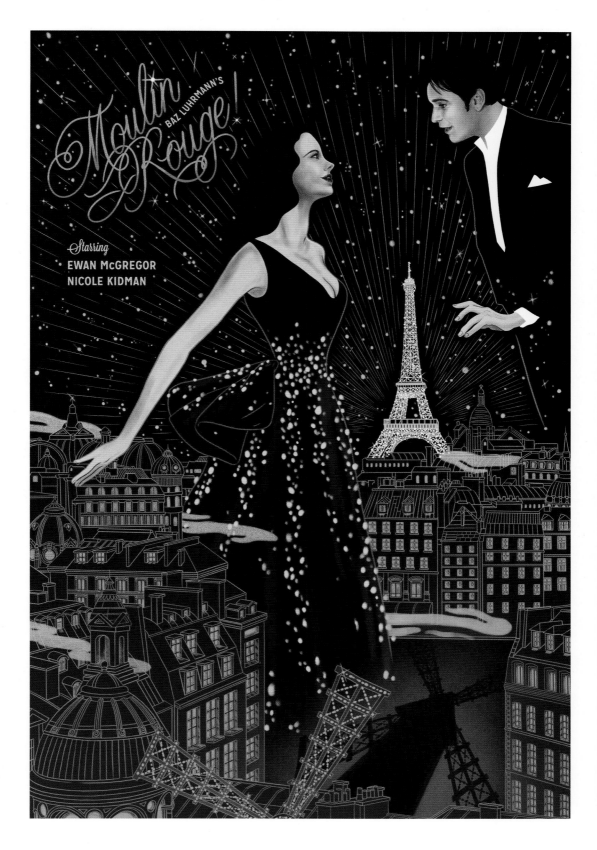

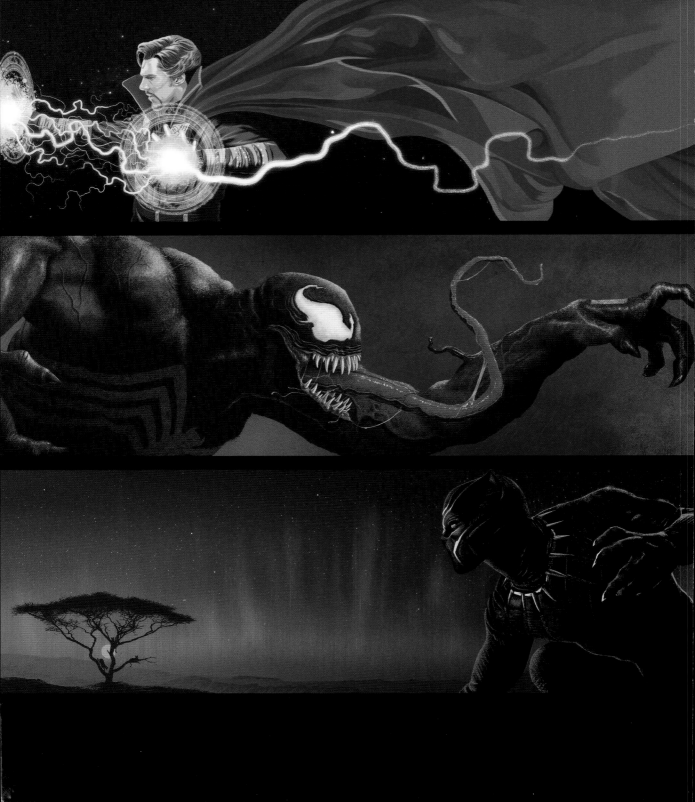

ANDREW SWAINSON

Andrew Swainson is an illustrator and graphic designer based in the United Kingdom. He is currently the "resident art person" for two music labels. As an illustrator he is a member of California-based agency Poster Posse with whom he has produced official artwork for the likes of Disney, Sony, Warner Bros., 20th Century Fox, and Netflix for films such as *Toy Story 4, Alien, Justice League, Kong: Skull Island, Cars 3,* and *Big Hero 6.*

WEBSITE: www.andrewswainson.com

> ❝ I don't think people can look at my work and know who has made it. I've tried and tried to settle on 'a style' but every new piece looks different from the last. It has always been this way. I'm comfortable with it and frustrated by it at the same time." ❞

Doctor Strange
2016

Venom
2018

Black Panther
2018

Guardians of the Galaxy Vol. 2
2017

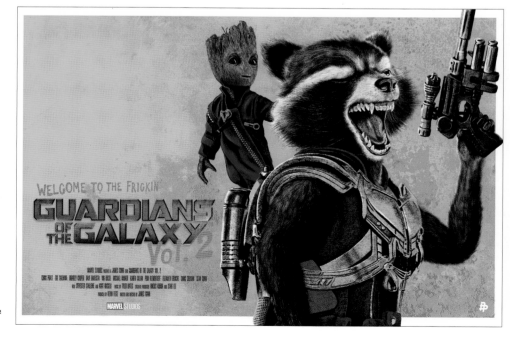

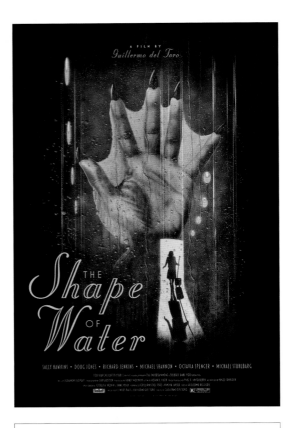

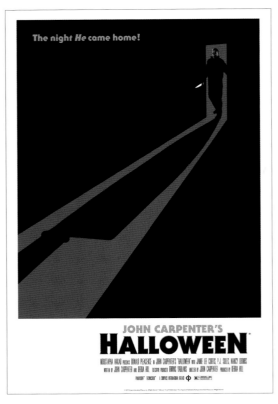

The Shape of Water
2018

Halloween
2018

The Maltese Falcon
2018

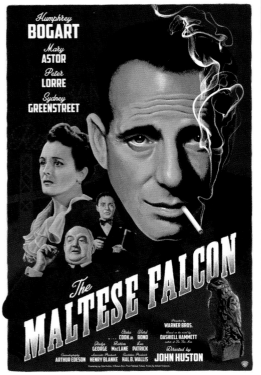

The Witch
2018

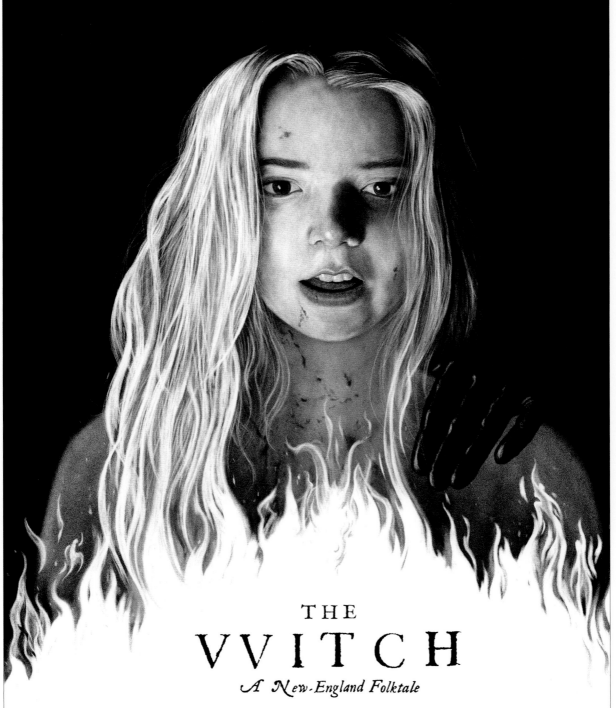

THE
VVITCH
A New-England Folktale

ANYA TAYLOR-JOY   RALPH INESON   KATE DICKIE   HARVEY SCRIMSHAW

Music by MARK KORVEN   *Cinematography by* JARIN BLASCHKE   *Film Editing by* LOUISE FORD   *Production Design by* CRAIG LATHROP
Art Direction by DEREK CONNELL *and* ANDREA KRISTOF   *Set Decoration by* MARY KIRKLAND   *Costume Design by* LINDA MUIR
Produced by Daniel Bekerman   *Written and Directed by* ROBERT EGGERS

A24

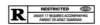

MATT TALBOT

Matt Talbot is a designer and illustrator from the New Hampshire seacoast. He's done work for clients that include Marvel Studios and shown his pop-culture work at Gallery1988 in Los Angeles. Matt can be found online at mattrobot.com.

WEBSITE: www.mattrobot.com
INSTAGRAM: @mattrobot
TWITTER: @mattrobot

" As a child of the eighties, I grew up with pop culture in my blood. Watching cartoons on Saturday morning was my gateway to a passion that never died. Today, I still read comics, love movies, and, even better, love making work that is informed by, and hopefully adds to, these great pieces of pop culture."

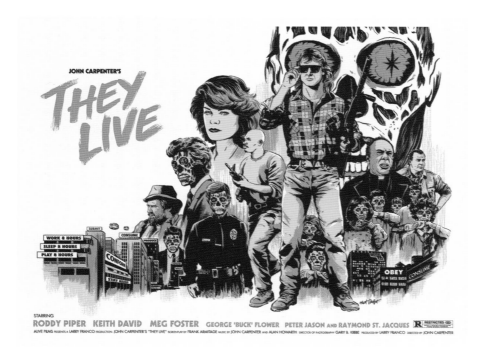

They Live
2018

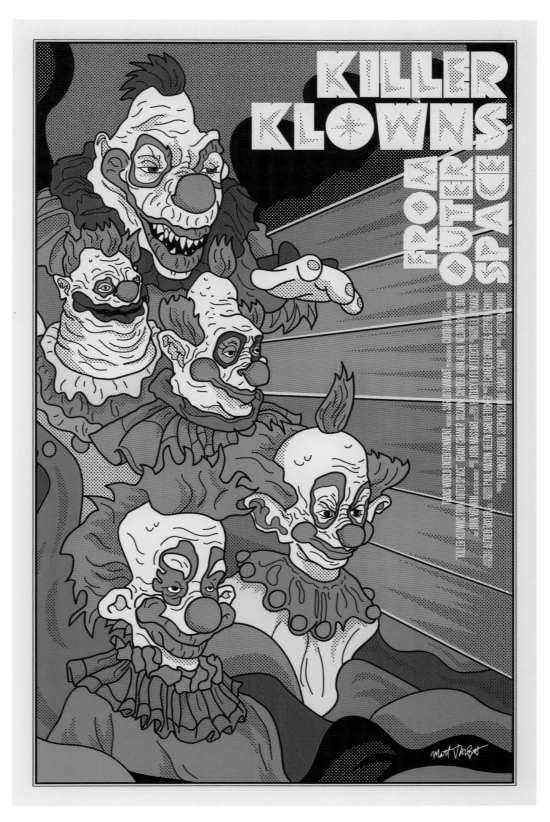

Killer Klowns
From Outer Space
2016

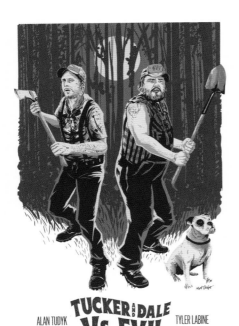

Tucker and Dale
2017

Crimson Peak
2016

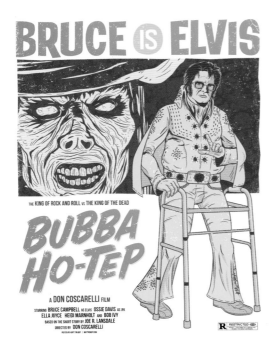

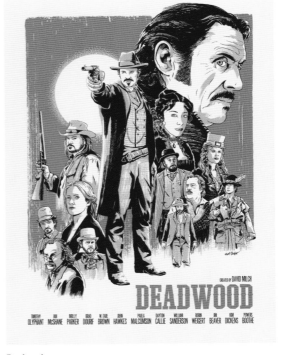

Bubba Ho-Tep
2018

Deadwood
2018

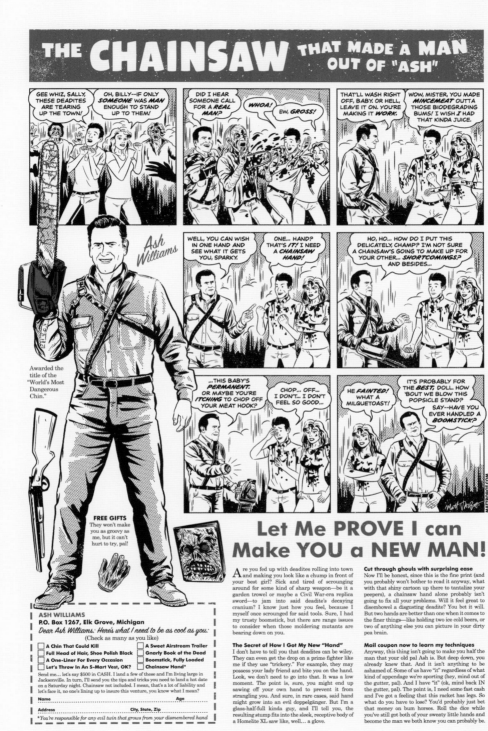

TIKKA

TikKa Ng began his artistic career in 2006. He is known for the "So Ha" and "Chìz" art styles, demonstrating different aspects of traditional Chinese culture with loveable baby characters.

TikKa's creativity has taken a deep root in China's traditional culture; he has incorporated strong Chinese traits in his artistic expression. Fusing the distinct Chinese characteristics with Western elements and Japanese superflat technique, TikKa ultimately creates his own narrative and recognizable style. In a recent body of work, TikKa investigates the traditional Chinese value of death and life. TikKa has collaborated with renowned commercial brands and corporations, such as Commercial Radio Hong Kong, 7-Eleven, Heineken, Coca-Cola, Nescafé, One2free, Tsui Wah Restaurant Group, Plaza Hollywood, Metro City Plaza, Henderson Land Development Company, Devilrobots, Artoyz, and Peugeot.

FACEBOOK: TikKaGallery/TikKafromEast
INSTAGRAM: @tikkafromeast

" I hope everyone can live like a child, happier."

Blossoming
2015

Cool
2015

Dàoshi
2016

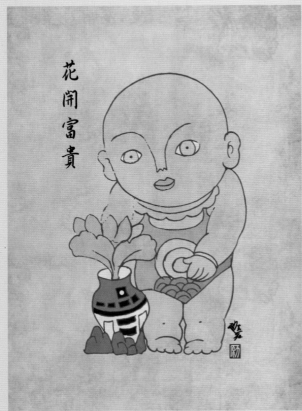

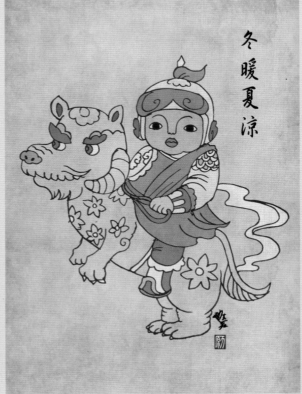

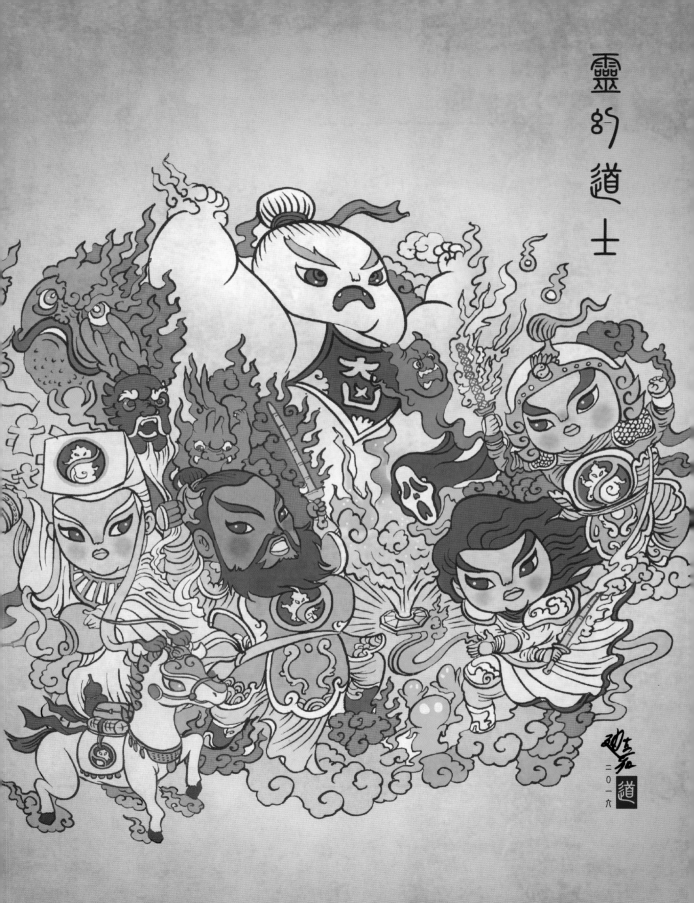

Evil Town House
2015

辟邪鎮宅

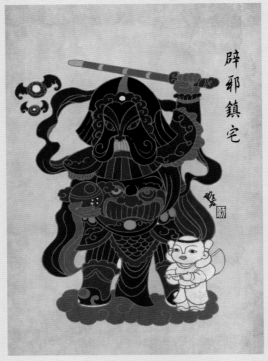

Good Fortune
2015

Wishing you boundless energy
2015

龍馬精神

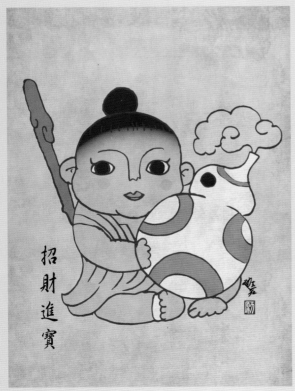

招財進寶

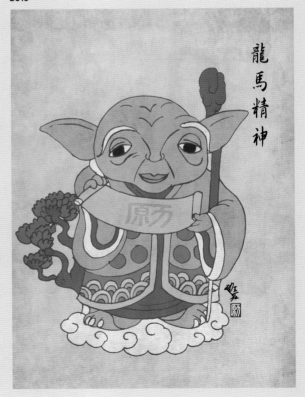

Patriot General
2016

Iron General
2016

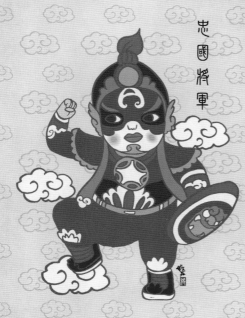

忠國將軍

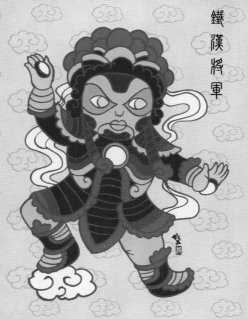

鐵漢將軍

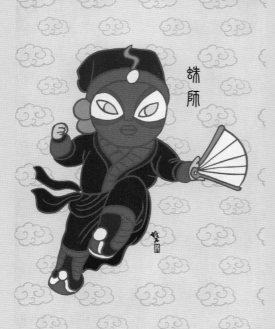

蛛師

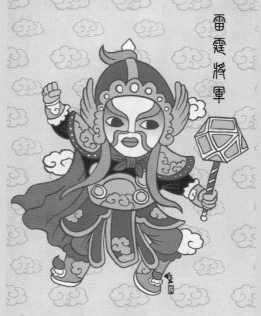

雷霆將軍

Spider Master
2016

Thunder General
2016

FELIX TINDALL

F elix Tindall is a Kiwi-based designer and illustrator especially fond of video game and movie culture. He likes poster art . . . like a lot! He has a passion for the world of art and design, and he is attracted to simple composition, minimalism, striking contrast, and monochromatic colors. It's something he has developed an eye for that has become his defining style. Being involved in this industry has put him in contact with galleries located in Los Angeles, Paris, and New York, which has given him the chance to work with official licenses for some of his favorite movies and TV shows. His persistent love for creating pop-culture poster art has helped create an identity for myself and has further expanded my possibilities as a freelance designer.

WEBSITE: www.felixtindall.com
INSTAGRAM: @f_tindall
TWITTER: @FT_in_NZ

Read Dead Redemption 2
2018

Wolfenstein II
2017

Mario
2018

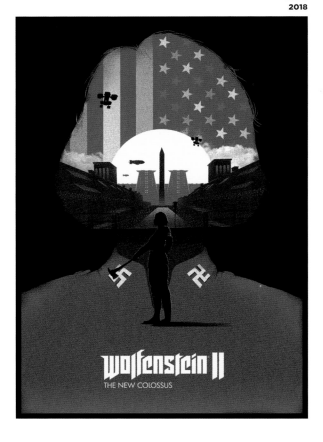

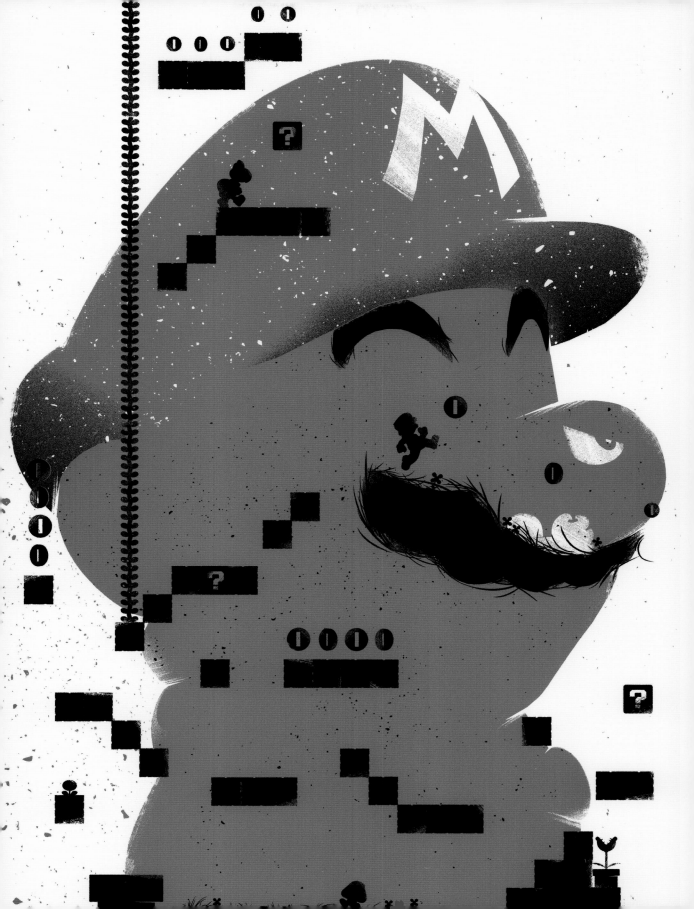

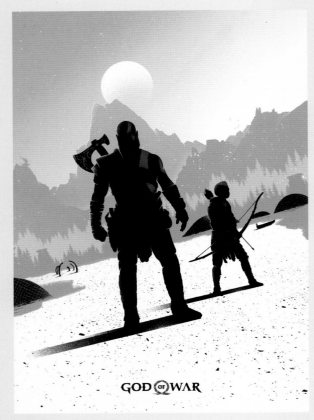

God of War
2018

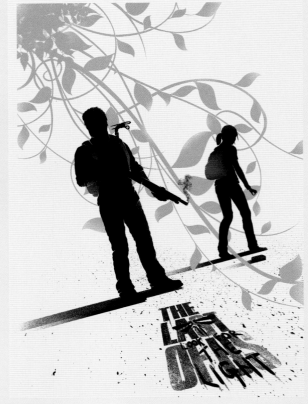

The Last of Us
2017

"The best part about pop culture, to me, or at least what I have discovered over the last few years, is the creativity behind the fans! Alternative poster art has grown to be a huge subculture movement over the last few years and has formed a brilliant and endlessly talented community of artists I am honoured to be a part of. I have discovered so many amazing artists through this community, many of which I am thrilled to be talking to today. I've made good friends and clients and have had opportunities (like this very book) I never thought I could ever have. Not only do the films or videogames inspire me, but the fans do as well."

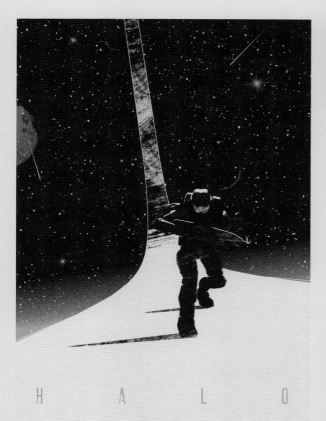

Halo
2018

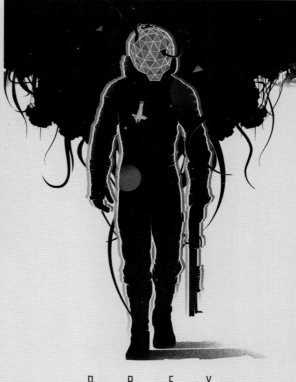

Prey
2017

DOM TSOI

Dom Tsoi is a stylistic visual illustrator. he loves drawing and producing artwork and he specializes in narrative storytelling.
   He is based in Cardiff, Wales, and was raised in a little town called Dinas Powys. Graduated in BA illustration at Plymouth College of Art and studied in the University of Worcester International College Art and Design Foundation.

CONTACT: domtsoi93@gmail.com
INSTAGRAM: d_tsoi1

> " Pop culture will forever inspire and influence and build such a unique, fun community."

Atyk-Senso Part II
2019

Atyk-Senso Part I
2019

Wonder Woman
2016

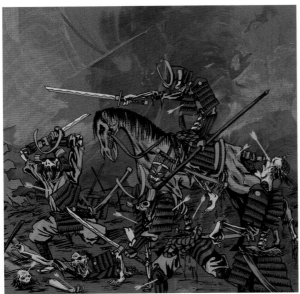

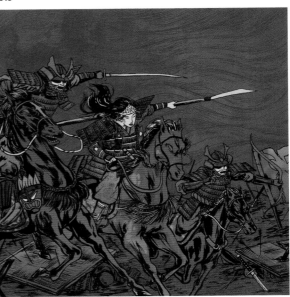

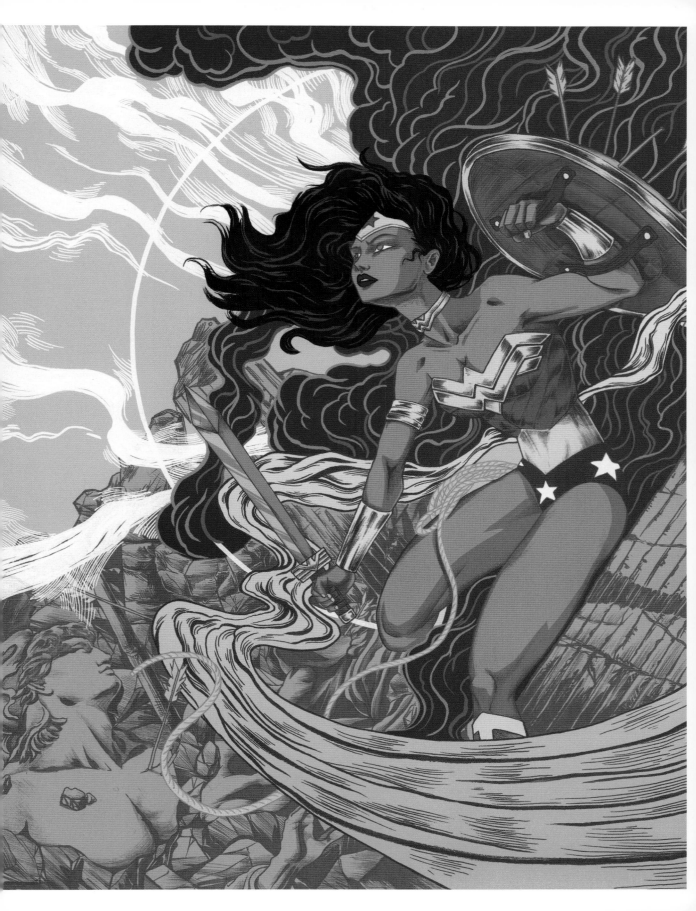

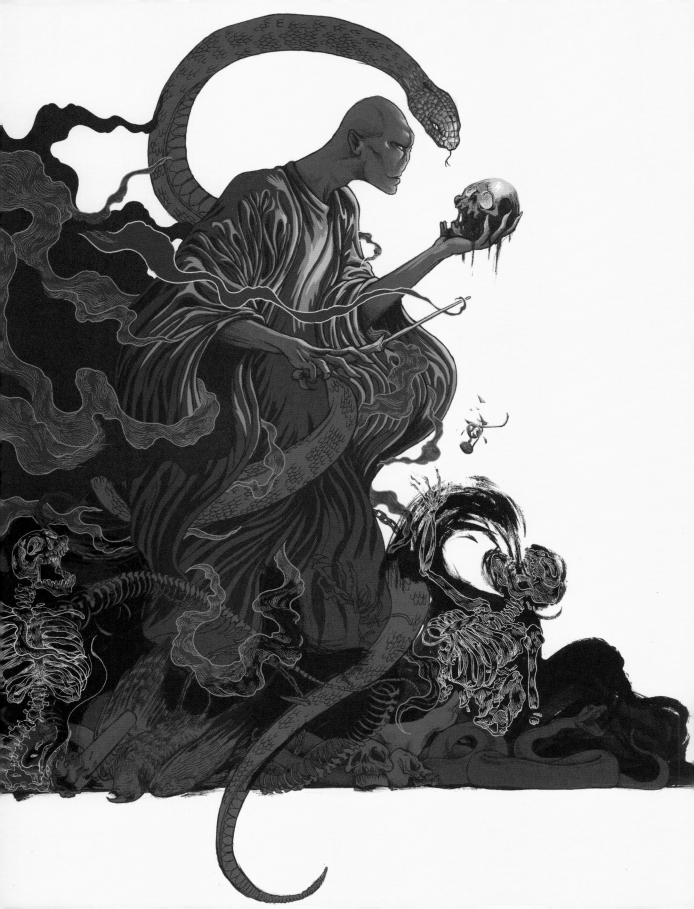

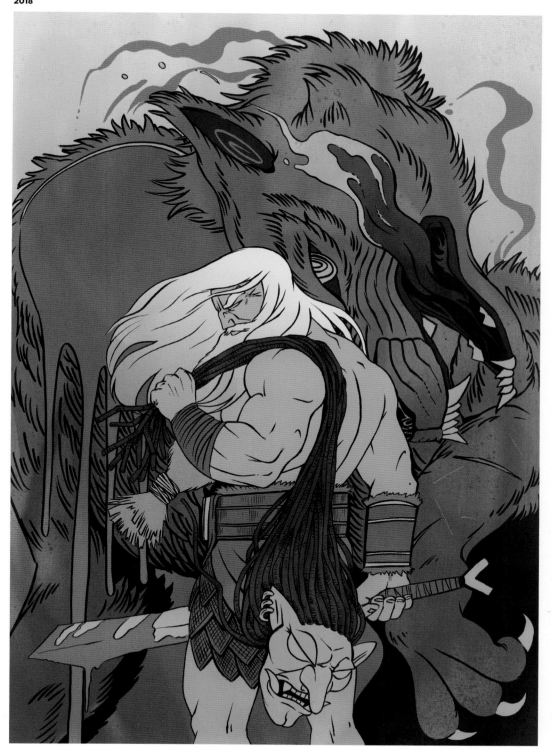

VAN ORTON DESIGN

Van Orton Design is twin brothers from Turin, Italy. Their art is influenced by pop culture and inspired by stained glass windows of churches. In their work, pop style is sometimes mixed with bright neon lines and very strong symmetric concepts. They started reinterpreting icons of cult movies of the eighties, and this allowed them to quickly get a lot of visibility, and to be contacted by major brands, such as ESPN, Marvel, Sky, *Rolling Stone*, and Universal Music. They are currently exhibiting for several American galleries between Los Angeles and San Francisco.

WEBSITE: www.vanortondesign.com
ONLINE STORE: www.vanortondesign.com/store
INSTAGRAM: @vanortondesign

> " The truth is at the end of the one perspective point."

The Shining
2015

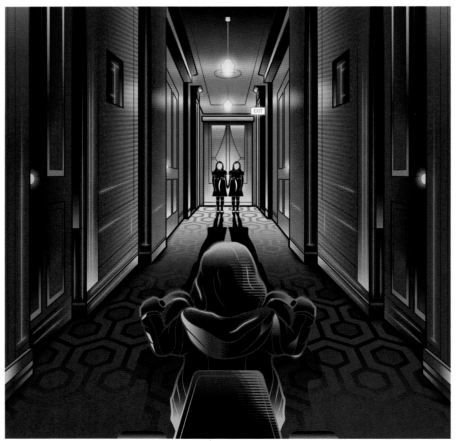

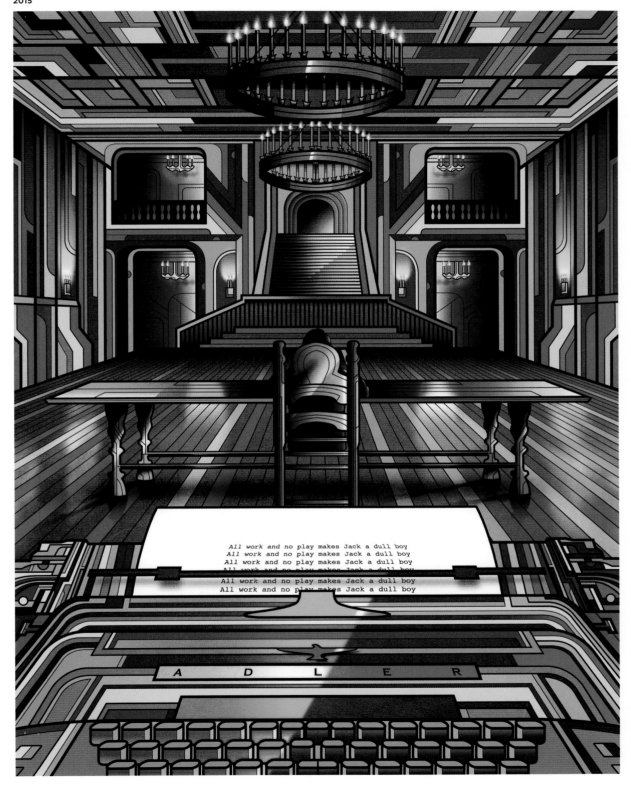

All work and no play makes Jack a dull boy
All work and no play makes Jack a dull boy
All work and no play makes Jack a dull boy
All work and no play makes Jack a dull boy
All work and no play makes Jack a dull boy
All work and no play makes Jack a dull boy

ADLER

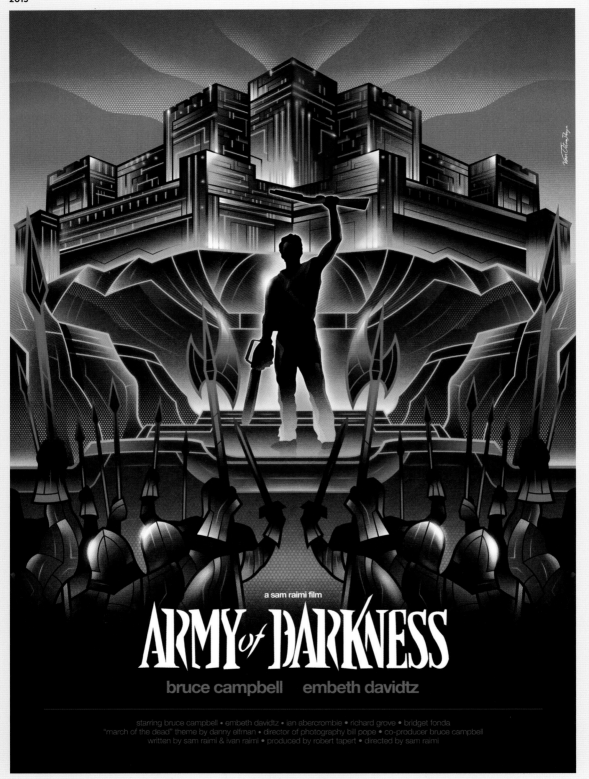

a sam raimi film

ARMY of DARKNESS

bruce campbell   embeth davidtz

starring bruce campbell • embeth davidtz • ian abercrombie • richard grove • bridget fonda
"march of the dead" theme by danny elfman • director of photography bill pope • co-producer bruce campbell
written by sam raimi & ivan raimi • produced by robert tapert • directed by sam raimi

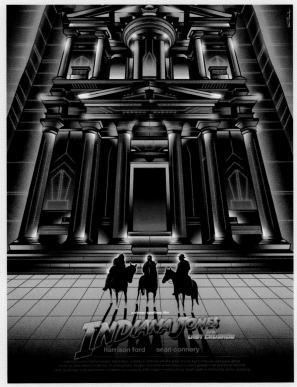

Indiana Jones
2015

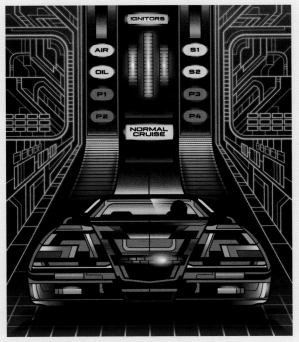

Knight Rider
2014

RICHARD WILKINSON

Like every other kid, Richard loved watching TV growing up, and he used to celebrate his passion for the shows and films he loved by drawing them. He also has always loved natural history. There's something about the adventure of discovery that always excited him.

He studied art at college and then, after a few diversions into electronic music, sound production, and music video production, decided to try to make a go of it as an illustrator.

He has been lucky enough to work extensively in editorial illustration, often for science-based magazines such as *New Scientist, Nature,* and *Aeon.* His illustration style has always been informed by natural history illustration and so the "Arthropoda Iconicus" project was a natural step for him.

He now lives and works in Brighton, England, with his wife and his son.

WEBSITE: www.arthropodaiconicus.com and www.richard-wilkinson.com
CONTACT: contact@richard-wilkinson.com
INSTAGRAM: @richardwilkinsonart
FACEBOOK: /richardwilkinsonart

" It's the inhabitants of our modern world. It's our flora and fauna."

Dokk volgatus
2018

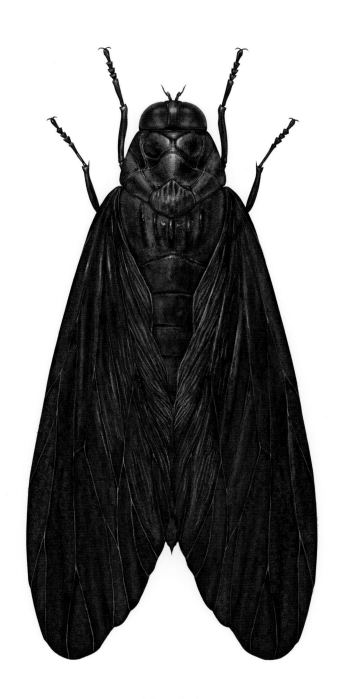

Dokk volgatus

Family: Atermedeisapiens

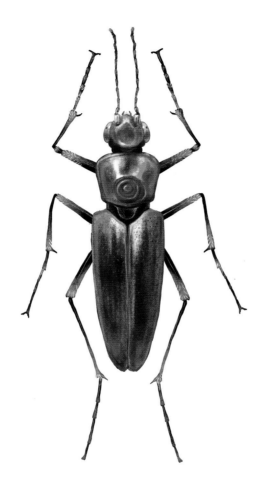

Consocius potiorpoetapolitus
Family: *Internuntimachinae*

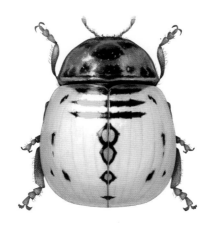

Roboduobus deoduobus

Family: *Astromachinae*

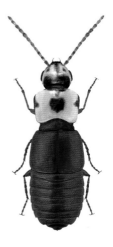

Lumeniter rubrumpentus
Family: *Medeisapiens*

Lumeniter rubrumpentus
2018

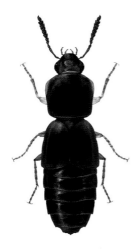

Ego solus
Family: *Opesparacida-reformati*

Ego solus
2018

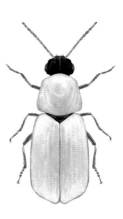

Filiae imperia
Family: *Luminhominestera*

Filiae imperia
2018

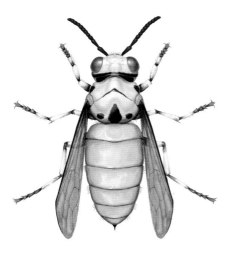

Equitem tempestus
Family: *Impermilitae*

Equitem tempestus
2018

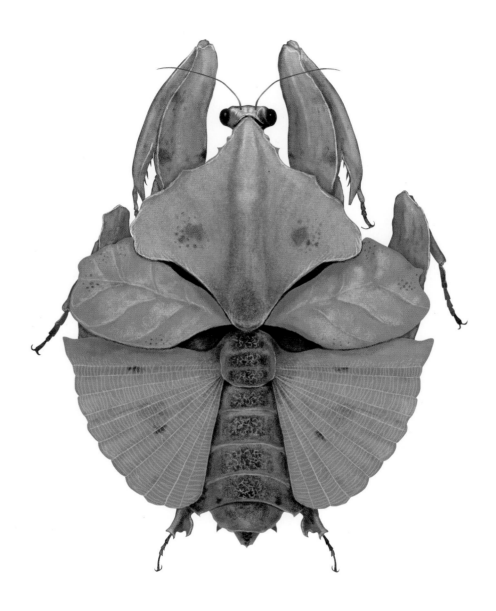

Malluvium volans

Family: *Naviculae*

Malluvium volans
2018

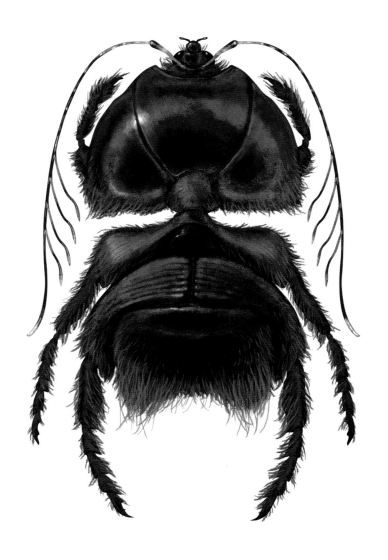

Chaetebarbatus bonamicii
Family: *Ursavistera*

Chaetebarbatus bonamicii
2018

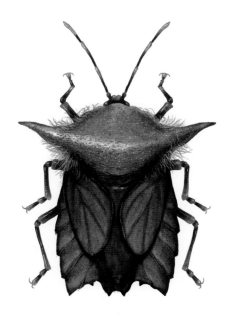

Dominus magister

Family: *Medeisapiens*

Dominus magister
2018

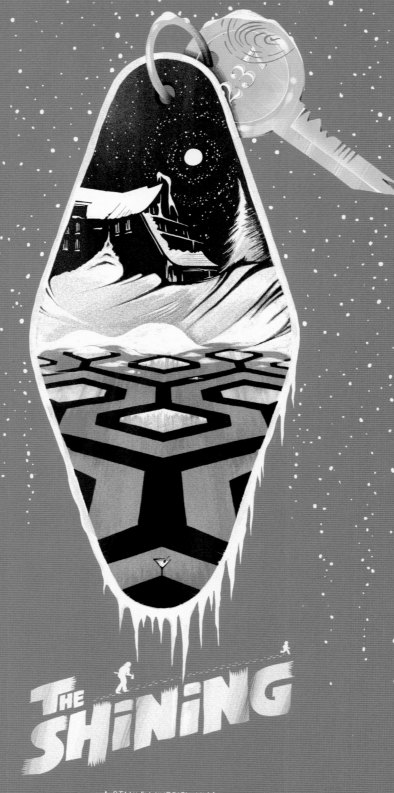

THE SHINING

A STANLEY KUBRICK FILM

STARRING JACK NICHOLSON   SHELLEY DUVALL   SCATMAN CROTHERS   DANNY LLOYD   BASED ON THE NOVEL BY STEPHEN KING

SCREENPLAY BY STANLEY KUBRICK + DIANE JOHNSON   PRODUCED AND DIRECTED BY STANLEY KUBRICK   EXECUTIVE PRODUCER JAN HARLAN   PRODUCED IN ASSOCIATION WITH THE PRODUCER CIRCLE CO.

R RESTRICTED UNDER 17 REQUIRES ACCOMPANYING PARENT OR ADULT GUARDIAN

LYNDON WILLOUGHBY

Lyndon Willoughby is a designer/illustrator living in McKinney, Texas. His primary passion lies in the creation of digital art for silkscreen printing. He attended college at Abilene Christian University where he received his bachelor of fine arts in graphic design. Since graduating in 2012 he has created art for a variety of clients and events, including gallery group shows, private commissions, and in conjunction with online retailers.

WEBSITE: www.willowstration.com

> **"** My passions and interests are many and varied, from film to music to gaming and much in between."

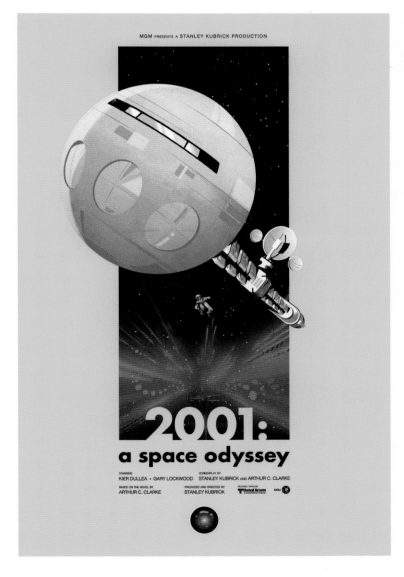

2001: A Space Odyssey
2017

The Shining
2016

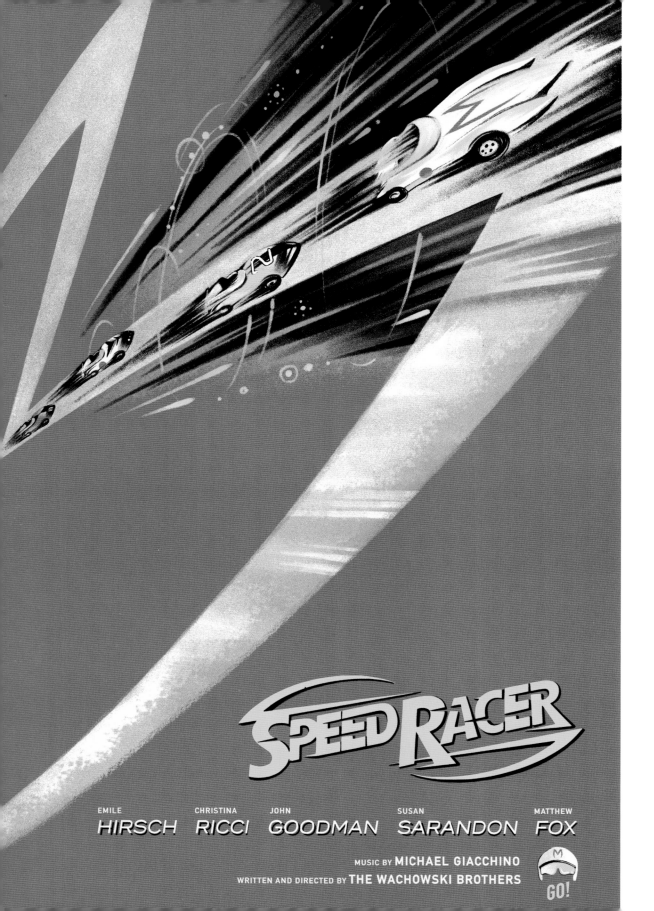

SPEED RACER

EMILE **HIRSCH** CHRISTINA **RICCI** JOHN **GOODMAN** SUSAN **SARANDON** MATTHEW **FOX**

MUSIC BY **MICHAEL GIACCHINO**
WRITTEN AND DIRECTED BY **THE WACHOWSKI BROTHERS**

GO!

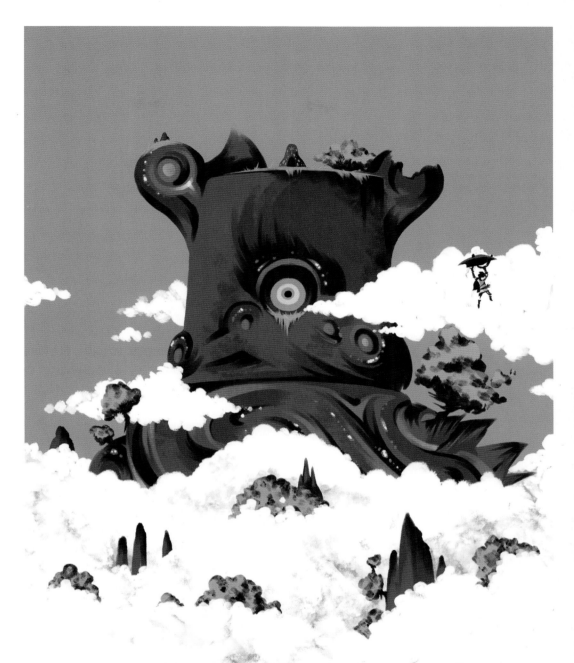

ゼルダの伝説

ブレス オブ ザ ワイルド

THE LEGEND OF ZELDA

BREATH OF THE WILD

Speed Race
2018

Breath of the Wild
2018

MIKE WROBEL

Mike Wrobel is a French illustrator based in Tokyo, Japan. After a *bac L (baccalauréat littéraire)*, he studied in an animation school for three years. Then, he worked as a graphic designer for different clients and then moved to Japan, where he began to focus on his art. He made himself known thanks to a series of illustrations on *Game of Thrones* six years ago, which gave him enough visibility to be able to live for his art. A big fan of pop culture, cinema, and TV series, he grew up with *the X-Files*, Teenage Mutant Ninja Turtles, and Super Nintendo.

WEBSITE: mikewrobel.shop
INSTAGRAM: @mikewrobel
FACEBOOK: /MoshiStudio

" I like to appropriate popular works by reworking them from a different angle. References to pop culture have always been a driving force in my work."

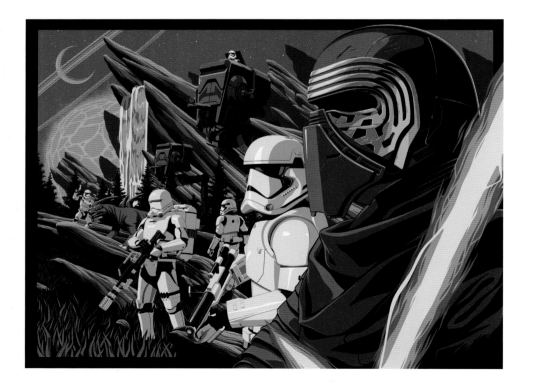

Kylo Ren
2018
Batman
2017
Joker
2017
Twoface
2017

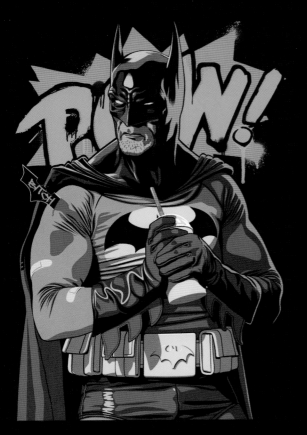
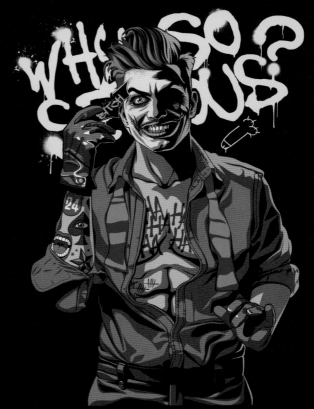
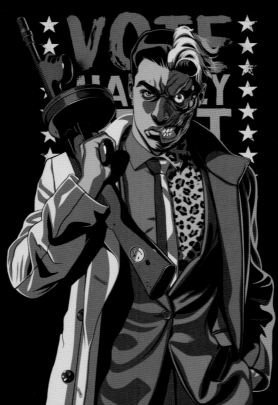

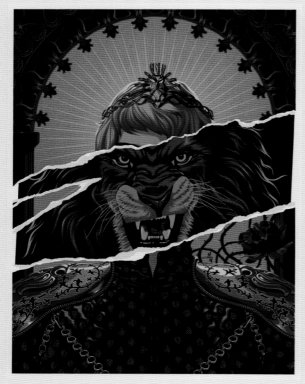

Cersei
2019

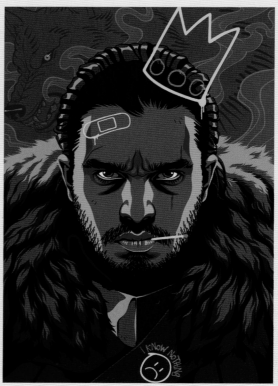

Jon Snow
2017

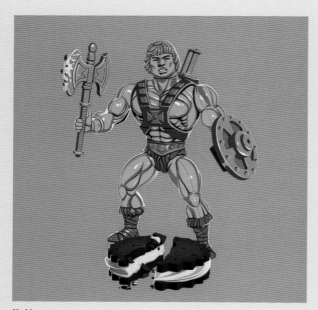

He-Man
2018

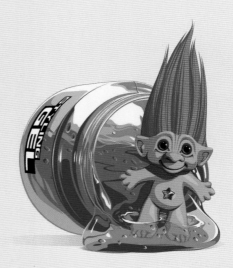

Treasure Troll
2018

Fujilan Rumble
2017

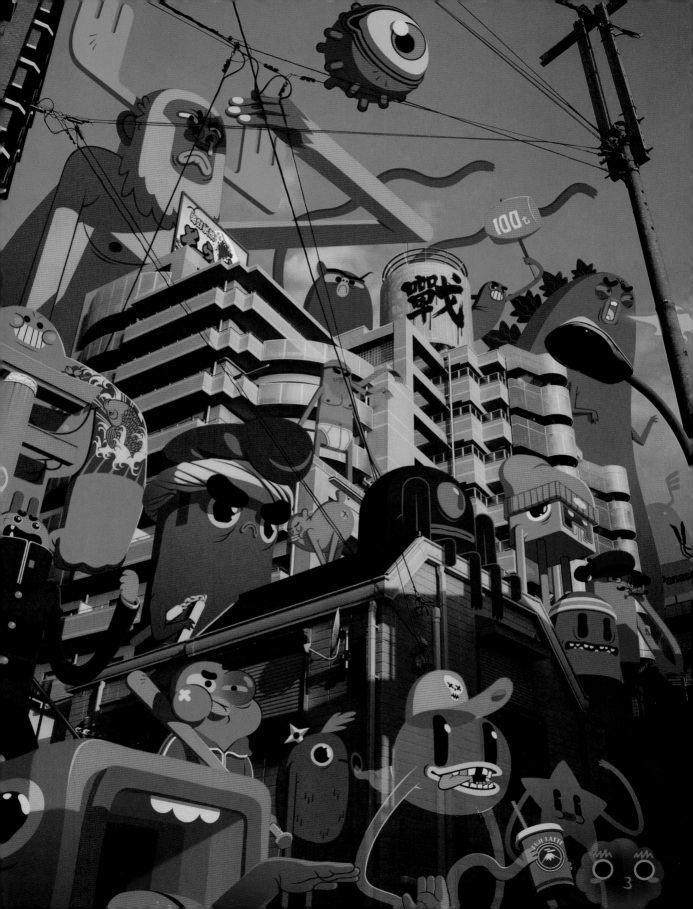

BRUCE YAN

Bruce Yan is an artist and graphic designer based in Seattle, Washington. He's known for his clever interpretations of pop culture from films, animation, and comics. His work ranges from screenprints to original paintings and sculptures. Bruce enjoys collecting art as much as creating it.

WEBSITE: www.bruceyan.com
INSTAGRAM: @mrbruceyan

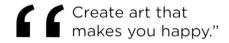

"Create art that makes you happy."

Play Dough
2014

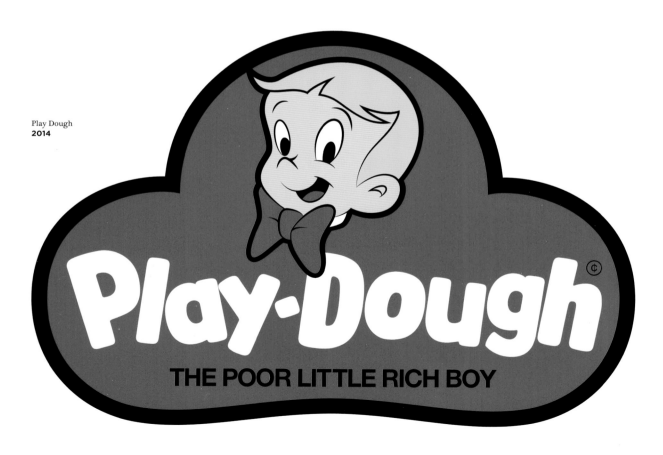

The Mermaid
2014

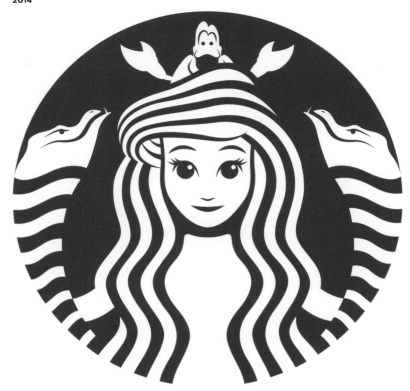

Stay Puft
2014

The Bunny
2014

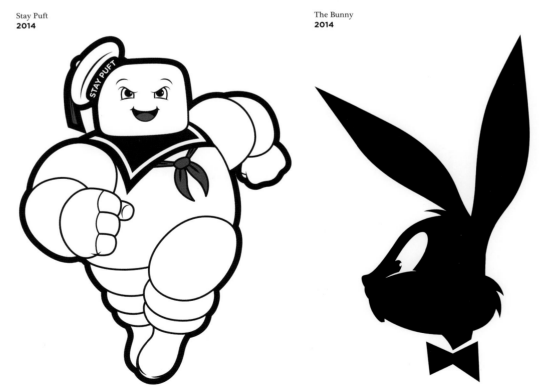

Ghibli Scouts
2014

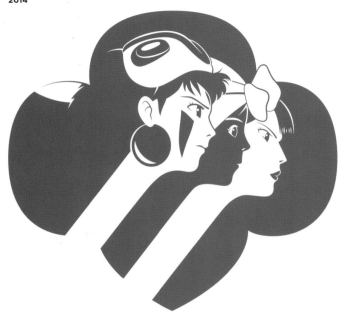

Hayao Airlines
2014

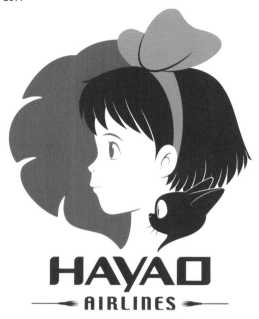

Shishi Gami
2014

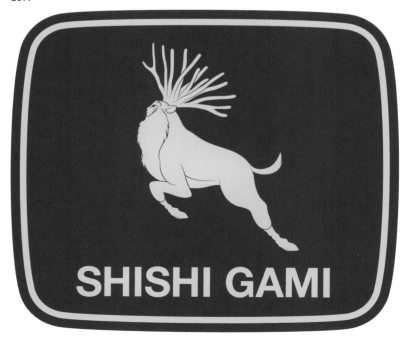

Miyazaki Salt
2014

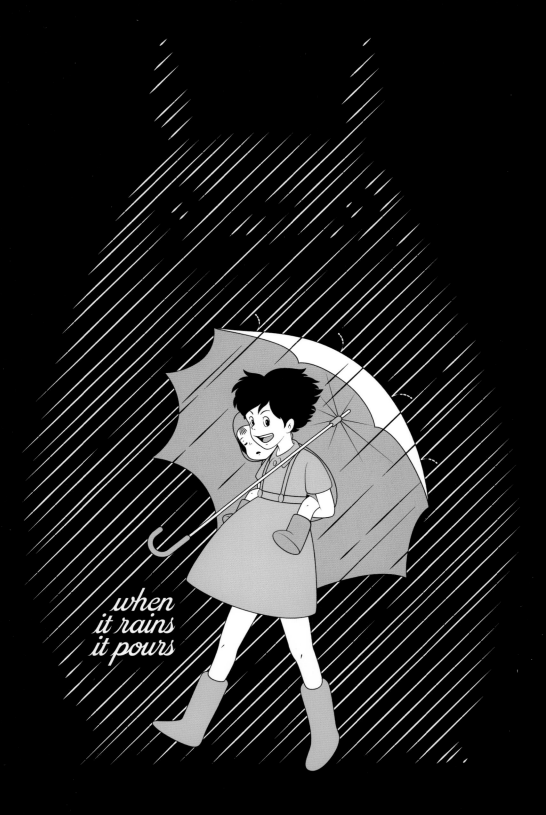

Also available from

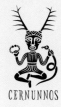

CERNUNNOS

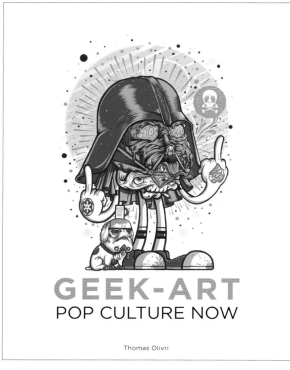

9782374950112 – $40.00

9782374951355 – $29.95

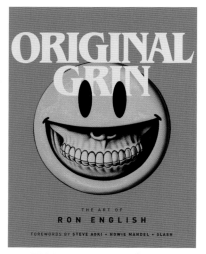

9782374950938 – $65.00

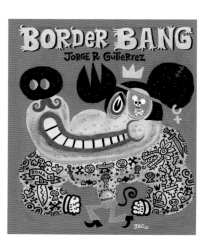

9782374950419 – $24.95

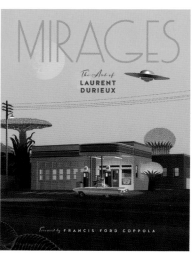

9782374951492 – $50.00